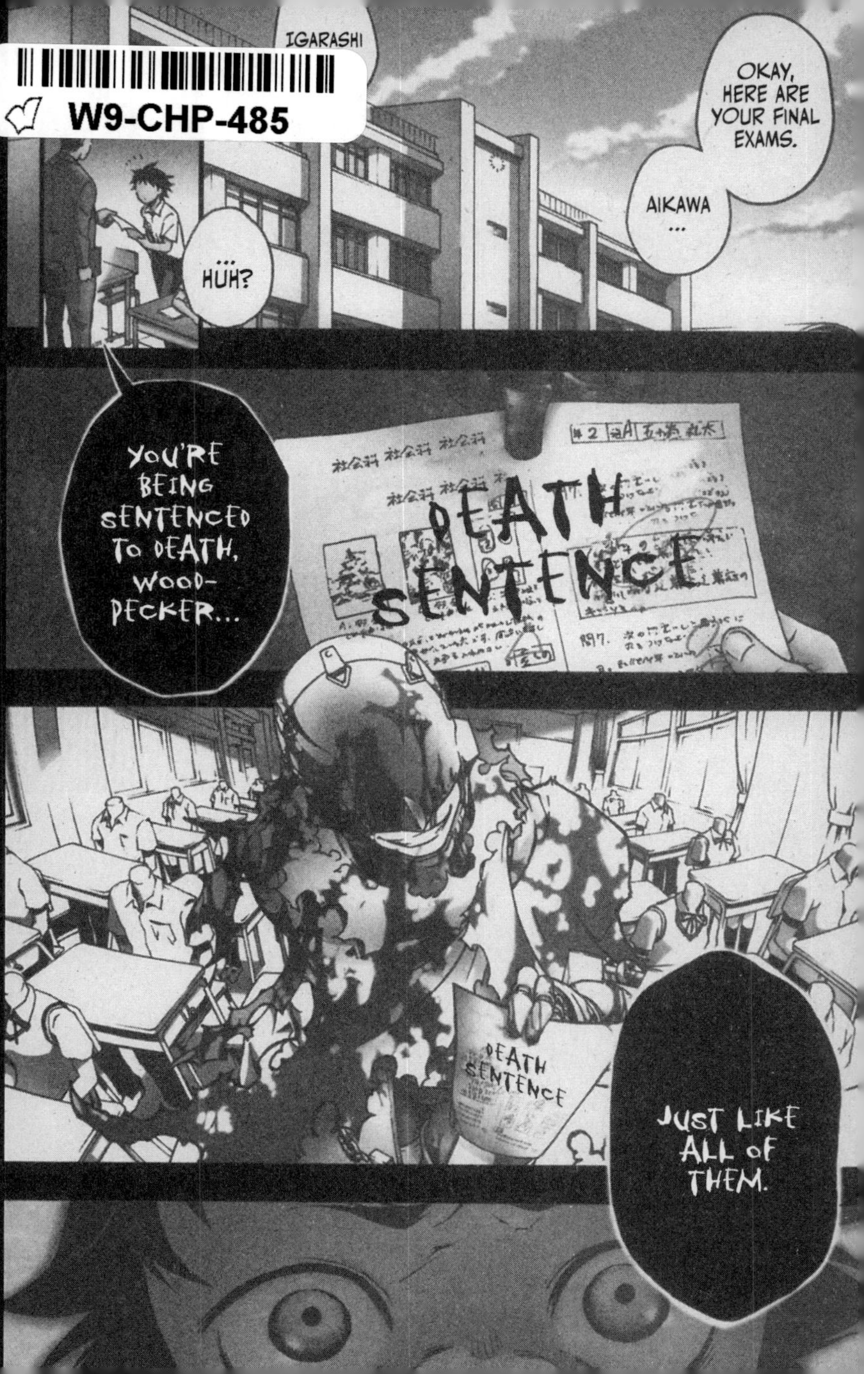
OKAY, HERE ARE YOUR FINAL EXAMS.
AIKAWA ...
IGARASHI
... HUH?
DEATH SENTENCE
YOU'RE BEING SENTENCED TO DEATH, WOOD-PECKER...
DEATH SENTENCE
JUST LIKE ALL OF THEM.

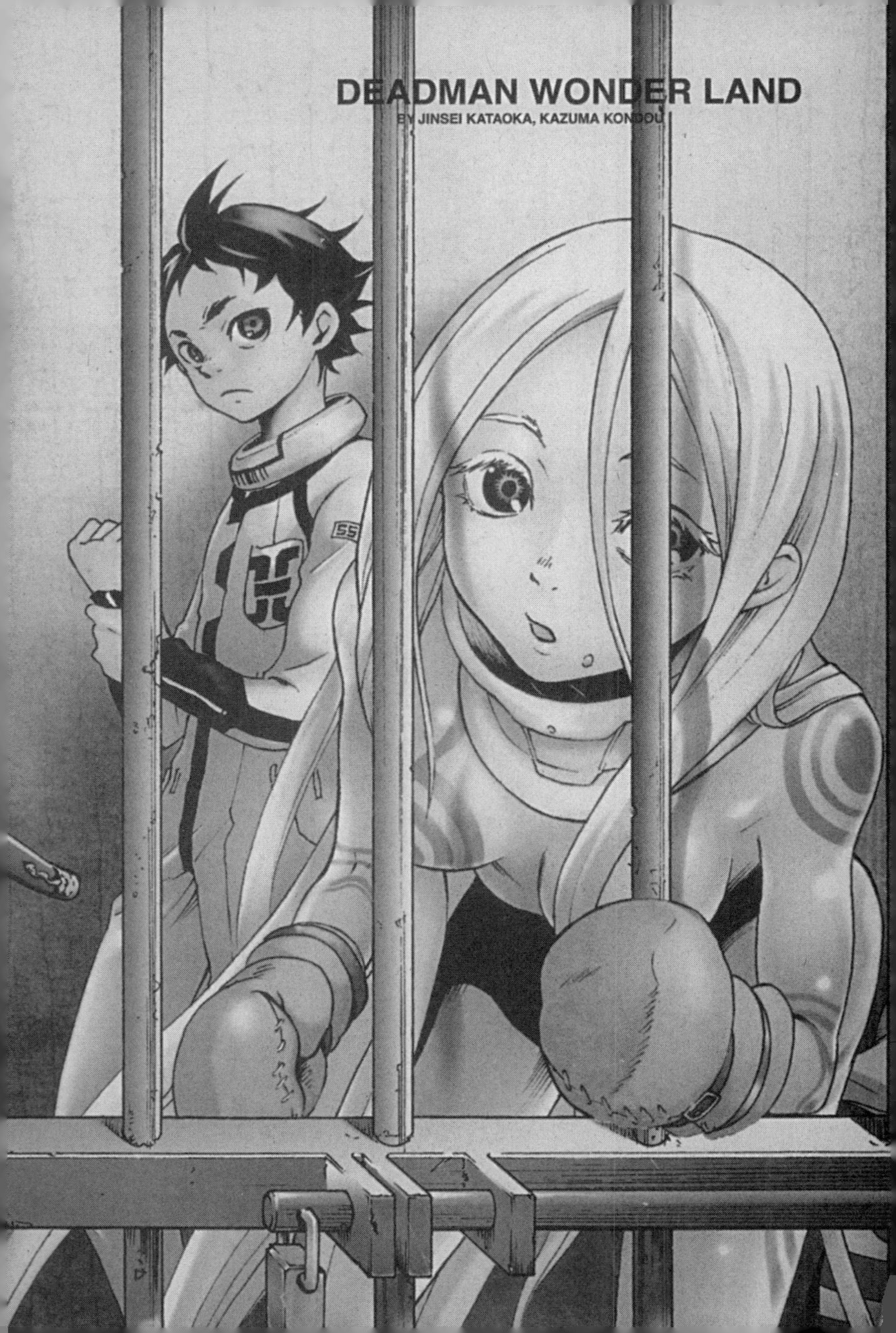
DEADMAN WONDER LAND
BY JINSEI KATAOKA, KAZUMA KONDOU

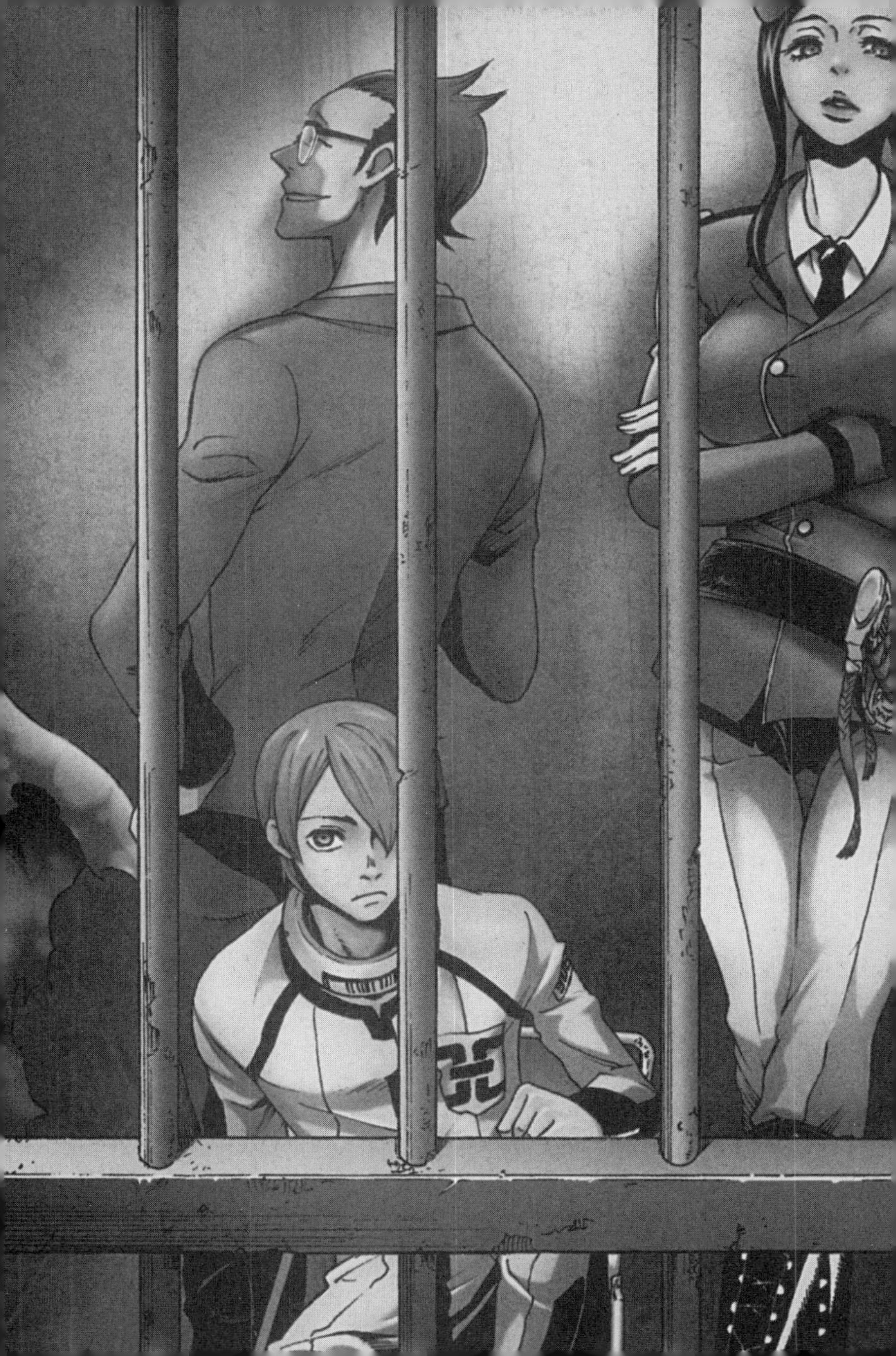

DEADMAN WONDERLAND
Volume 2
CONTENTS
Cartoon by JINSEI KATAOKA & KAZUMA KONDOU
Book design by TSUYOSHI KUSANO

# DEADMAN
## WONDERLAND

VOLUME 2

STORY BY JINSEI KATAOKA
ART BY KAZUMA KONDOU

HAMBURG // LONDON // LOS ANGELES // TOKYO

## *Deadman Wonderland Volume 2*
## Created by JINSEI KATAOKA, KAZUMA KONDOU

Translation - Ray Yoshimoto
English Adaptation - Bryce P. Coleman
Copy Editor - Shannon Watters
Retouch and Lettering - Star Print Brokers
Production Artist - Rui Kyo
Graphic Designer - Chelsea Windlinger

Editor - Cindy Suzuki
Print Production Manager - Lucas Rivera
Managing Editor - Vy Nguyen
Senior Designer - Louis Csontos
Art Director - Al-Insan Lashley
Director of Sales and Manufacturing - Allyson De Simone
Associate Publisher - Marco F. Pavia
President and C.O.O. - John Parker
C.E.O. and Chief Creative Officer - Stu Levy

A  Manga

TOKYOPOP Inc.
5900 Wilshire Blvd. Suite 2000
Los Angeles, CA 90036

E-mail: info@TOKYOPOP.com
Come visit us online at www.TOKYOPOP.com

DEAD MAN WONDERLAND vol.2
© Jinsei KATAOKA 2007 © Kazuma KONDOU 2007
First published in Japan in 2007 by KADOKAWA SHOTEN
Publishing Co., Ltd., Tokyo.
English translation rights arranged with KADOKAWA
SHOTEN Publishing Co., Ltd., Tokyo
through TUTTLE–MORI AGENCY, INC., Tokyo.
English text copyright © 2010 TOKYOPOP Inc.

ISBN: 978-1-4278-1742-6

First TOKYOPOP printing: June 2010
10 9 8 7 6 5 4 3 2 1
Printed in the USA

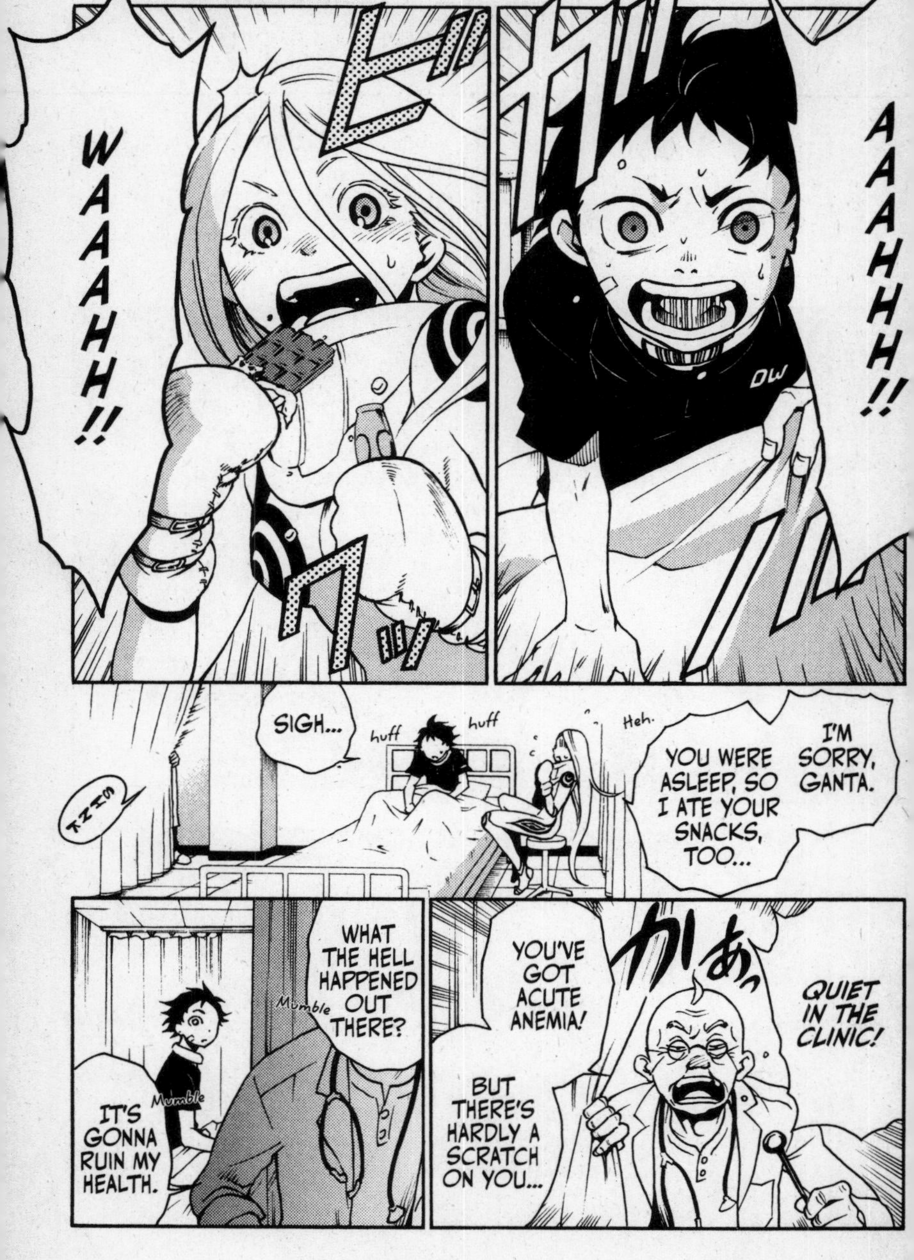
AAAAHHH!!
WAAAAHH!!
I'M SORRY, GANTA.
YOU WERE ASLEEP, SO I ATE YOUR SNACKS, TOO...
Heh.
huff
huff
SIGH...
QUIET IN THE CLINIC!
YOU'VE GOT ACUTE ANEMIA!
BUT THERE'S HARDLY A SCRATCH ON YOU...
WHAT THE HELL HAPPENED OUT THERE?
Mumble
IT'S GONNA RUIN MY HEALTH.
Mumble

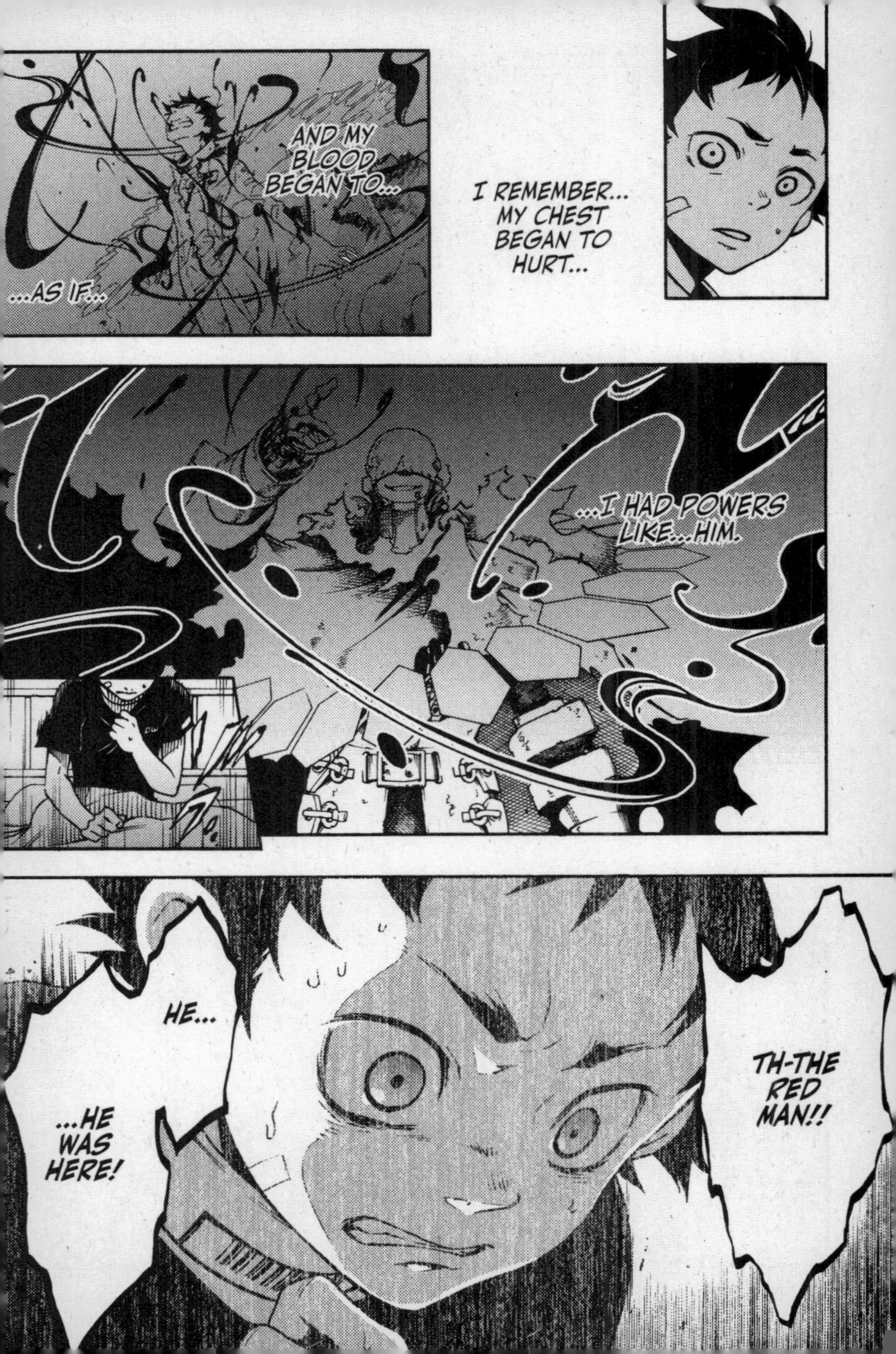
I REMEMBER... MY CHEST BEGAN TO HURT...
AND MY BLOOD BEGAN TO...
...AS IF...
...I HAD POWERS LIKE...HIM.
TH-THE RED MAN!!
HE...
...HE WAS HERE!

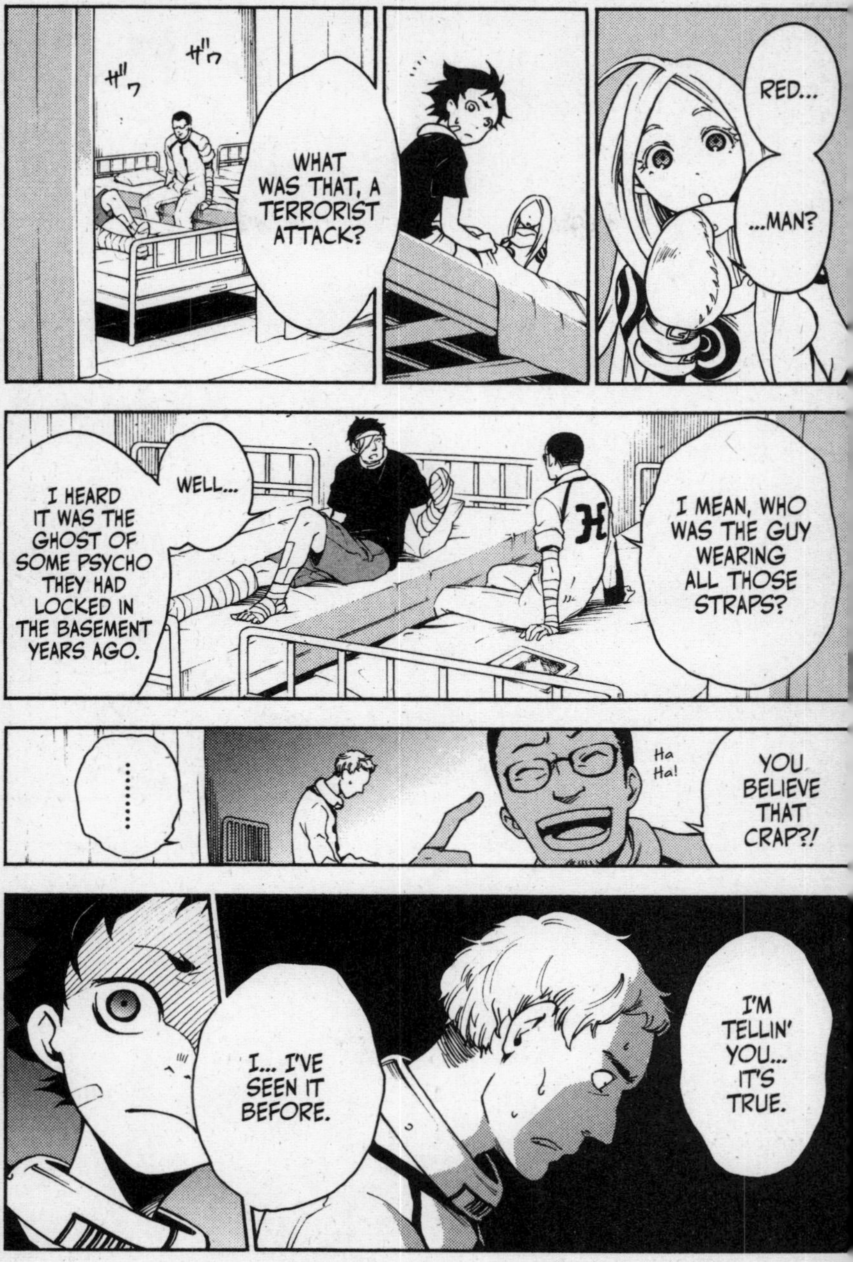
RED...
...MAN?
WHAT WAS THAT, A TERRORIST ATTACK?
ザワ
ザワ
I MEAN, WHO WAS THE GUY WEARING ALL THOSE STRAPS?
WELL...
I HEARD IT WAS THE GHOST OF SOME PSYCHO THEY HAD LOCKED IN THE BASEMENT YEARS AGO.
YOU BELIEVE THAT CRAP?!
Ha Ha!
......
I'M TELLIN' YOU... IT'S TRUE.
I... I'VE SEEN IT BEFORE.

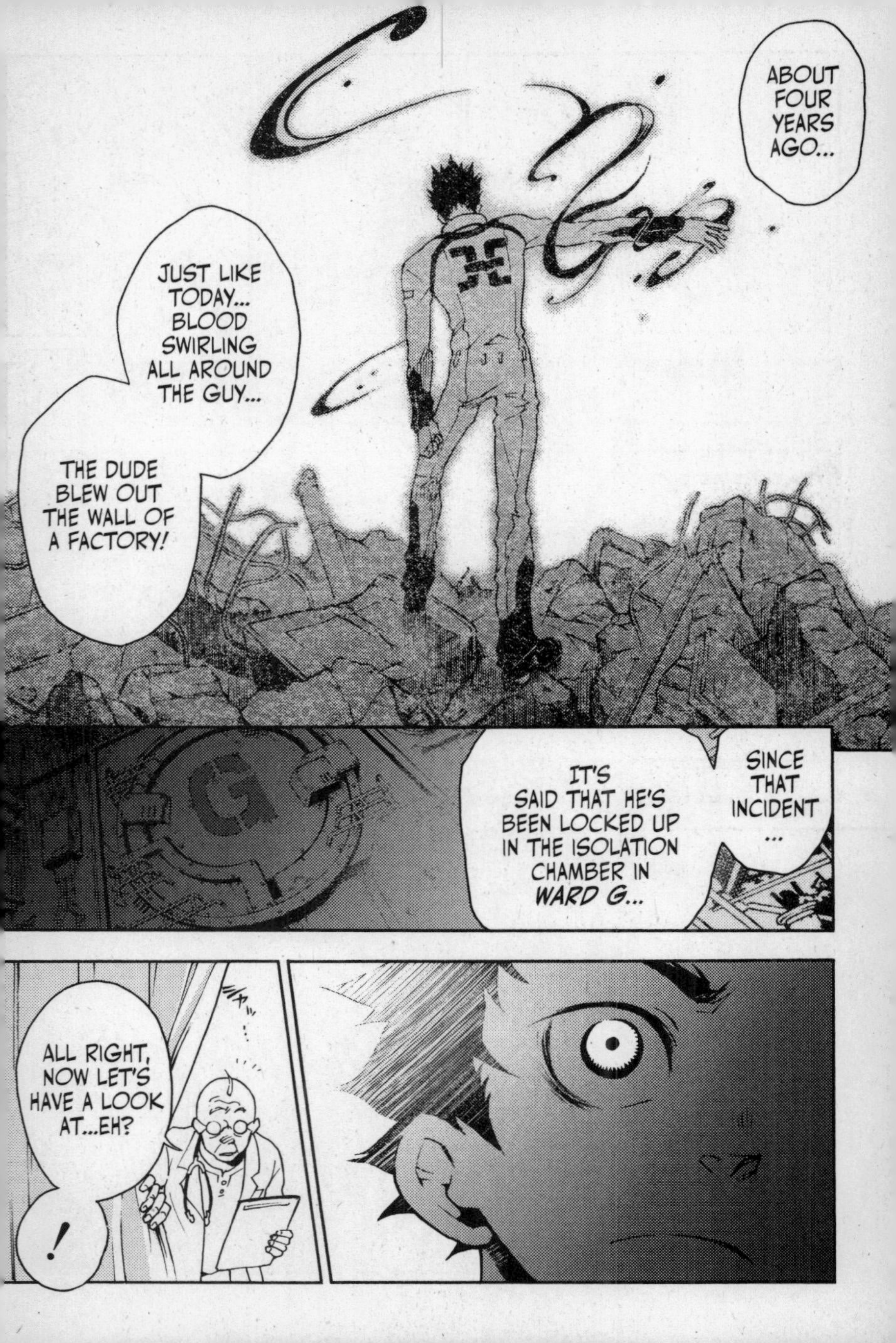
ABOUT FOUR YEARS AGO...
JUST LIKE TODAY... BLOOD SWIRLING ALL AROUND THE GUY...
THE DUDE BLEW OUT THE WALL OF A FACTORY!
SINCE THAT INCIDENT ...
IT'S SAID THAT HE'S BEEN LOCKED UP IN THE ISOLATION CHAMBER IN *WARD G*...
ALL RIGHT, NOW LET'S HAVE A LOOK AT...EH?
!

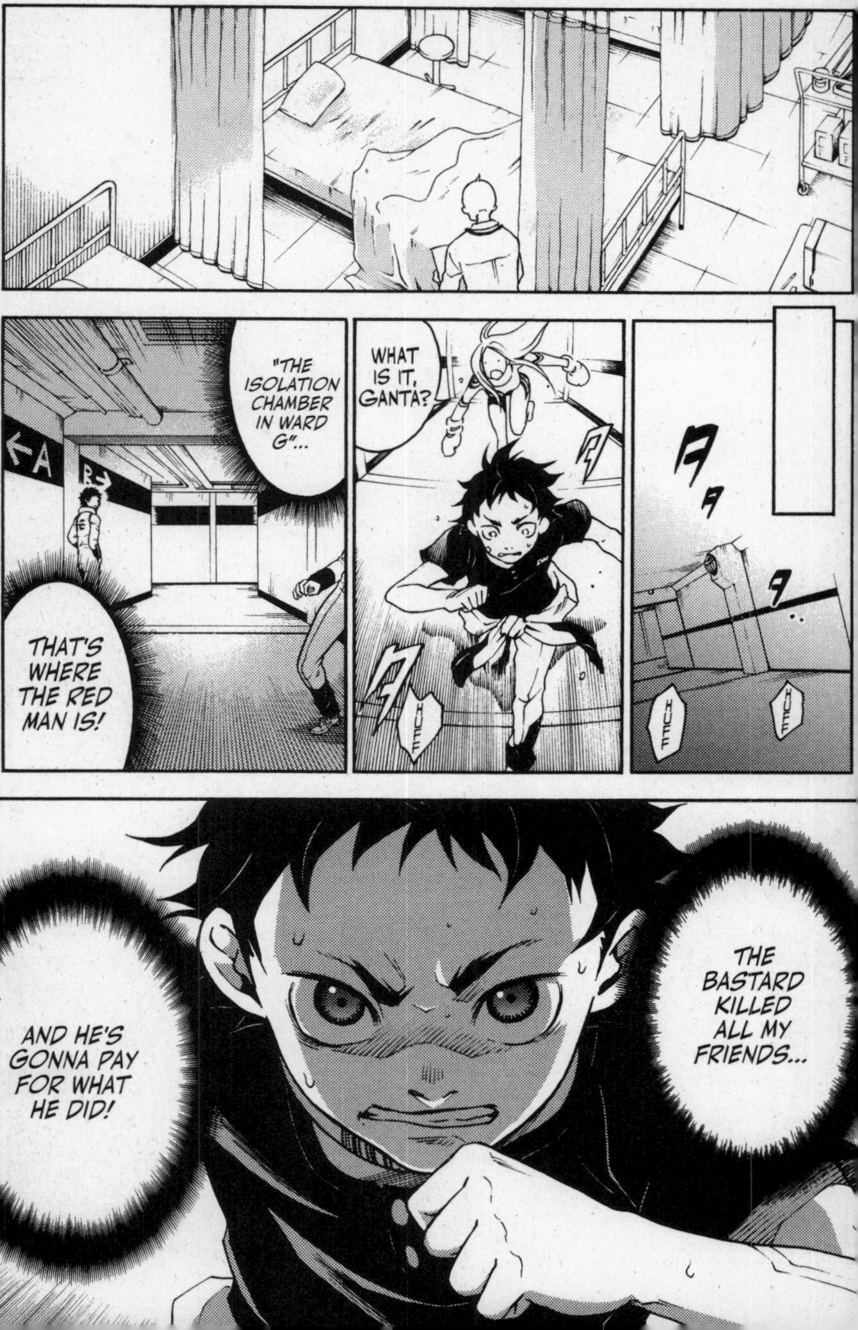
HUFF
HUFF
WHAT IS IT, GANTA?
HUFF
"THE ISOLATION CHAMBER IN WARD G"...
THAT'S WHERE THE RED MAN IS!
THE BASTARD KILLED ALL MY FRIENDS...
AND HE'S GONNA PAY FOR WHAT HE DID!

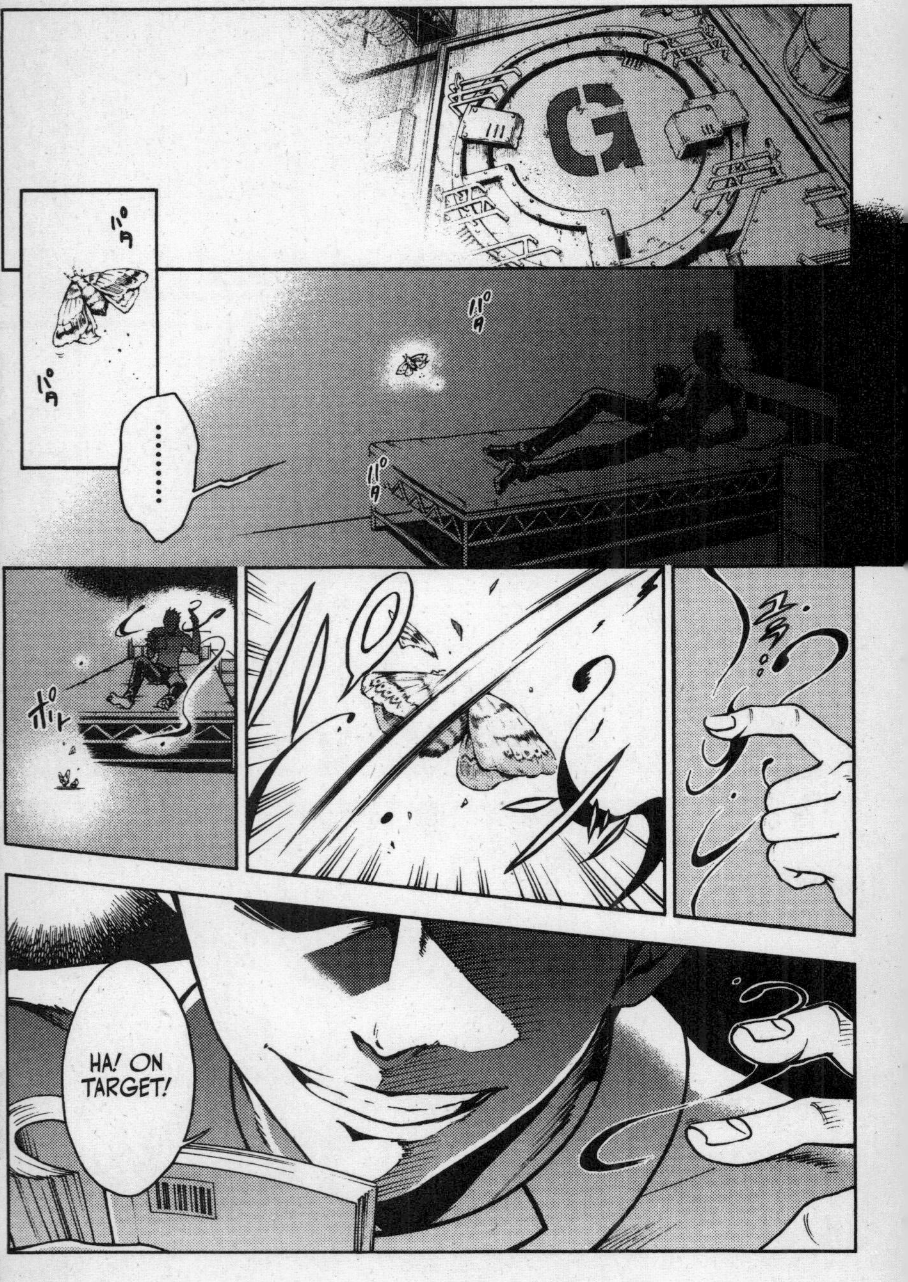

パタ
パタ
..........
パタ
パタ
ポト
HA! ON TARGET!

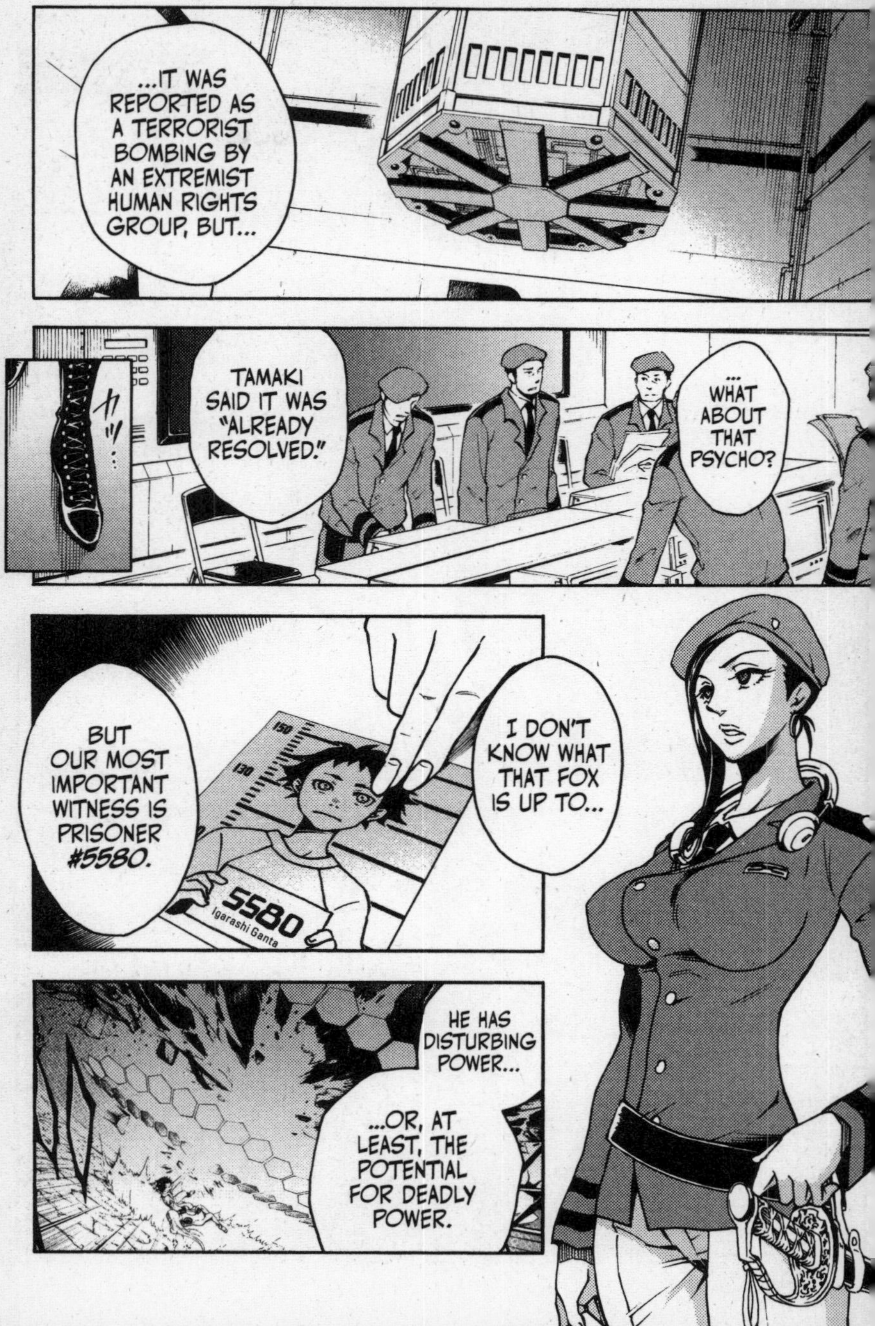

...IT WAS REPORTED AS A TERRORIST BOMBING BY AN EXTREMIST HUMAN RIGHTS GROUP, BUT...
... WHAT ABOUT THAT PSYCHO?
TAMAKI SAID IT WAS "ALREADY RESOLVED."
カッ…
I DON'T KNOW WHAT THAT FOX IS UP TO...
BUT OUR MOST IMPORTANT WITNESS IS PRISONER #5580.
150
130
5580
Igarashi Ganta
HE HAS DISTURBING POWER...
...OR, AT LEAST, THE POTENTIAL FOR DEADLY POWER.

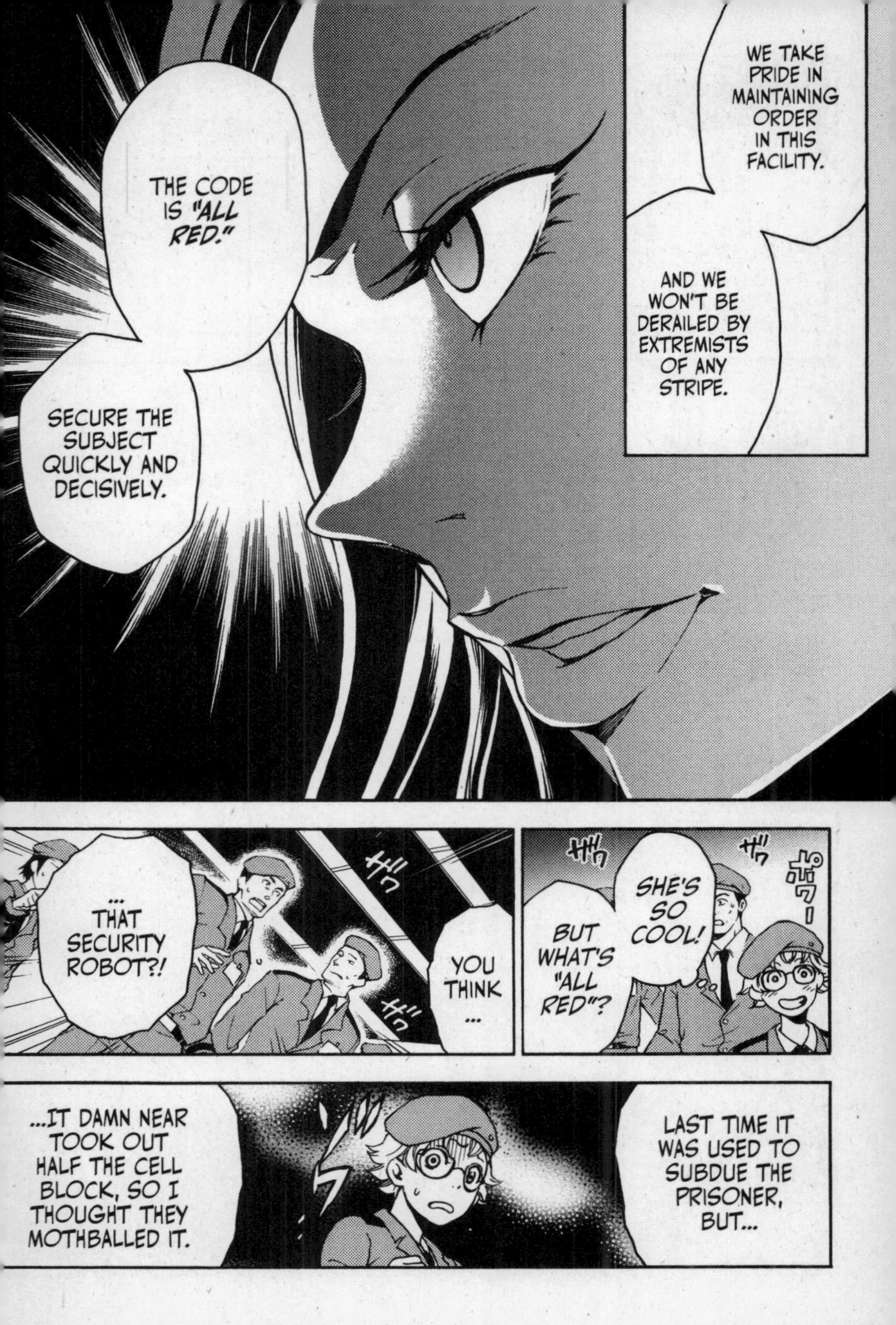
WE TAKE PRIDE IN MAINTAINING ORDER IN THIS FACILITY.
AND WE WON'T BE DERAILED BY EXTREMISTS OF ANY STRIPE.
THE CODE IS "ALL RED."
SECURE THE SUBJECT QUICKLY AND DECISIVELY.
SHE'S SO COOL!
BUT WHAT'S "ALL RED"?
YOU THINK ...
... THAT SECURITY ROBOT?!
LAST TIME IT WAS USED TO SUBDUE THE PRISONER, BUT...
...IT DAMN NEAR TOOK OUT HALF THE CELL BLOCK, SO I THOUGHT THEY MOTHBALLED IT.

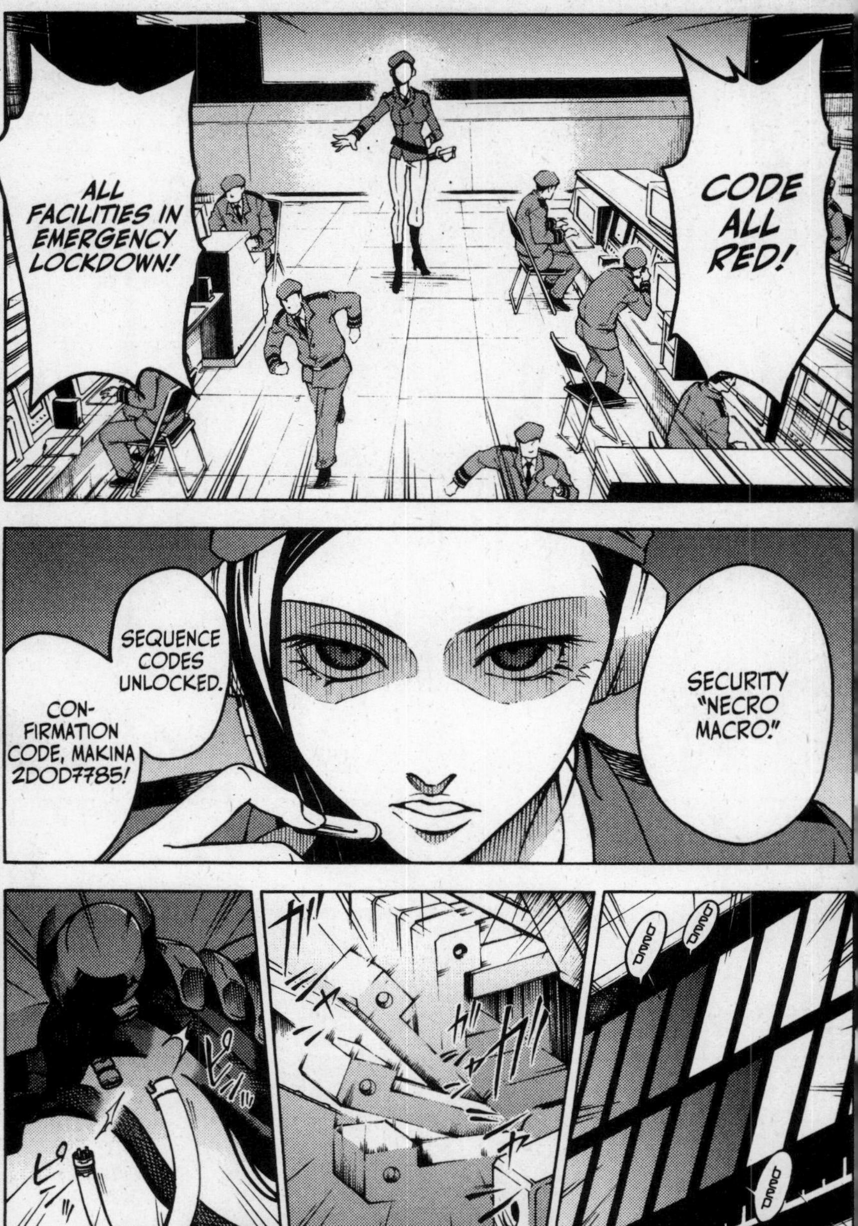
CODE ALL RED!
ALL FACILITIES IN EMERGENCY LOCKDOWN!
SECURITY "NECRO MACRO."
SEQUENCE CODES UNLOCKED.
CON-FIRMATION CODE, MAKINA 2DOD7785!

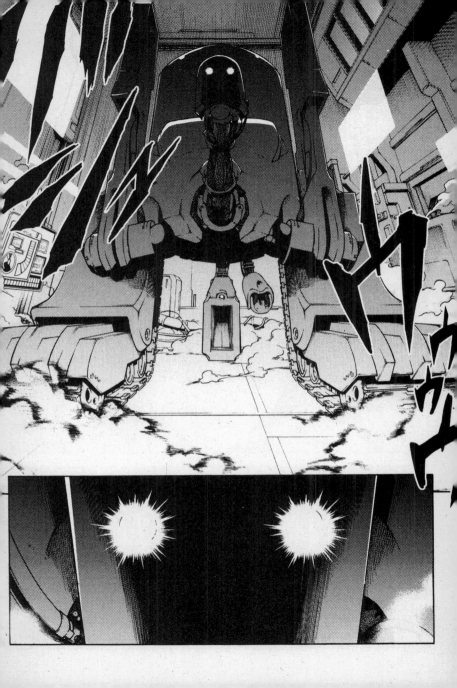

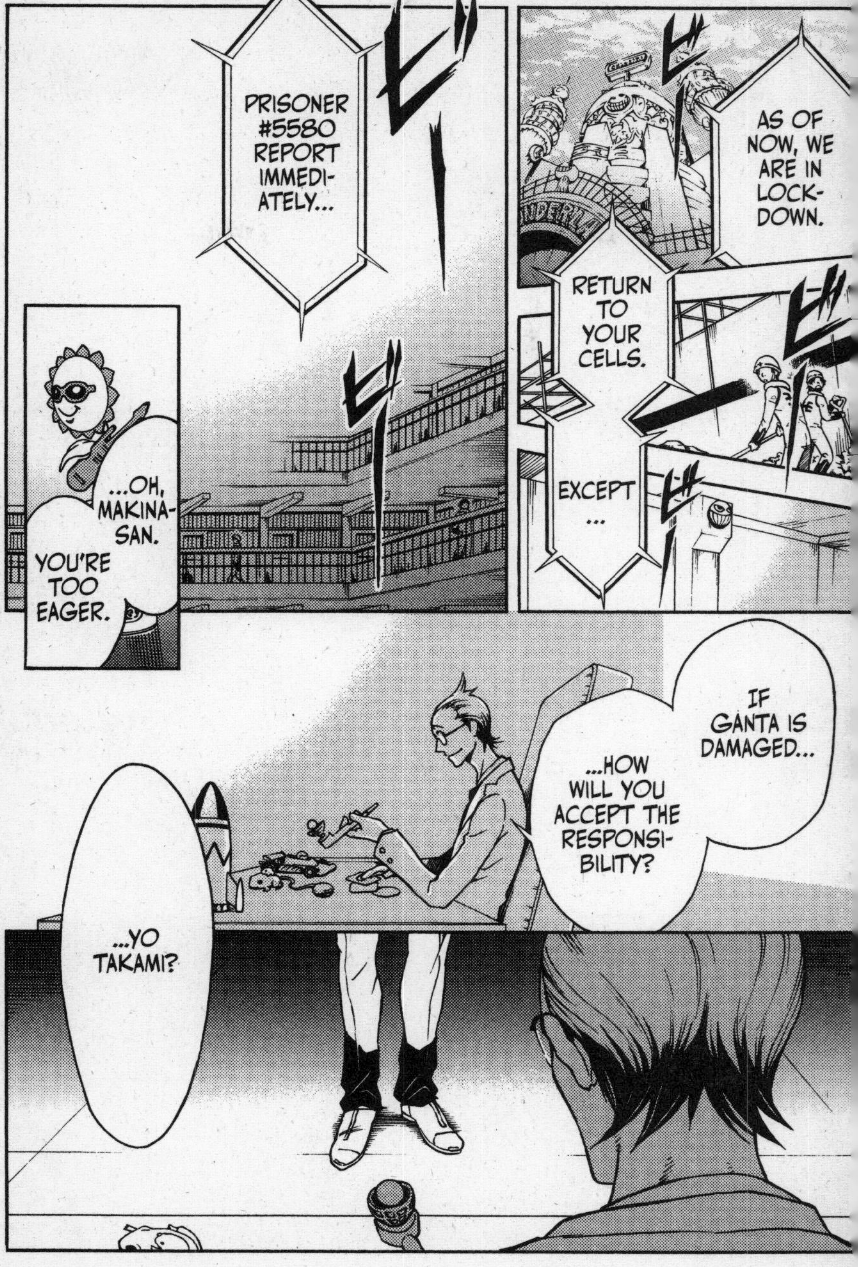
AS OF NOW, WE ARE IN LOCK-DOWN.
RETURN TO YOUR CELLS.
EXCEPT ...
PRISONER #5580 REPORT IMMEDI-ATELY...
...OH, MAKINA-SAN.
YOU'RE TOO EAGER.
IF GANTA IS DAMAGED...
...HOW WILL YOU ACCEPT THE RESPONSI-BILITY?
...YO TAKAMI?

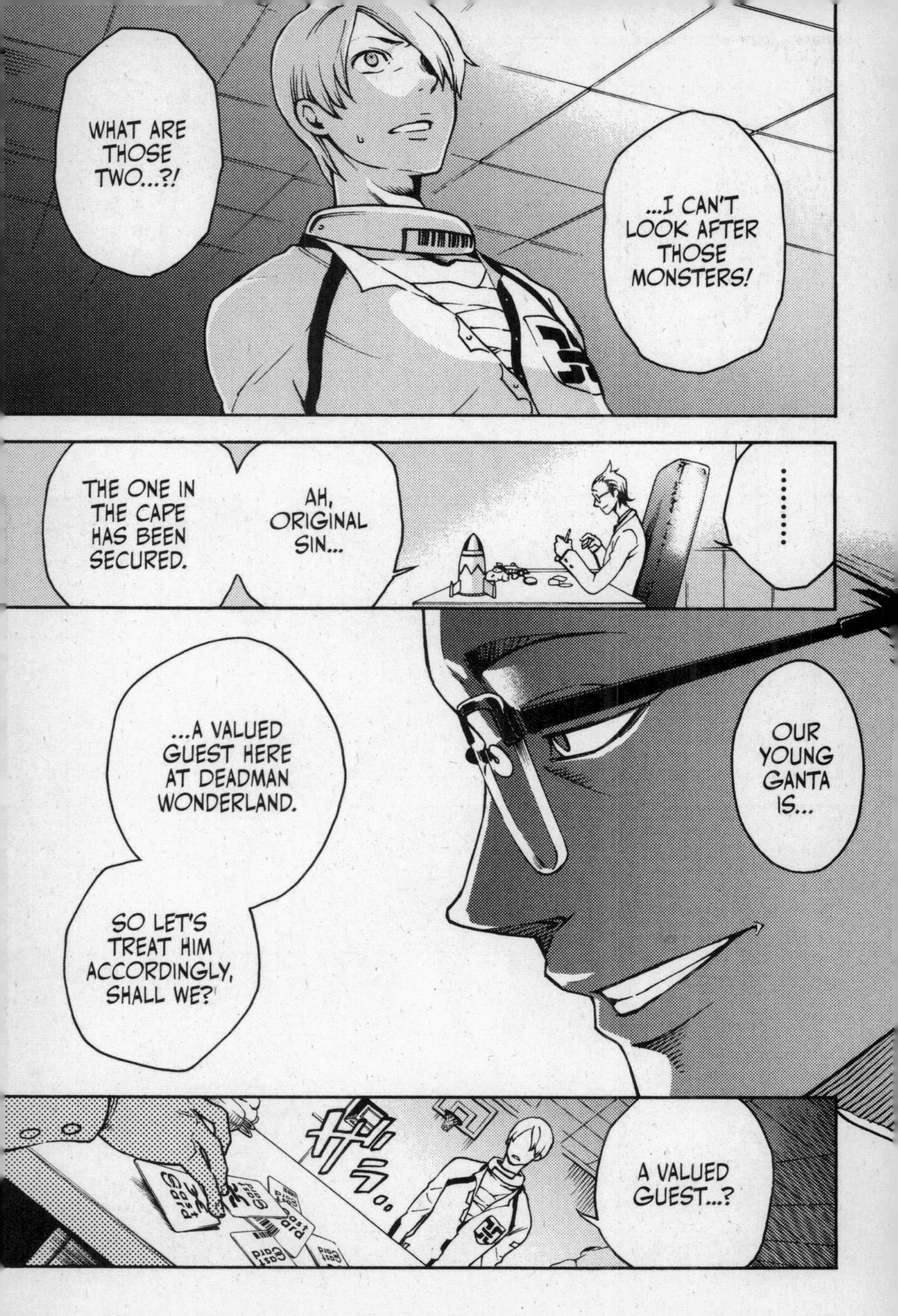
...I CAN'T LOOK AFTER THOSE MONSTERS!
WHAT ARE THOSE TWO...?!
......
AH, ORIGINAL SIN...
THE ONE IN THE CAPE HAS BEEN SECURED.
OUR YOUNG GANTA IS...
...A VALUED GUEST HERE AT DEADMAN WONDERLAND.
SO LET'S TREAT HIM ACCORDINGLY, SHALL WE?
A VALUED GUEST...?

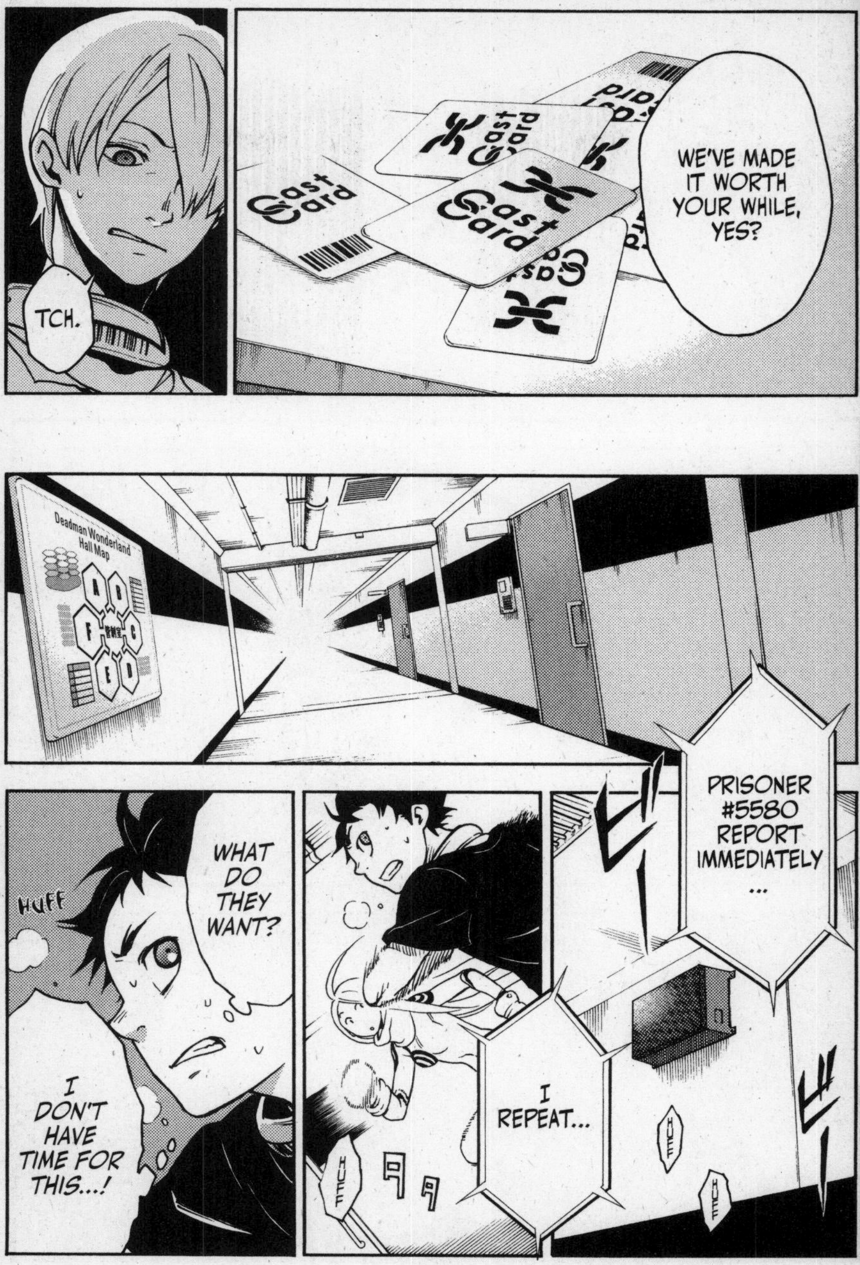
WE'VE MADE IT WORTH YOUR WHILE, YES?
Cast Card
TCH.
Deadman Wonderland
Hall Map
PRISONER #5580 REPORT IMMEDIATELY ...
I REPEAT...
HUFF
HUFF
HUFF
WHAT DO THEY WANT?
HUFF
I DON'T HAVE TIME FOR THIS...!

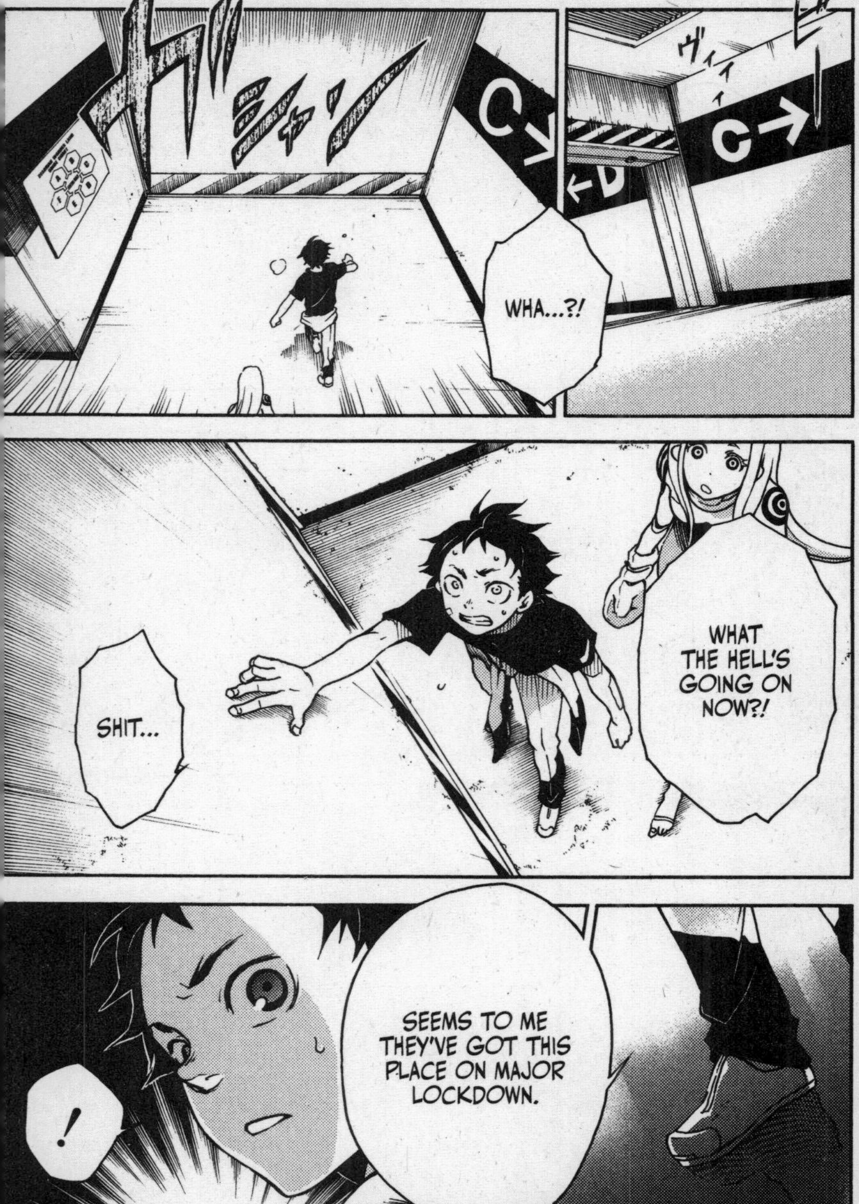

ビー
ヴィイイ
C→
←D
WHA...?!
ガシャン
WHAT THE HELL'S GOING ON NOW?!
SHIT...
SEEMS TO ME THEY'VE GOT THIS PLACE ON MAJOR LOCKDOWN.
!

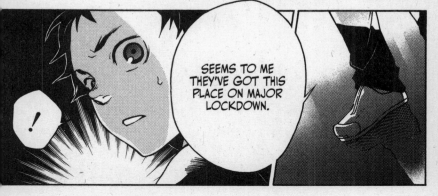

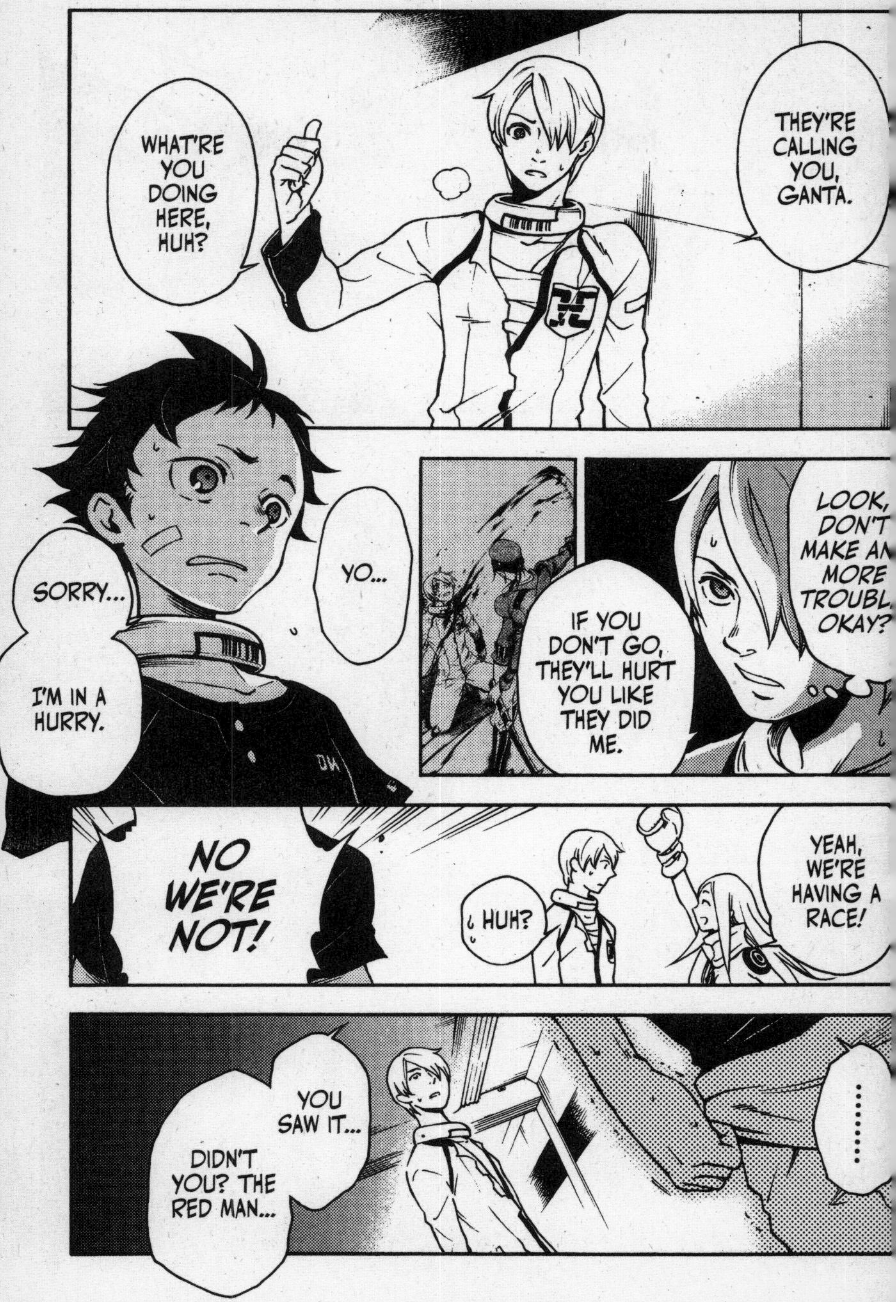
THEY'RE CALLING YOU, GANTA.
WHAT'RE YOU DOING HERE, HUH?
LOOK, DON'T MAKE AN MORE TROUBL, OKAY?
IF YOU DON'T GO, THEY'LL HURT YOU LIKE THEY DID ME.
YO...
SORRY...
I'M IN A HURRY.
YEAH, WE'RE HAVING A RACE!
¿ HUH?
NO WE'RE NOT!
......
YOU SAW IT...
DIDN'T YOU? THE RED MAN...

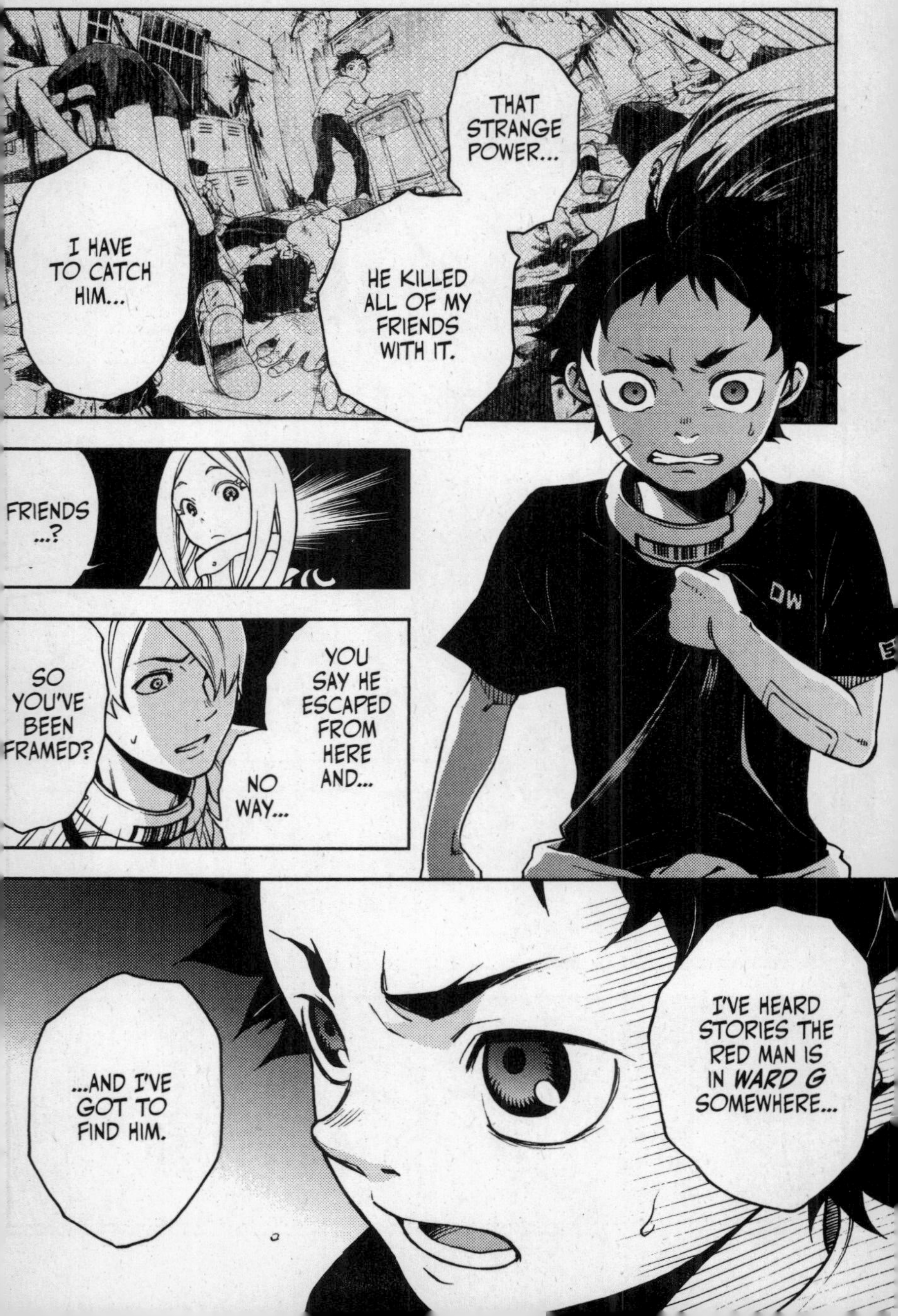
THAT STRANGE POWER...
HE KILLED ALL OF MY FRIENDS WITH IT.
I HAVE TO CATCH HIM...
FRIENDS ...?
YOU SAY HE ESCAPED FROM HERE AND...
NO WAY...
SO YOU'VE BEEN FRAMED?
I'VE HEARD STORIES THE RED MAN IS IN *WARD G* SOMEWHERE...
...AND I'VE GOT TO FIND HIM.

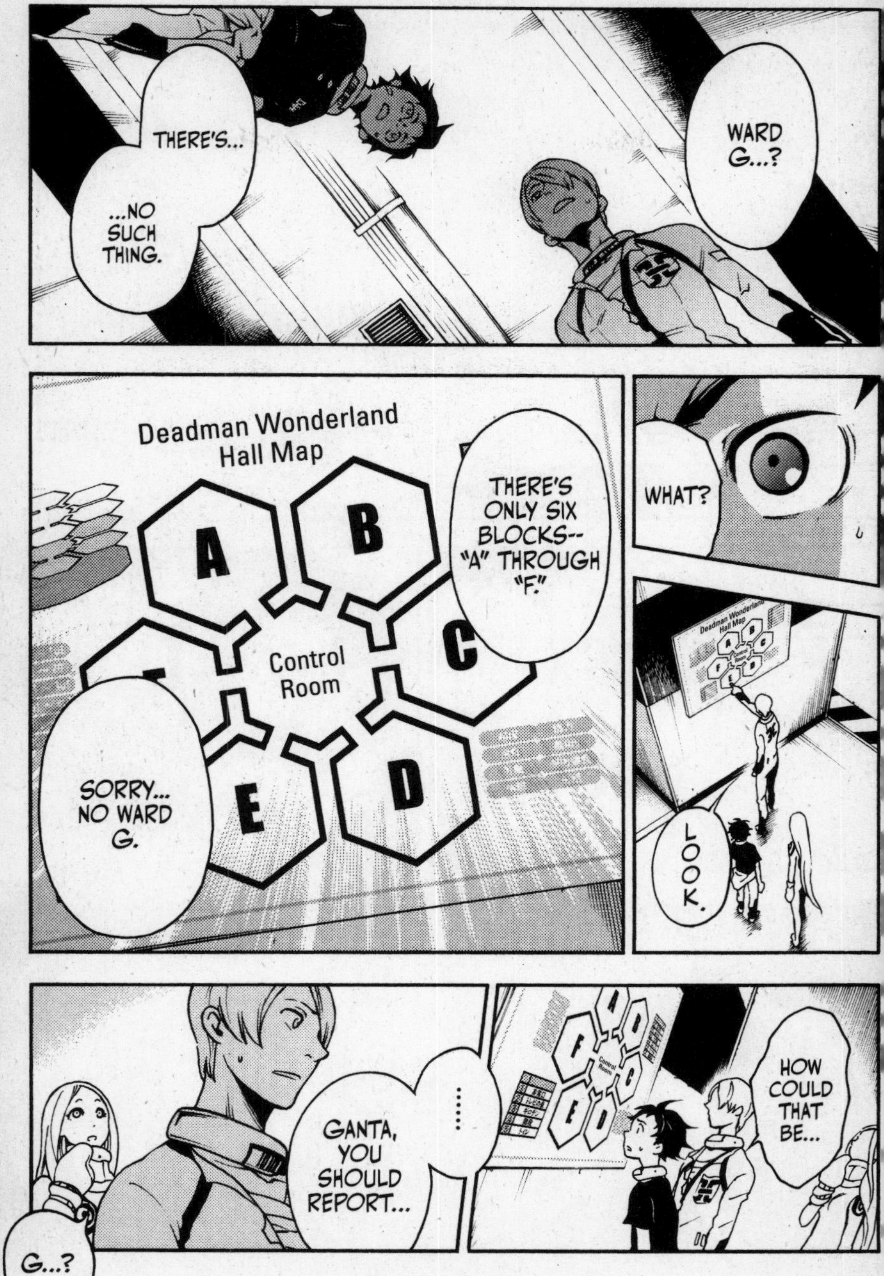

WARD G...?
THERE'S...
...NO SUCH THING.
WHAT?
LOOK.
Deadman Wonderland Hall Map
A
B
C
D
E
Control Room
THERE'S ONLY SIX BLOCKS-- "A" THROUGH "F."
SORRY... NO WARD G.
HOW COULD THAT BE...
......
GANTA, YOU SHOULD REPORT...
G...?

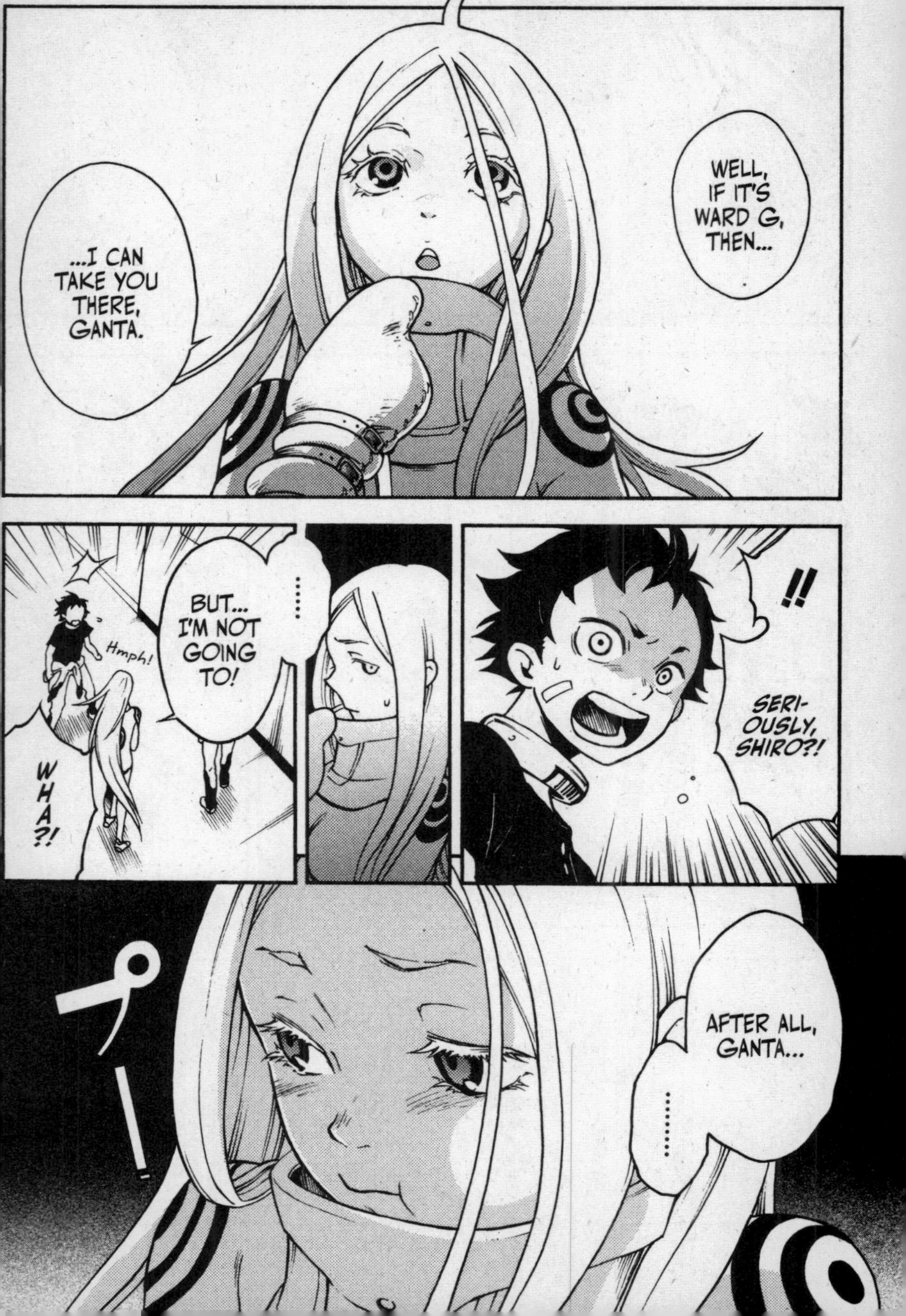
WELL, IF IT'S WARD G, THEN...
...I CAN TAKE YOU THERE, GANTA.
!!
SERI-OUSLY, SHIRO?!
......
BUT... I'M NOT GOING TO!
Hmph!
WHA?!
AFTER ALL, GANTA...
......

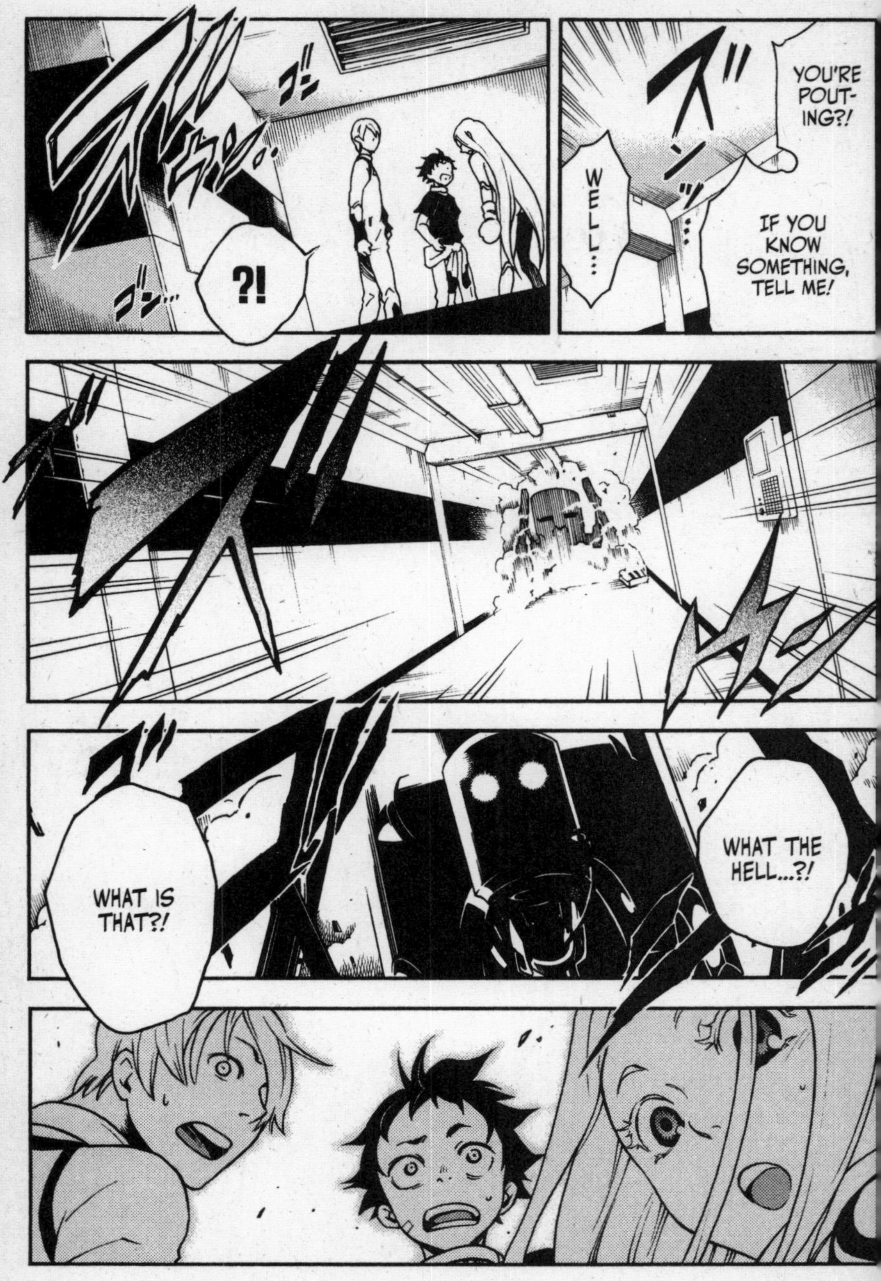
YOU'RE POUT-ING?!
IF YOU KNOW SOMETHING, TELL ME!
WELL...
?!
WHAT THE HELL...?!
WHAT IS THAT?!

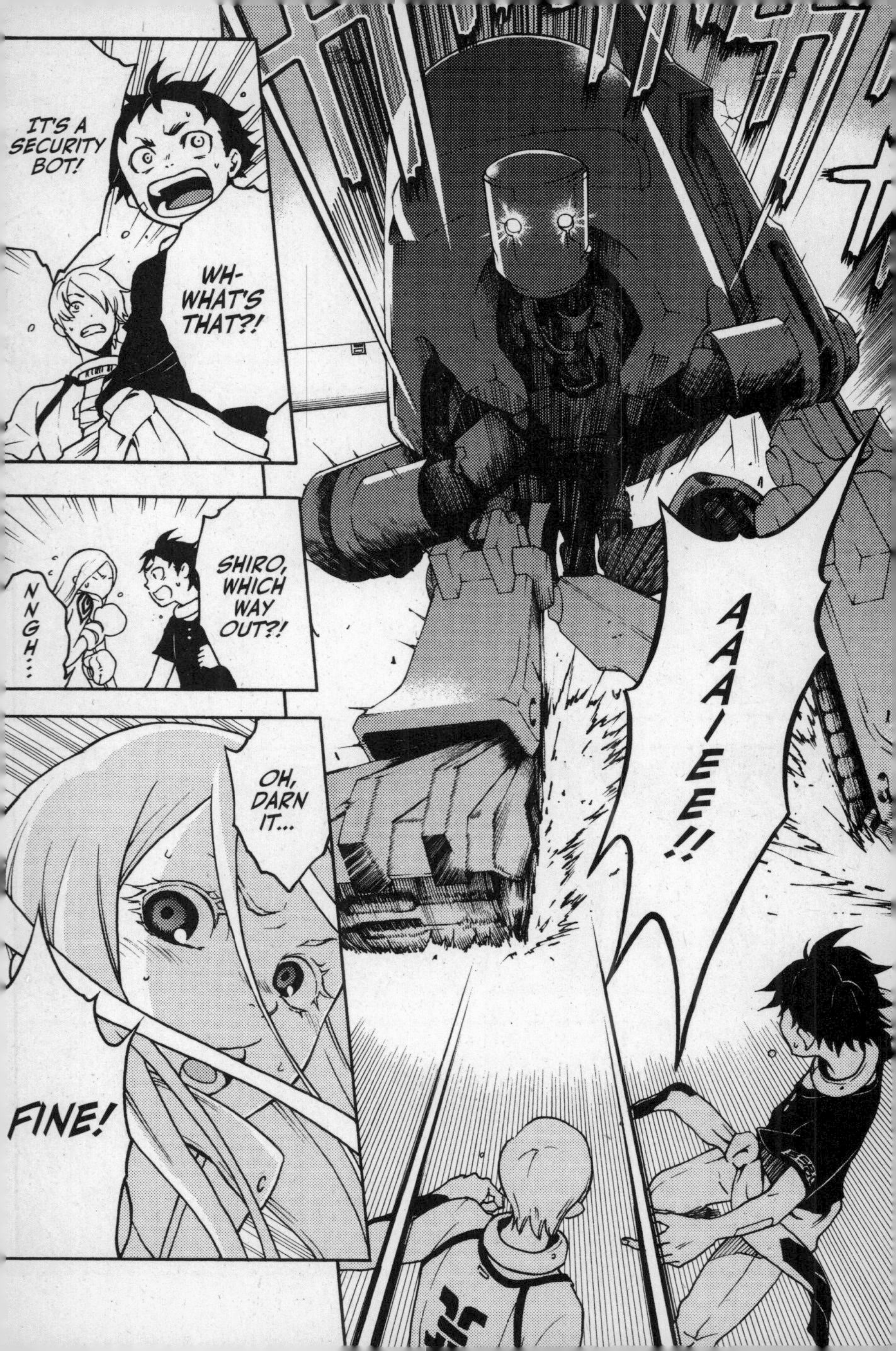
AAAIEEE!!
WH-WHAT'S THAT?!
IT'S A SECURITY BOT!
SHIRO, WHICH WAY OUT?!
NNGH...
OH, DARN IT...
FINE!

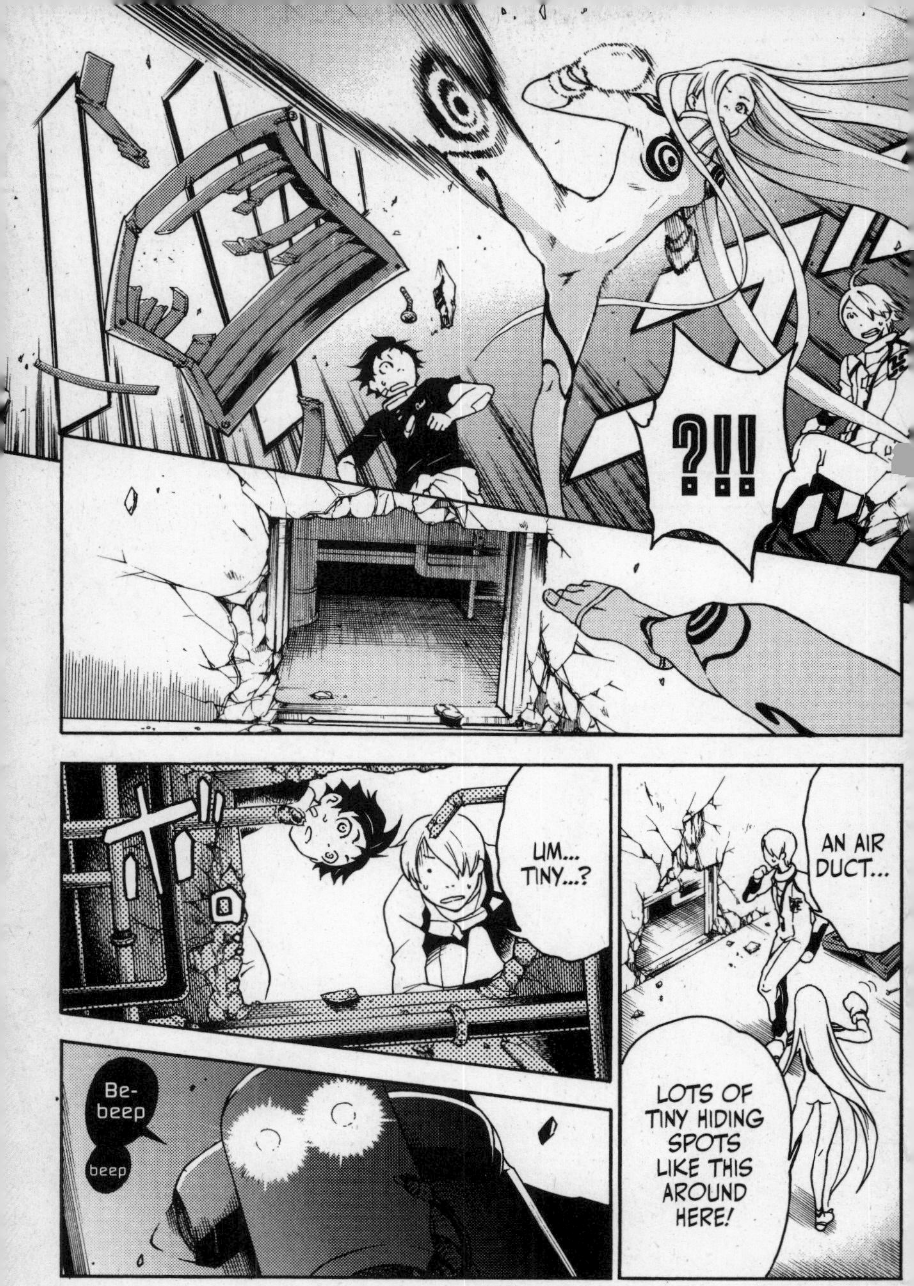
?!!
AN AIR DUCT...
LOTS OF TINY HIDING SPOTS LIKE THIS AROUND HERE!
UM... TINY...?
Be-beep
beep

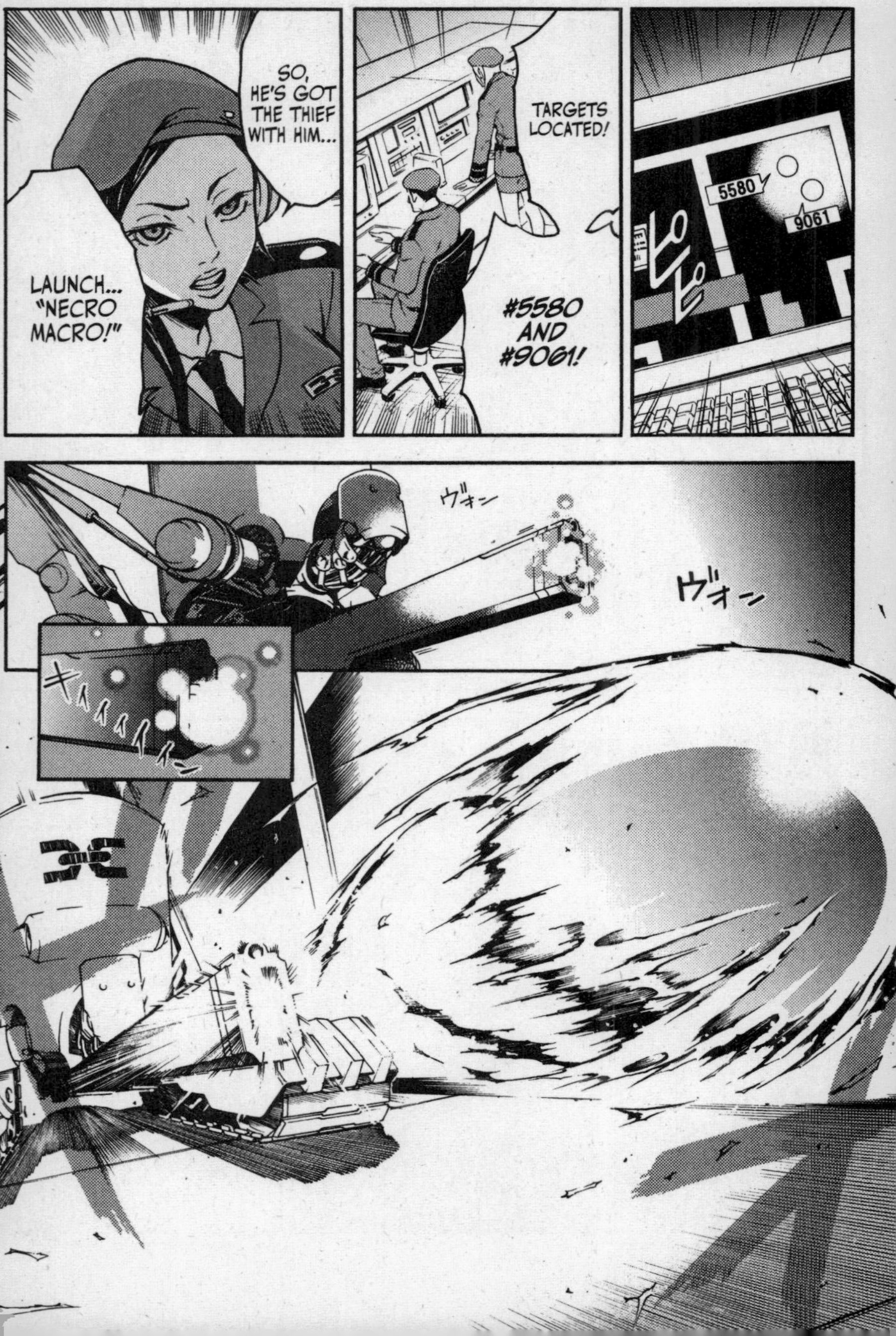
5580
9061
ピピ
TARGETS LOCATED!
#5580 AND #9061!
SO, HE'S GOT THE THIEF WITH HIM...
LAUNCH... "NECRO MACRO!"
ヴォーン
ヴォーン
キィィィィィン

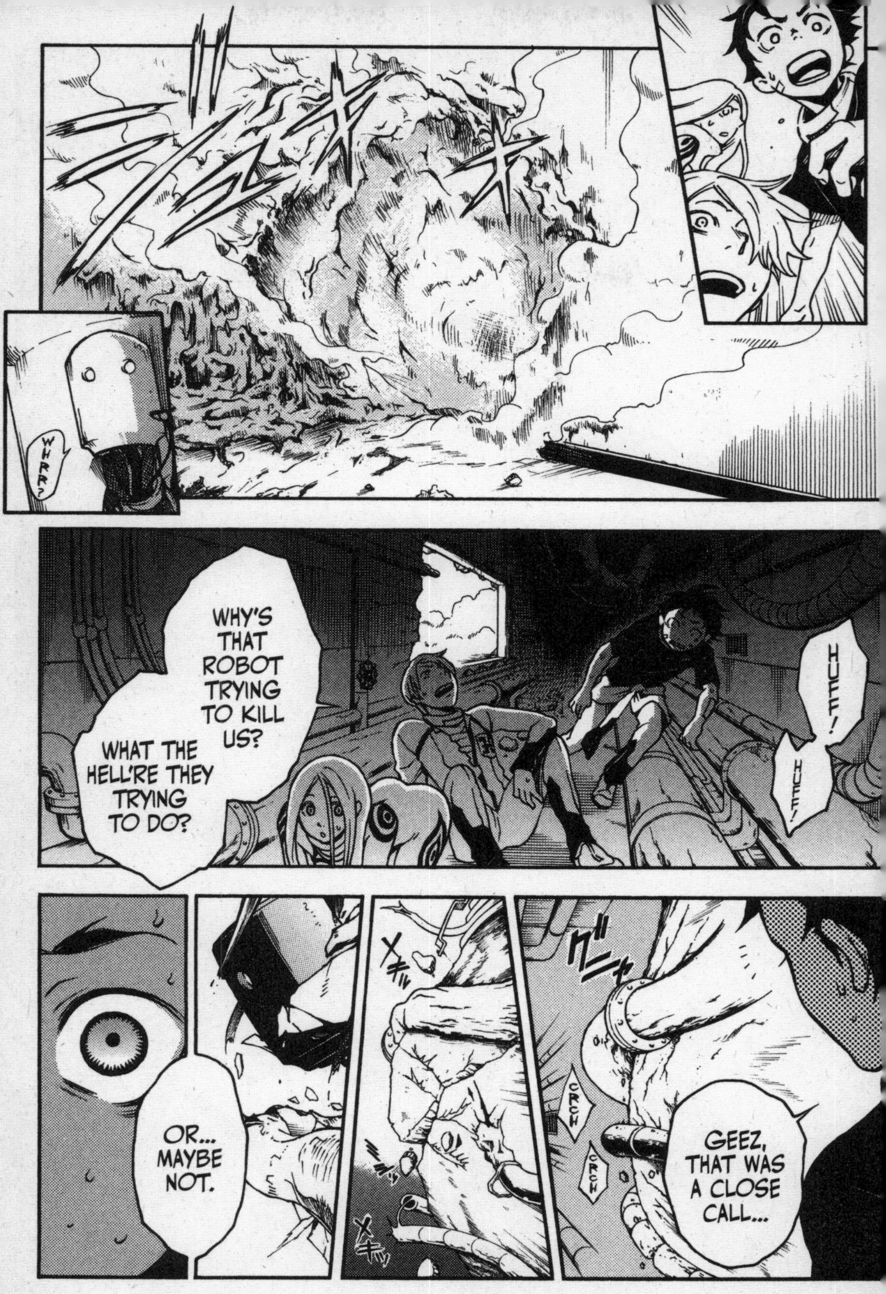
WHRR?
HUFF!
HUFF!
WHY'S THAT ROBOT TRYING TO KILL US?
WHAT THE HELL'RE THEY TRYING TO DO?
GEEZ, THAT WAS A CLOSE CALL...
CRCH
CRCH
OR... MAYBE NOT.

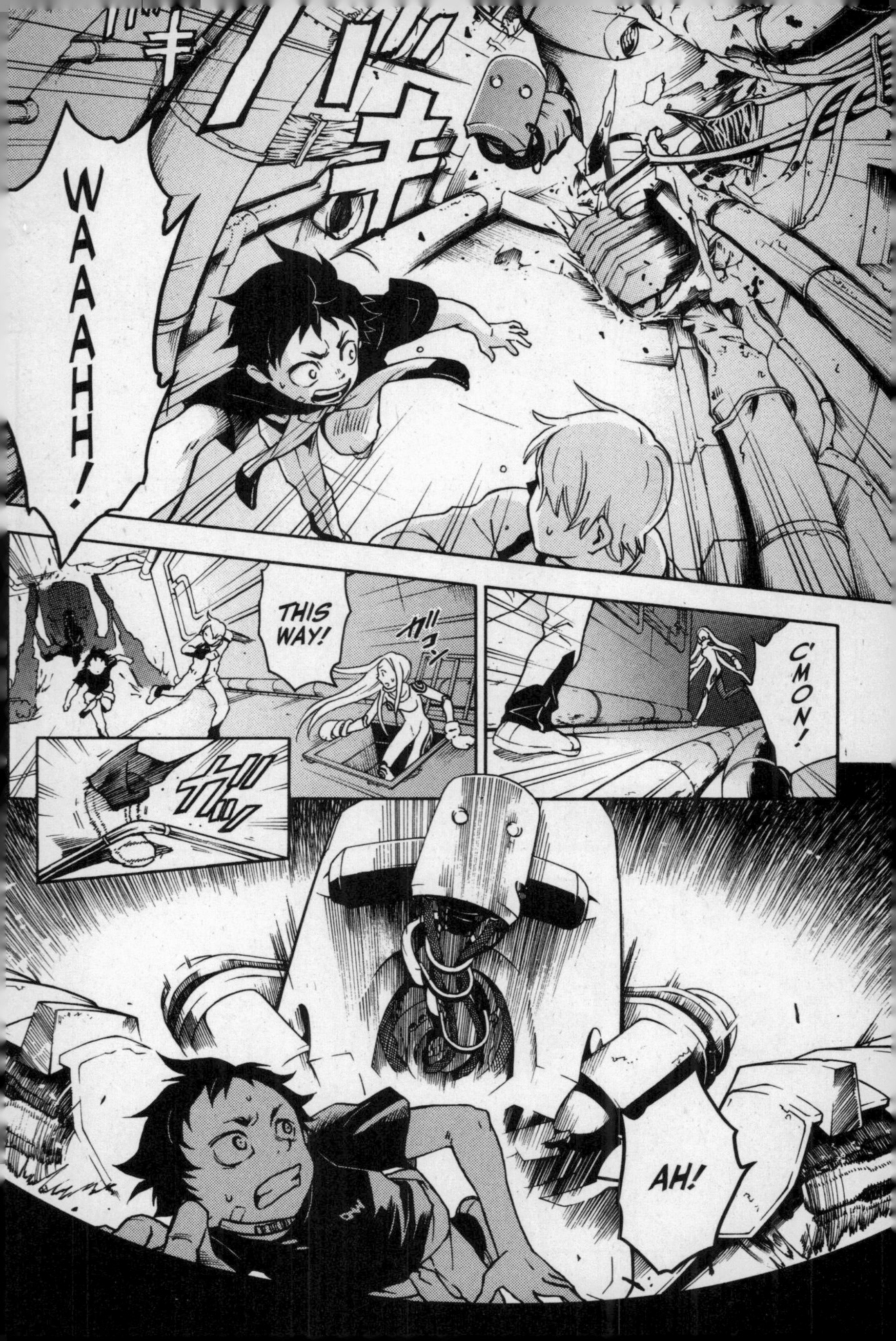
WAAAAHH!
C'MON!
THIS WAY!
AH!

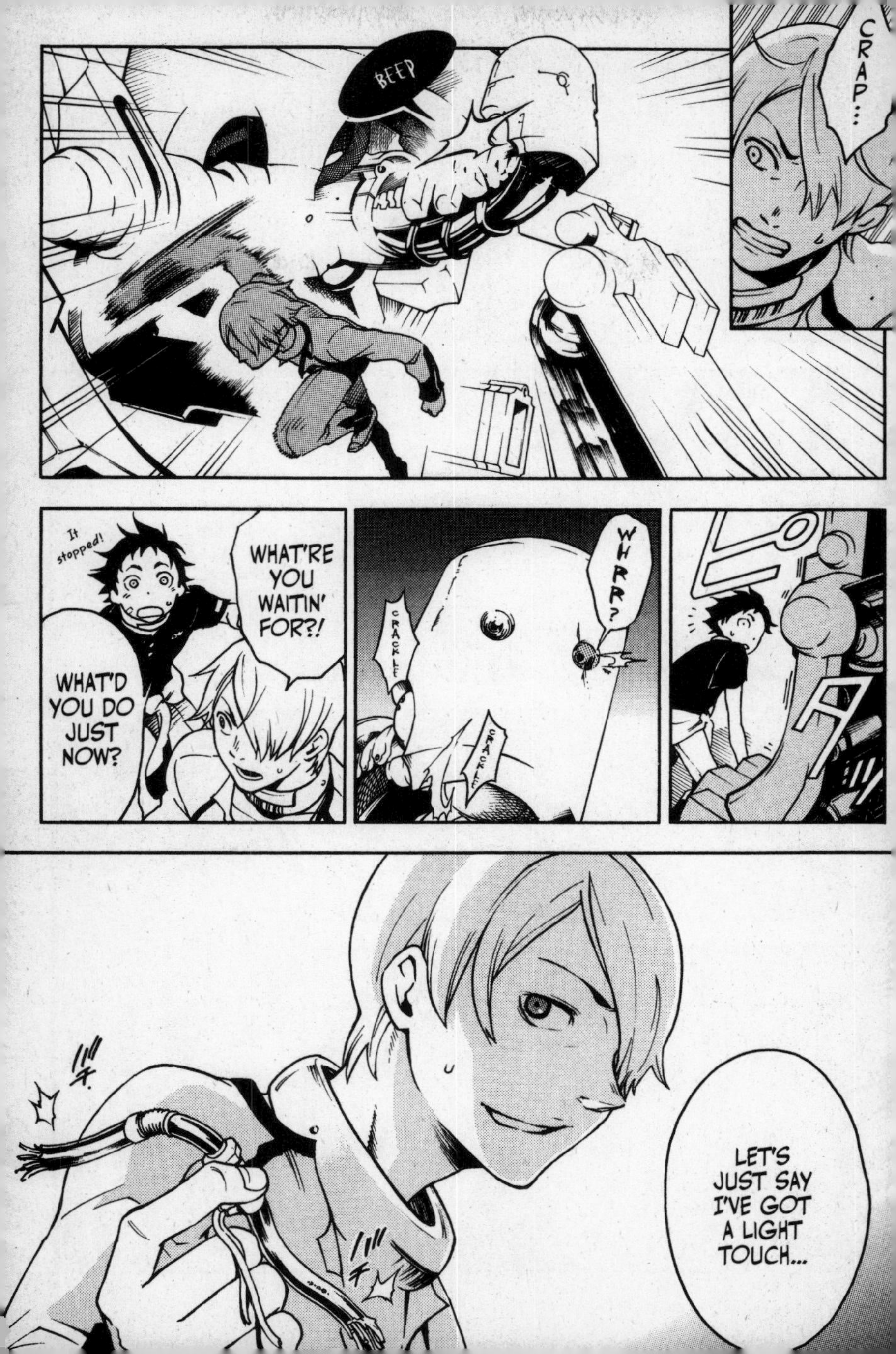
CRAP...
BEEP
WHRR?
CRACKLE
CRACKLE
WHAT'RE YOU WAITIN' FOR?!
It stopped!
WHAT'D YOU DO JUST NOW?
LET'S JUST SAY I'VE GOT A LIGHT TOUCH...

LIGHT TOUCH?

TCH, FORGET ABOUT IT...

...?

...WHY DID SHE GET SO TICKED OFF BACK THERE?

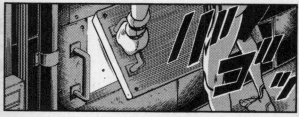

WHOA...!

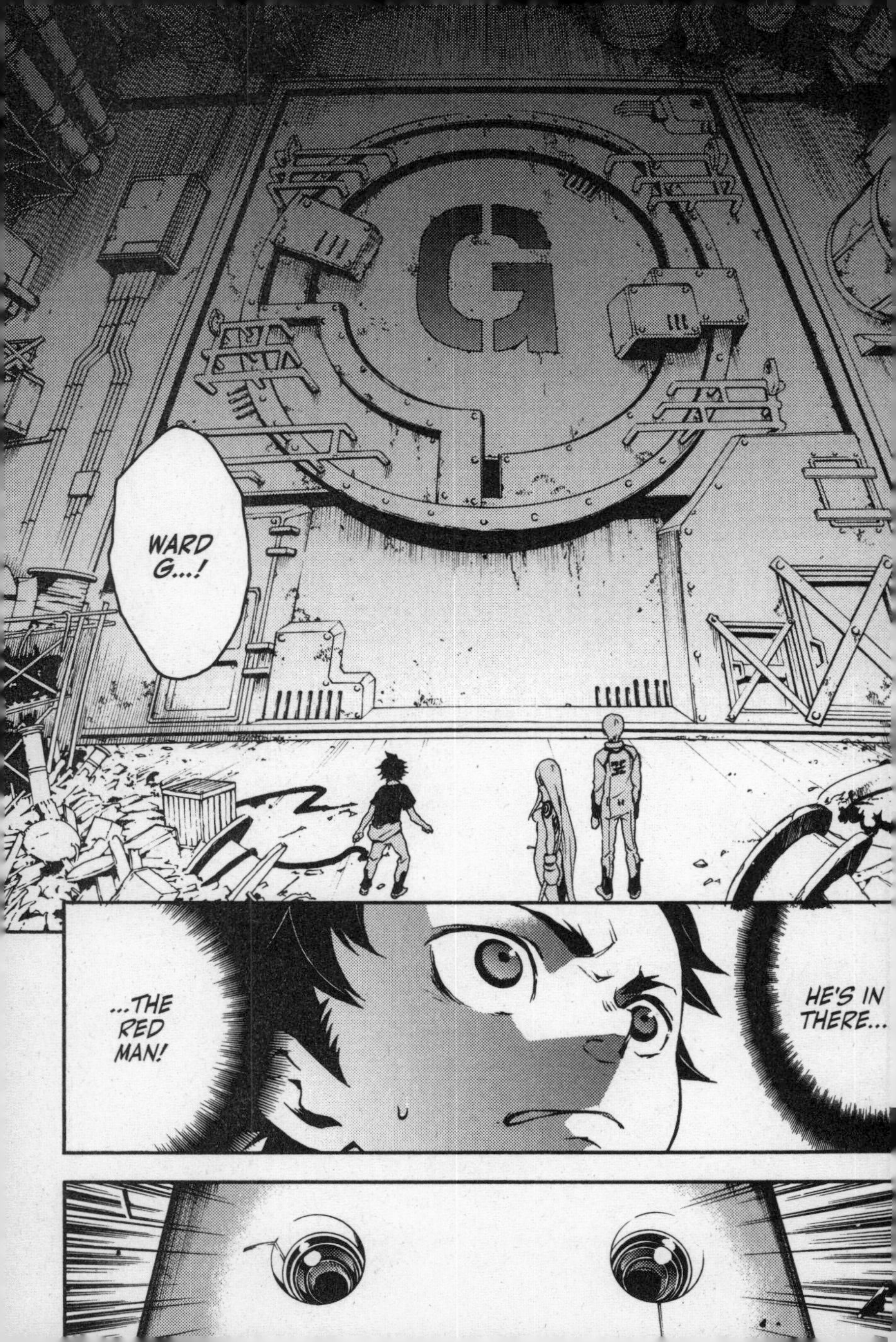
WARD G...!
HE'S IN THERE...
...THE RED MAN!

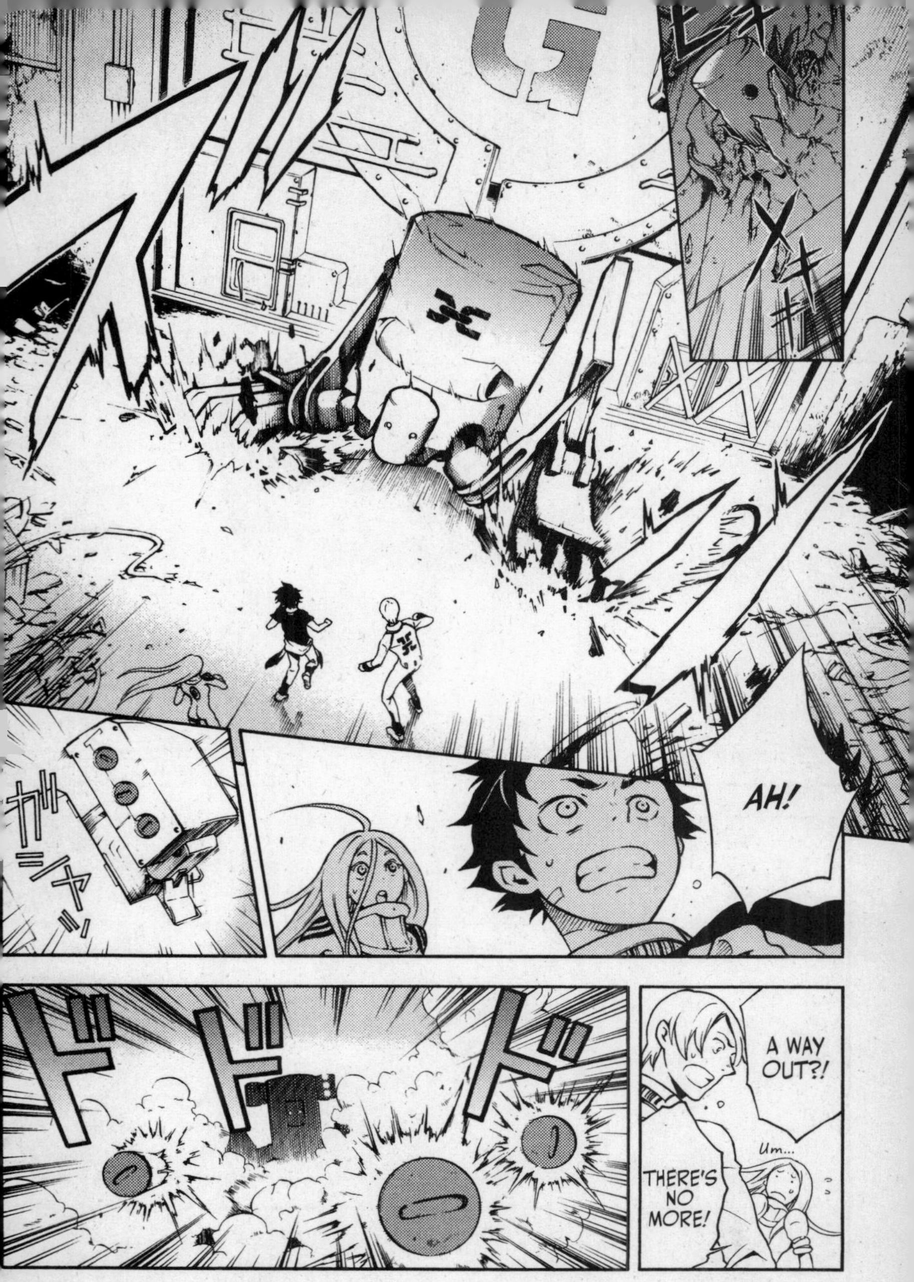
AH!
A WAY OUT?!
Um...
THERE'S NO MORE!
ドドド

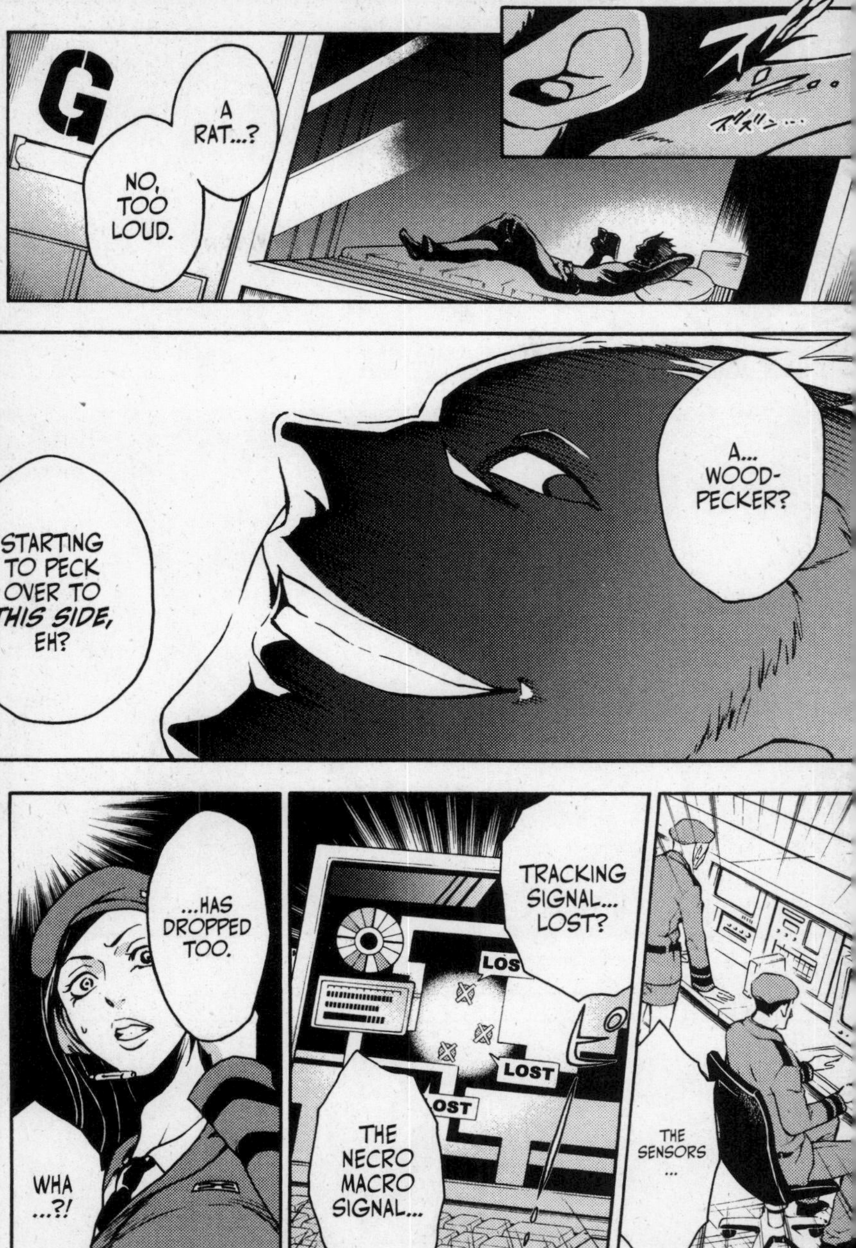
A RAT...?
NO, TOO LOUD.
A... WOOD-PECKER?
STARTING TO PECK OVER TO *THIS SIDE,* EH?
THE SENSORS ...
TRACKING SIGNAL... LOST?
LOST
LOST
LOST
THE NECRO MACRO SIGNAL...
...HAS DROPPED TOO.
WHA ...?!

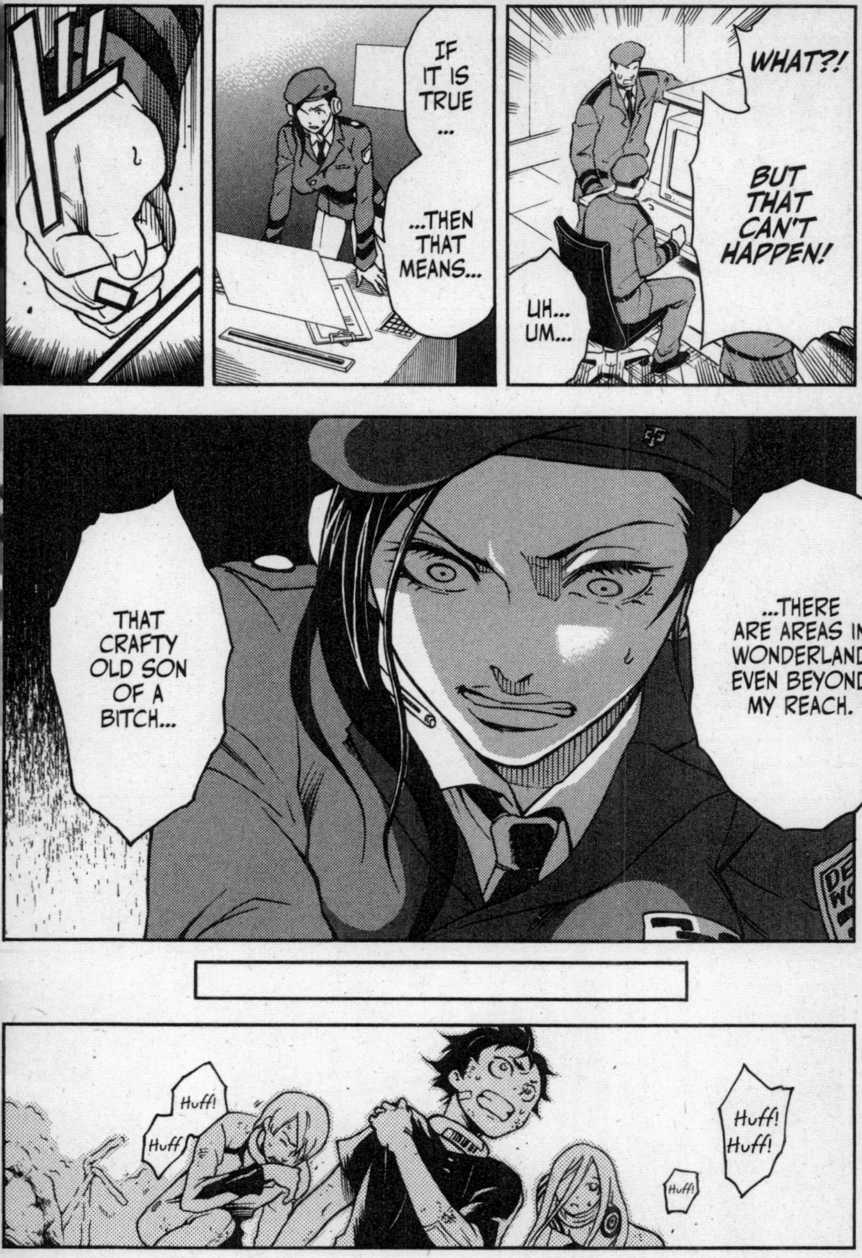
WHAT?!
BUT THAT CAN'T HAPPEN!
UH... UM...
IF IT IS TRUE ...
...THEN THAT MEANS...
...THERE ARE AREAS IN WONDERLAND EVEN BEYOND MY REACH.
THAT CRAFTY OLD SON OF A BITCH...
Huff! Huff!
Huff!
Huff!
Huff

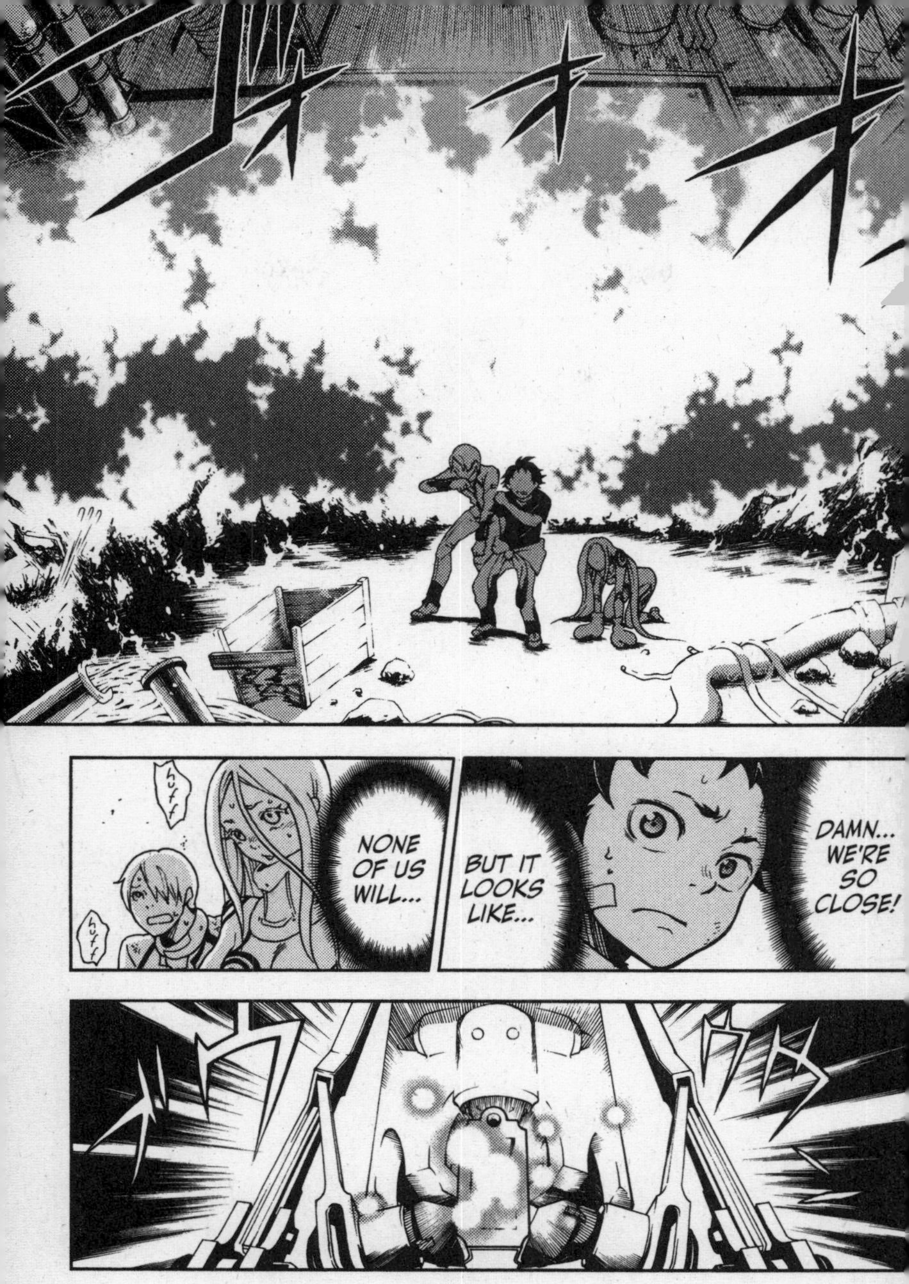
DAMN... WE'RE SO CLOSE!
BUT IT LOOKS LIKE...
NONE OF US WILL...

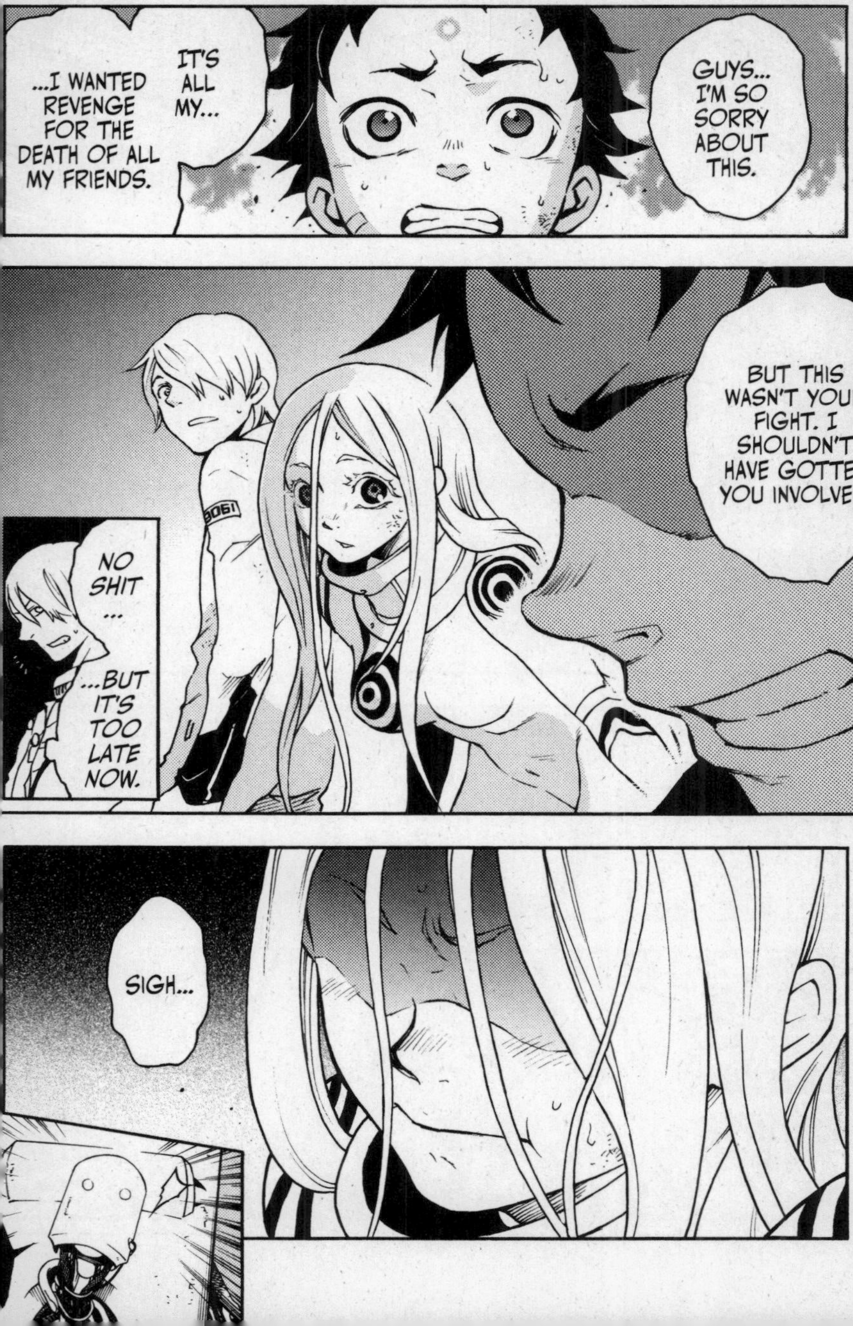
GUYS... I'M SO SORRY ABOUT THIS.
IT'S ALL MY...
...I WANTED REVENGE FOR THE DEATH OF ALL MY FRIENDS.
BUT THIS WASN'T YOUR FIGHT. I SHOULDN'T HAVE GOTTEN YOU INVOLVED.
NO SHIT...
...BUT IT'S TOO LATE NOW.
SIGH...

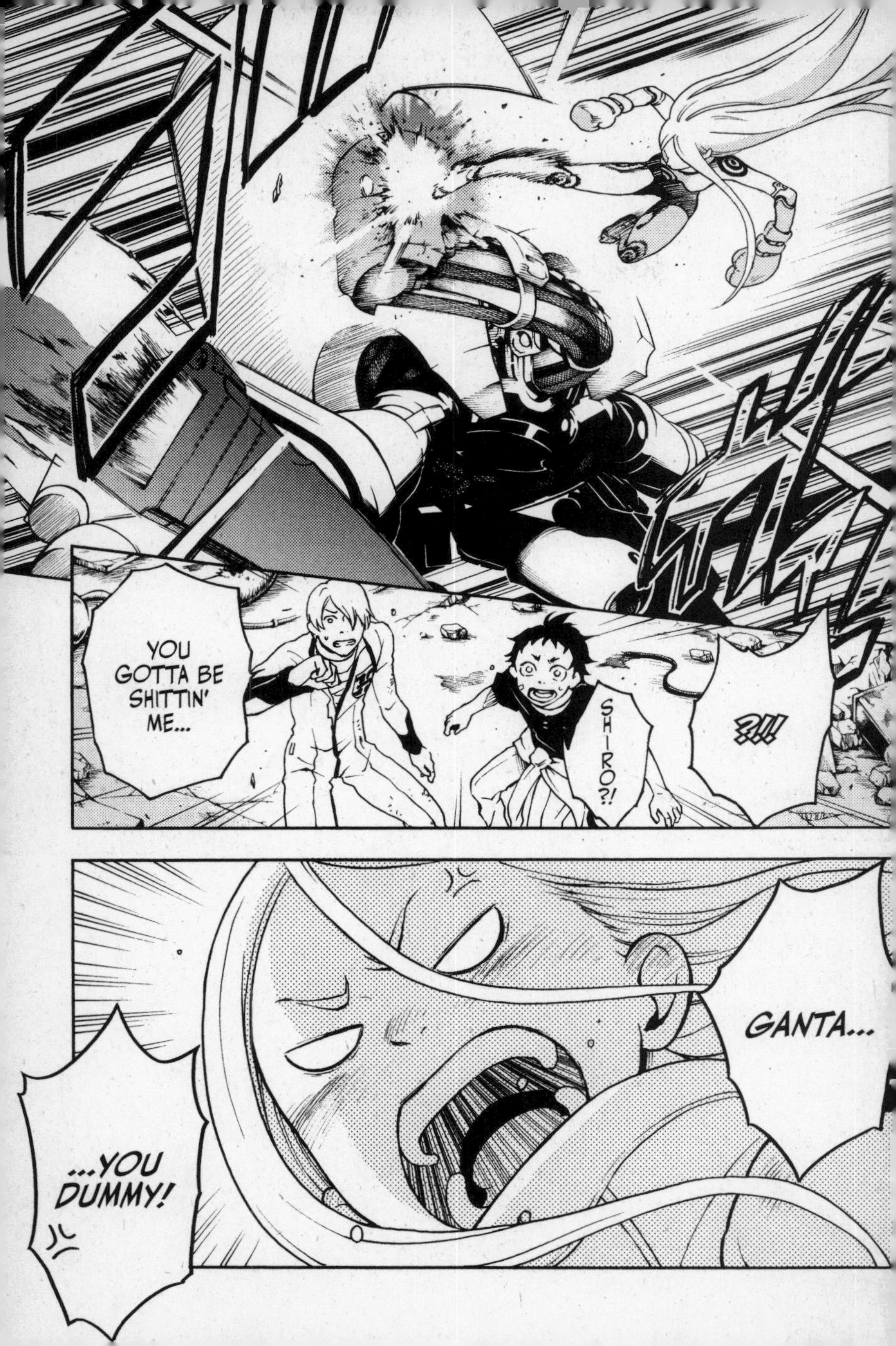
?!!
SHIRO?!
YOU GOTTA BE SHITTIN' ME...
GANTA...
...YOU DUMMY!

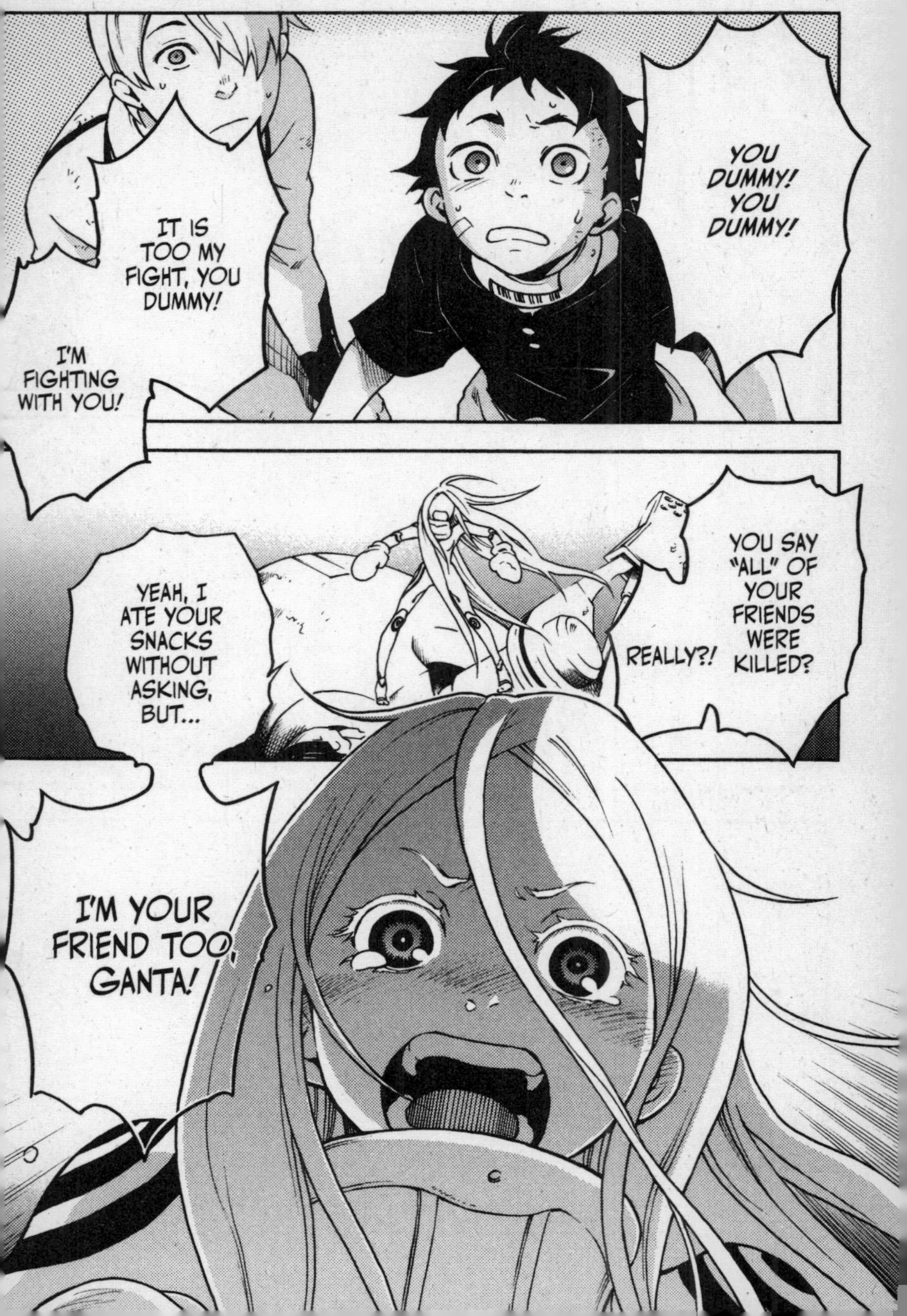
YOU DUMMY! YOU DUMMY!
IT IS TOO MY FIGHT, YOU DUMMY!
I'M FIGHTING WITH YOU!
YOU SAY "ALL" OF YOUR FRIENDS WERE KILLED?
REALLY?!
YEAH, I ATE YOUR SNACKS WITHOUT ASKING, BUT...
I'M YOUR FRIEND TOO, GANTA!

OH, YEAH...

I...

THAT'S WHAT YOU'RE MAD ABOUT?

I MADE A NEW FRIEND...

WHETHER I KNEW IT OR NOT...

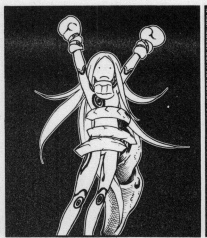

SORRY...

...SHIRO.

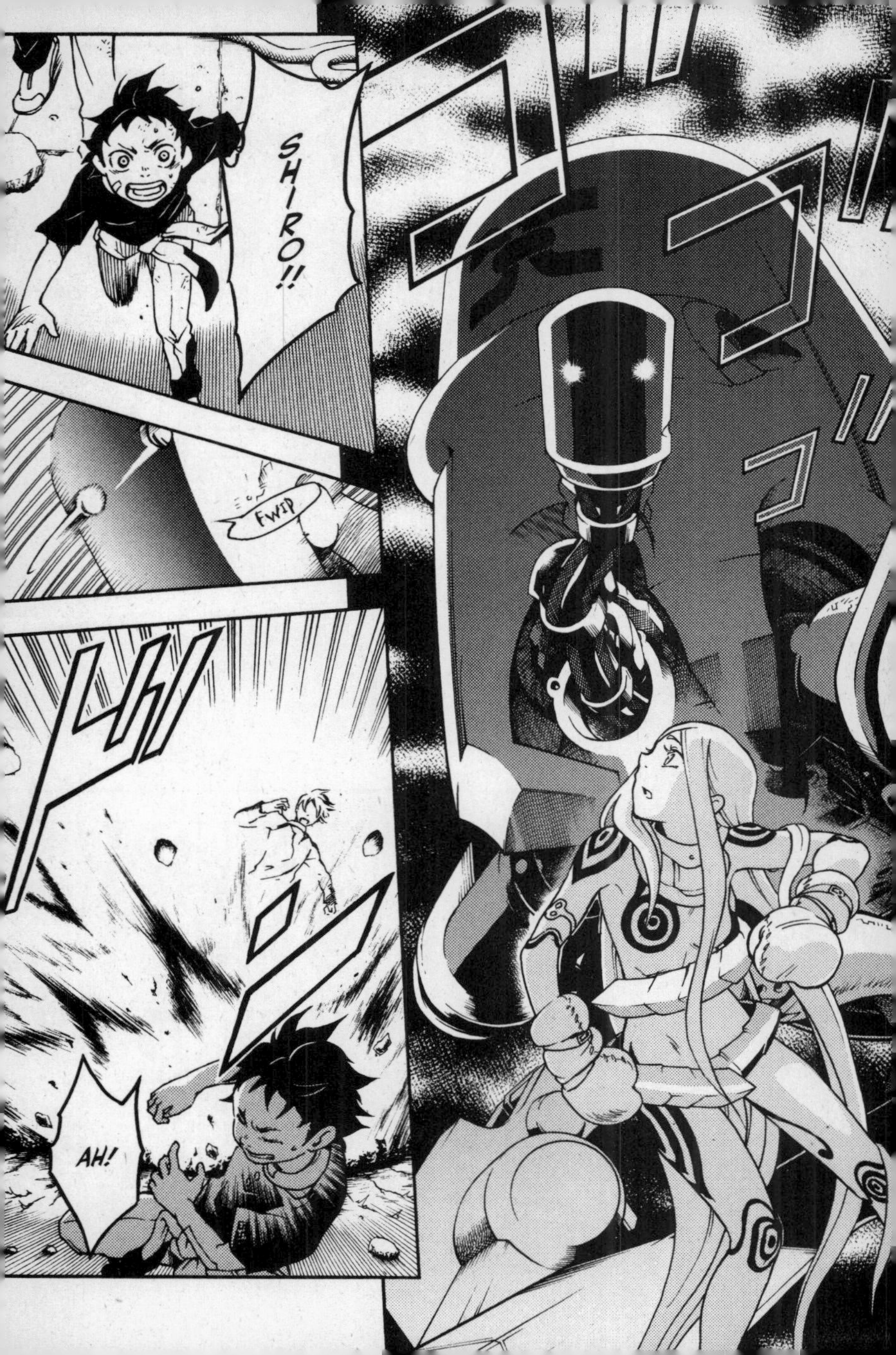
SHIRO!!
FWIP
AH!

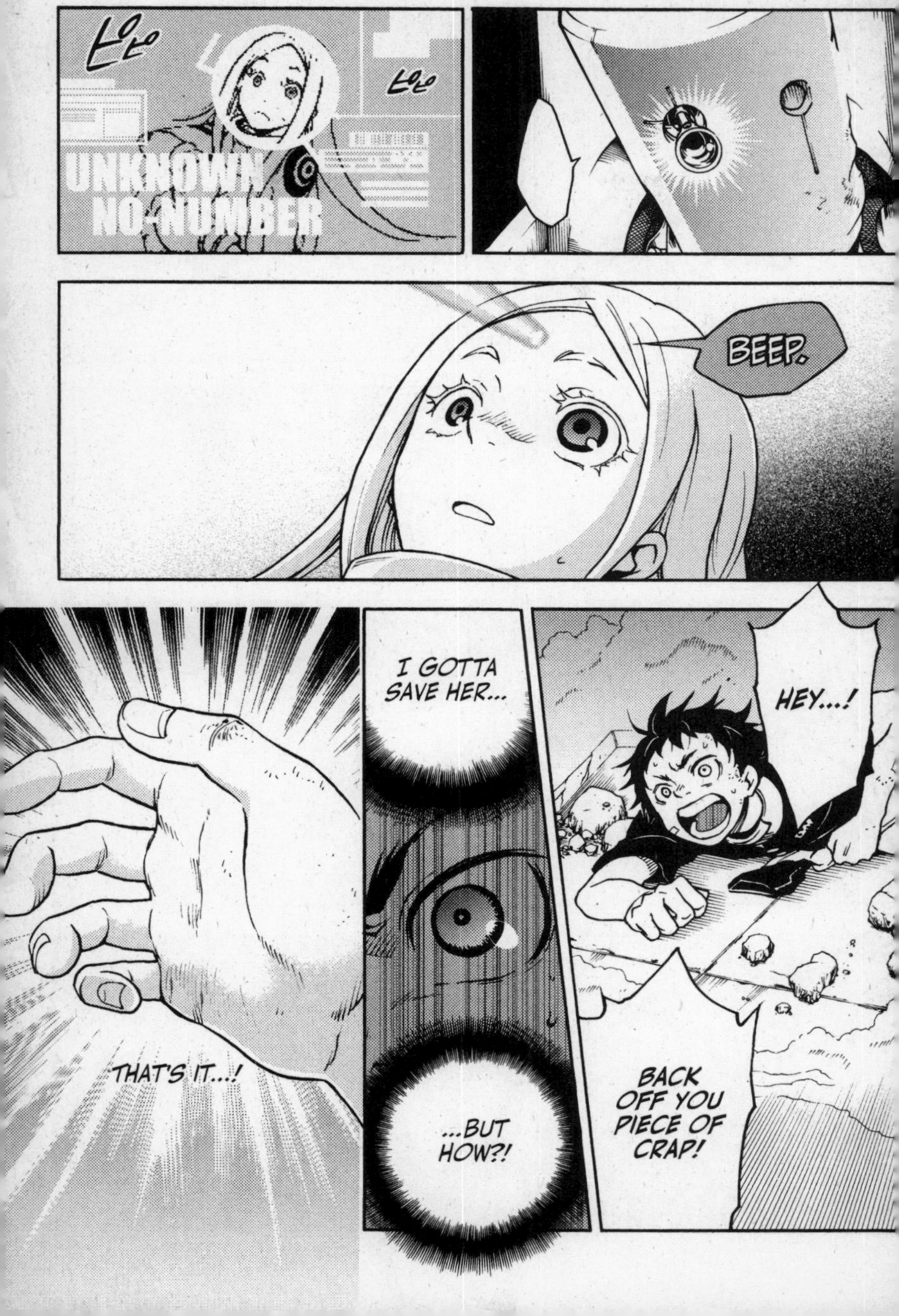
ピピ
ピピ
UNKNOWN NO-NUMBER
BEEP.
HEY...!
BACK OFF YOU PIECE OF CRAP!
I GOTTA SAVE HER...
...BUT HOW?!
THAT'S IT...!

COME
ON!!

THAT POWER...!

COME
OUT,
DAMN
YOU!

C'MON!

...IN MY
BLOOD!

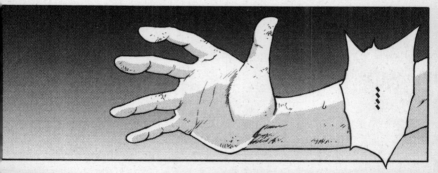

PLEASE!

C'MON
...

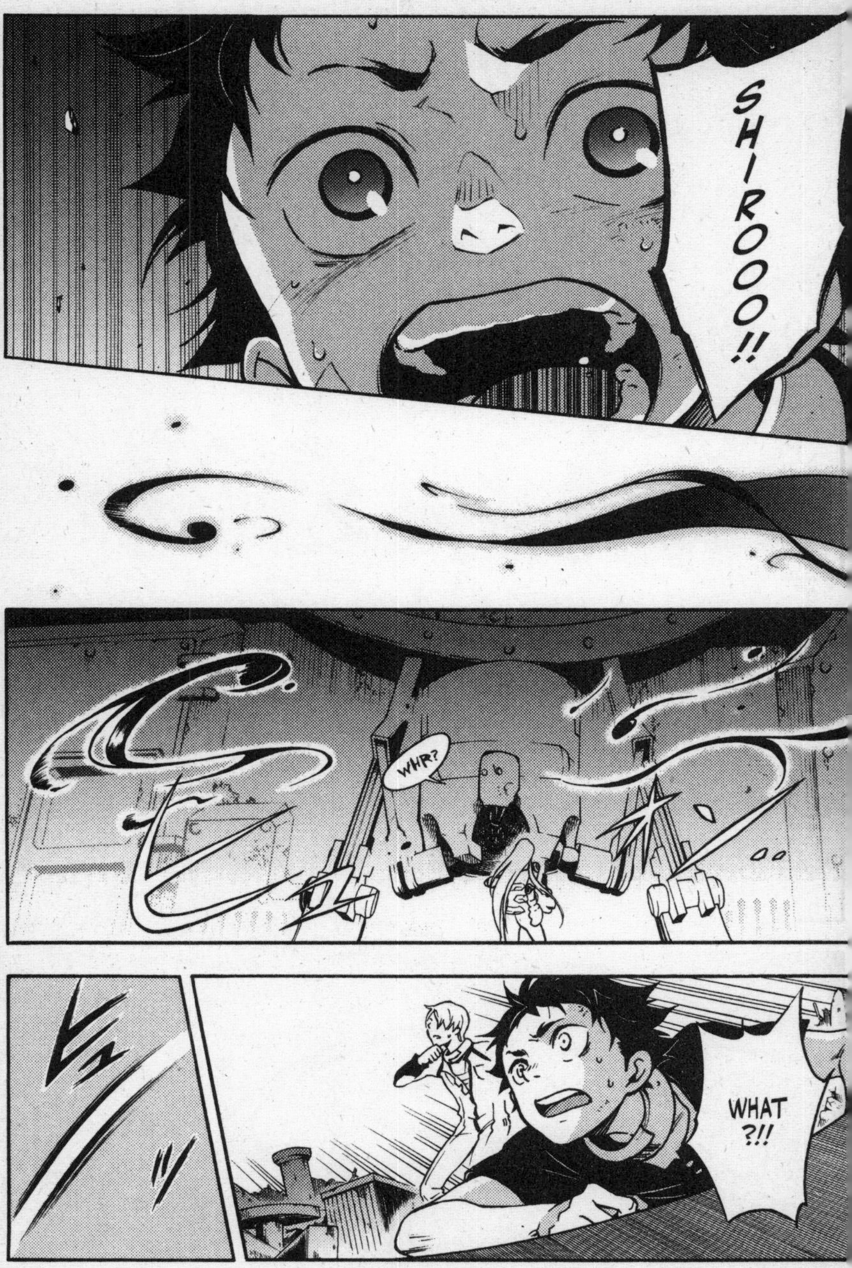
SHIROOO!!
WHR?
WHAT ?!!

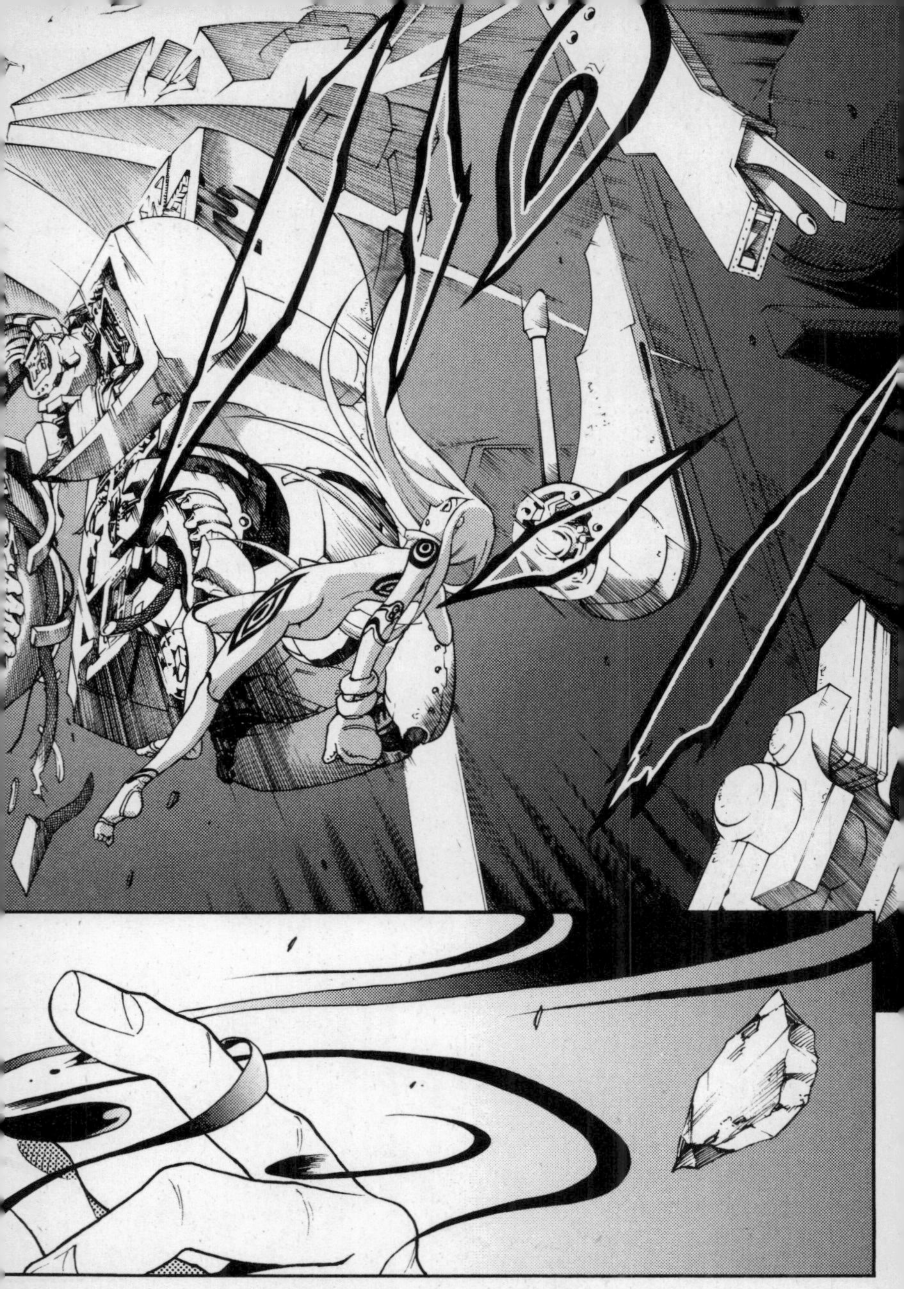

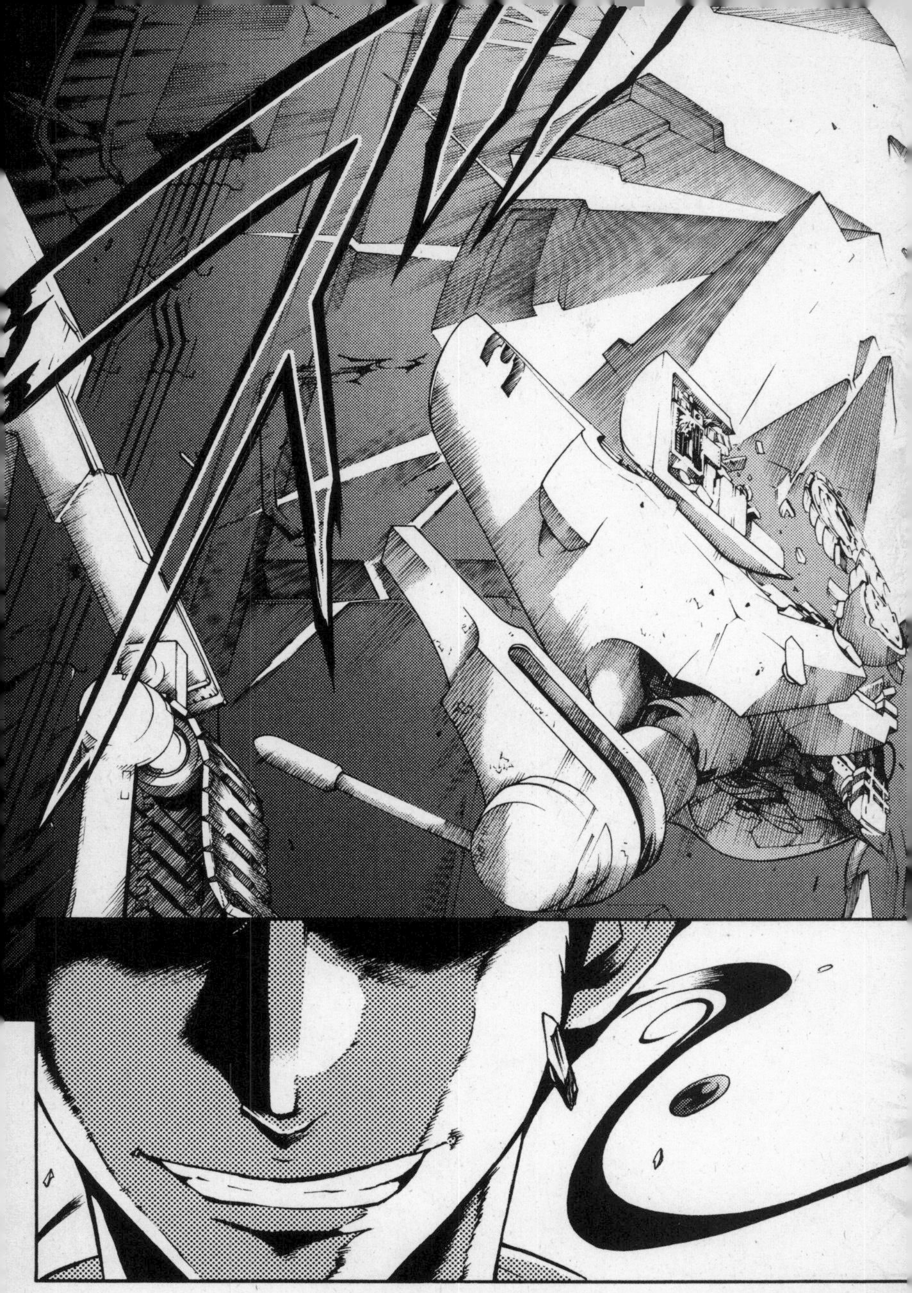

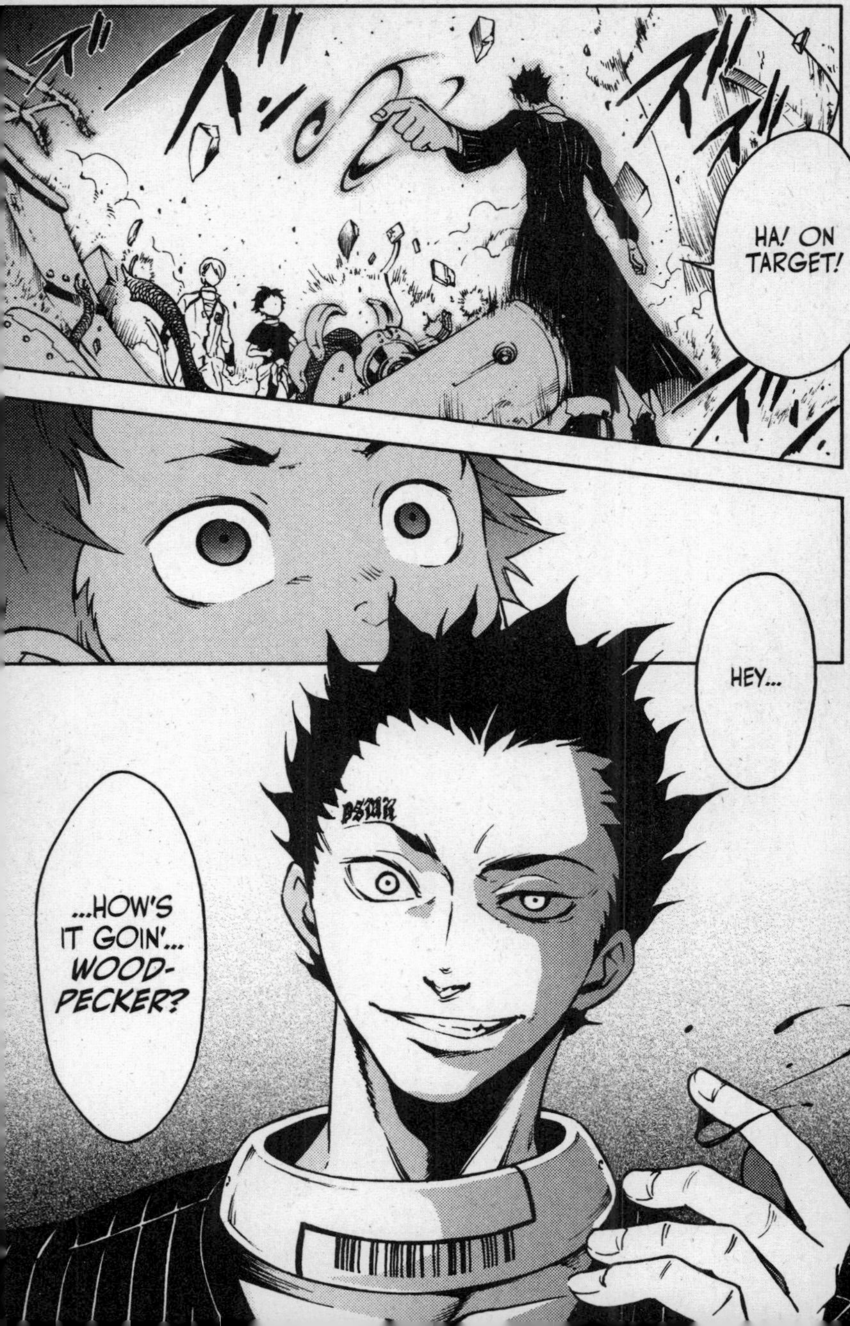
HA! ON TARGET!
HEY...
...HOW'S IT GOIN'... WOOD-PECKER?

# 06 Crow Craw

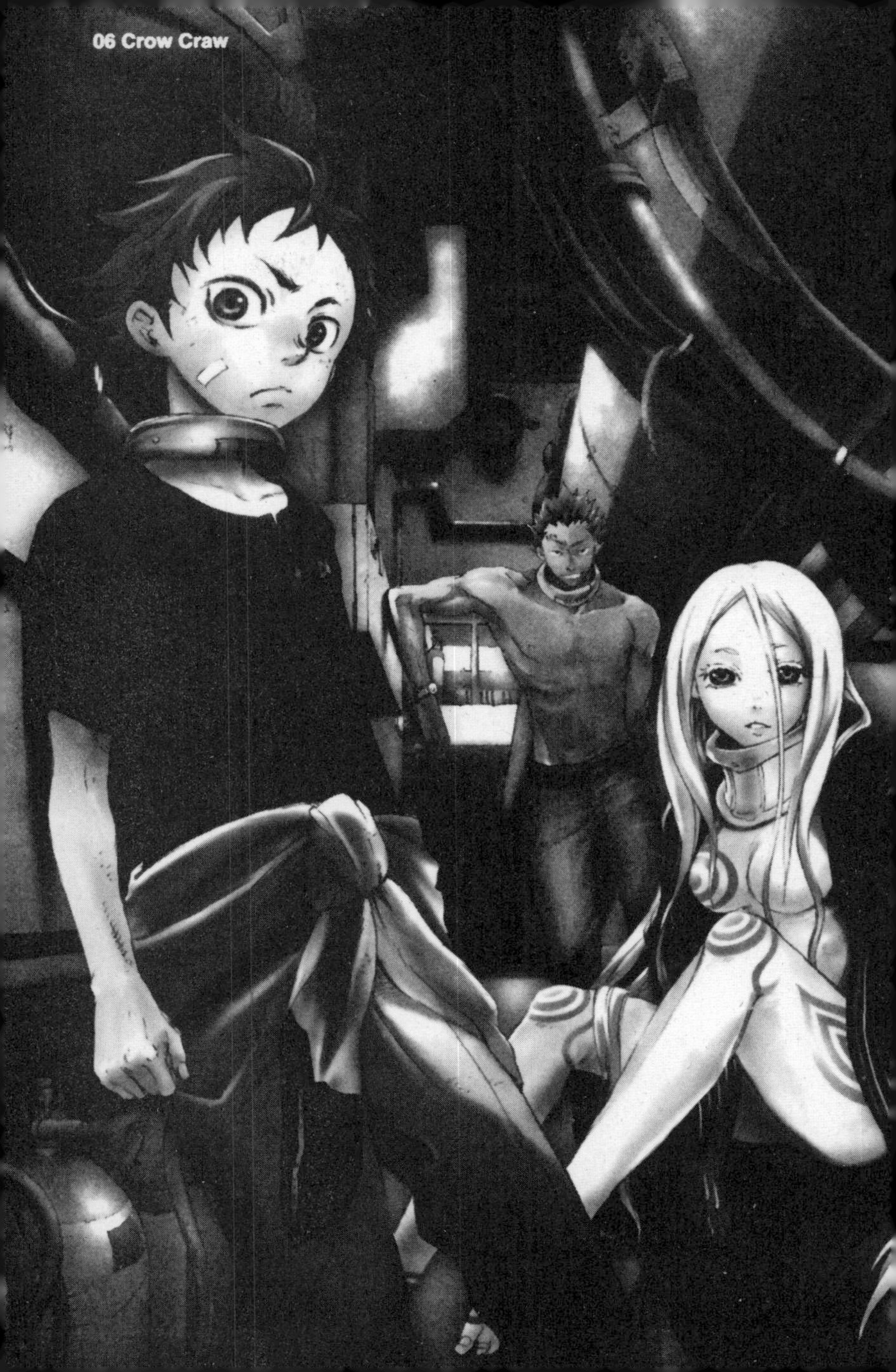

# DEADMAN WONDER LAND

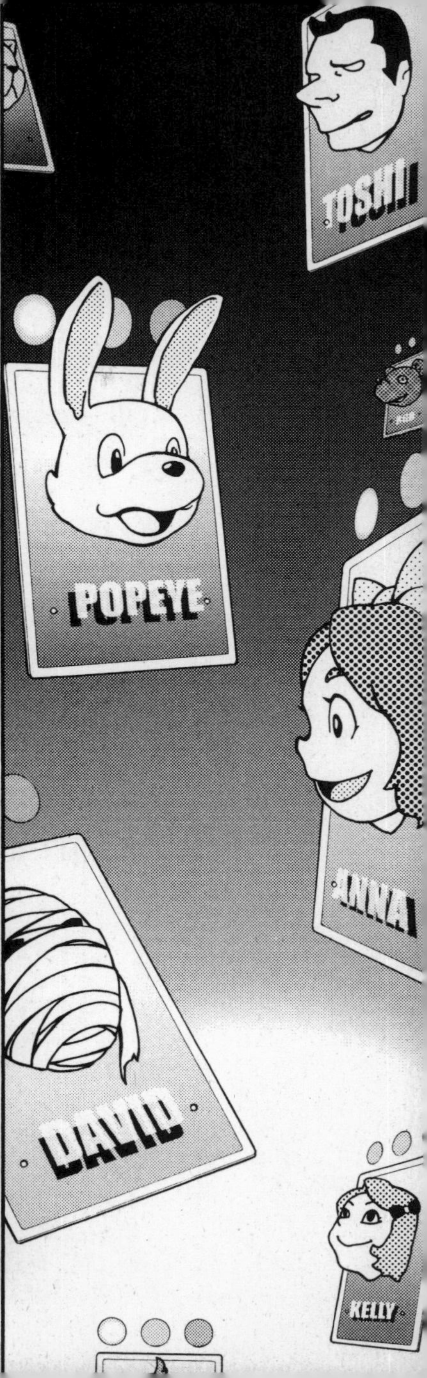
TOSHI
POPEYE
ANNA
DAVID
KELLY
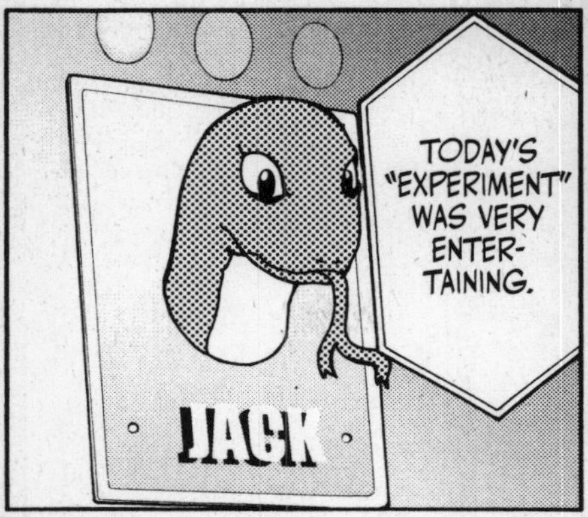
JACK
TODAY'S "EXPERIMENT" WAS VERY ENTER-TAINING.
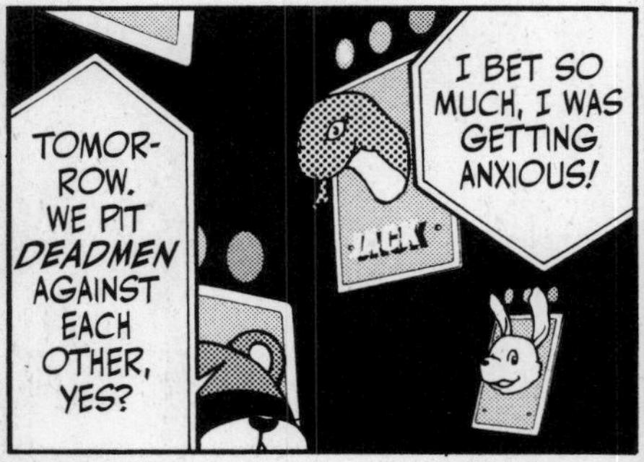
I BET SO MUCH, I WAS GETTING ANXIOUS!
JACK
TOMOR-ROW. WE PIT *DEADMEN* AGAINST EACH OTHER, YES?
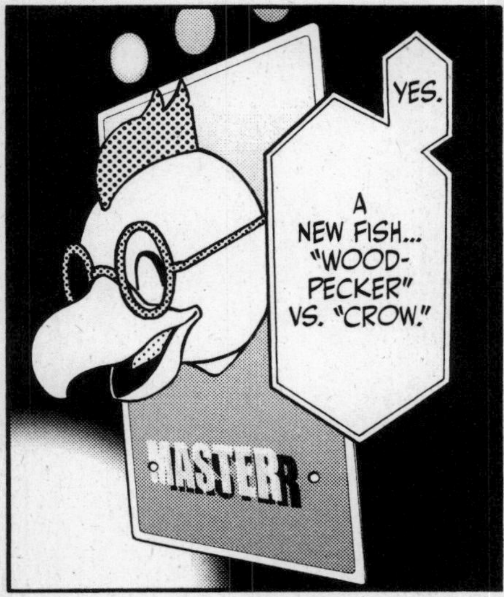
YES.
A NEW FISH... "WOOD-PECKER" VS. "CROW."
MASTER

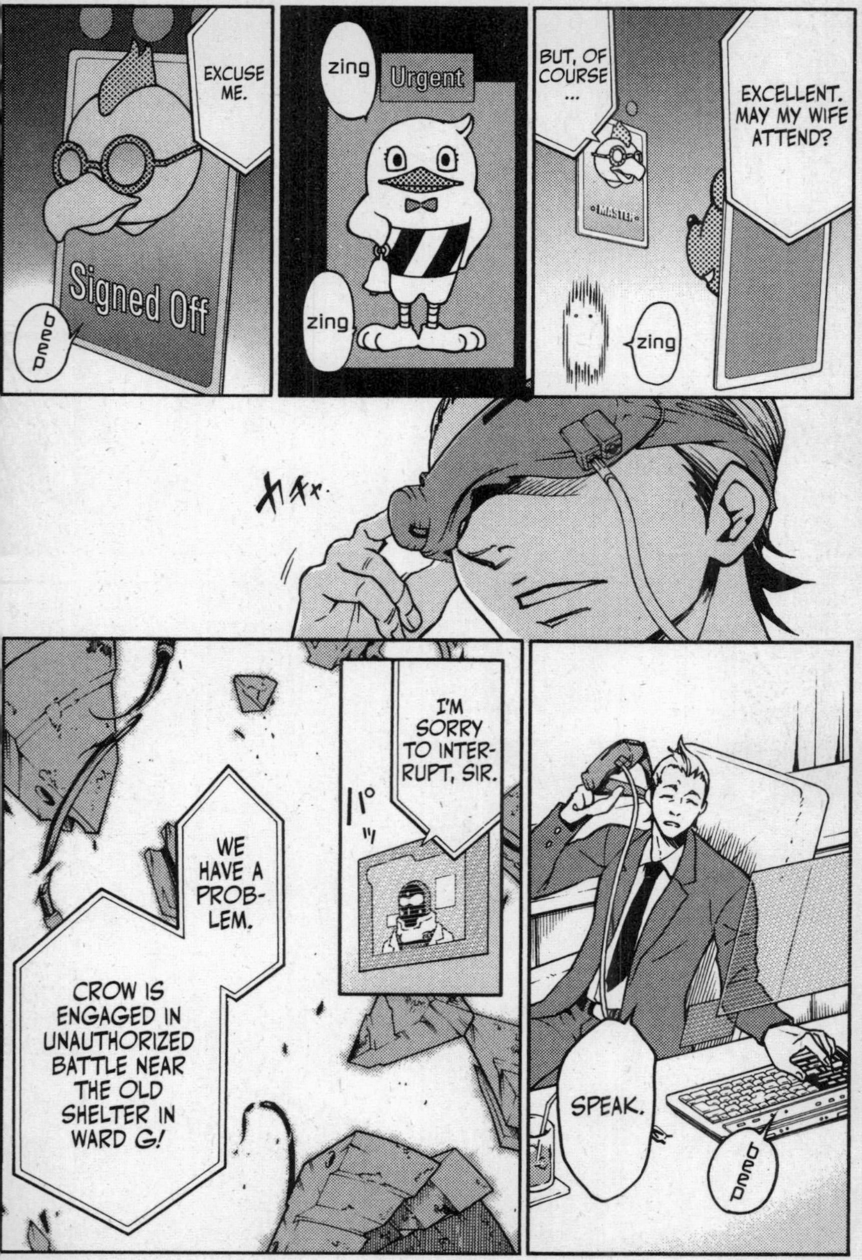
EXCELLENT. MAY MY WIFE ATTEND?
BUT, OF COURSE ...
zing
zing
Urgent
zing
EXCUSE ME.
Signed Off
beep
カチャ
SPEAK.
beep
I'M SORRY TO INTER-RUPT, SIR.
パッ
WE HAVE A PROB-LEM.
CROW IS ENGAGED IN UNAUTHORIZED BATTLE NEAR THE OLD SHELTER IN WARD G!

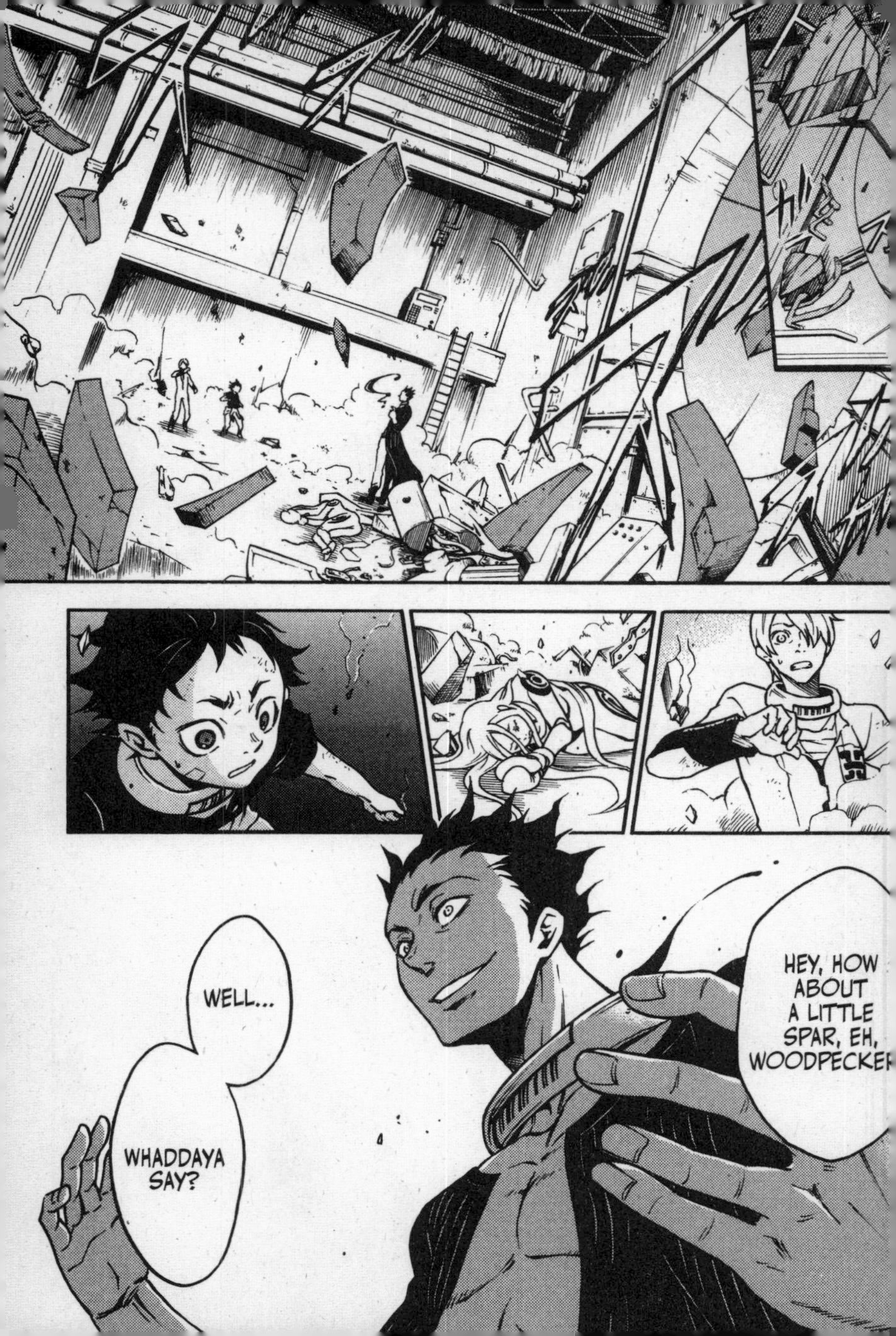
HEY, HOW ABOUT A LITTLE SPAR, EH, WOODPECKER
WELL...
WHADDAYA SAY?

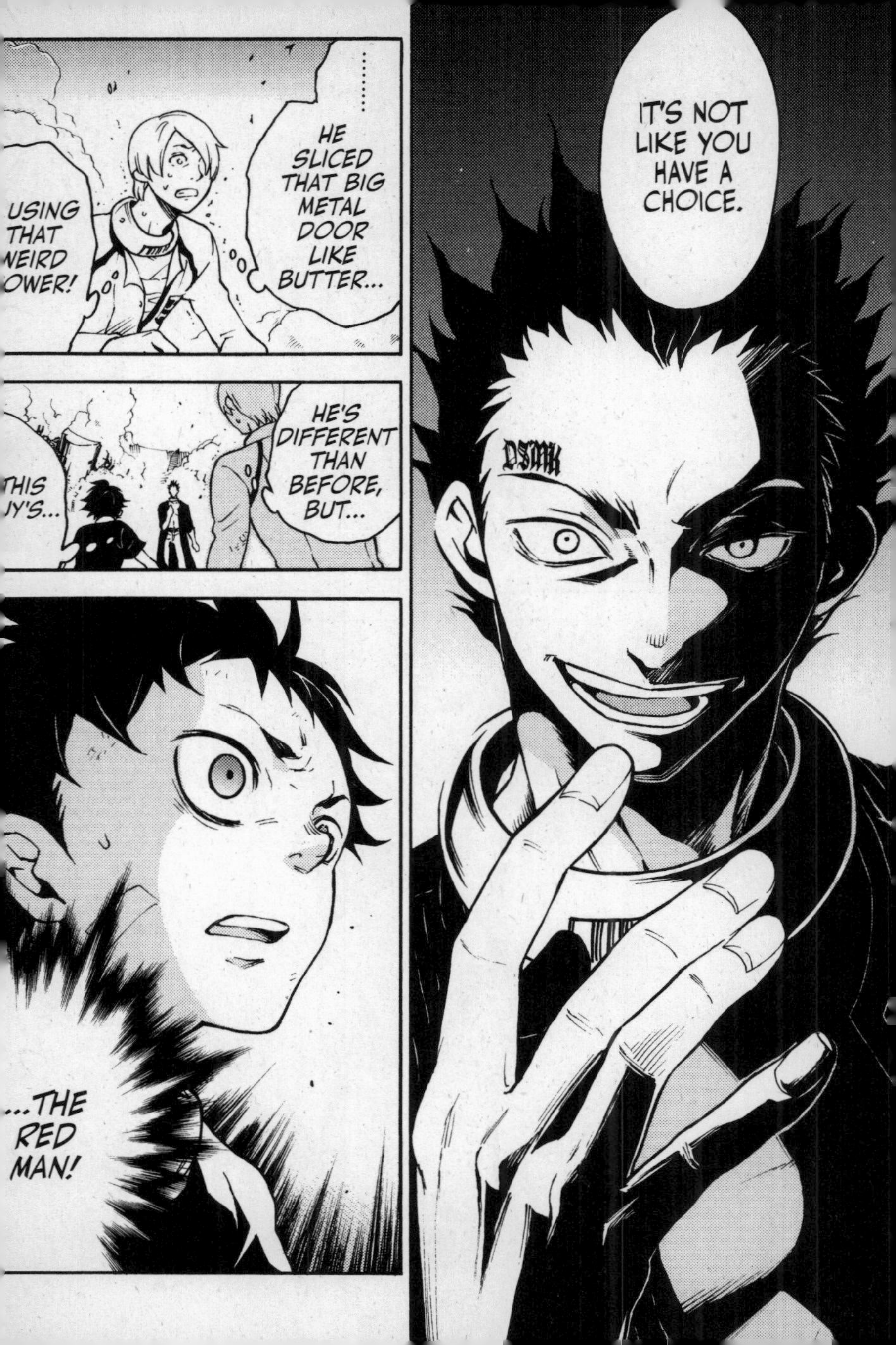
IT'S NOT LIKE YOU HAVE A CHOICE.
HE SLICED THAT BIG METAL DOOR LIKE BUTTER...
USING THAT WEIRD OWER!
HE'S DIFFERENT THAN BEFORE, BUT...
THIS UY'S...
...THE RED MAN!

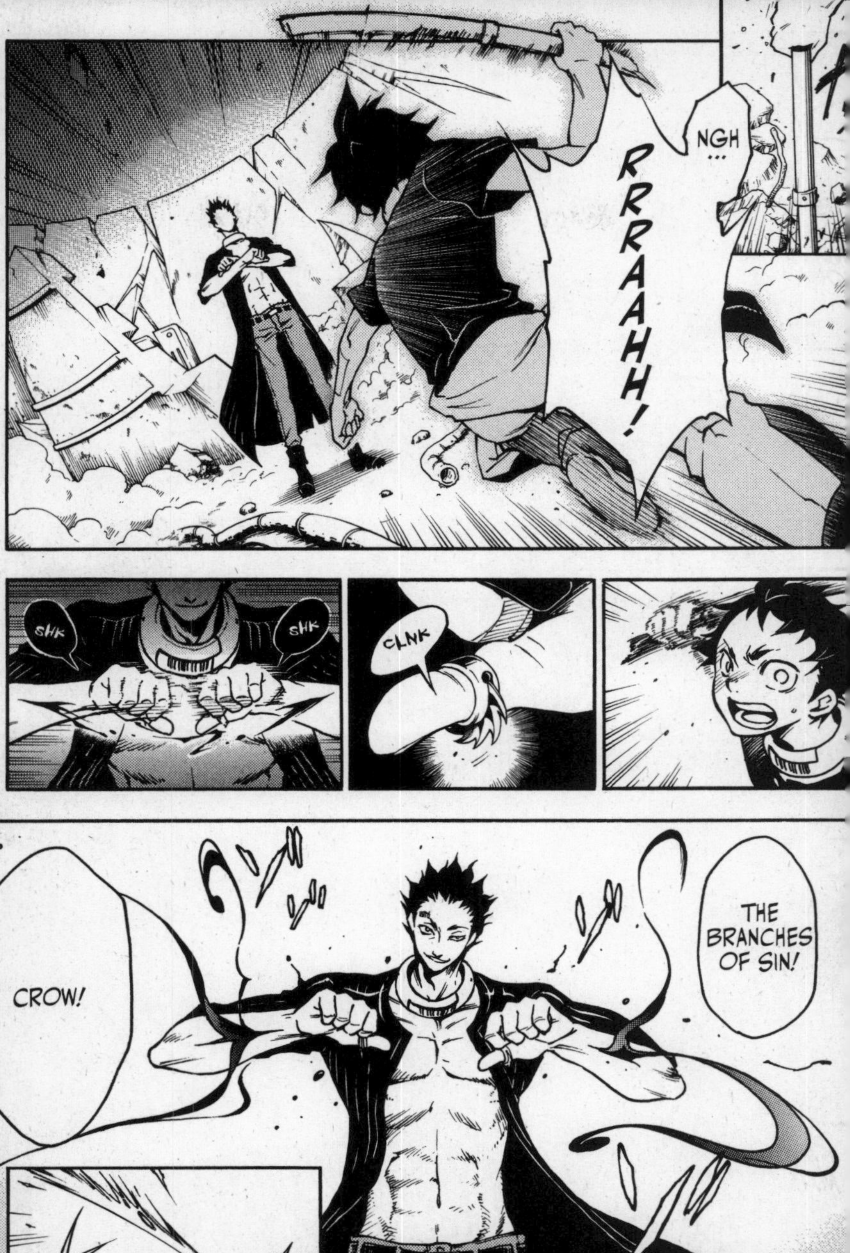
NGH ...
RRRAAHHH!
CLNK
SHK
SHK
THE BRANCHES OF SIN!
CROW!

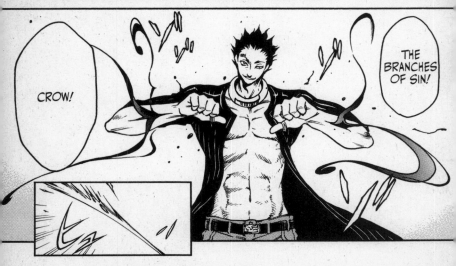

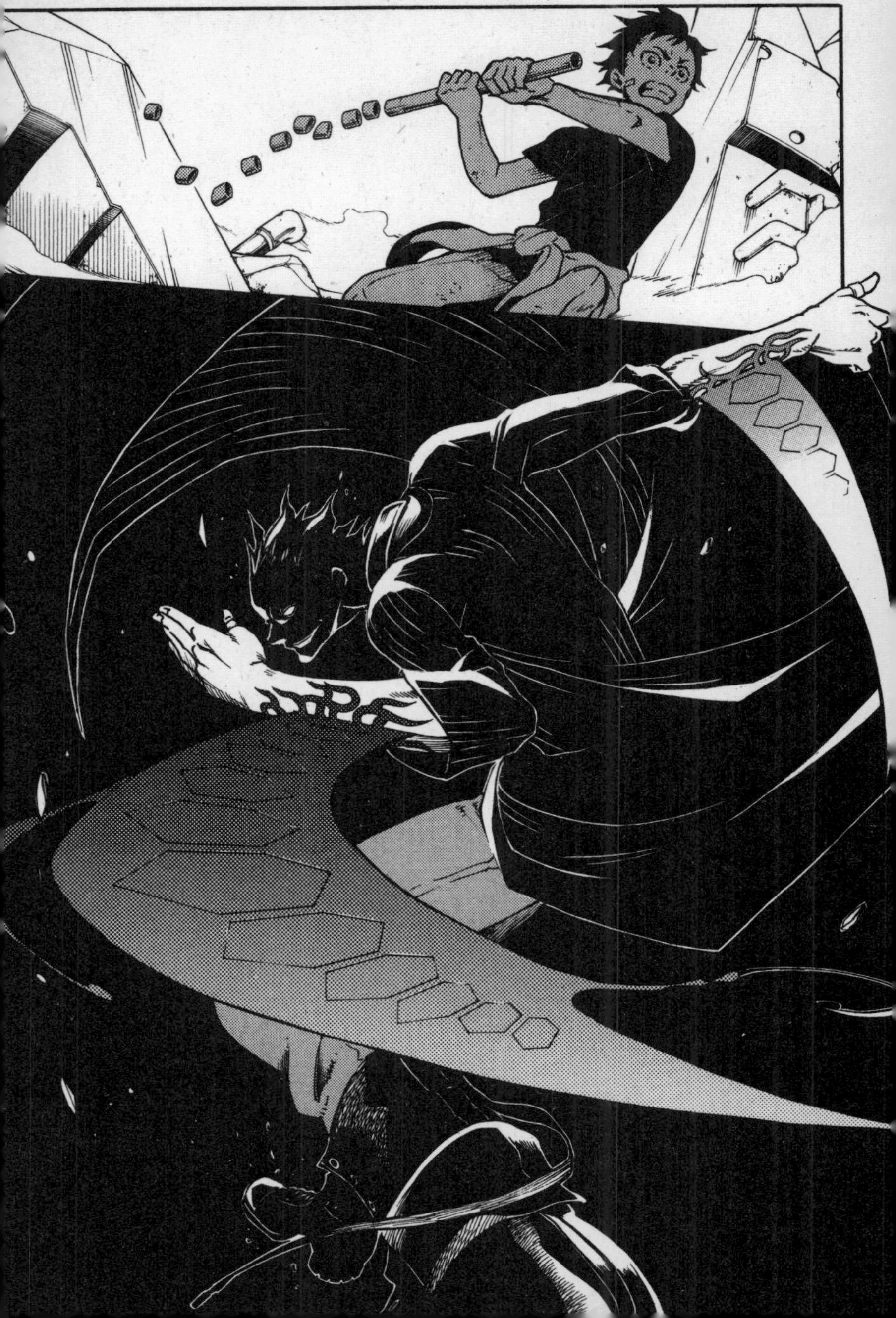

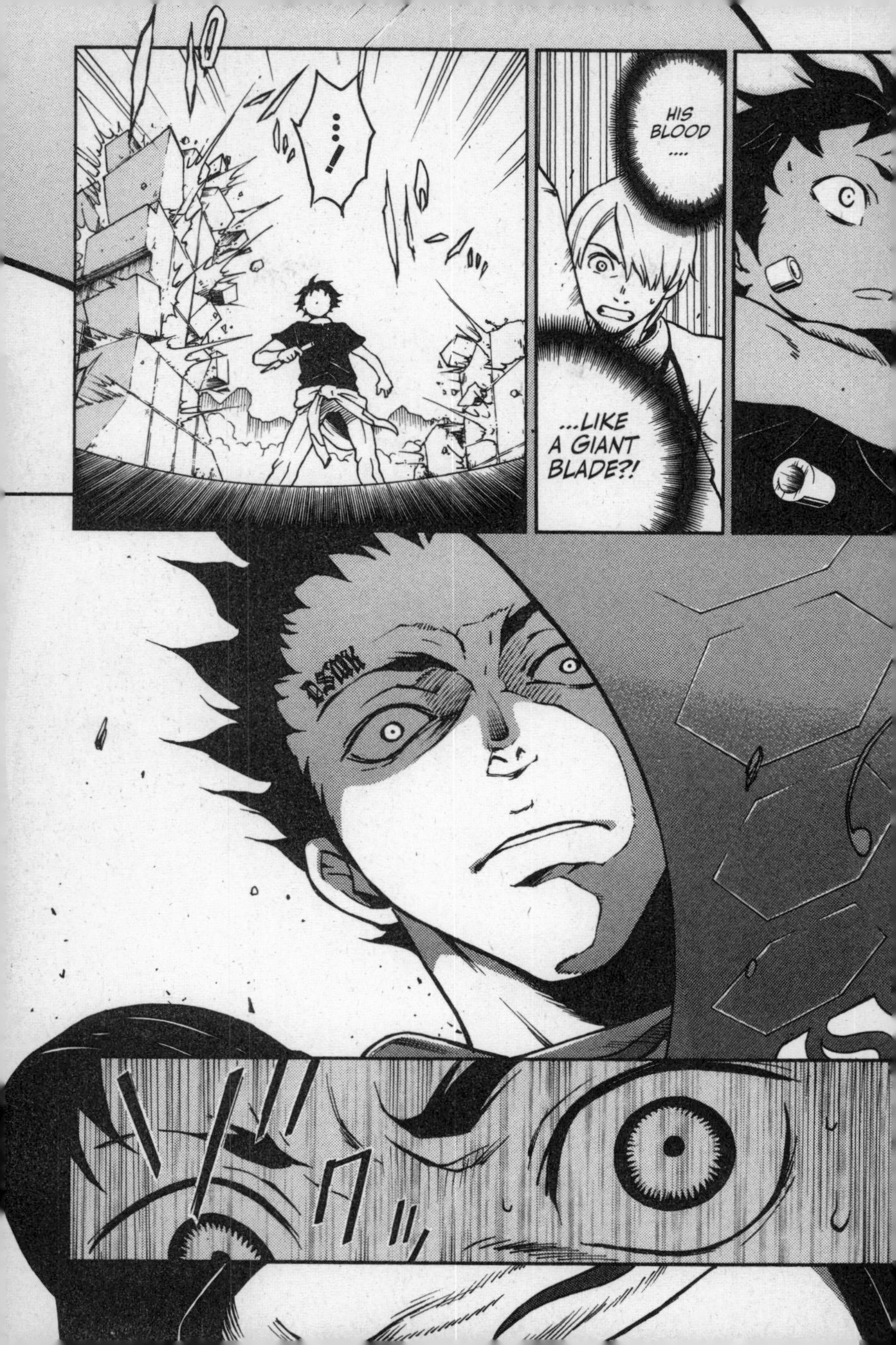
HIS BLOOD ....
...LIKE A GIANT BLADE?!
...!

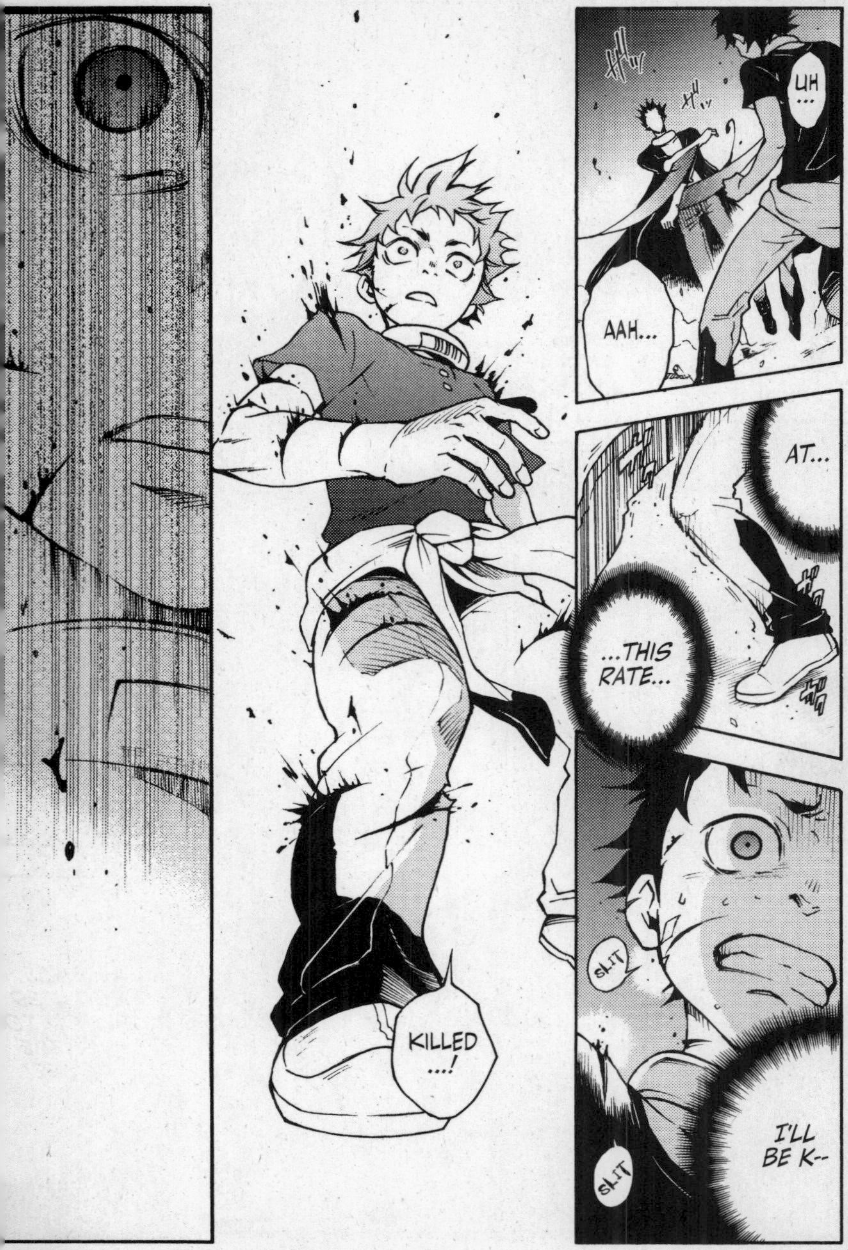
UH ...
AAH...
AT...
...THIS RATE...
SLIT
I'LL BE K--
SLIT
KILLED ...!

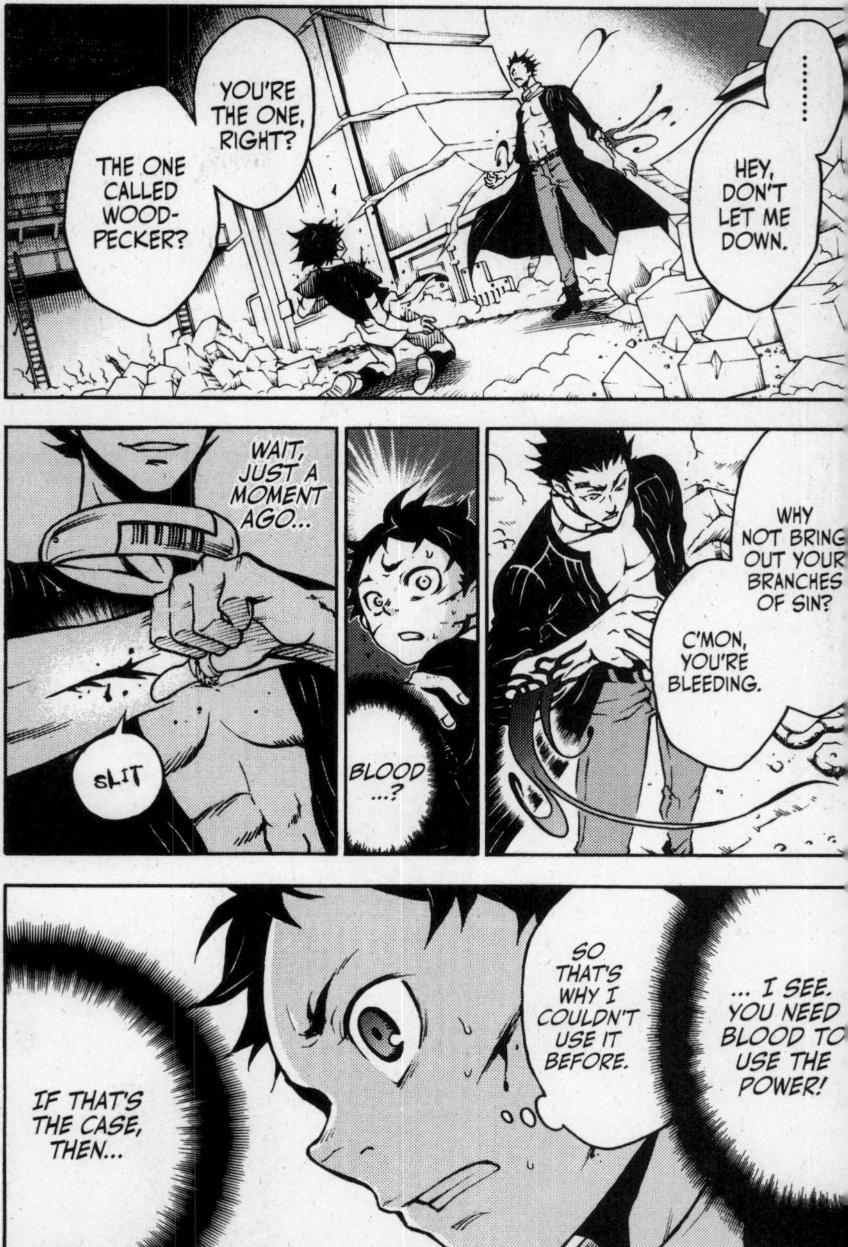
......
HEY, DON'T LET ME DOWN.
YOU'RE THE ONE, RIGHT?
THE ONE CALLED WOOD-PECKER?
WHY NOT BRING OUT YOUR BRANCHES OF SIN?
C'MON, YOU'RE BLEEDING.
BLOOD ...?
WAIT, JUST A MOMENT AGO...
SLIT
... I SEE. YOU NEED BLOOD TO USE THE POWER!
SO THAT'S WHY I COULDN'T USE IT BEFORE.
IF THAT'S THE CASE, THEN...

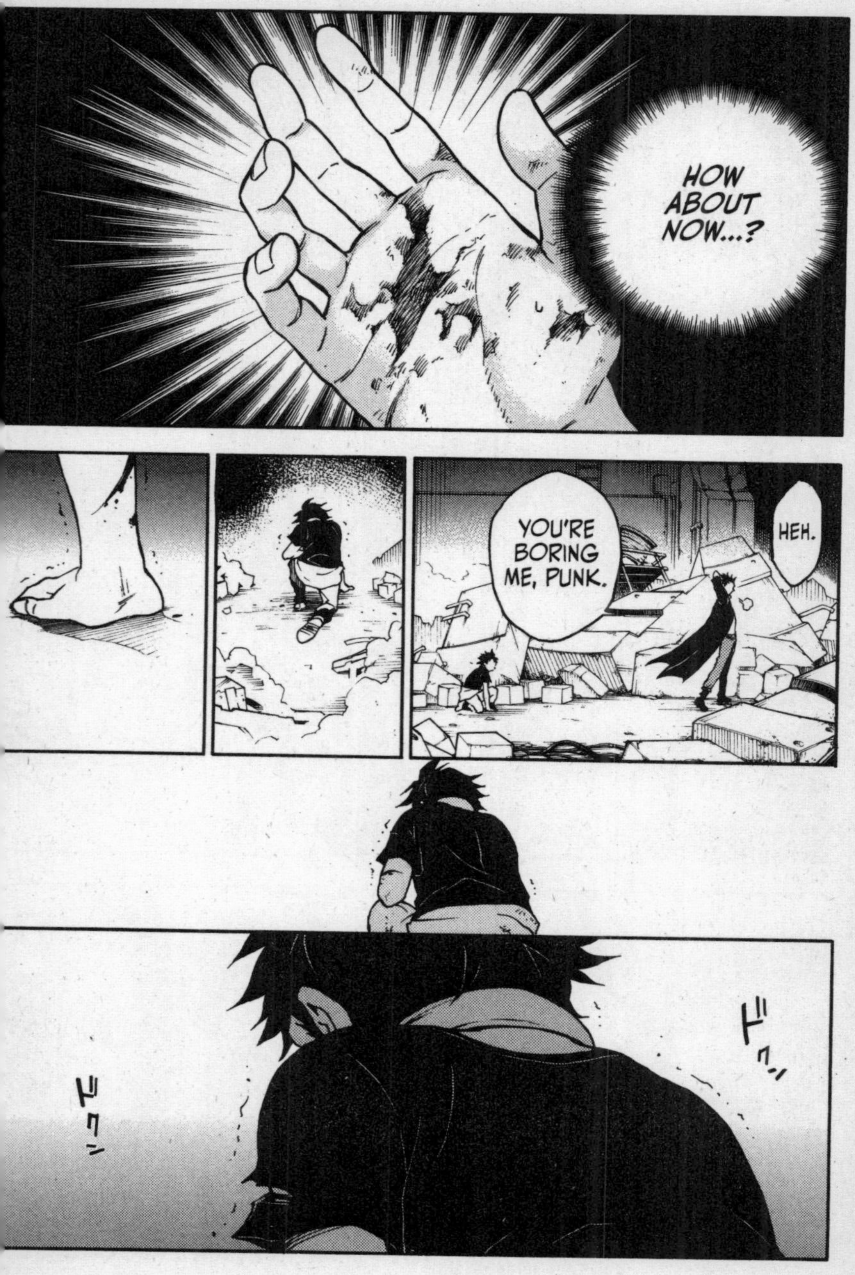
HOW ABOUT NOW...?
HEH.
YOU'RE BORING ME, PUNK.
ドクッ

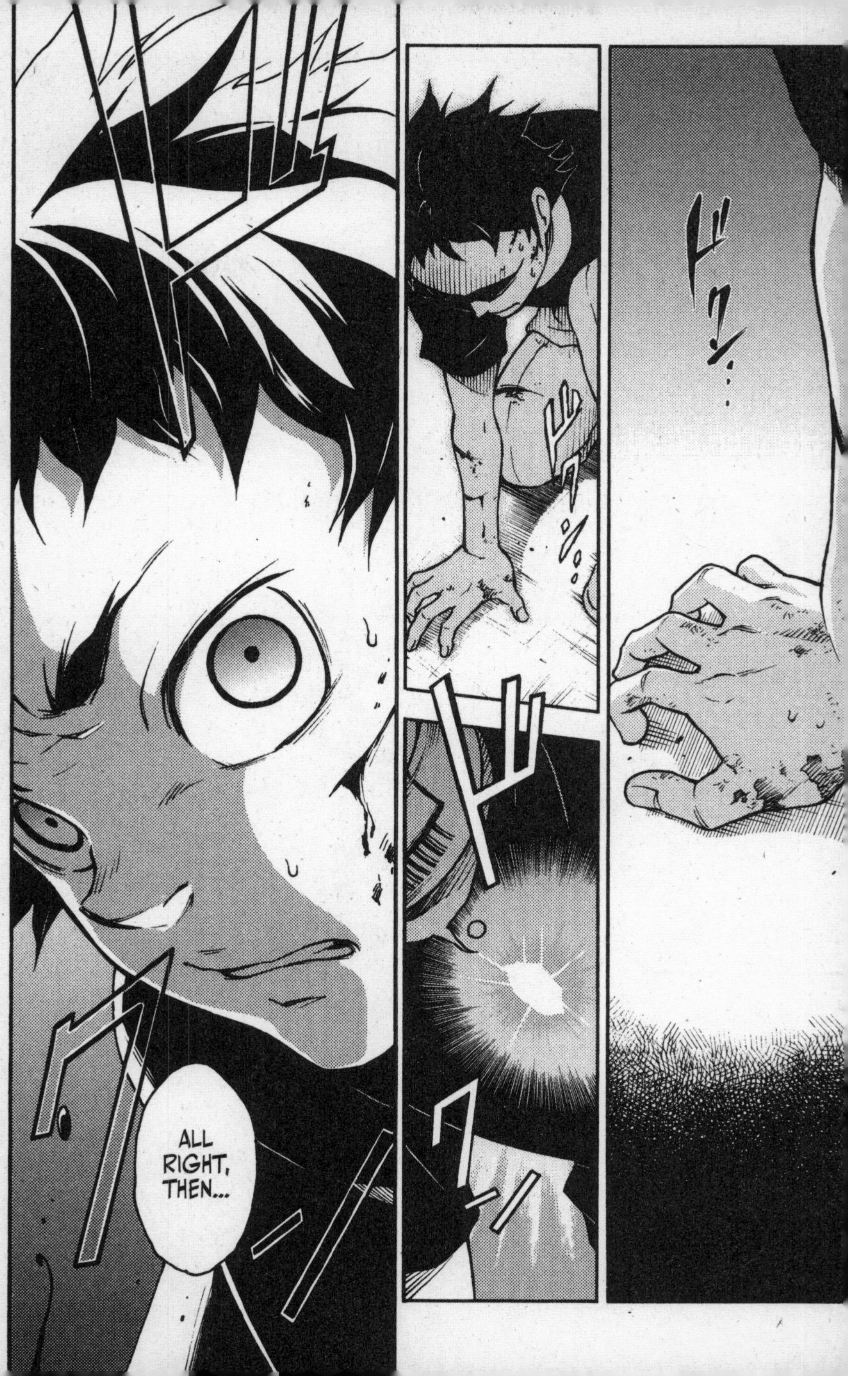
ALL RIGHT, THEN...

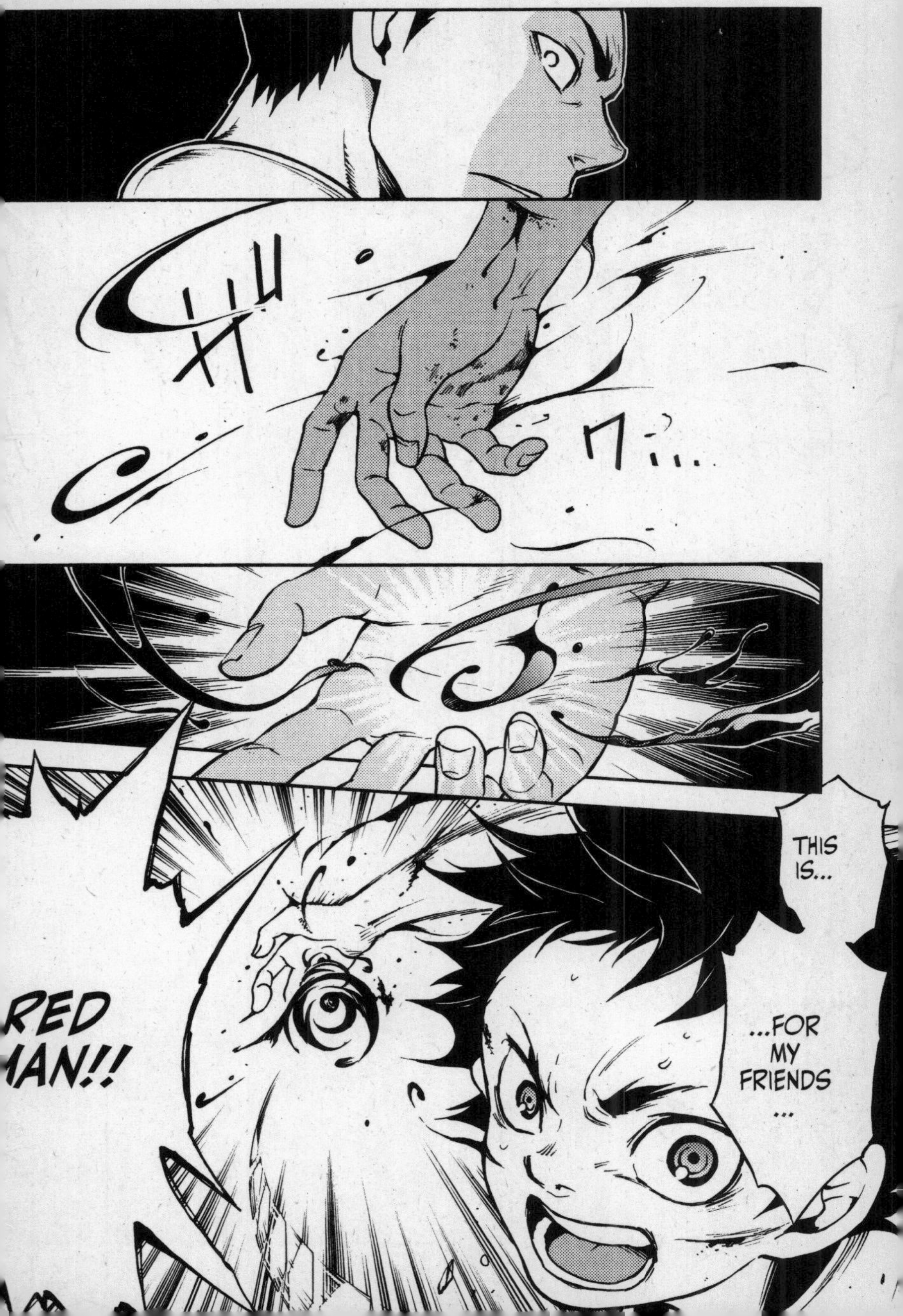
THIS IS...
...FOR MY FRIENDS ...
RED
AN!!

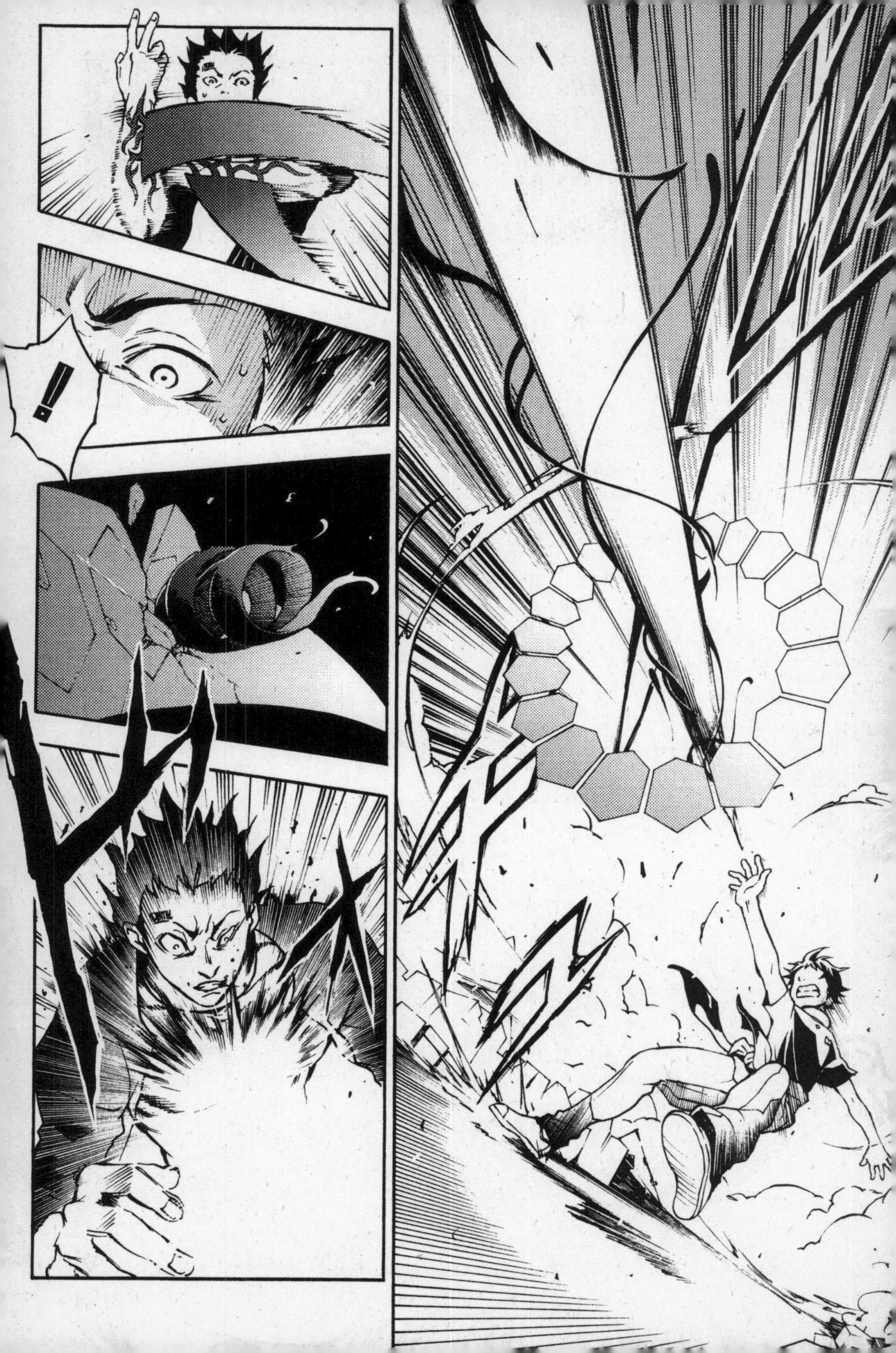
!

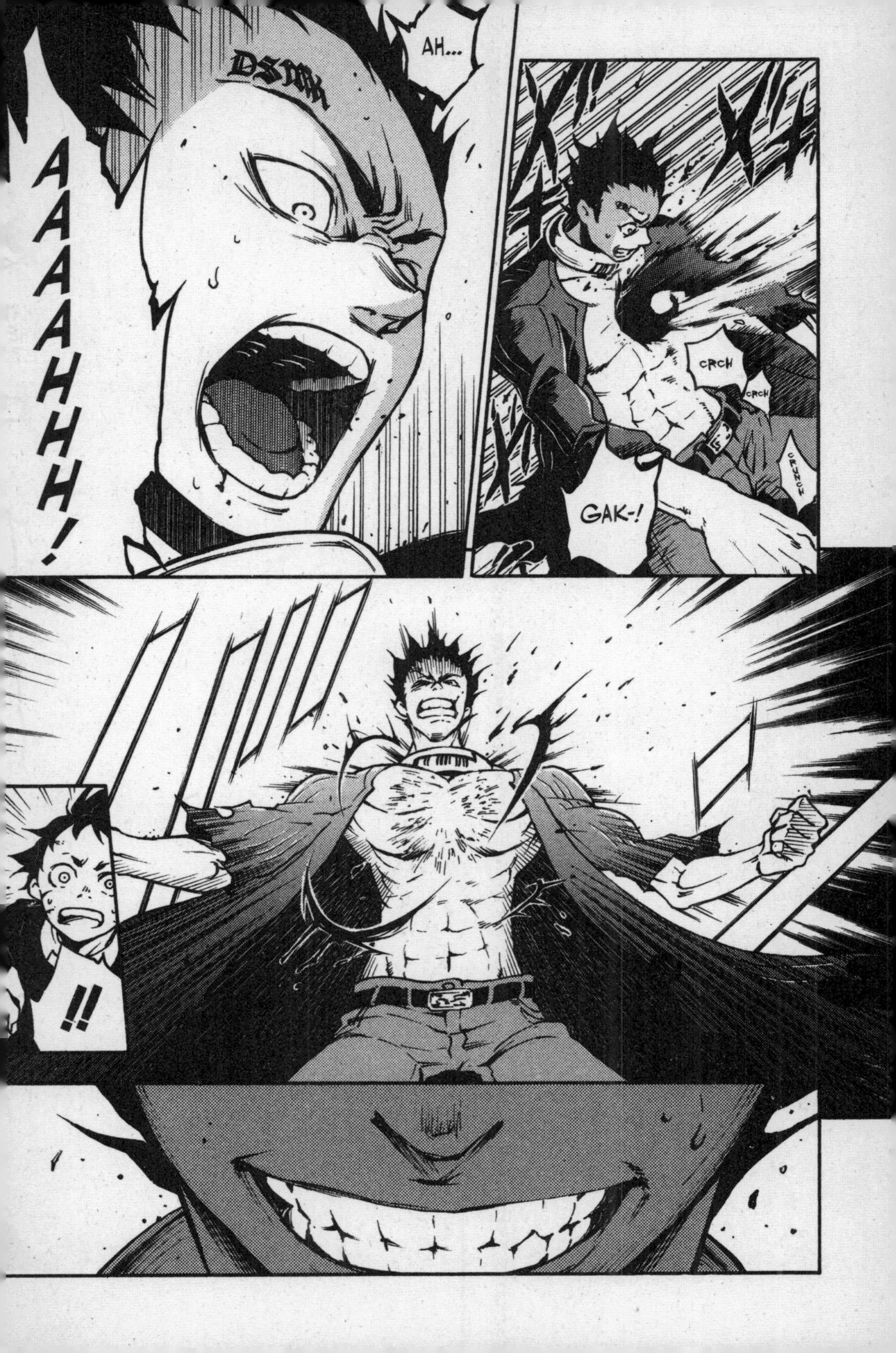
CRCH
CRCH
CRUNCH
GAK-!
AH...
AAAAHHH!
!!

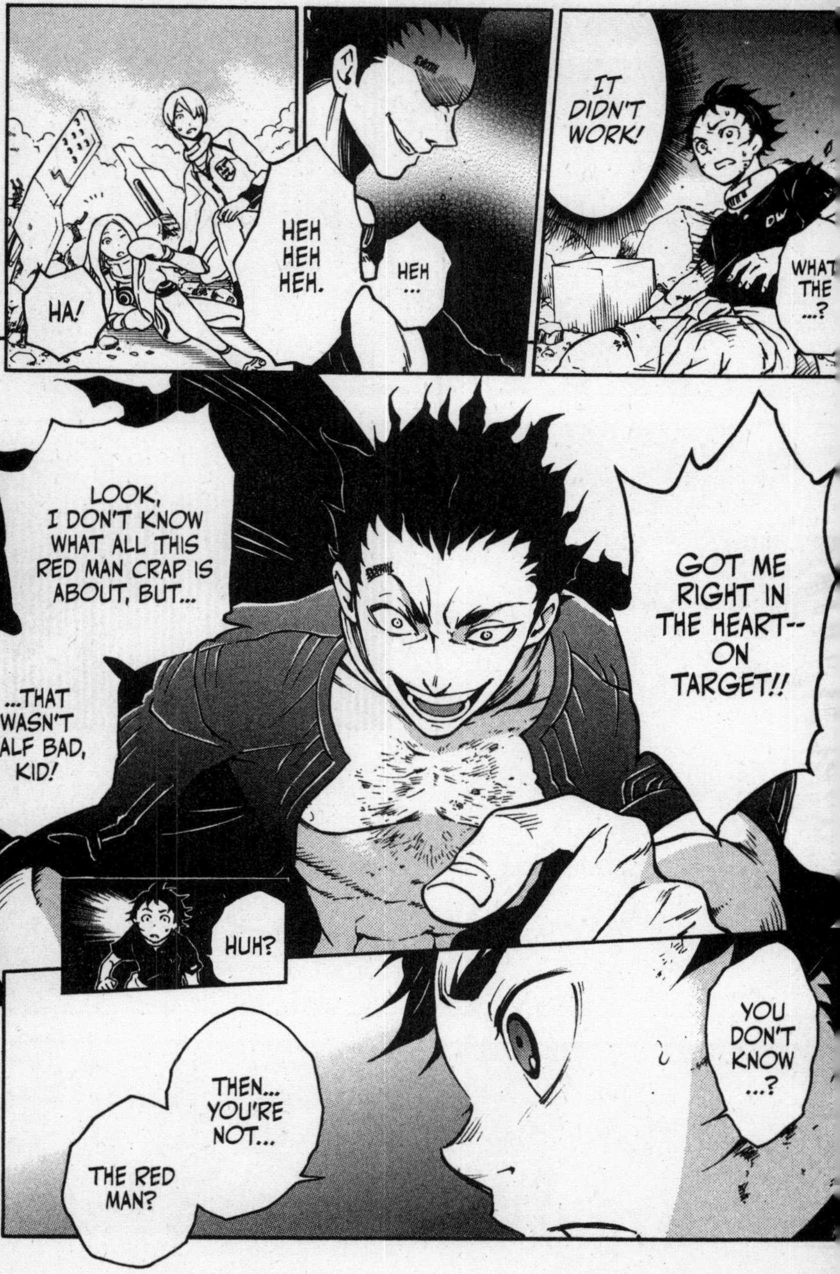
IT DIDN'T WORK!
WHAT THE ...?
HEH HEH HEH.
HEH ...
HA!
GOT ME RIGHT IN THE HEART-- ON TARGET!!
LOOK, I DON'T KNOW WHAT ALL THIS RED MAN CRAP IS ABOUT, BUT...
...THAT WASN'T HALF BAD, KID!
HUH?
YOU DON'T KNOW ...?
THEN... YOU'RE NOT...
THE RED MAN?

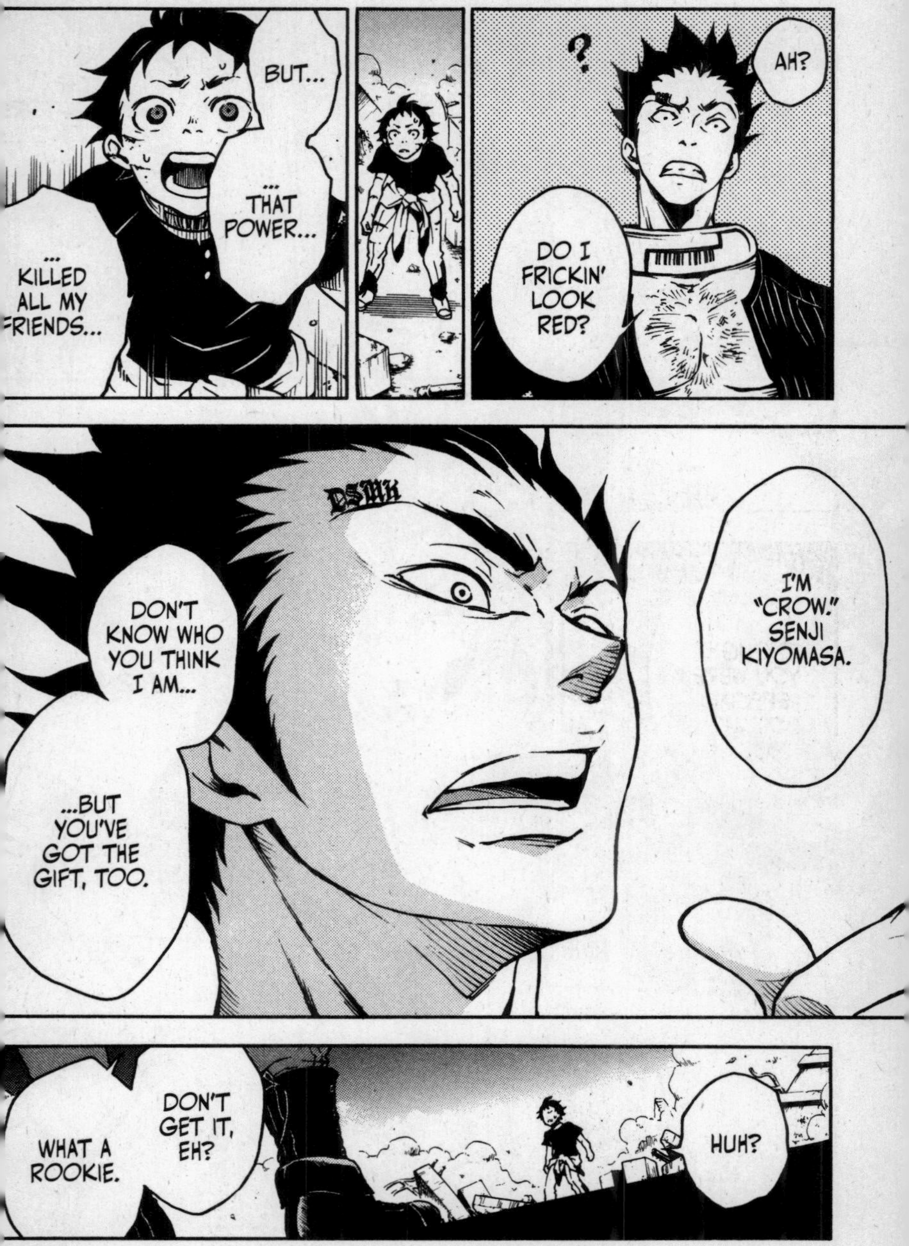
?
AH?
DO I FRICKIN' LOOK RED?
BUT...
...THAT POWER...
...KILLED ALL MY FRIENDS...
I'M "CROW." SENJI KIYOMASA.
DON'T KNOW WHO YOU THINK I AM...
...BUT YOU'VE GOT THE GIFT, TOO.
HUH?
DON'T GET IT, EH?
WHAT A ROOKIE.

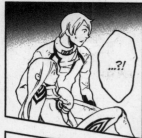

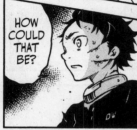

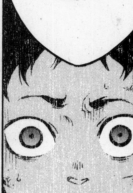

THE MANIPULATORS OF BLOOD ...
WE'RE CALLED DEADMEN.
YOU THOUGHT YOU AND RED DUDE WERE THE ONLY ONES?
WE'RE IN THE HEART OF DEADMAN WONDERLAND, KID.
JUST WHO DO YOU THINK THEY'VE GOT LOCKED UP HERE?
...?!
HOW COULD THAT BE?
THOUGHT YOU WERE SPECIAL, DID'JA?
JUST LIKE A KID.
WELL ...

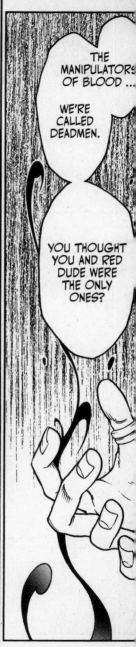

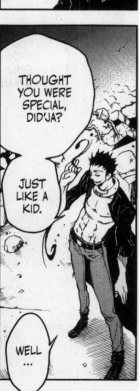

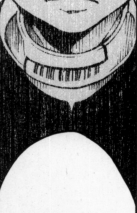

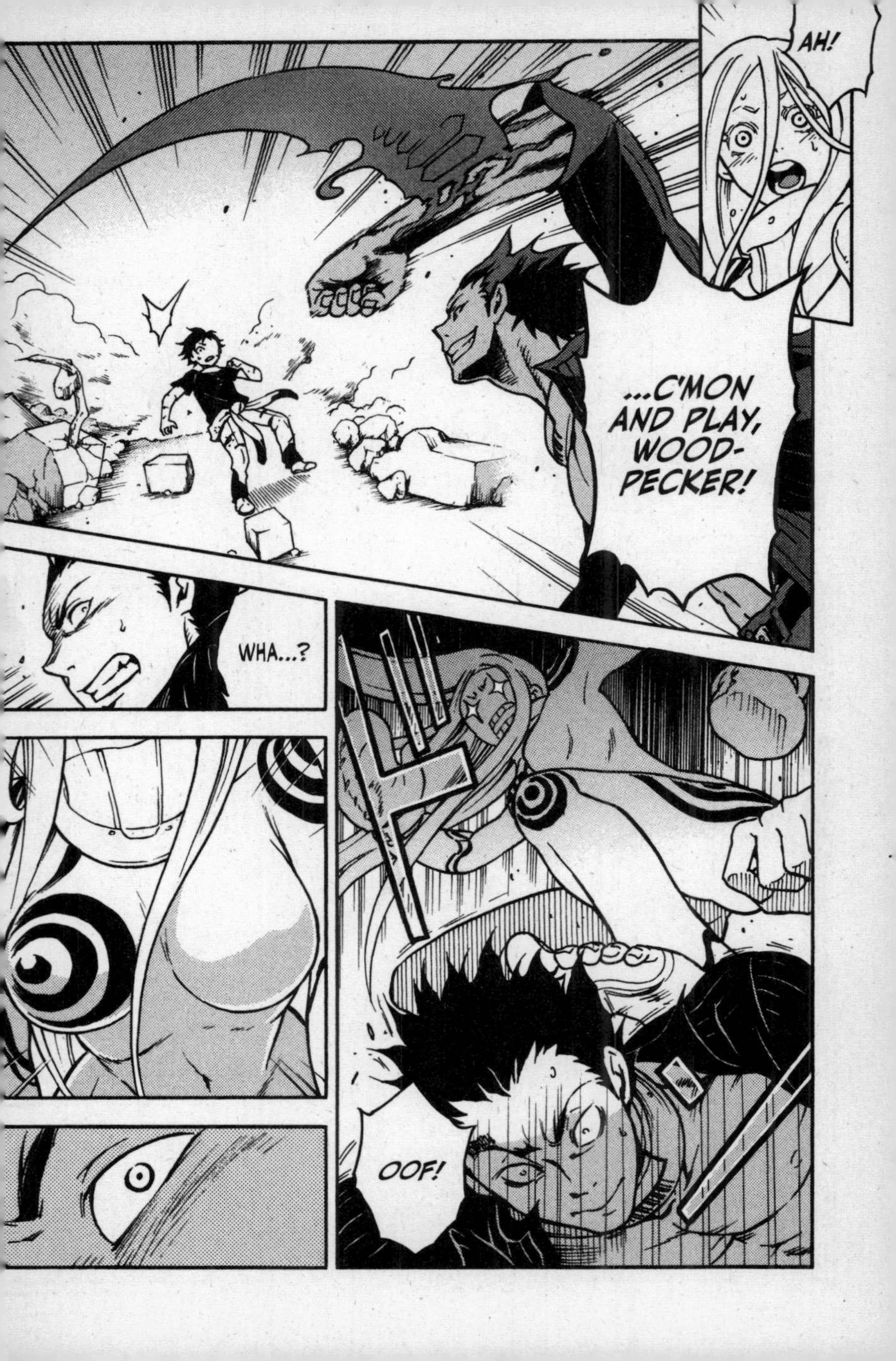
AH!
...C'MON AND PLAY, WOOD-PECKER!
OOF!
WHA...?

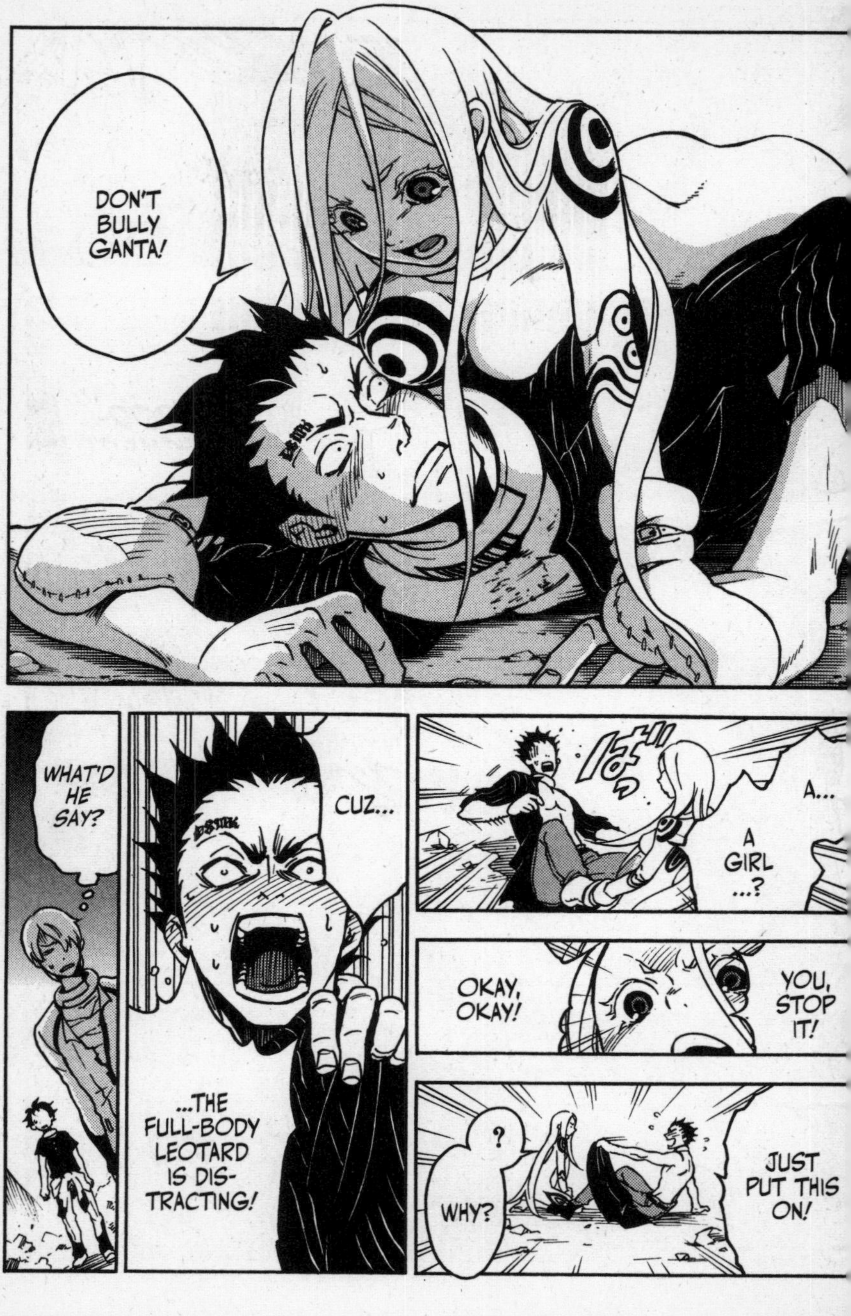
DON'T BULLY GANTA!
A...
A GIRL ...?
YOU, STOP IT!
OKAY, OKAY!
JUST PUT THIS ON!
?
WHY?
CUZ...
...THE FULL-BODY LEOTARD IS DIS-TRACTING!
WHAT'D HE SAY?

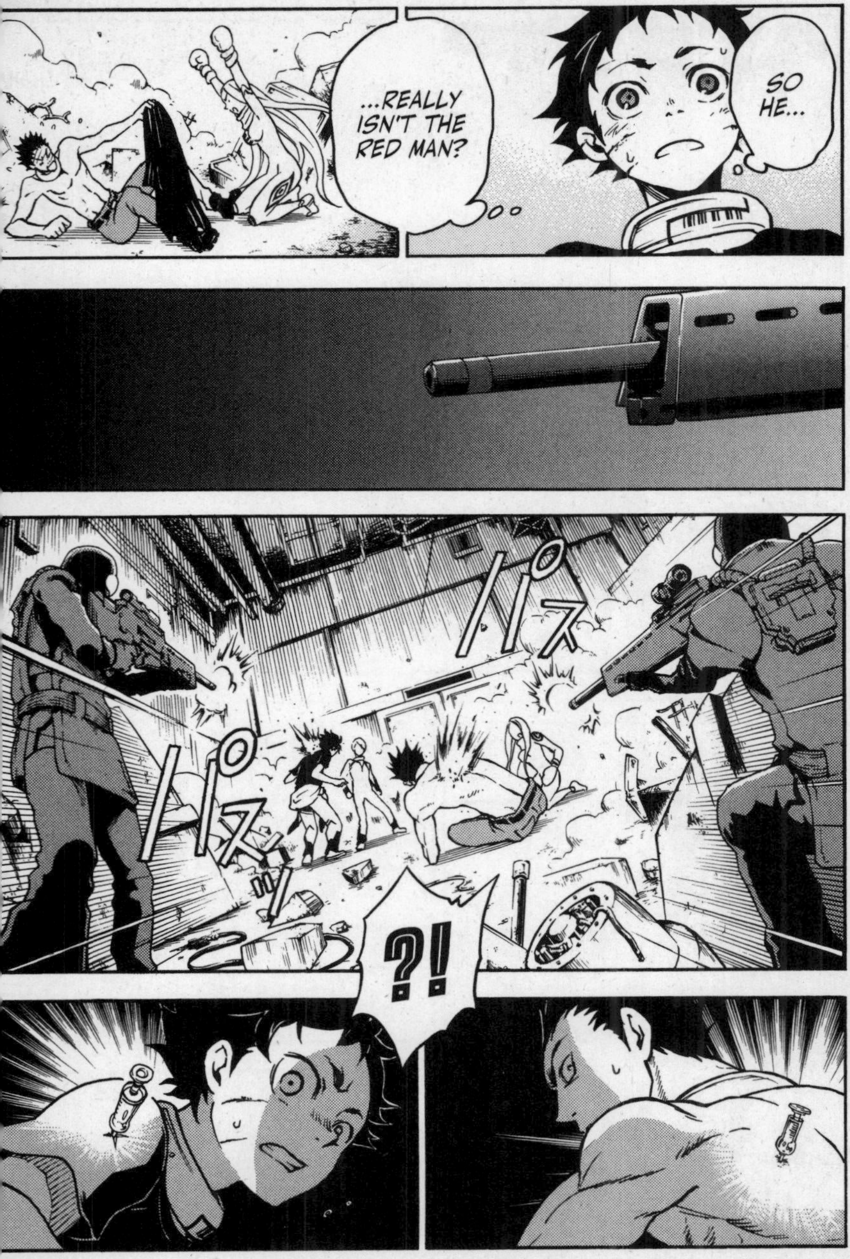
SO HE...
...REALLY ISN'T THE RED MAN?
パス
パス
?!

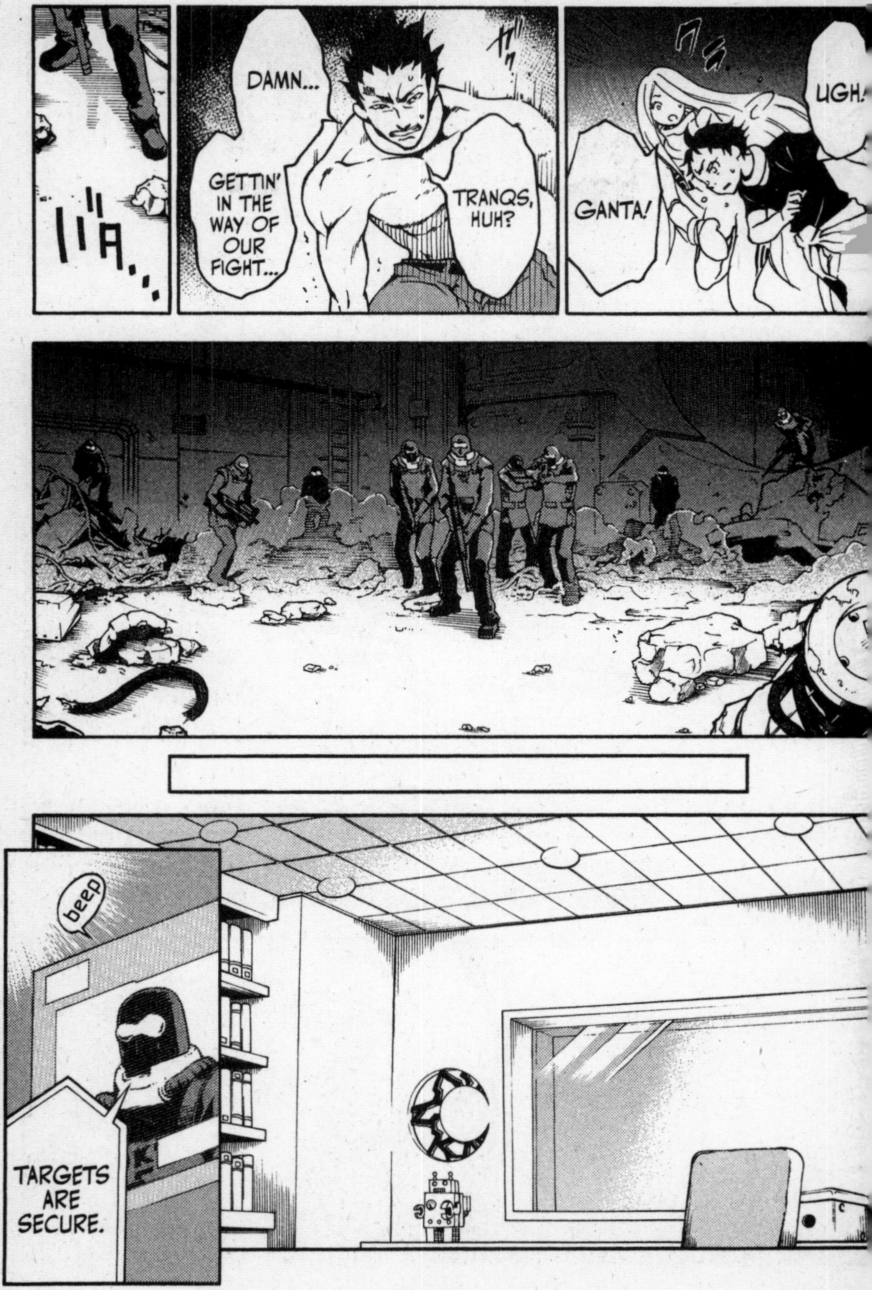
UGH!
GANTA!
DAMN...
TRANQS, HUH?
GETTIN' IN THE WAY OF OUR FIGHT...
beep
TARGETS ARE SECURE.

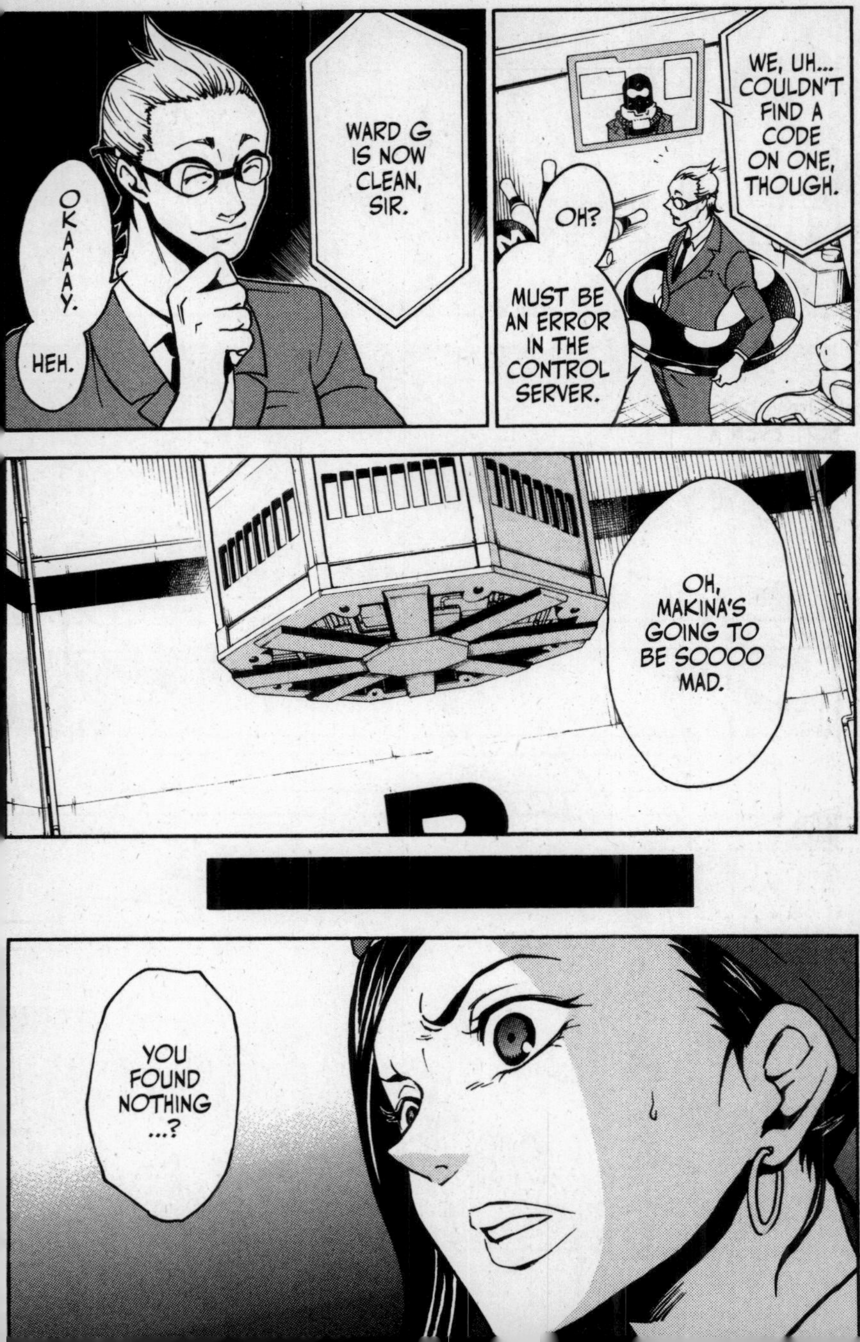
WE, UH... COULDN'T FIND A CODE ON ONE, THOUGH.
OH?
MUST BE AN ERROR IN THE CONTROL SERVER.
WARD G IS NOW CLEAN, SIR.
OKAAAY.
HEH.
OH, MAKINA'S GOING TO BE SOOOO MAD.
YOU FOUND NOTHING ...?

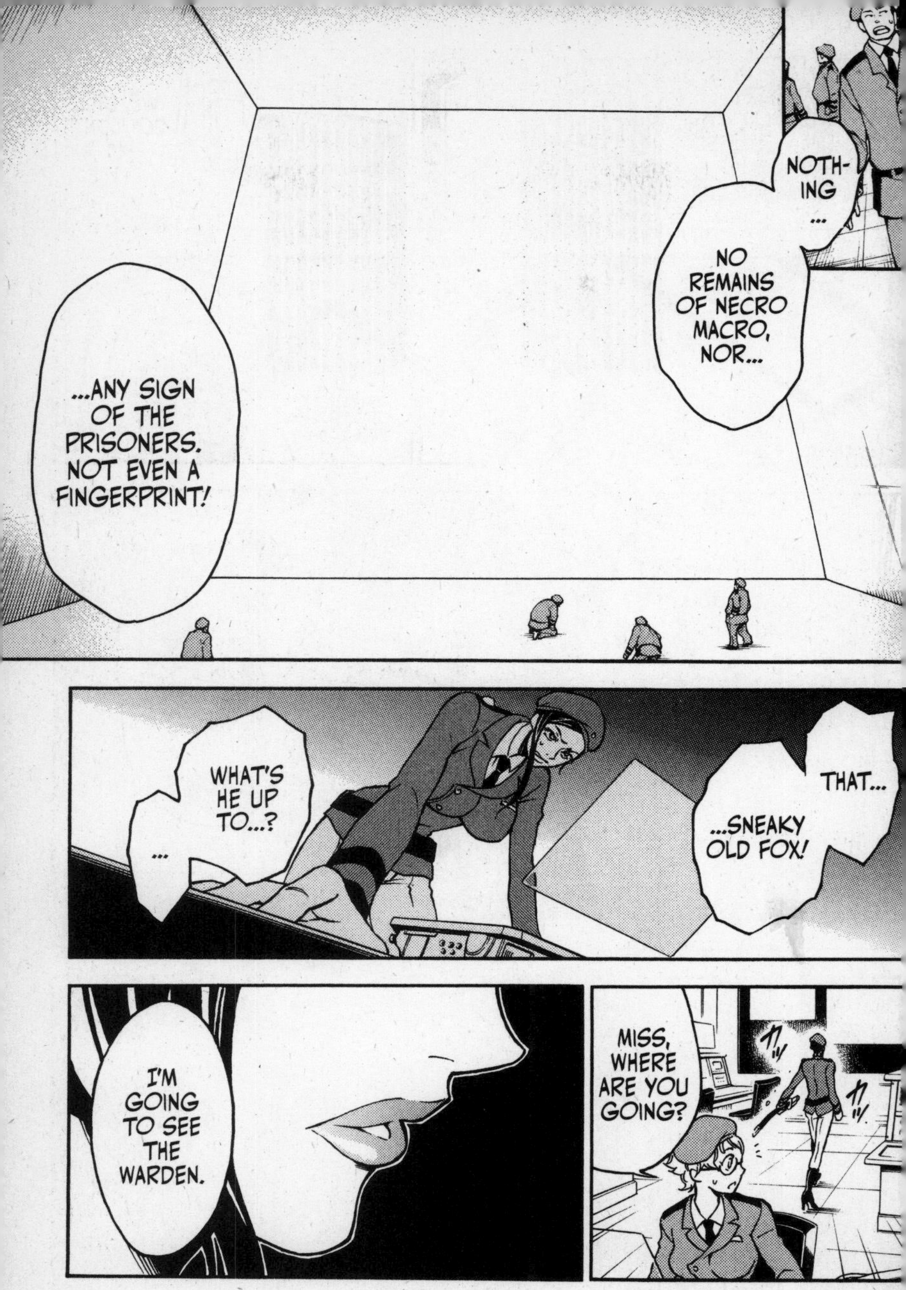
NOTH-ING ...
NO REMAINS OF NECRO MACRO, NOR...
...ANY SIGN OF THE PRISONERS. NOT EVEN A FINGERPRINT!
THAT...
...SNEAKY OLD FOX!
WHAT'S HE UP TO...?
...
MISS, WHERE ARE YOU GOING?
I'M GOING TO SEE THE WARDEN.

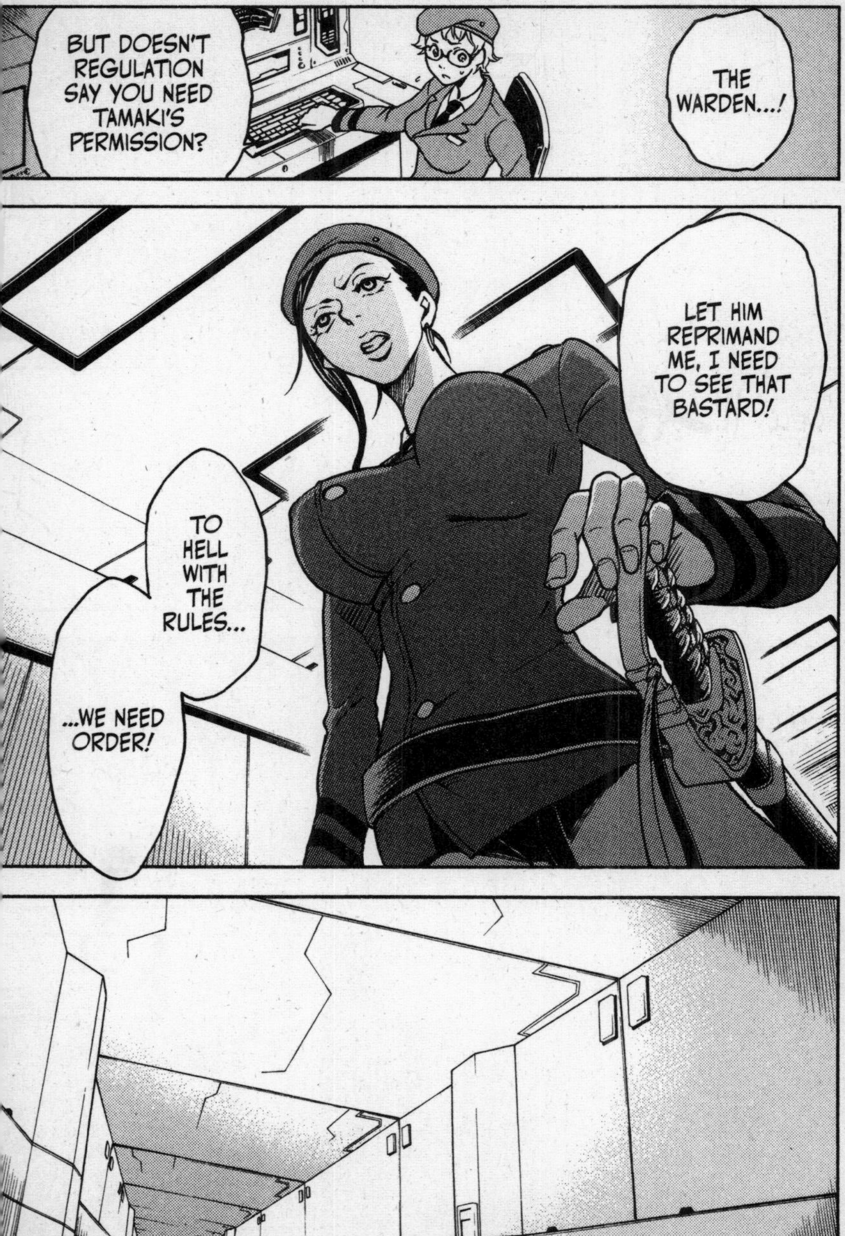
THE WARDEN...!
BUT DOESN'T REGULATION SAY YOU NEED TAMAKI'S PERMISSION?
LET HIM REPRIMAND ME, I NEED TO SEE THAT BASTARD!
TO HELL WITH THE RULES...
...WE NEED ORDER!

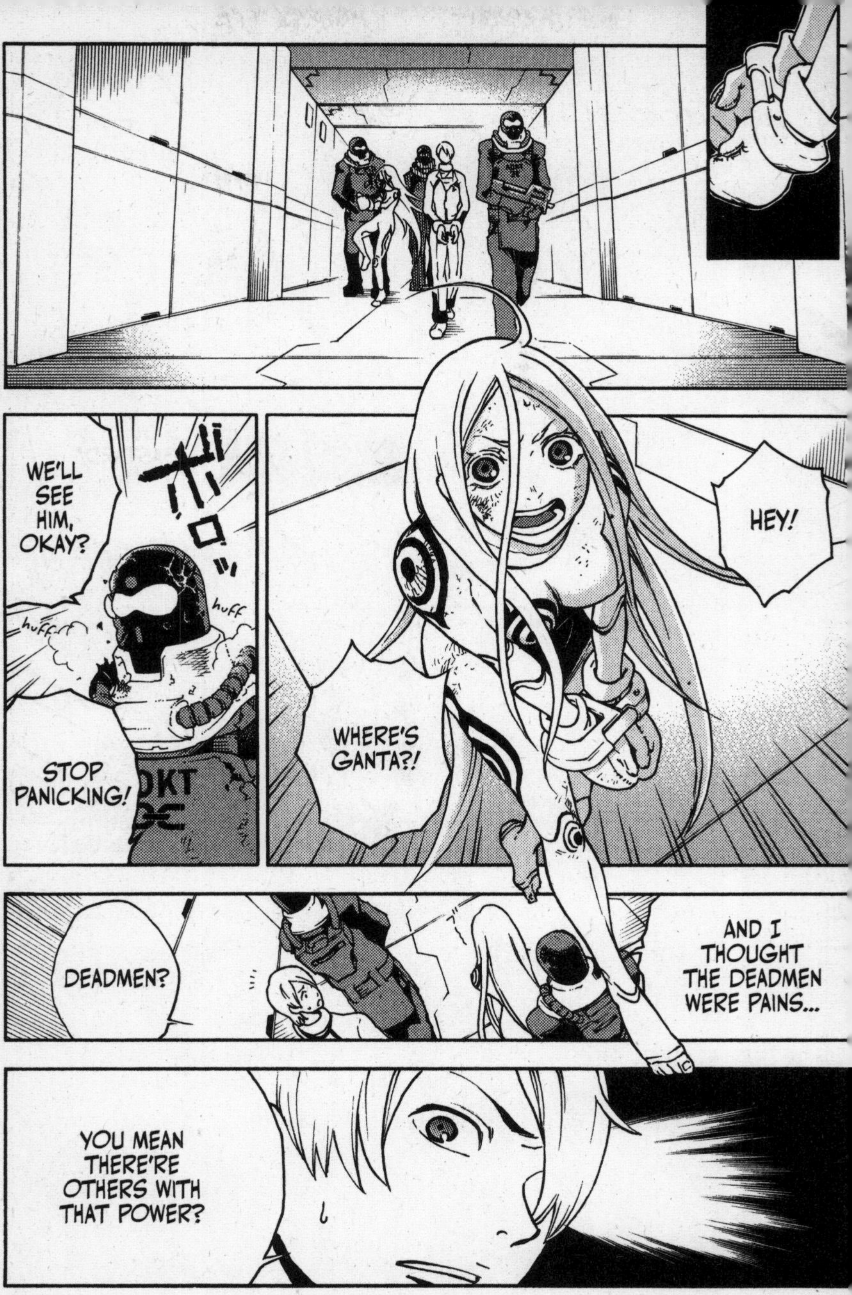
HEY!
WHERE'S GANTA?!
WE'LL SEE HIM, OKAY?
ボロッ
huff
huff
STOP PANICKING!
AND I THOUGHT THE DEADMEN WERE PAINS...
DEADMEN?
YOU MEAN THERE'RE OTHERS WITH THAT POWER?

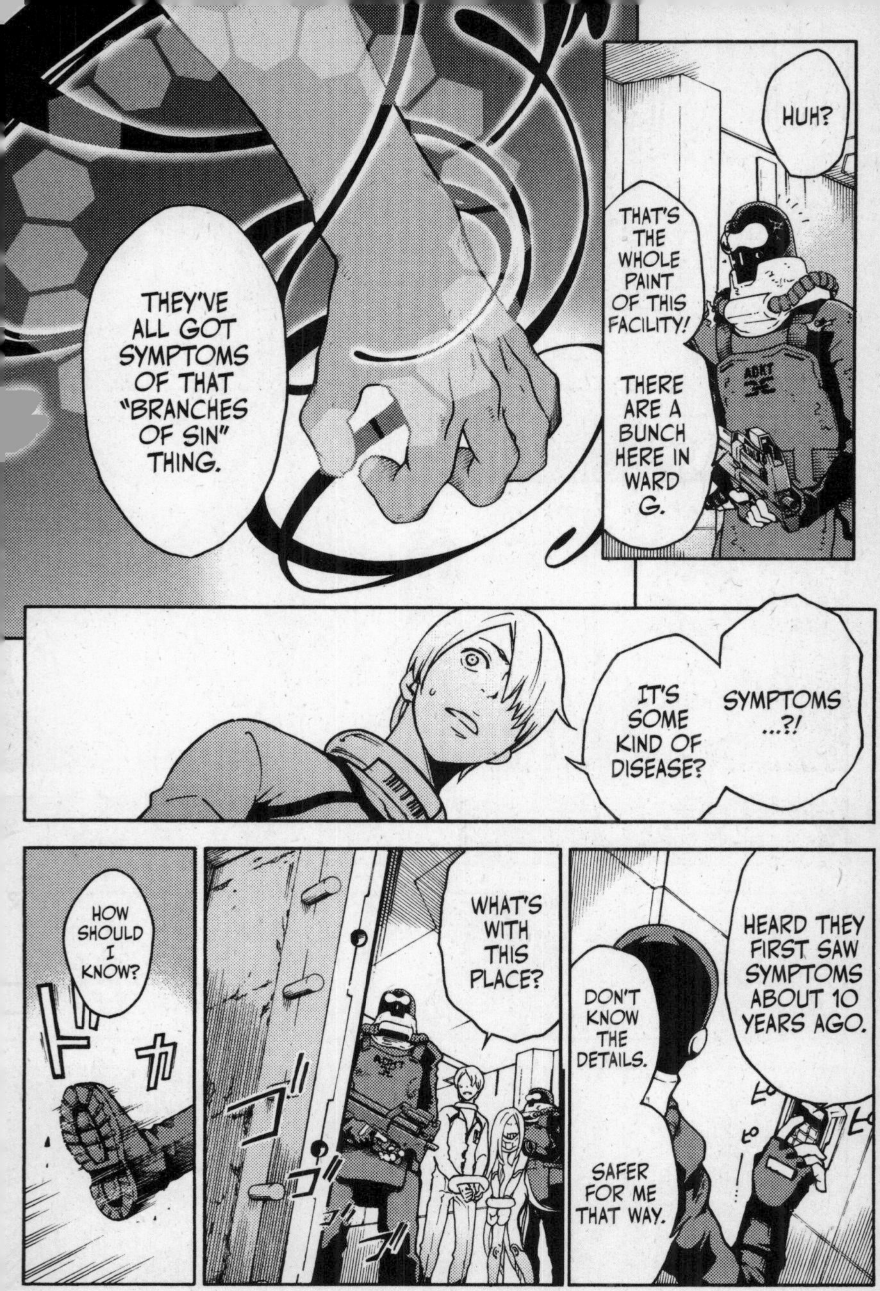
HUH?
THAT'S THE WHOLE PAINT OF THIS FACILITY!
THERE ARE A BUNCH HERE IN WARD G.
THEY'VE ALL GOT SYMPTOMS OF THAT "BRANCHES OF SIN" THING.
SYMPTOMS ...?!
IT'S SOME KIND OF DISEASE?
HEARD THEY FIRST SAW SYMPTOMS ABOUT 10 YEARS AGO.
DON'T KNOW THE DETAILS.
SAFER FOR ME THAT WAY.
WHAT'S WITH THIS PLACE?
HOW SHOULD I KNOW?

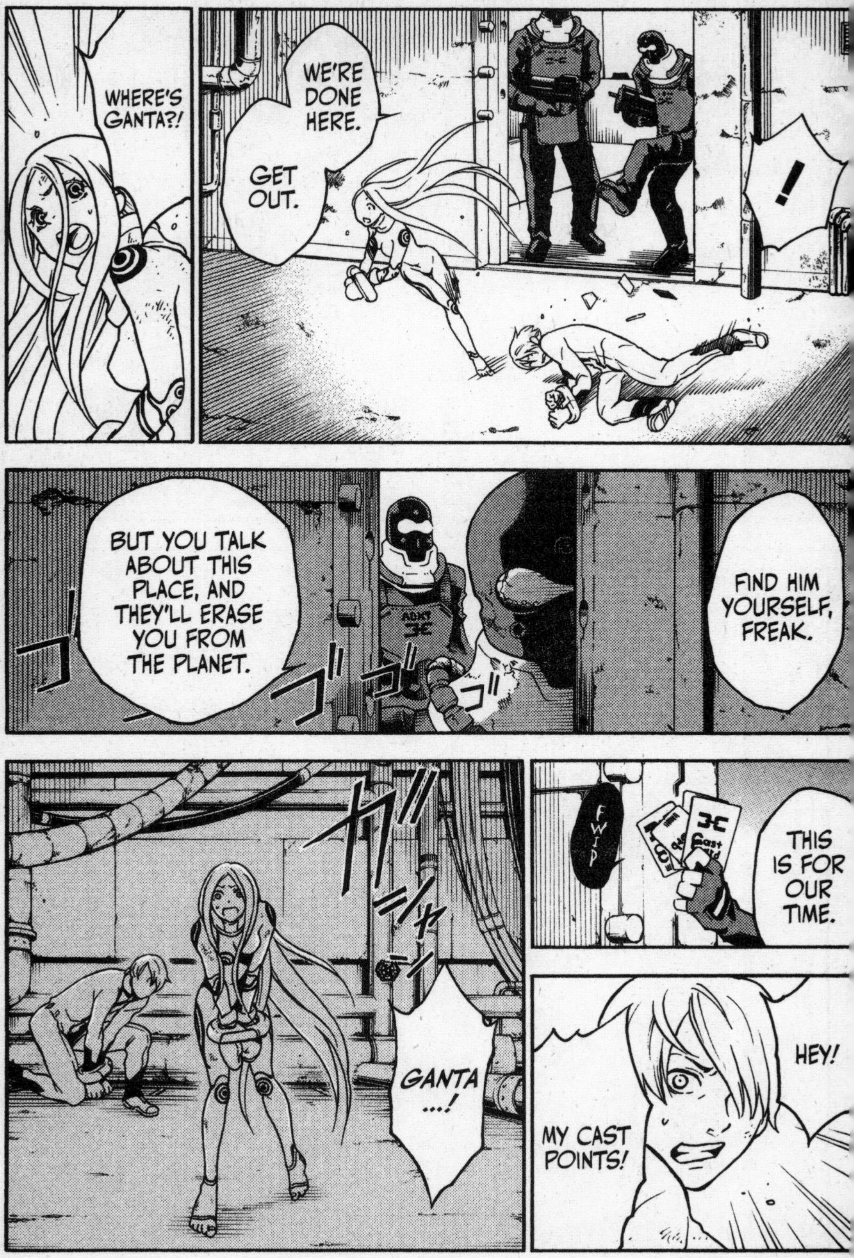
!
WE'RE DONE HERE.
GET OUT.
WHERE'S GANTA?!
FIND HIM YOURSELF, FREAK.
BUT YOU TALK ABOUT THIS PLACE, AND THEY'LL ERASE YOU FROM THE PLANET.
FWIP
THIS IS FOR OUR TIME.
HEY!
MY CAST POINTS!
GANTA ...!

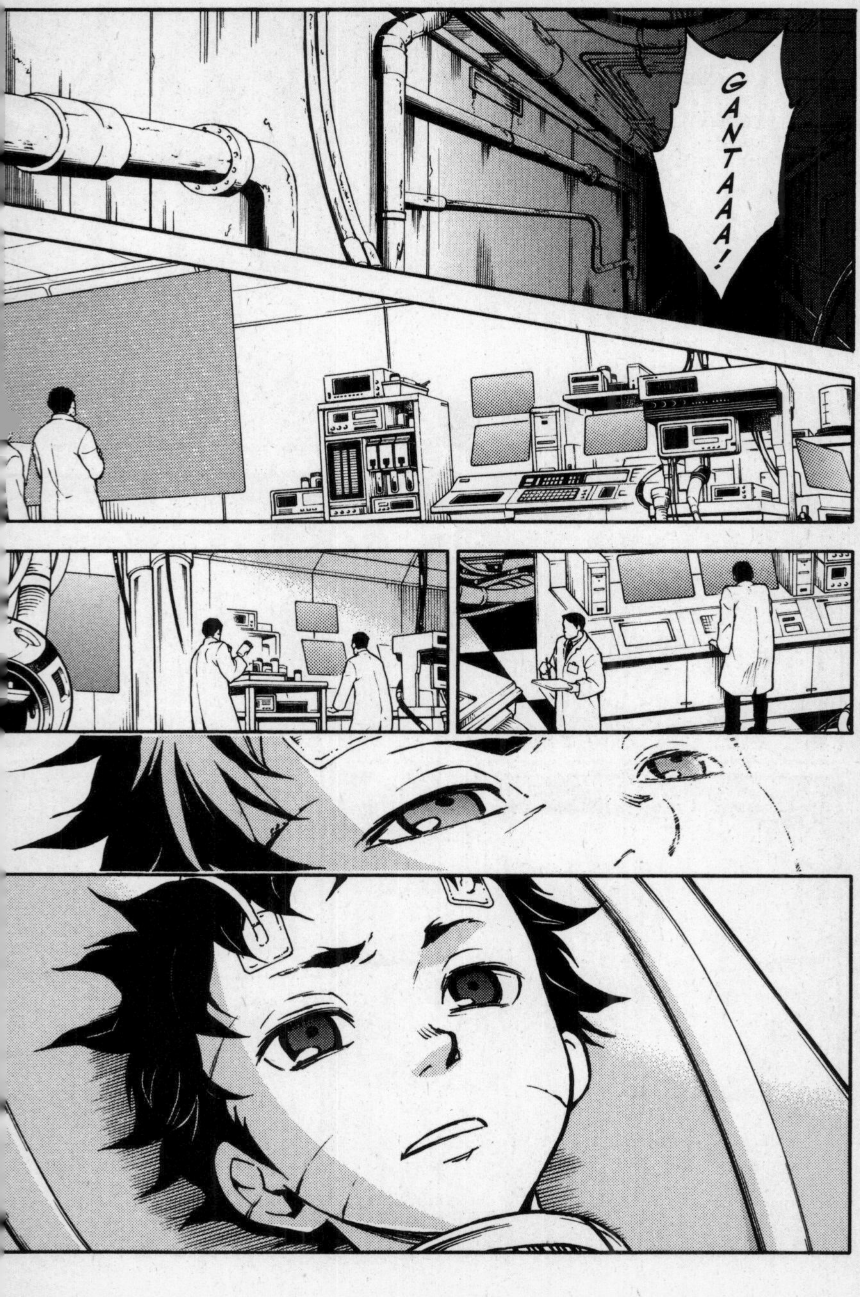
GANTAAA!

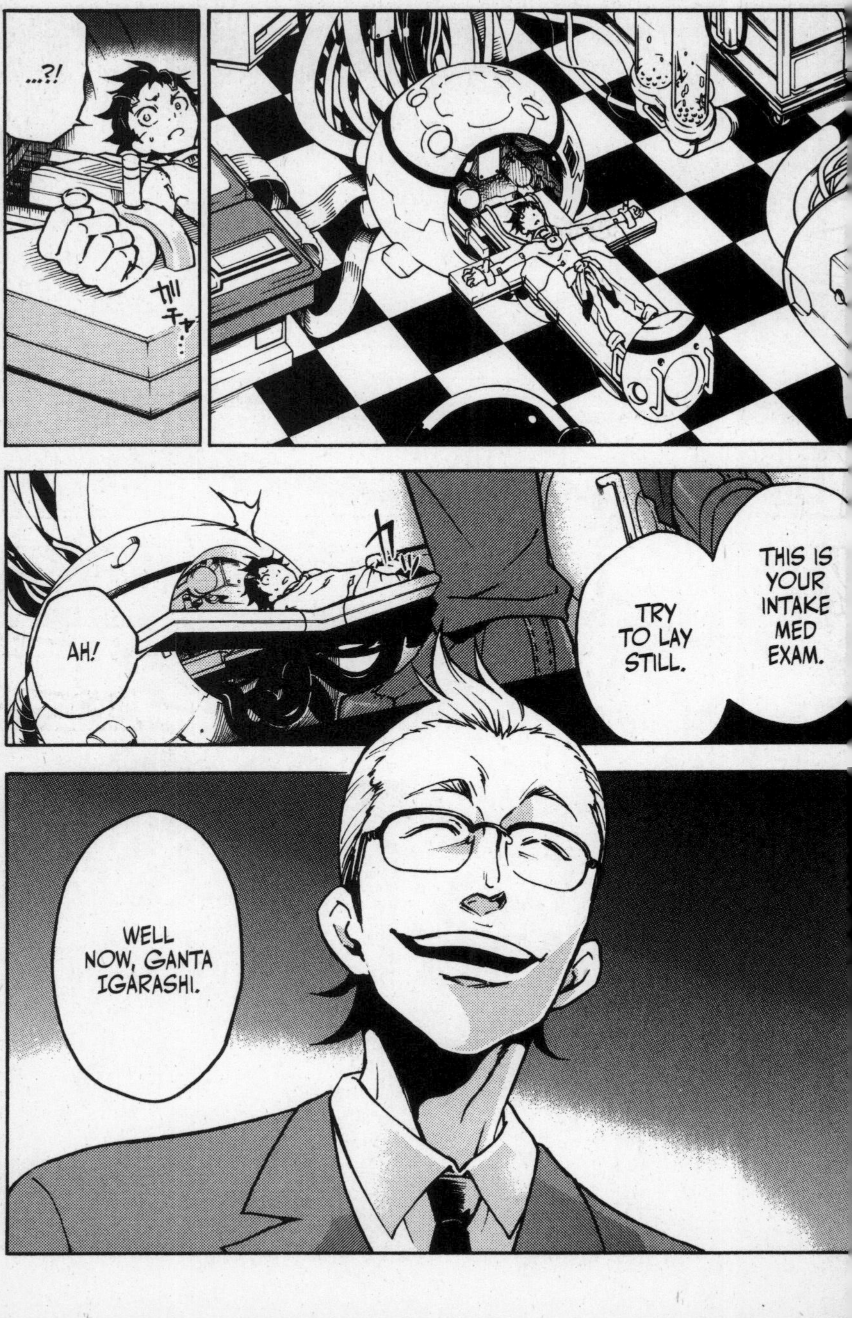
...?!
ガチャ…
THIS IS YOUR INTAKE MED EXAM.
TRY TO LAY STILL.
AH!
WELL NOW, GANTA IGARASHI.

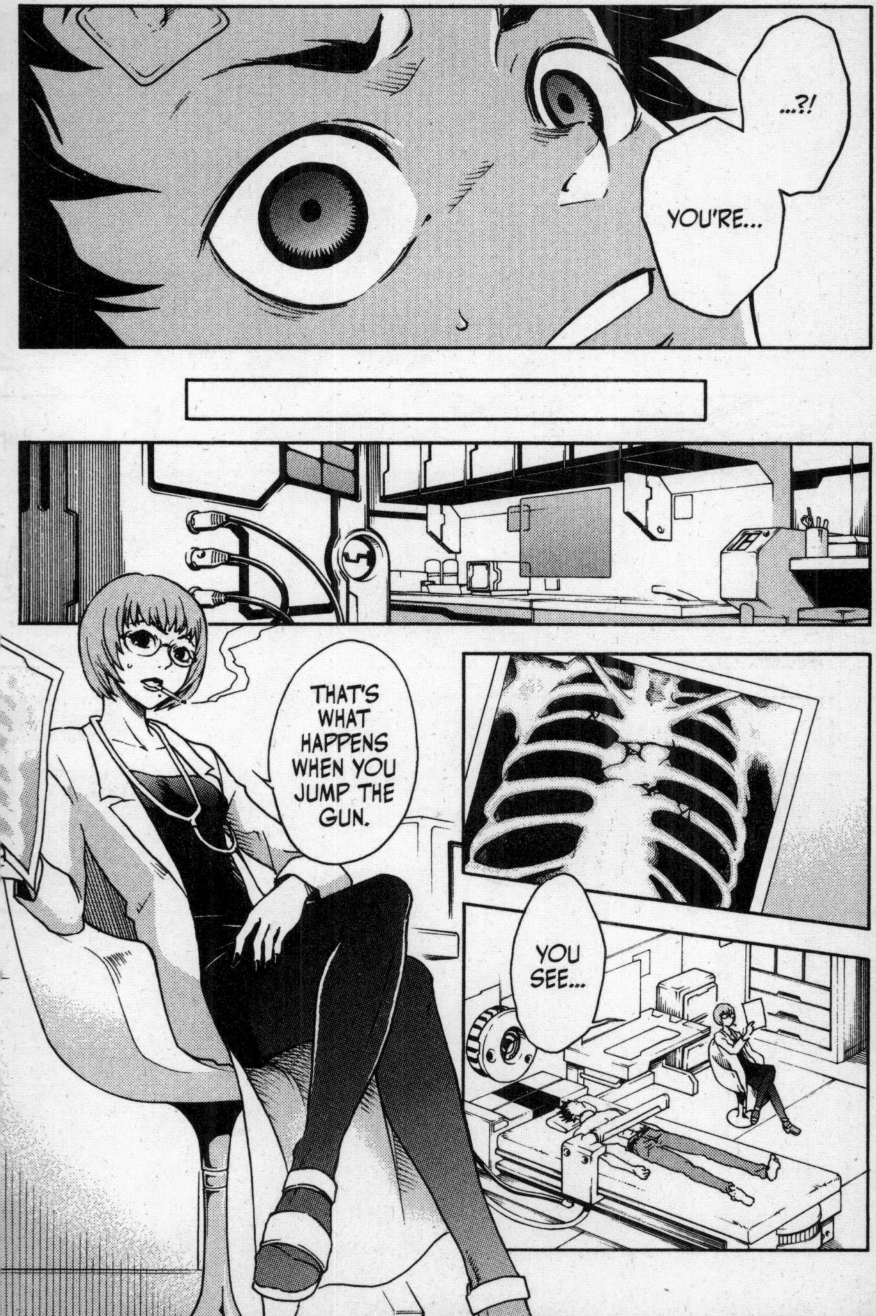

...?!
YOU'RE...
YOU SEE...
THAT'S WHAT HAPPENS WHEN YOU JUMP THE GUN.

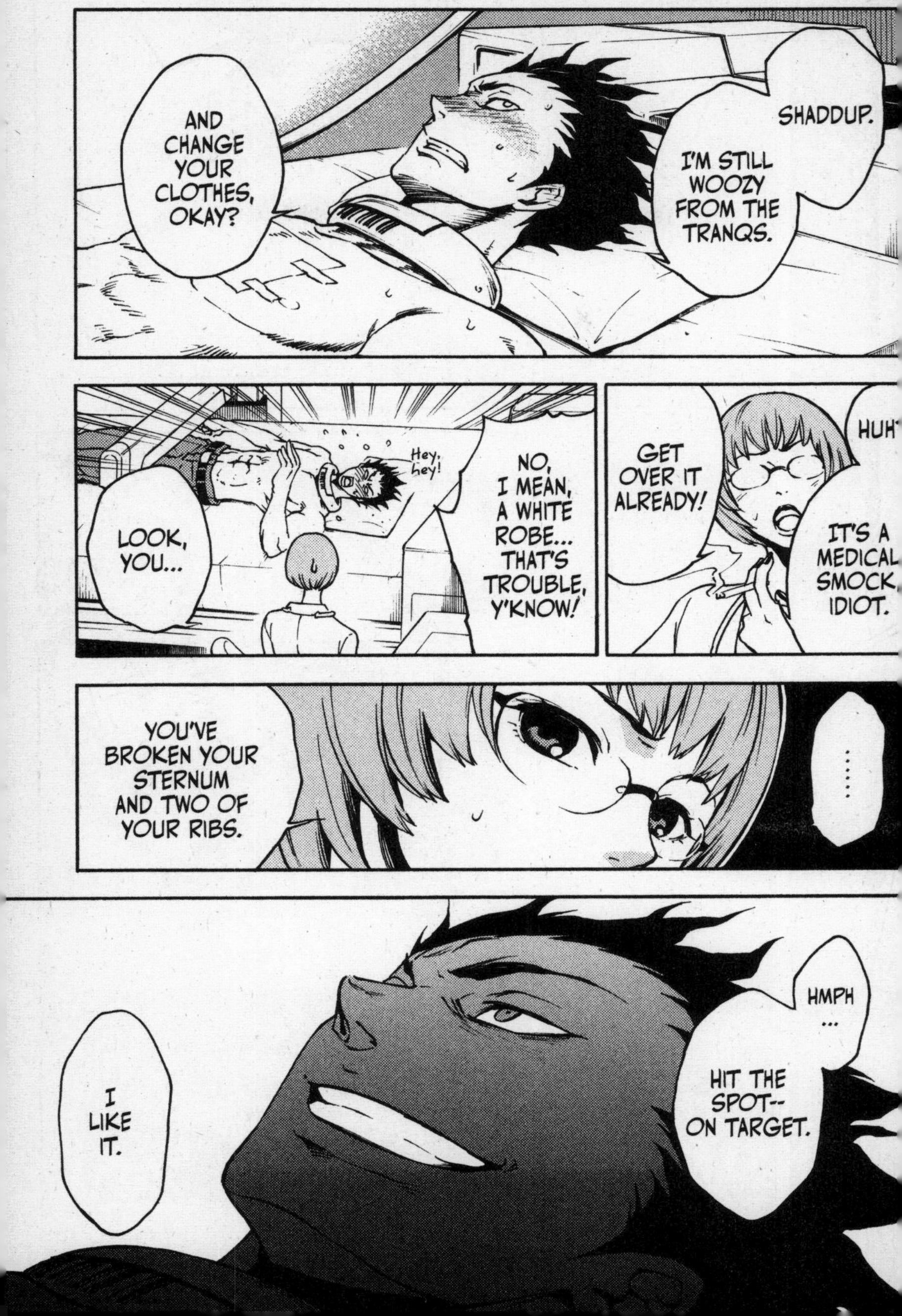
SHADDUP.
I'M STILL WOOZY FROM THE TRANQS.
AND CHANGE YOUR CLOTHES, OKAY?
HUH
IT'S A MEDICAL SMOCK, IDIOT.
GET OVER IT ALREADY!
NO, I MEAN, A WHITE ROBE... THAT'S TROUBLE, Y'KNOW!
Hey, hey!
LOOK, YOU...
......
YOU'VE BROKEN YOUR STERNUM AND TWO OF YOUR RIBS.
HMPH ...
HIT THE SPOT-- ON TARGET.
I LIKE IT.

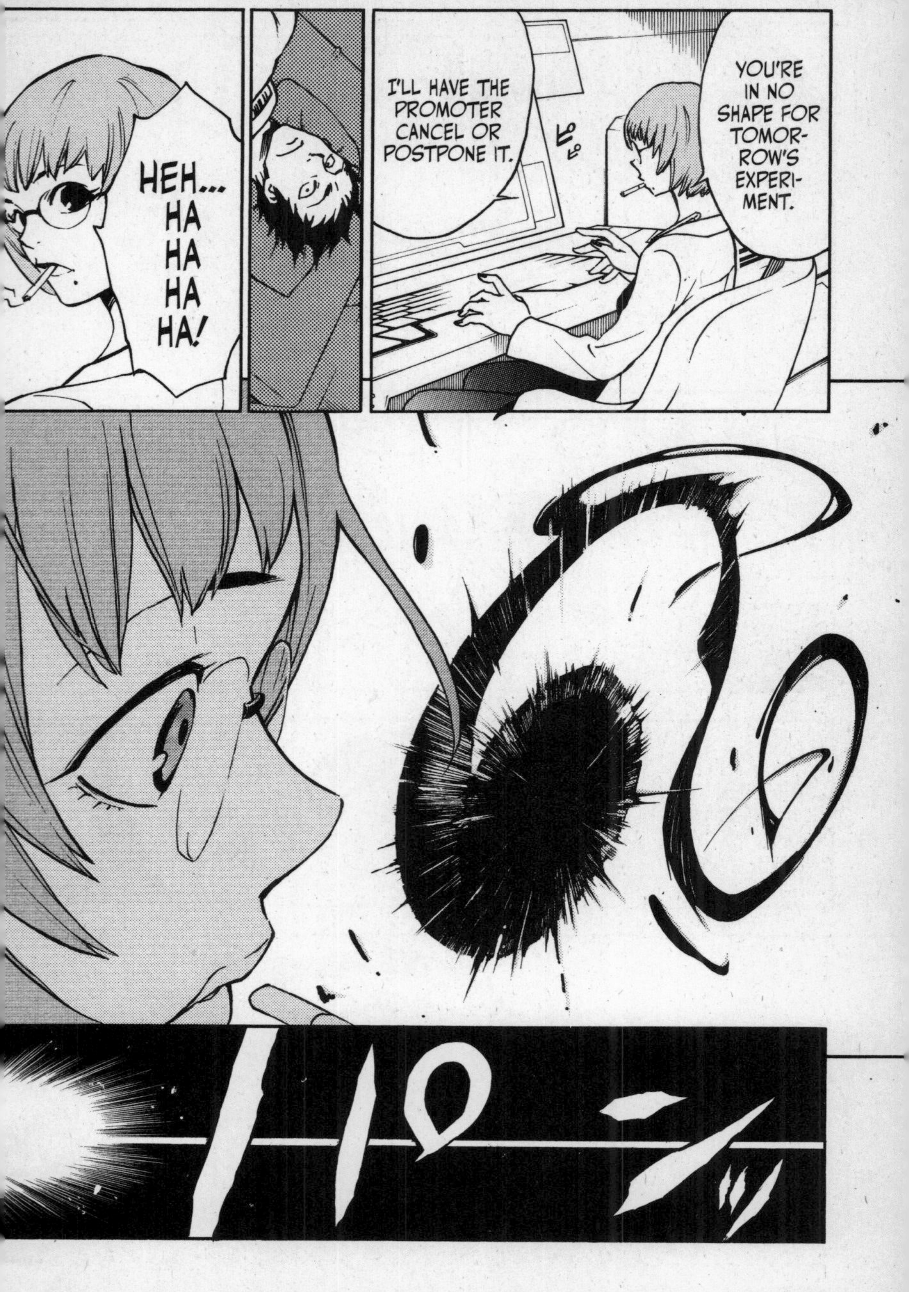
YOU'RE IN NO SHAPE FOR TOMOR-ROW'S EXPERI-MENT.
I'LL HAVE THE PROMOTER CANCEL OR POSTPONE IT.
HEH... HA HA HA HA!

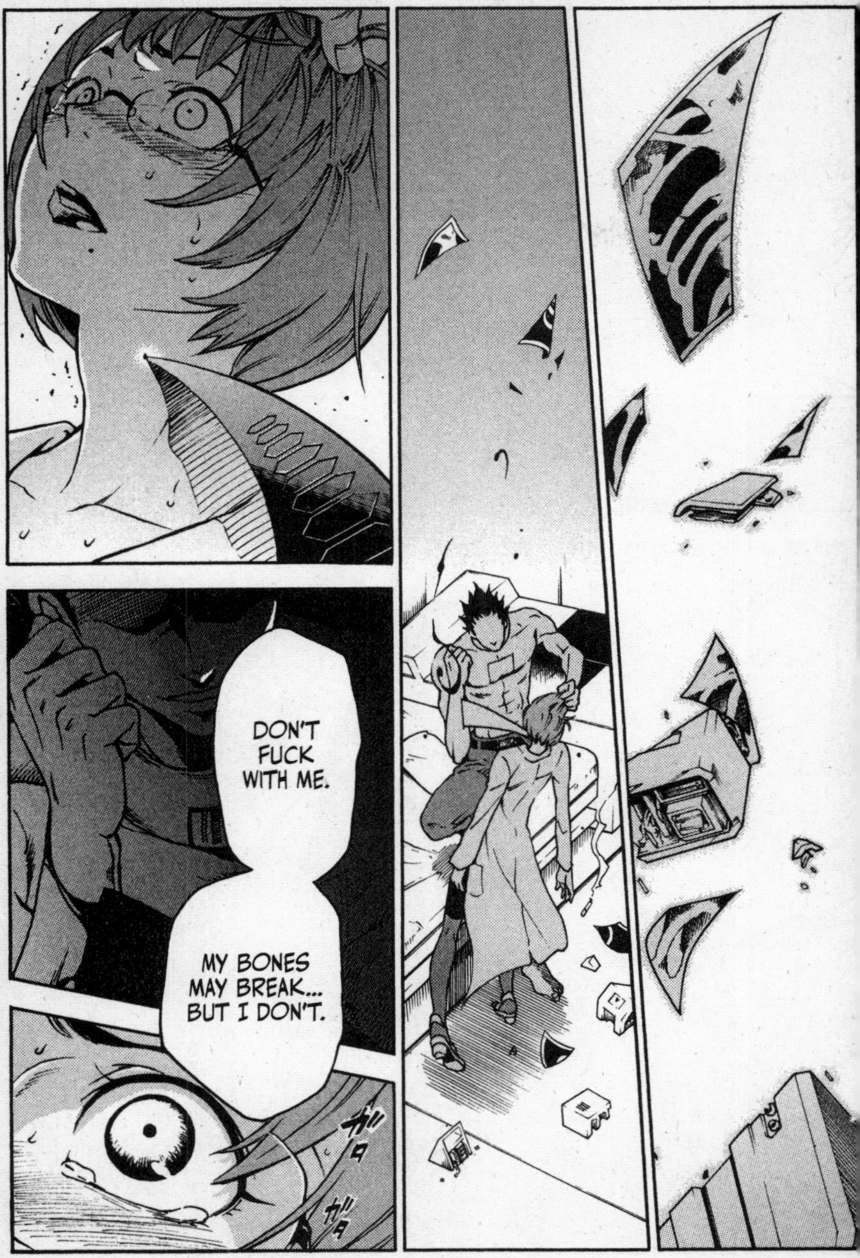
DON'T FUCK WITH ME.
MY BONES MAY BREAK... BUT I DON'T.
ガタ
ガタ

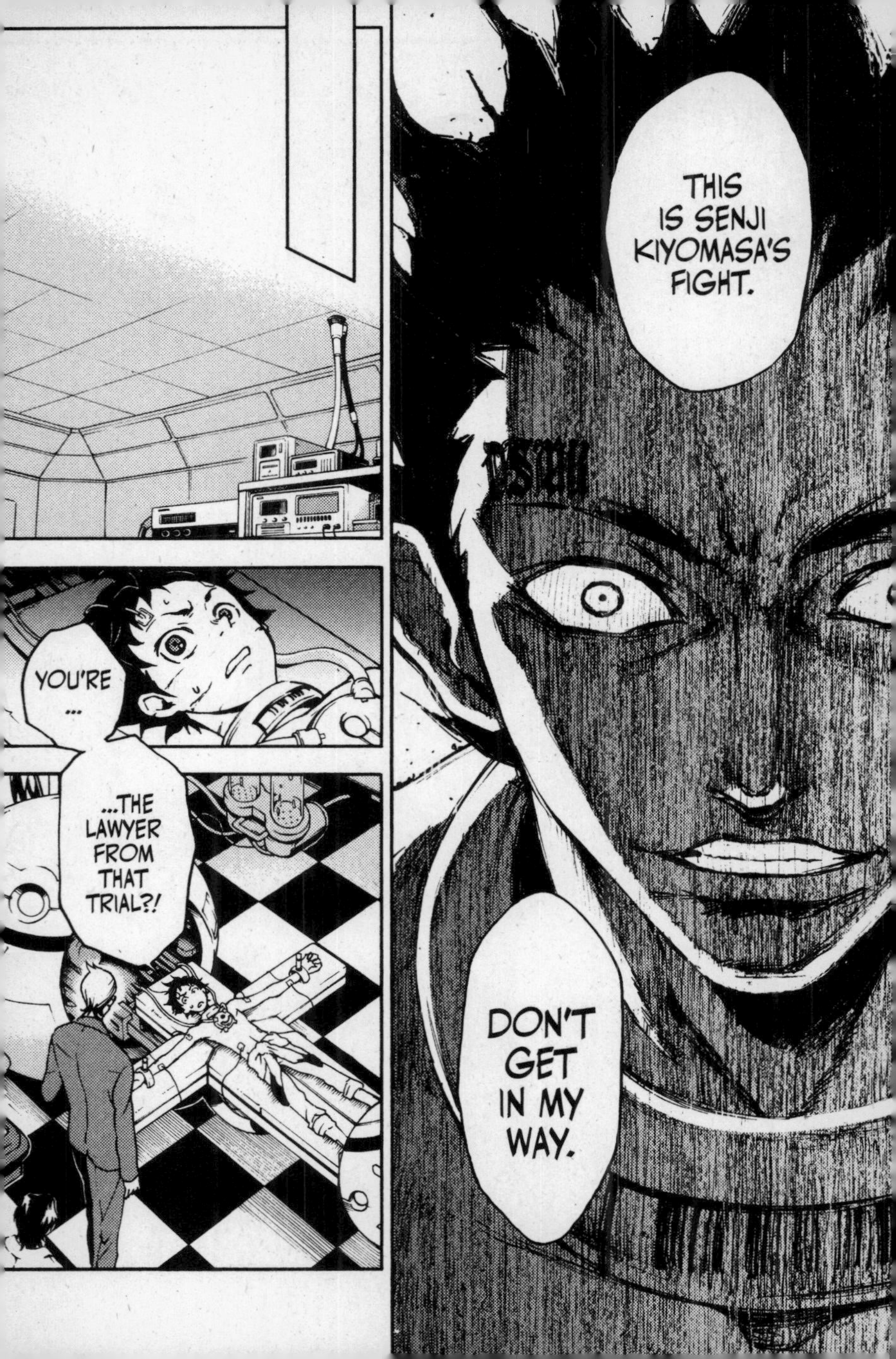
THIS IS SENJI KIYOMASA'S FIGHT.
DON'T GET IN MY WAY.
YOU'RE ...
...THE LAWYER FROM THAT TRIAL?!

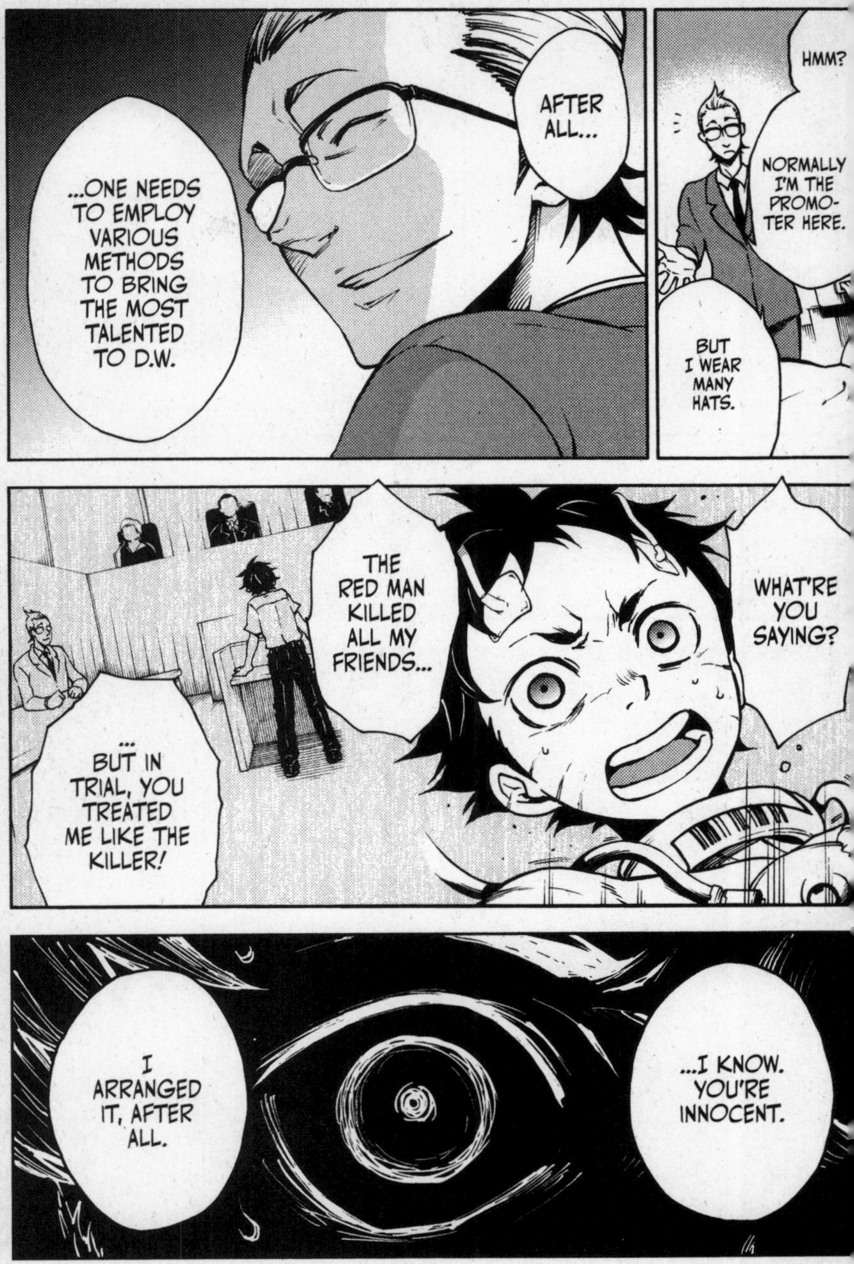
HMM?
NORMALLY I'M THE PROMOTER HERE.
BUT I WEAR MANY HATS.
AFTER ALL...
...ONE NEEDS TO EMPLOY VARIOUS METHODS TO BRING THE MOST TALENTED TO D.W.
WHAT'RE YOU SAYING?
THE RED MAN KILLED ALL MY FRIENDS...
...BUT IN TRIAL, YOU TREATED ME LIKE THE KILLER!
...I KNOW. YOU'RE INNOCENT.
I ARRANGED IT, AFTER ALL.

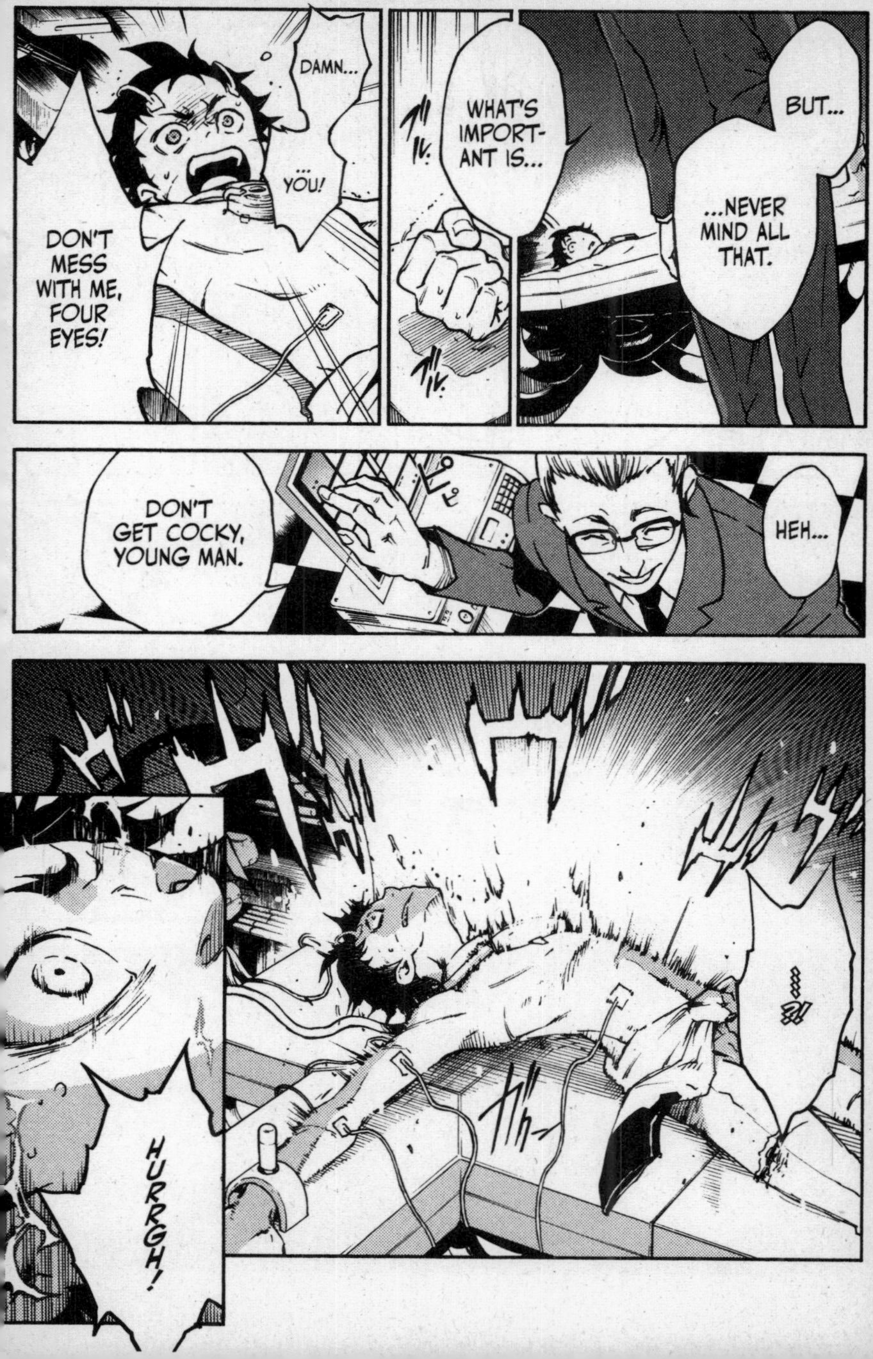
BUT...
...NEVER MIND ALL THAT.
WHAT'S IMPORT-ANT IS...
DAMN...
...YOU!
DON'T MESS WITH ME, FOUR EYES!
HEH...
DON'T GET COCKY, YOUNG MAN.
...!?
HURRGH!

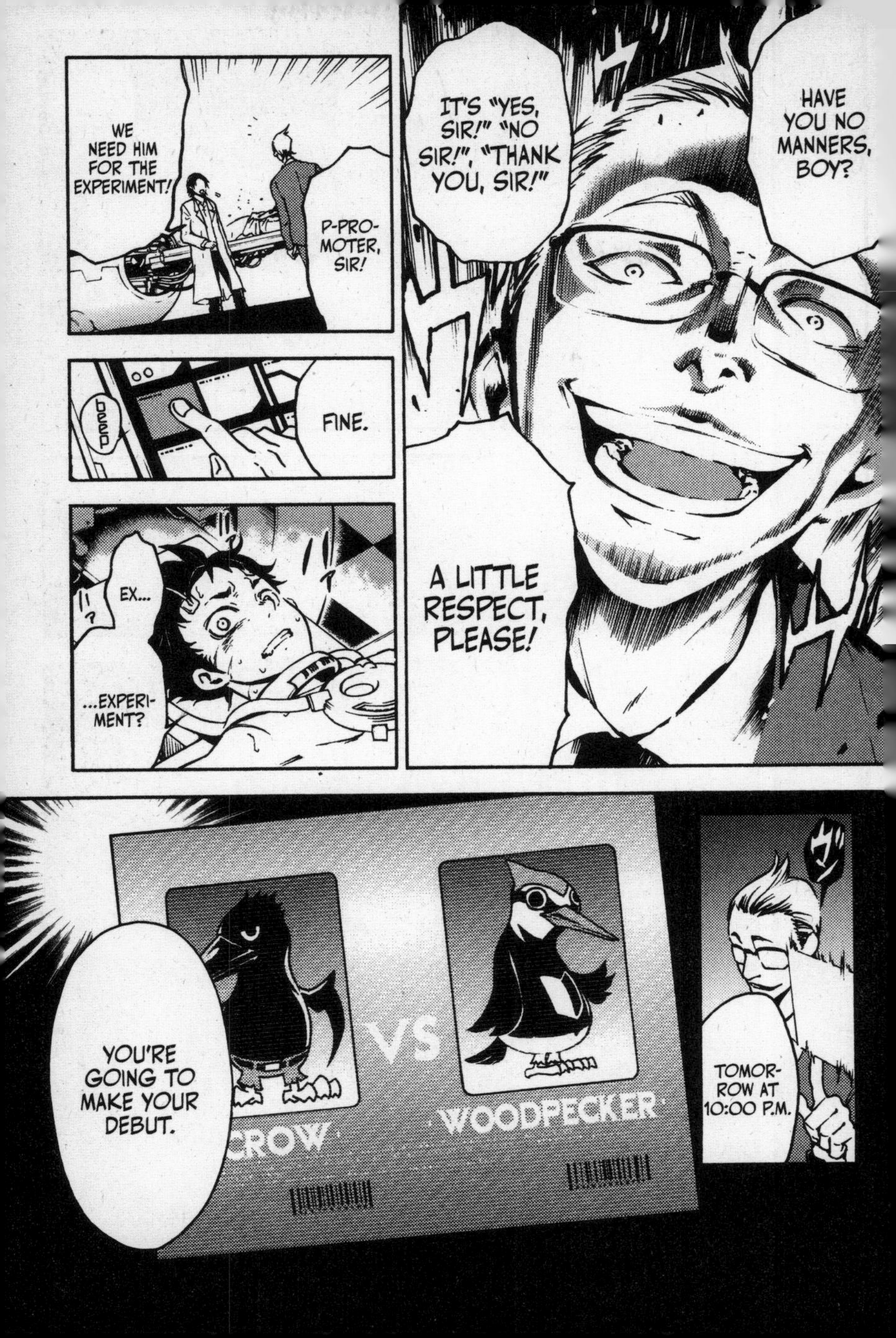
HAVE YOU NO MANNERS, BOY?
IT'S "YES, SIR!" "NO SIR!", "THANK YOU, SIR!"
A LITTLE RESPECT, PLEASE!
P-PROMOTER, SIR!
WE NEED HIM FOR THE EXPERIMENT!
FINE.
beep
EX...
!?
...EXPERIMENT?
TOMORROW AT 10:00 P.M.
WOODPECKER
VS
CROW
YOU'RE GOING TO MAKE YOUR DEBUT.

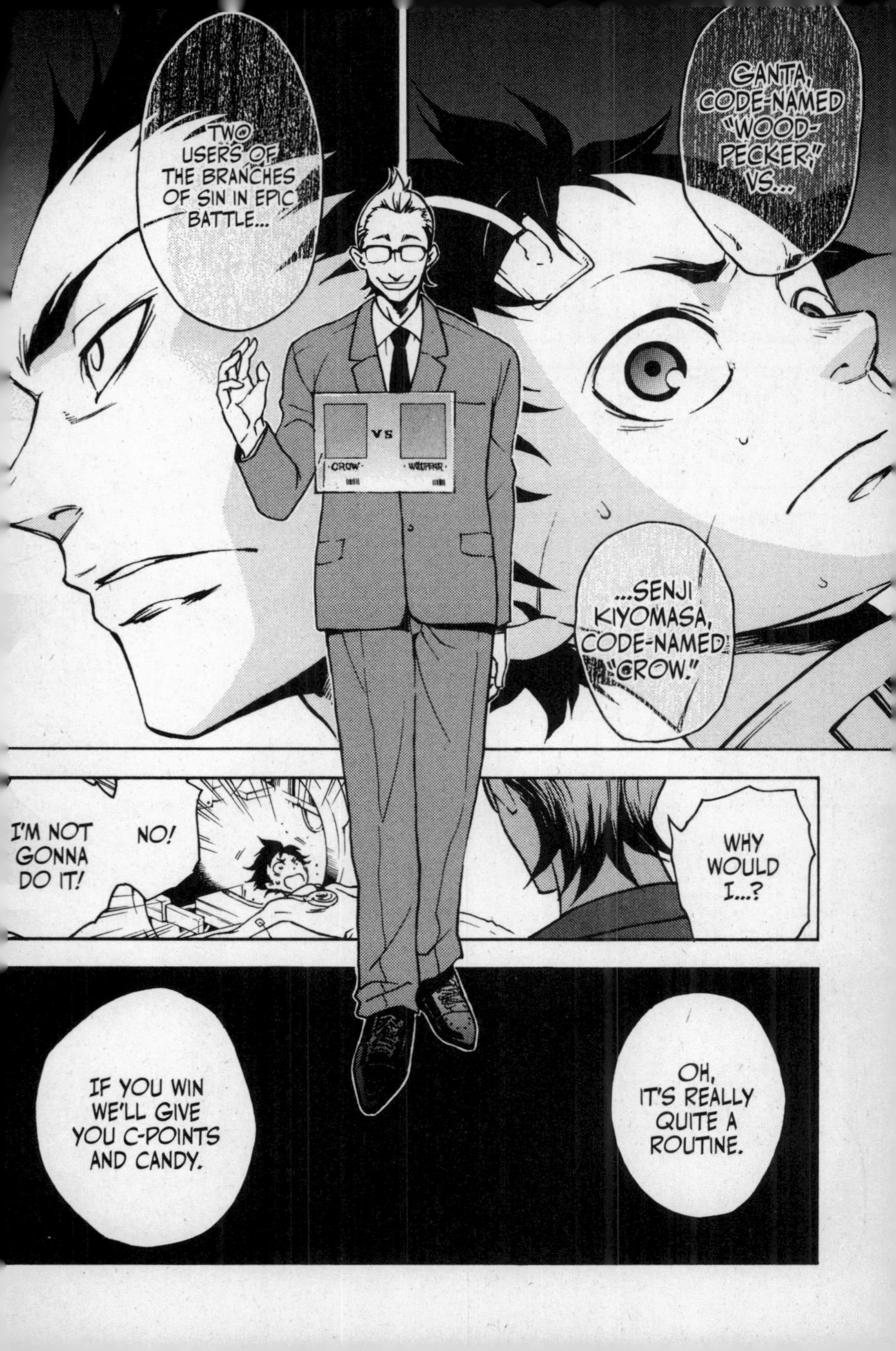
GANTA, CODE-NAMED "WOOD-PECKER," VS...
...SENJI KIYOMASA, CODE-NAMED "CROW."
TWO USERS OF THE BRANCHES OF SIN IN EPIC BATTLE...
CROW
VS
WHY WOULD I...?
NO!
I'M NOT GONNA DO IT!
OH, IT'S REALLY QUITE A ROUTINE.
IF YOU WIN WE'LL GIVE YOU C-POINTS AND CANDY.

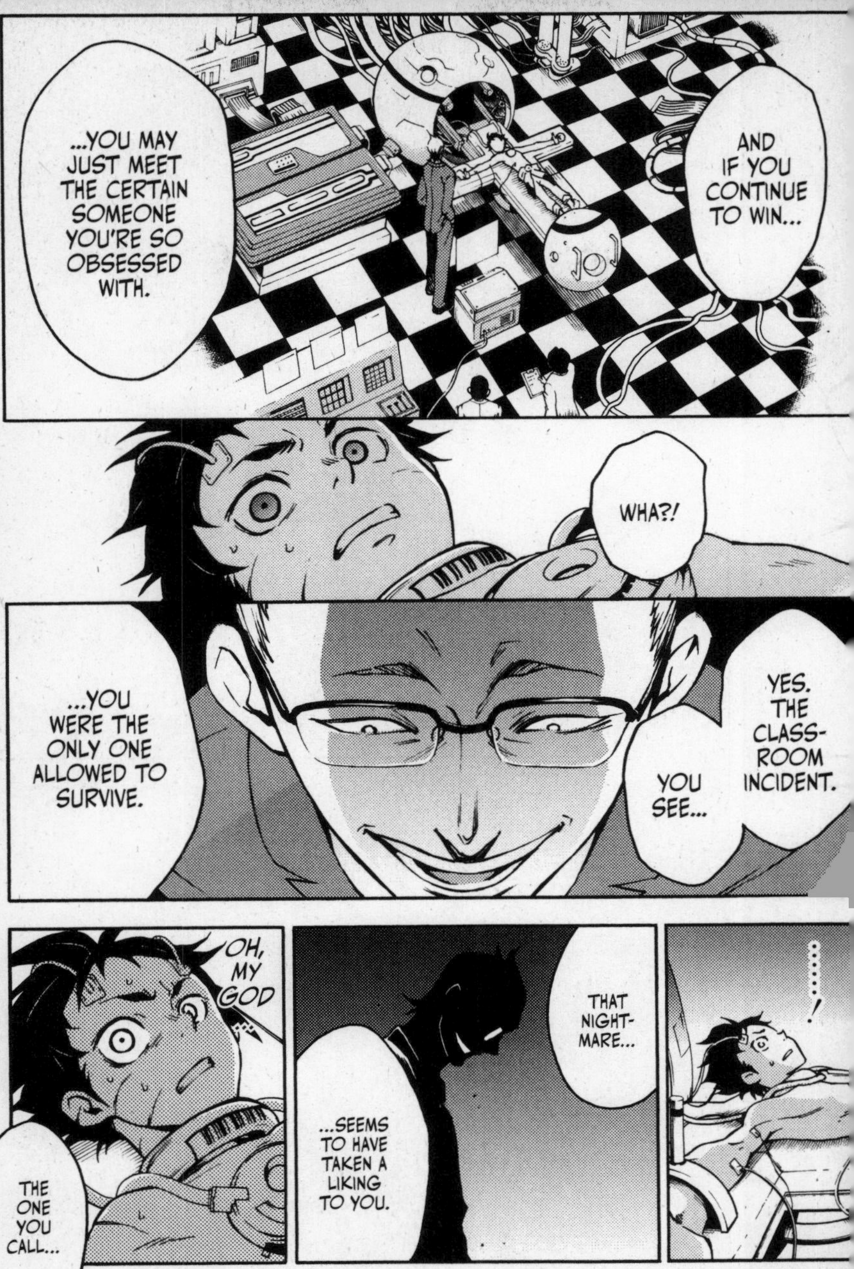
AND IF YOU CONTINUE TO WIN...
...YOU MAY JUST MEET THE CERTAIN SOMEONE YOU'RE SO OBSESSED WITH.
WHA?!
YES. THE CLASS-ROOM INCIDENT.
YOU SEE...
...YOU WERE THE ONLY ONE ALLOWED TO SURVIVE.
......!
THAT NIGHT-MARE...
...SEEMS TO HAVE TAKEN A LIKING TO YOU.
OH, MY GOD
THE ONE YOU CALL...

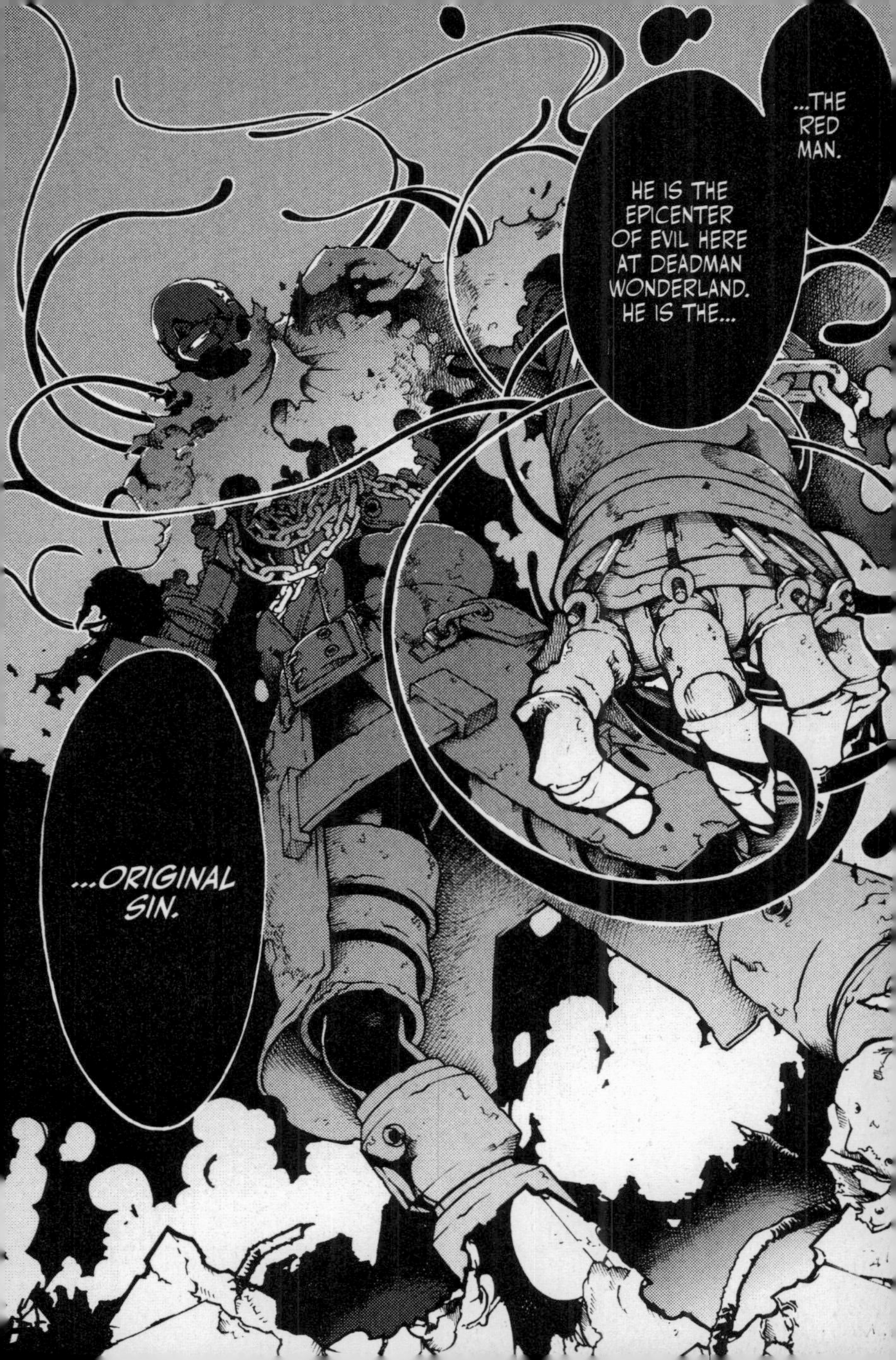
...THE RED MAN.
HE IS THE EPICENTER OF EVIL HERE AT DEADMAN WONDERLAND. HE IS THE...
...ORIGINAL SIN.

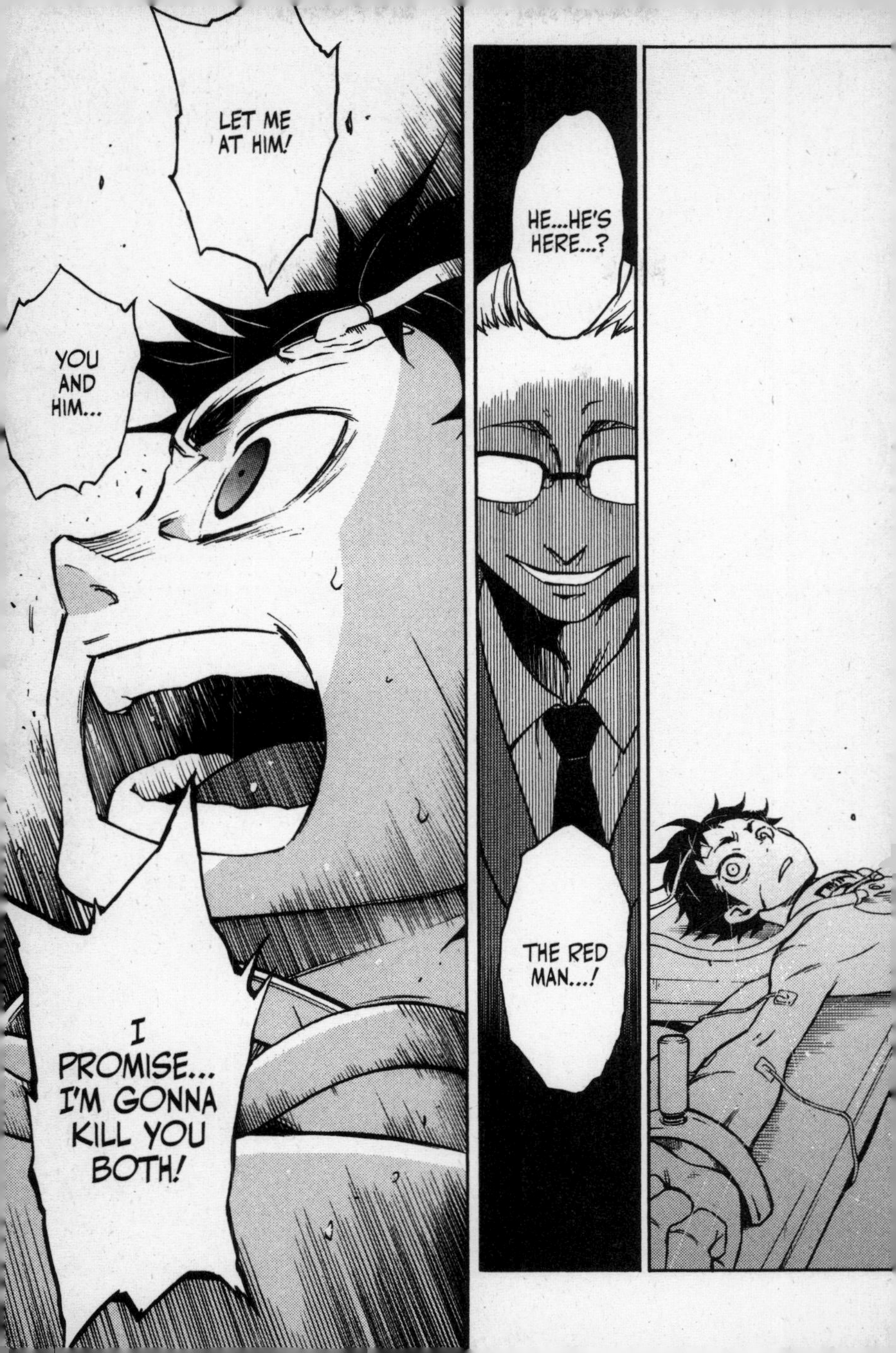
HE...HE'S HERE...?
THE RED MAN...!
LET ME AT HIM!
YOU AND HIM...
I PROMISE... I'M GONNA KILL YOU BOTH!

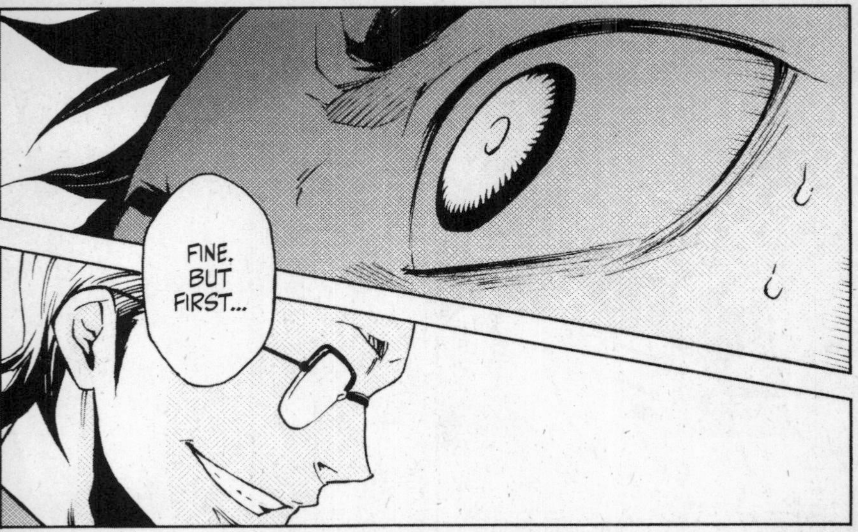
FINE. BUT FIRST...

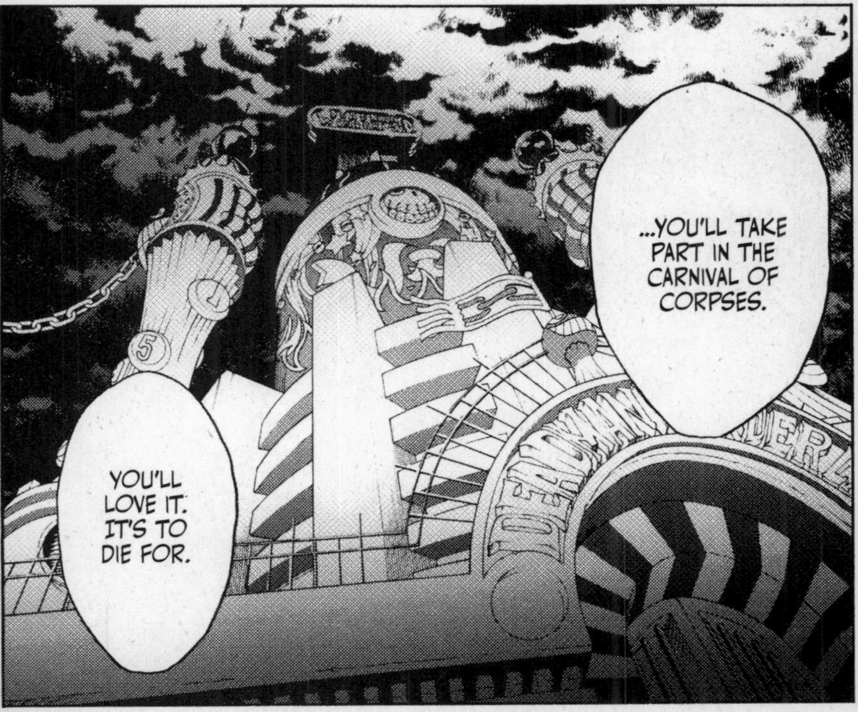
...YOU'LL TAKE PART IN THE CARNIVAL OF CORPSES.
YOU'LL LOVE IT. IT'S TO DIE FOR.

# DW

DEADMAN WONDER
LAND

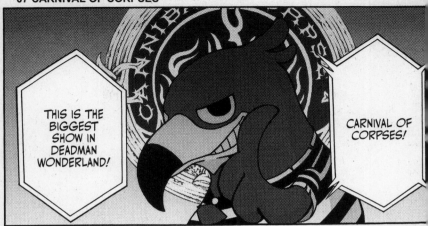

CARNIVAL OF CORPSES!
THIS IS THE BIGGEST SHOW IN DEADMAN WONDERLAND!
DEAD-MEN...
...THOSE INFECTED WITH THE "BRANCHES OF SIN," WHO BEGAN TO APPEAR AFTER THE GREAT TOKYO EARTH-QUAKE.
THIS IS AN EXPERIMENT TO DRAW OUT THOSE ABILITIES TO THEIR FULLEST EXTENT.
BASICALLY, IT ENTAILS...
...BATTLES TO THE DEATH BETWEEN DEADMEN. ♪

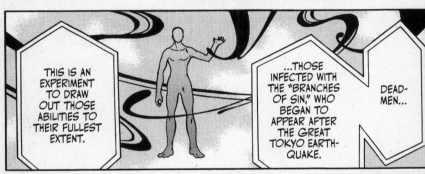

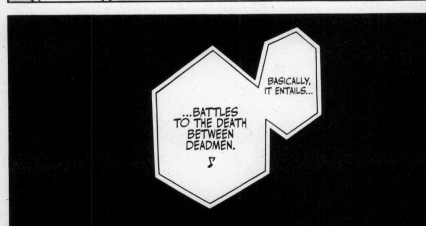

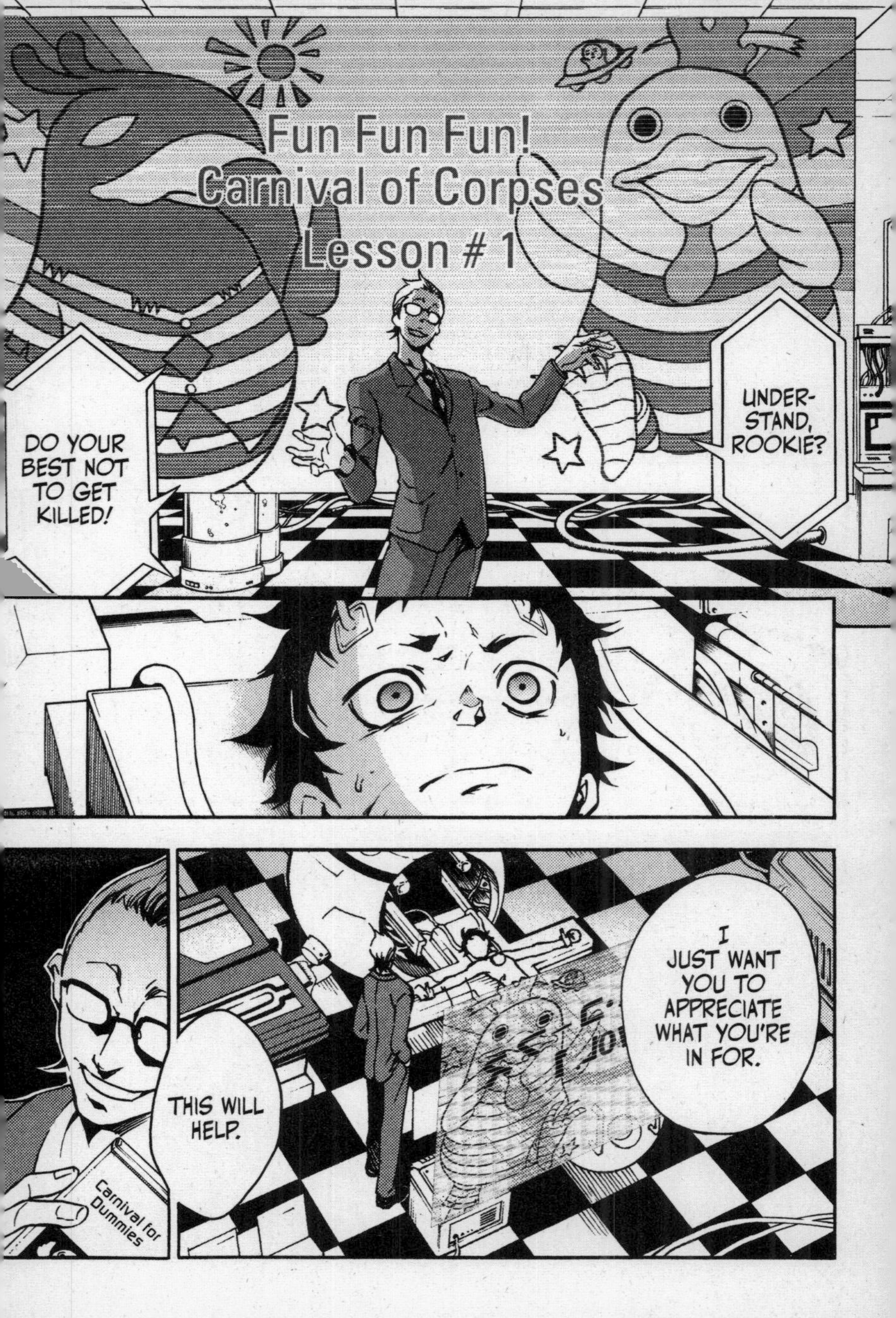
Fun Fun Fun!
Carnival of Corpses
Lesson # 1
UNDER-STAND, ROOKIE?
DO YOUR BEST NOT TO GET KILLED!
I JUST WANT YOU TO APPRECIATE WHAT YOU'RE IN FOR.
THIS WILL HELP.
Carnival for Dummies

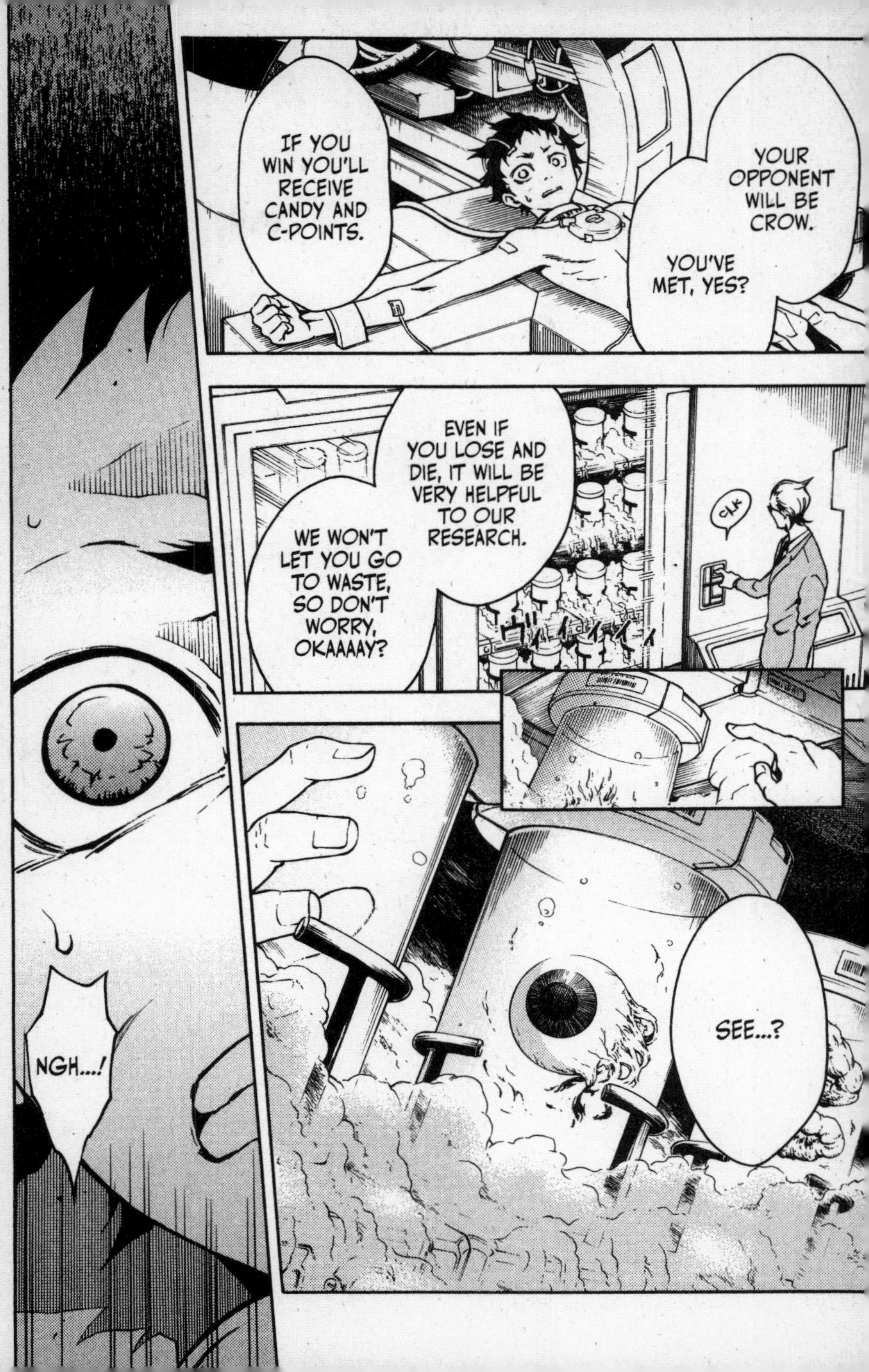

YOUR OPPONENT WILL BE CROW.
YOU'VE MET, YES?
IF YOU WIN YOU'LL RECEIVE CANDY AND C-POINTS.
EVEN IF YOU LOSE AND DIE, IT WILL BE VERY HELPFUL TO OUR RESEARCH.
WE WON'T LET YOU GO TO WASTE, SO DON'T WORRY, OKAAAAY?
CLIK
ヴィイイイイ
SEE...?
NGH...!

# 07 CARNIVAL OF CORPSES

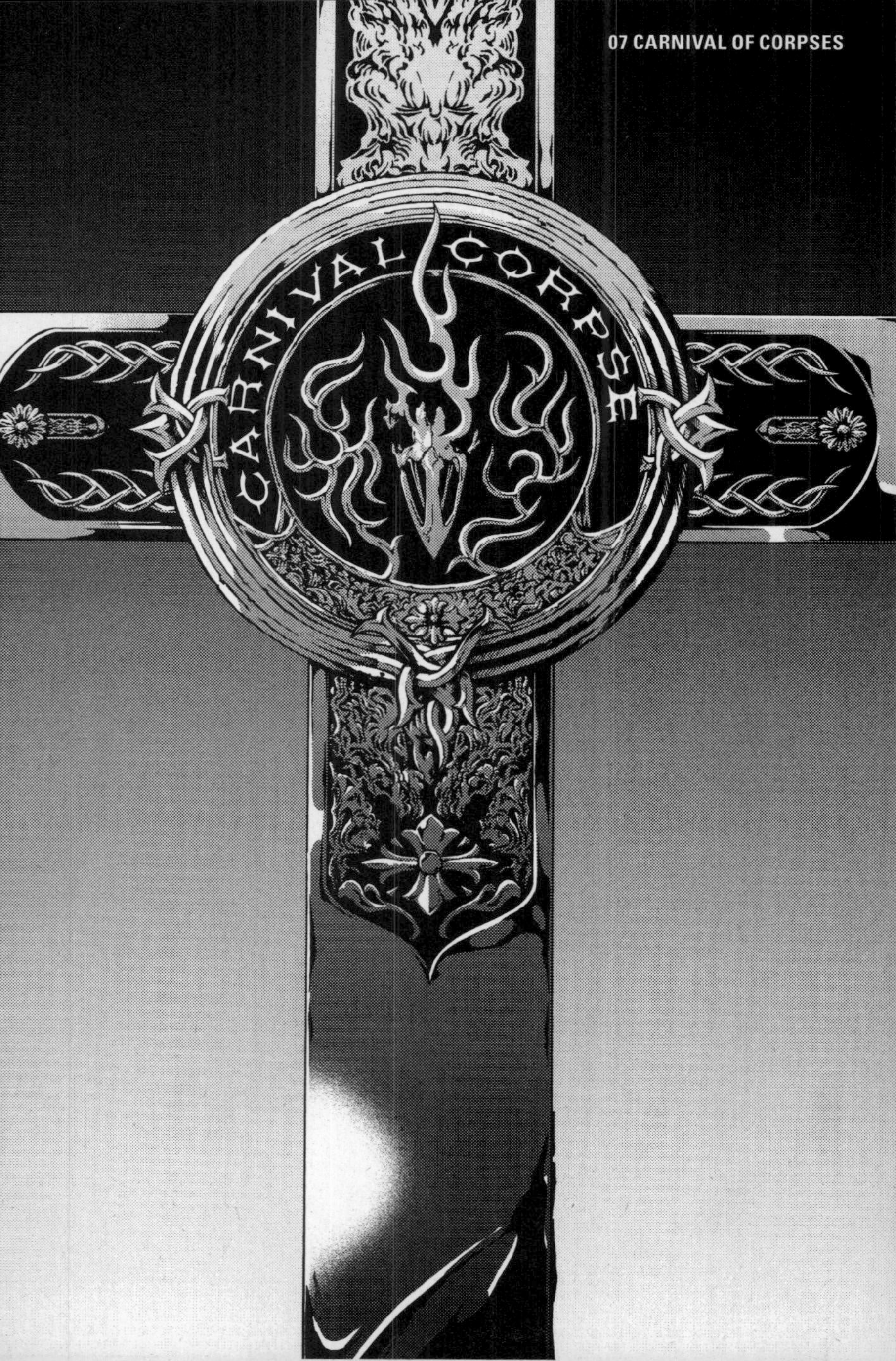
CARNIVAL CORPSE

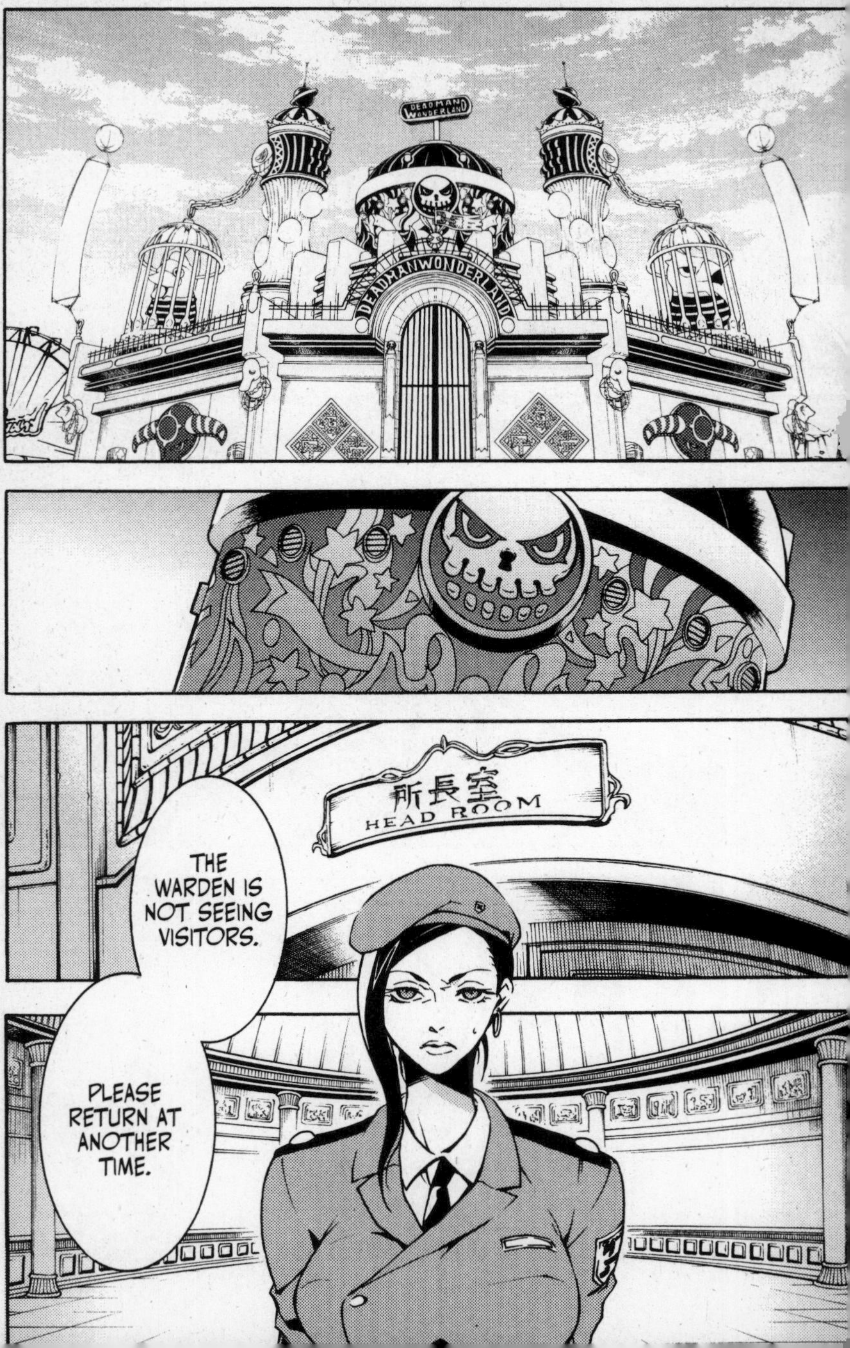
DEADMAN WONDERLAND
DEADMANWONDERLAND
所長室
HEAD ROOM
THE WARDEN IS NOT SEEING VISITORS.
PLEASE RETURN AT ANOTHER TIME.

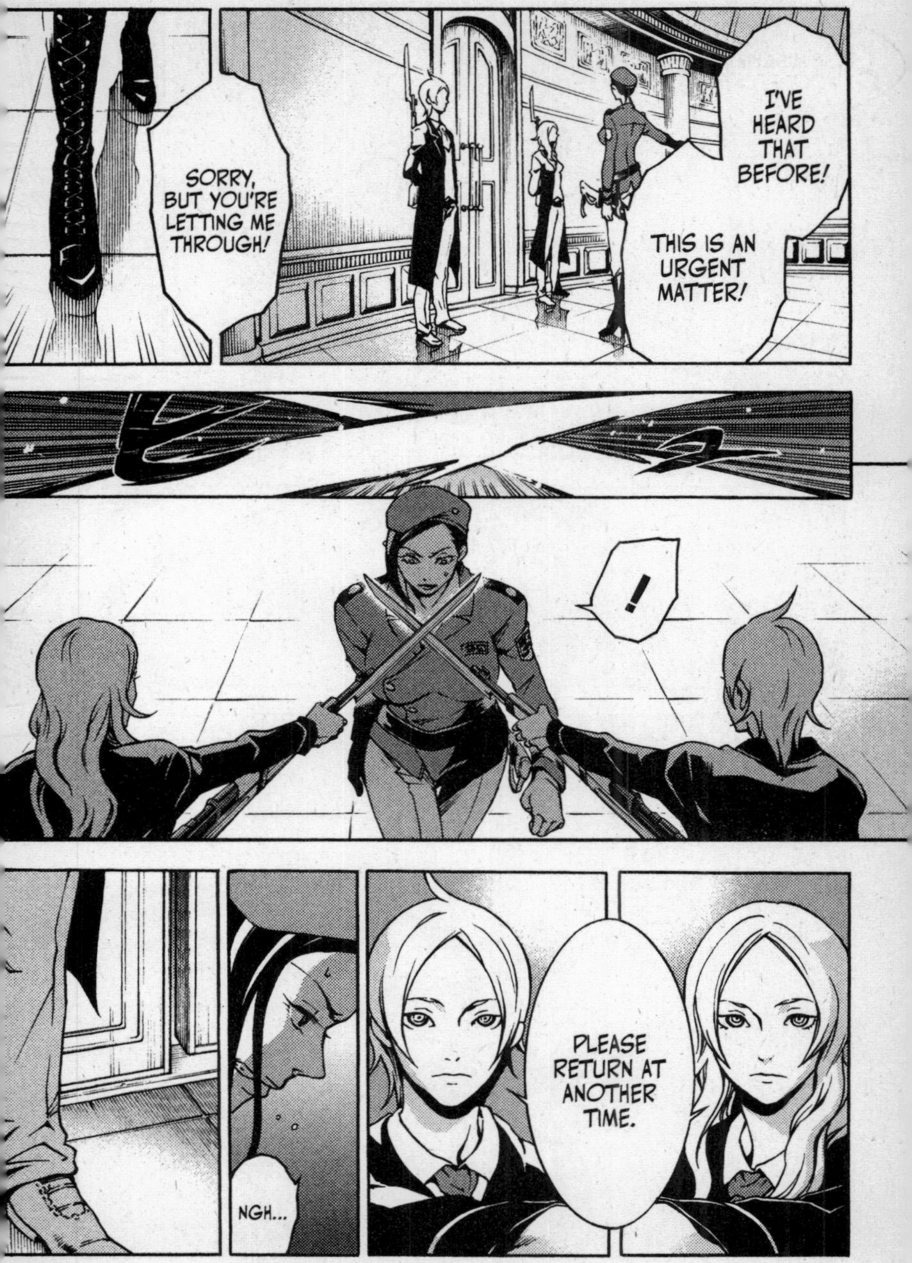
I'VE HEARD THAT BEFORE!
THIS IS AN URGENT MATTER!
SORRY, BUT YOU'RE LETTING ME THROUGH!
!
PLEASE RETURN AT ANOTHER TIME.
NGH...

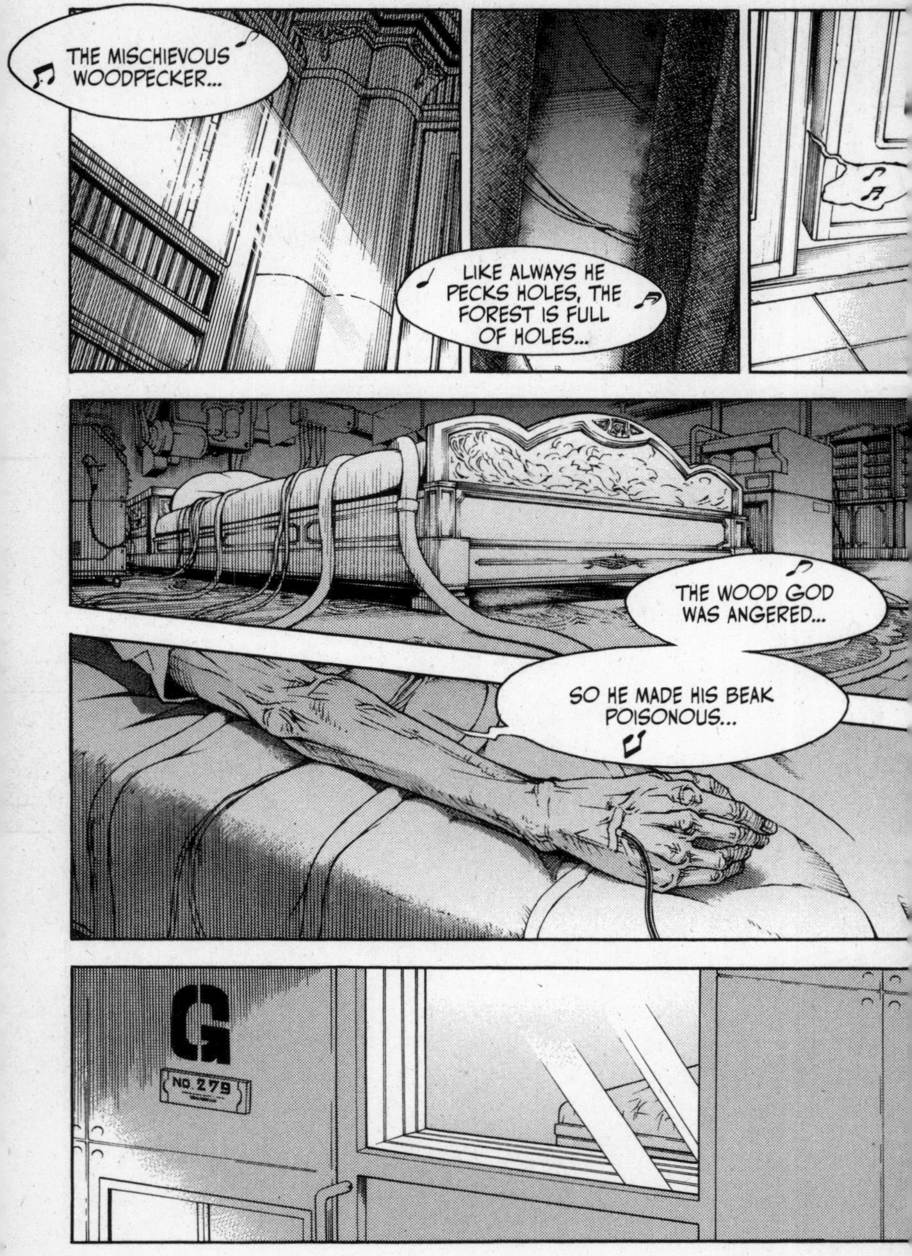
THE MISCHIEVOUS WOODPECKER...
LIKE ALWAYS HE PECKS HOLES, THE FOREST IS FULL OF HOLES...
THE WOOD GOD WAS ANGERED...
SO HE MADE HIS BEAK POISONOUS...
G
NO. 279

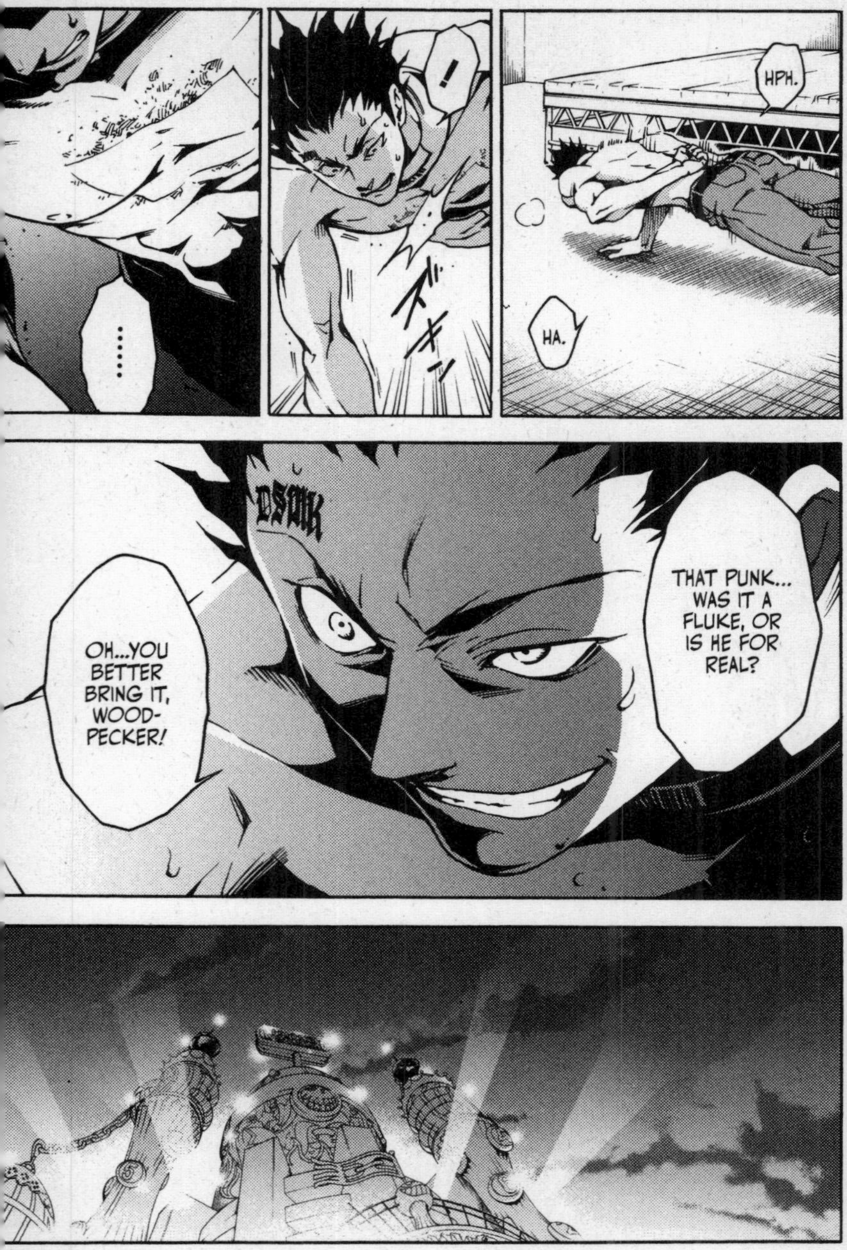
HPH.
HA.
!
......
THAT PUNK... WAS IT A FLUKE, OR IS HE FOR REAL?
OH...YOU BETTER BRING IT, WOOD-PECKER!

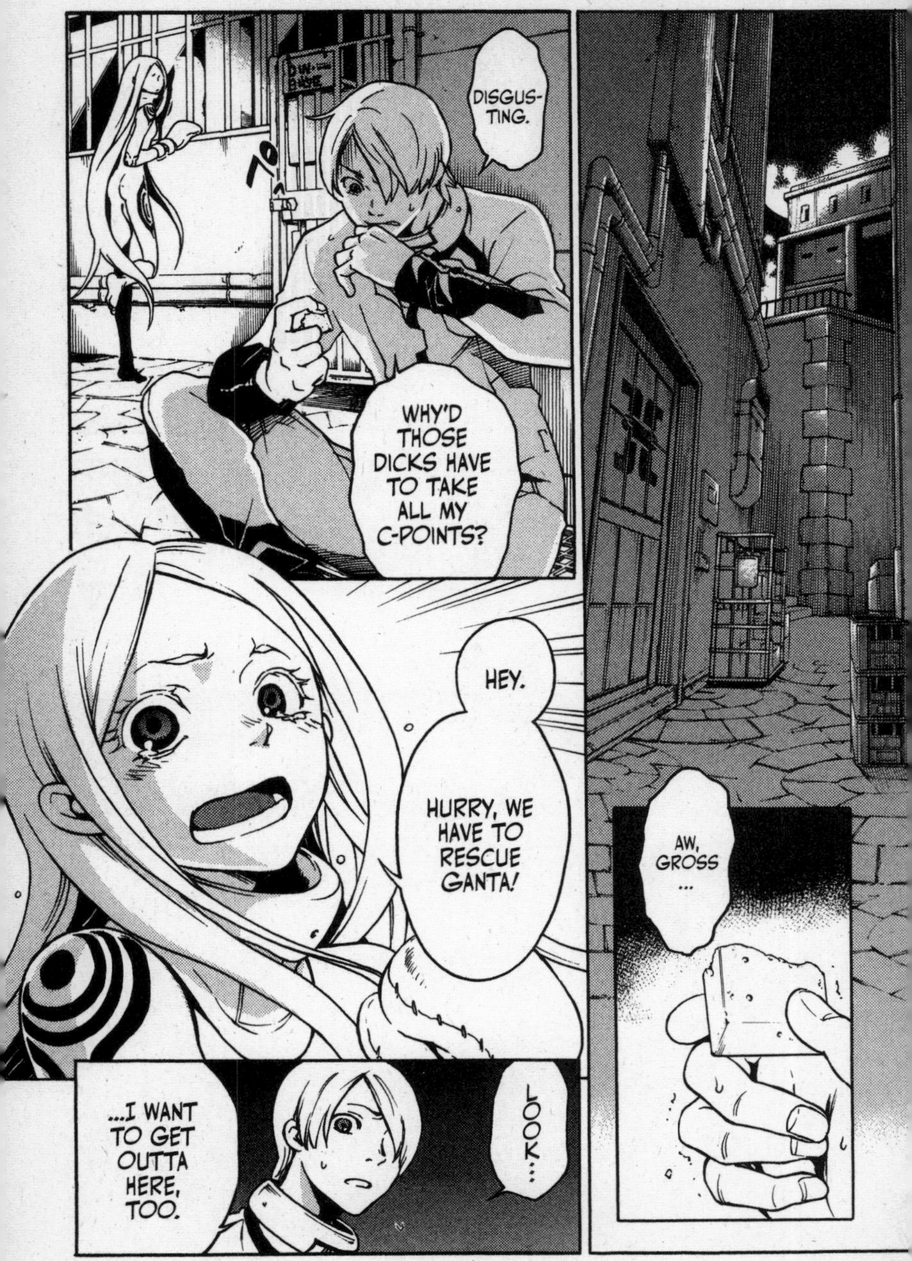
AW, GROSS ...
DISGUS-TING.
WHY'D THOSE DICKS HAVE TO TAKE ALL MY C-POINTS?
HEY.
HURRY, WE HAVE TO RESCUE GANTA!
LOOK...
...I WANT TO GET OUTTA HERE, TOO.

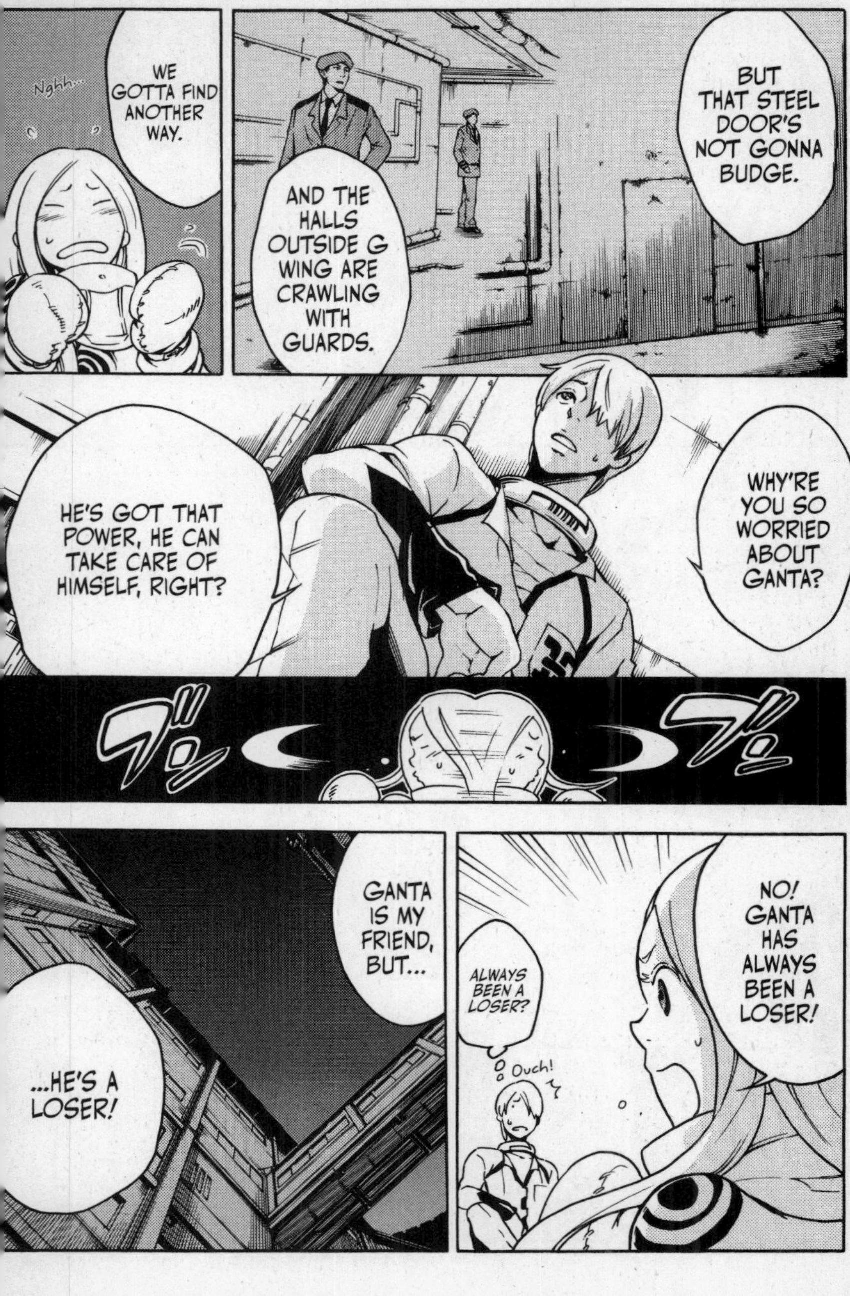

BUT THAT STEEL DOOR'S NOT GONNA BUDGE.
AND THE HALLS OUTSIDE G WING ARE CRAWLING WITH GUARDS.
Nghh...
WE GOTTA FIND ANOTHER WAY.
WHY'RE YOU SO WORRIED ABOUT GANTA?
HE'S GOT THAT POWER, HE CAN TAKE CARE OF HIMSELF, RIGHT?
ブン
ブン
NO! GANTA HAS ALWAYS BEEN A LOSER!
ALWAYS BEEN A LOSER?
Ouch!
GANTA IS MY FRIEND, BUT...
...HE'S A LOSER!

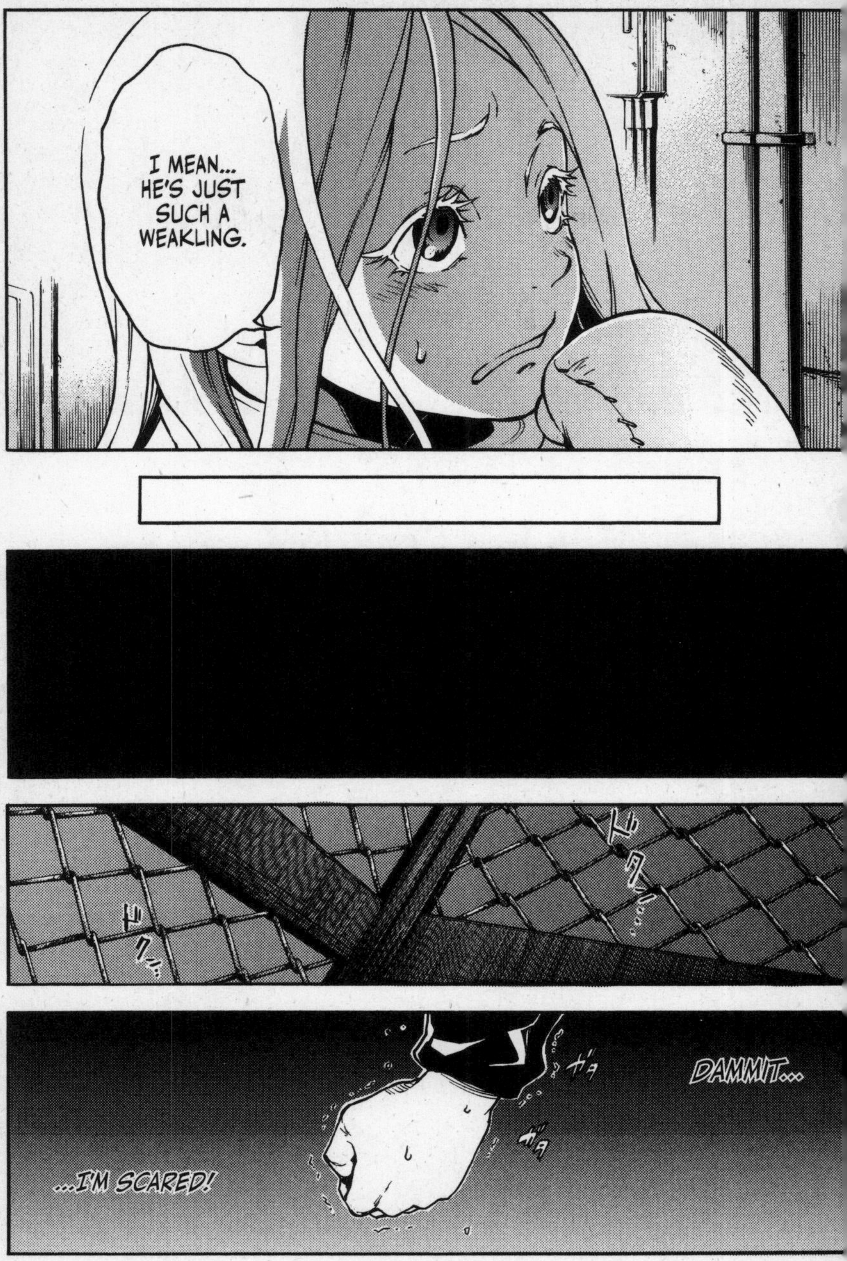
I MEAN... HE'S JUST SUCH A WEAKLING.
DAMMIT...
...I'M SCARED!

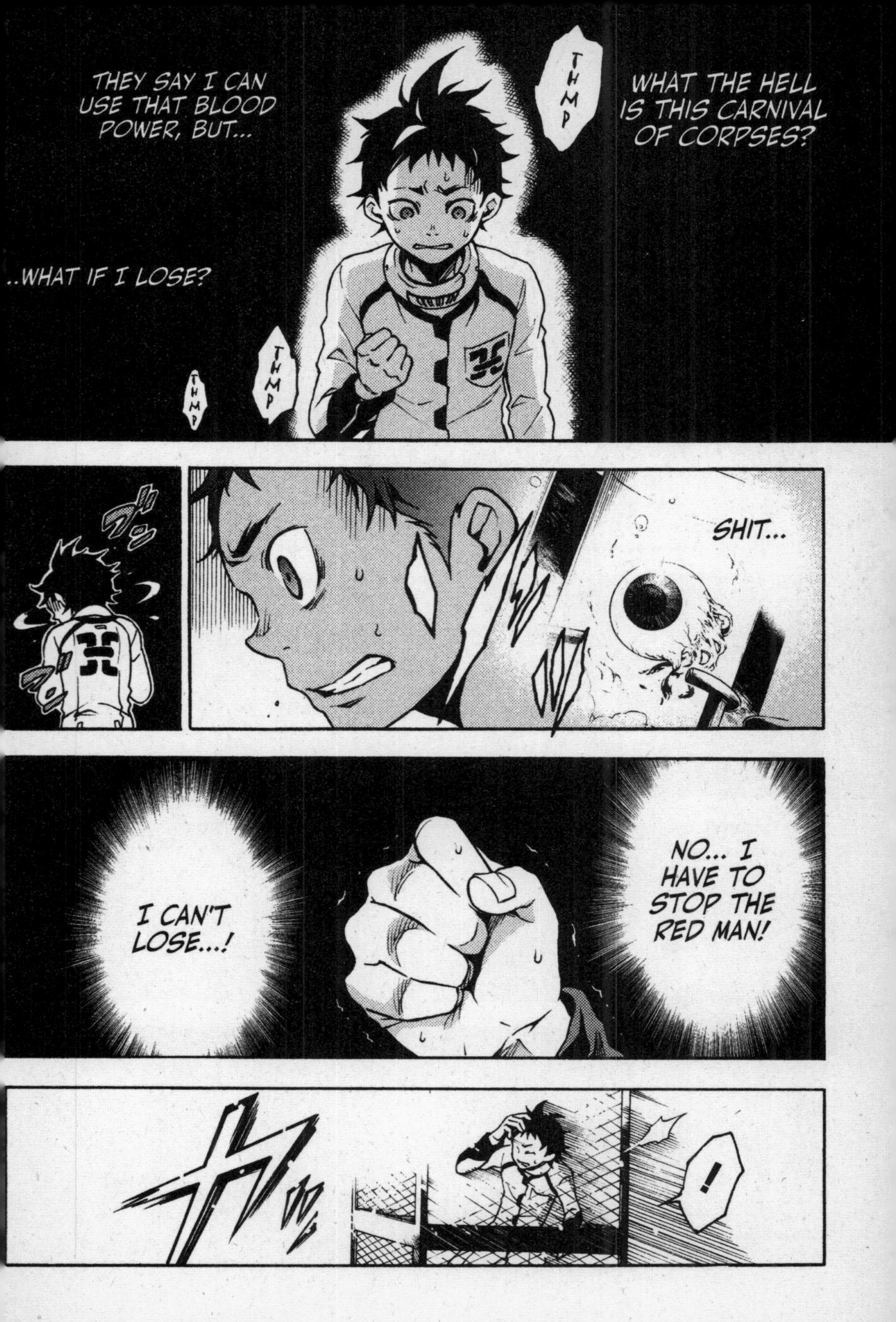
WHAT THE HELL IS THIS CARNIVAL OF CORPSES?
THMP
THEY SAY I CAN USE THAT BLOOD POWER, BUT...
..WHAT IF I LOSE?
THMP
THMP
SHIT...
NO... I HAVE TO STOP THE RED MAN!
I CAN'T LOSE...!
!

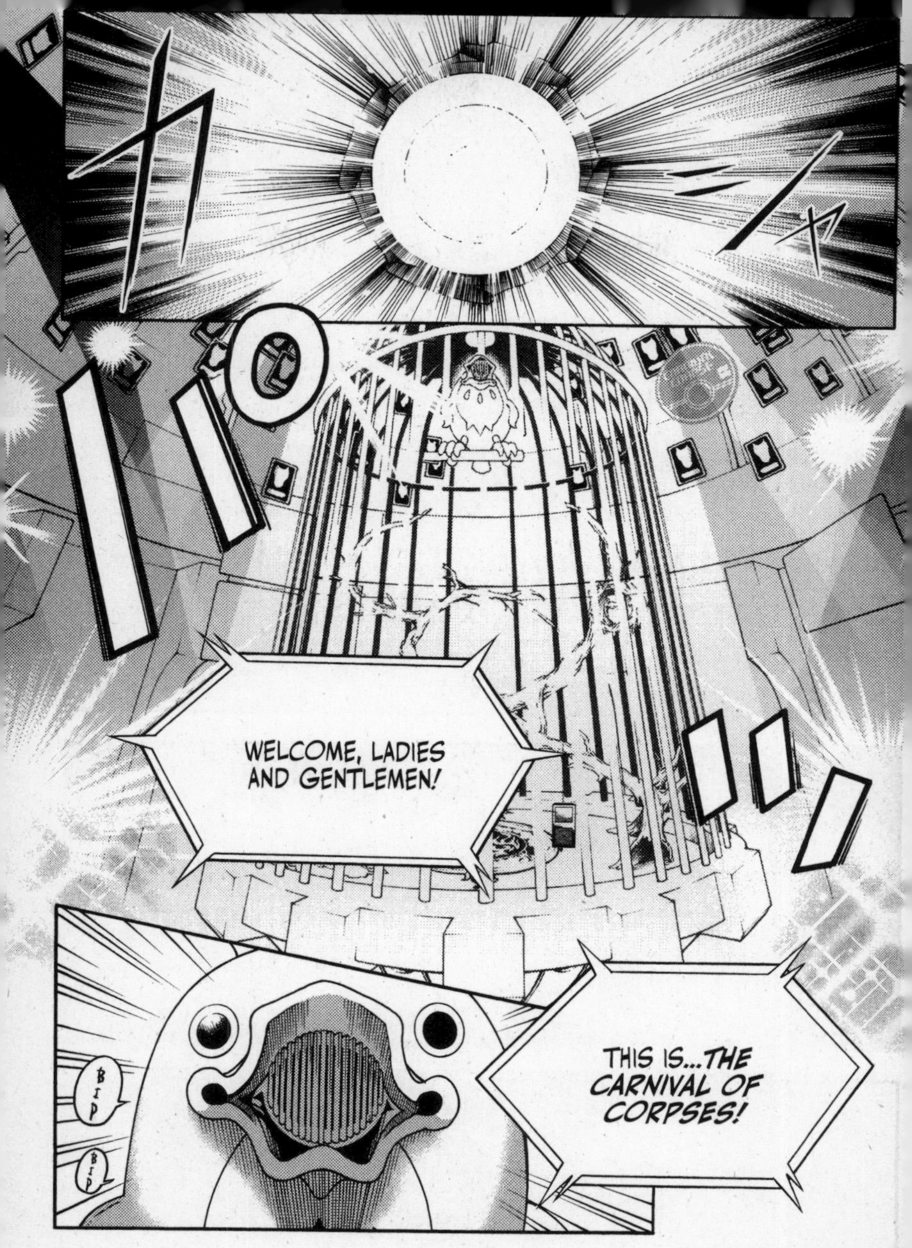
WELCOME, LADIES AND GENTLEMEN!
THIS IS...THE CARNIVAL OF CORPSES!
BIP
BIP

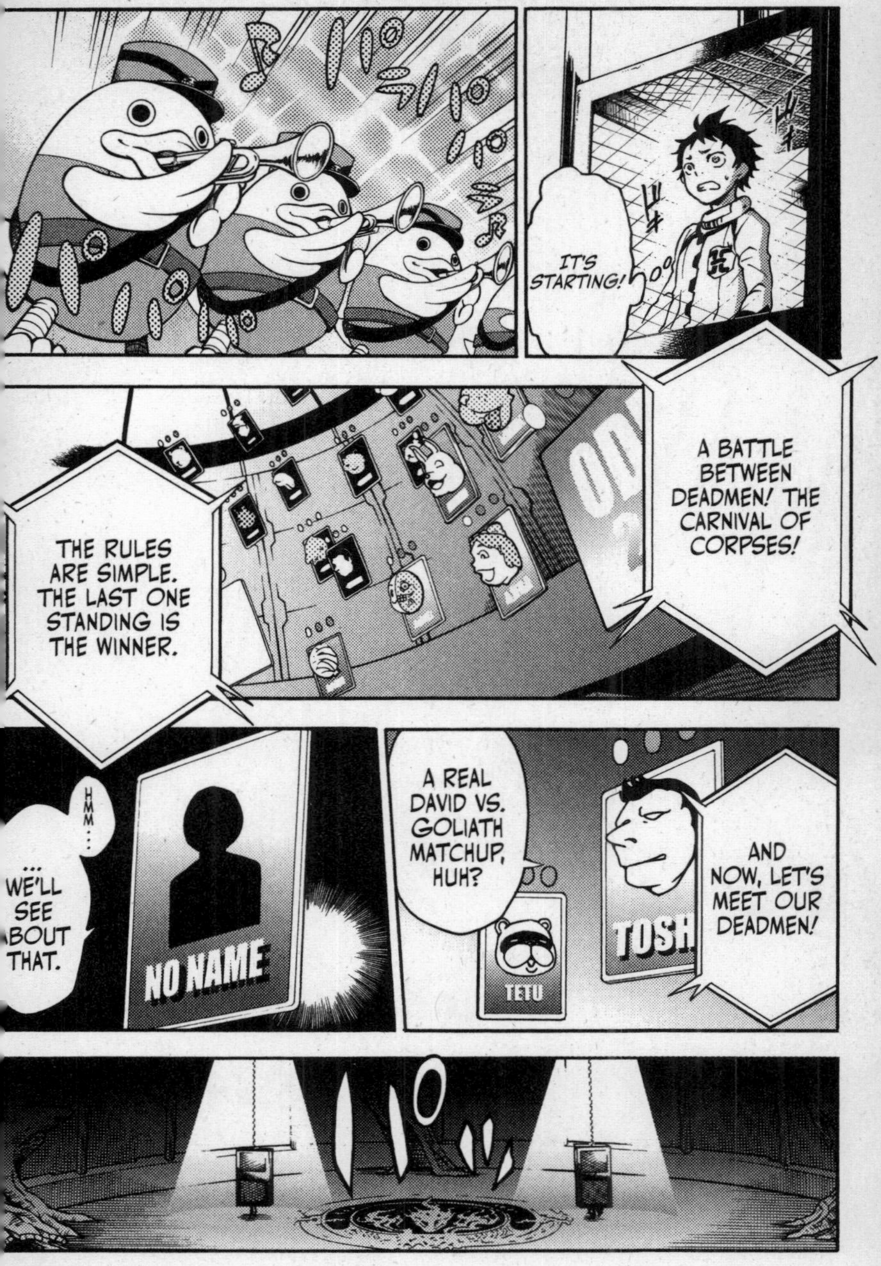
IT'S STARTING!
A BATTLE BETWEEN DEADMEN! THE CARNIVAL OF CORPSES!
THE RULES ARE SIMPLE. THE LAST ONE STANDING IS THE WINNER.
AND NOW, LET'S MEET OUR DEADMEN!
TOSH
TETU
A REAL DAVID VS. GOLIATH MATCHUP, HUH?
NO NAME
HMM...
...WE'LL SEE ABOUT THAT.

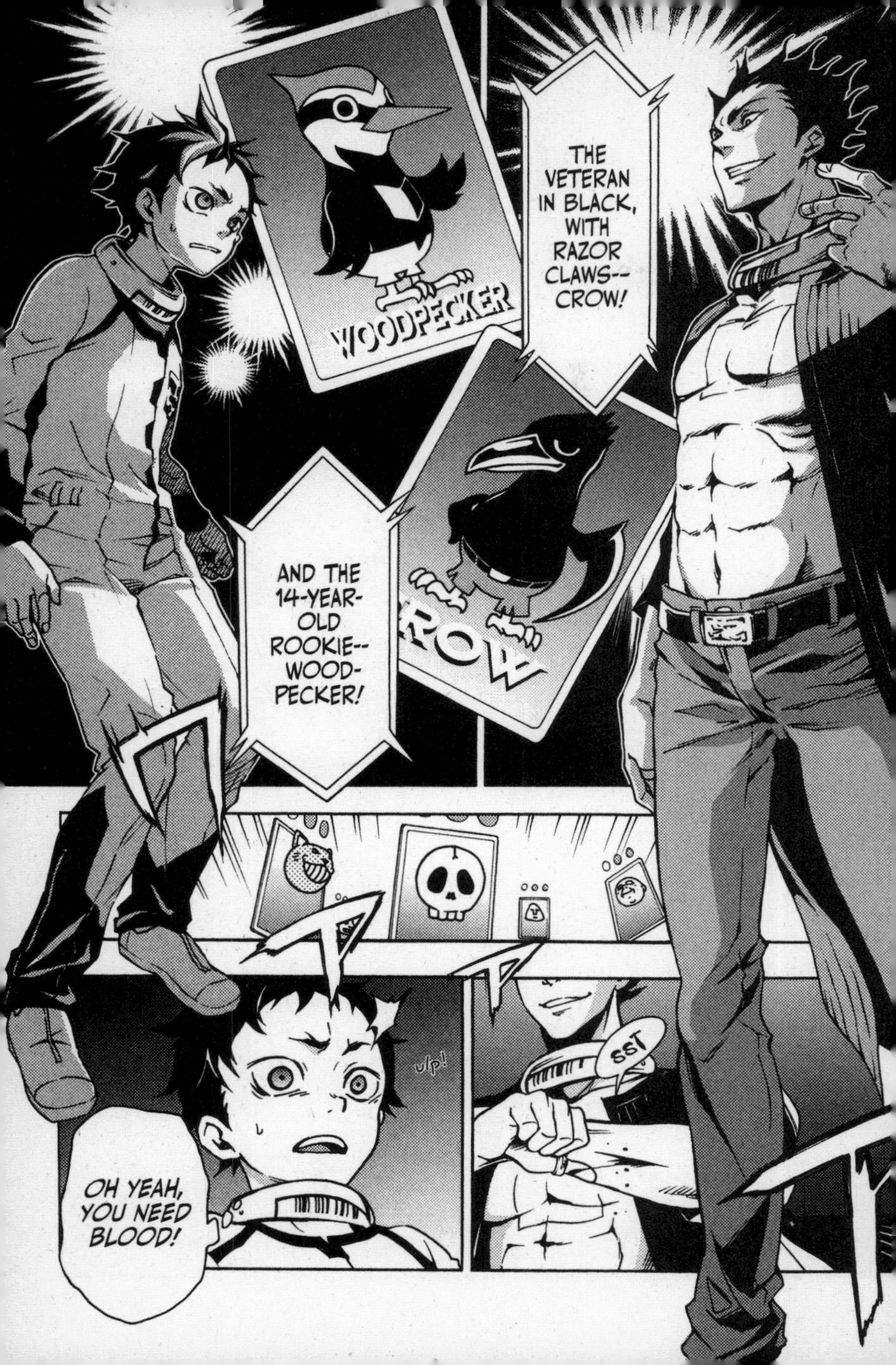
THE VETERAN IN BLACK, WITH RAZOR CLAWS-- CROW!
WOODPECKER
AND THE 14-YEAR-OLD ROOKIE-- WOOD-PECKER!
SST
ulp!
OH YEAH, YOU NEED BLOOD!

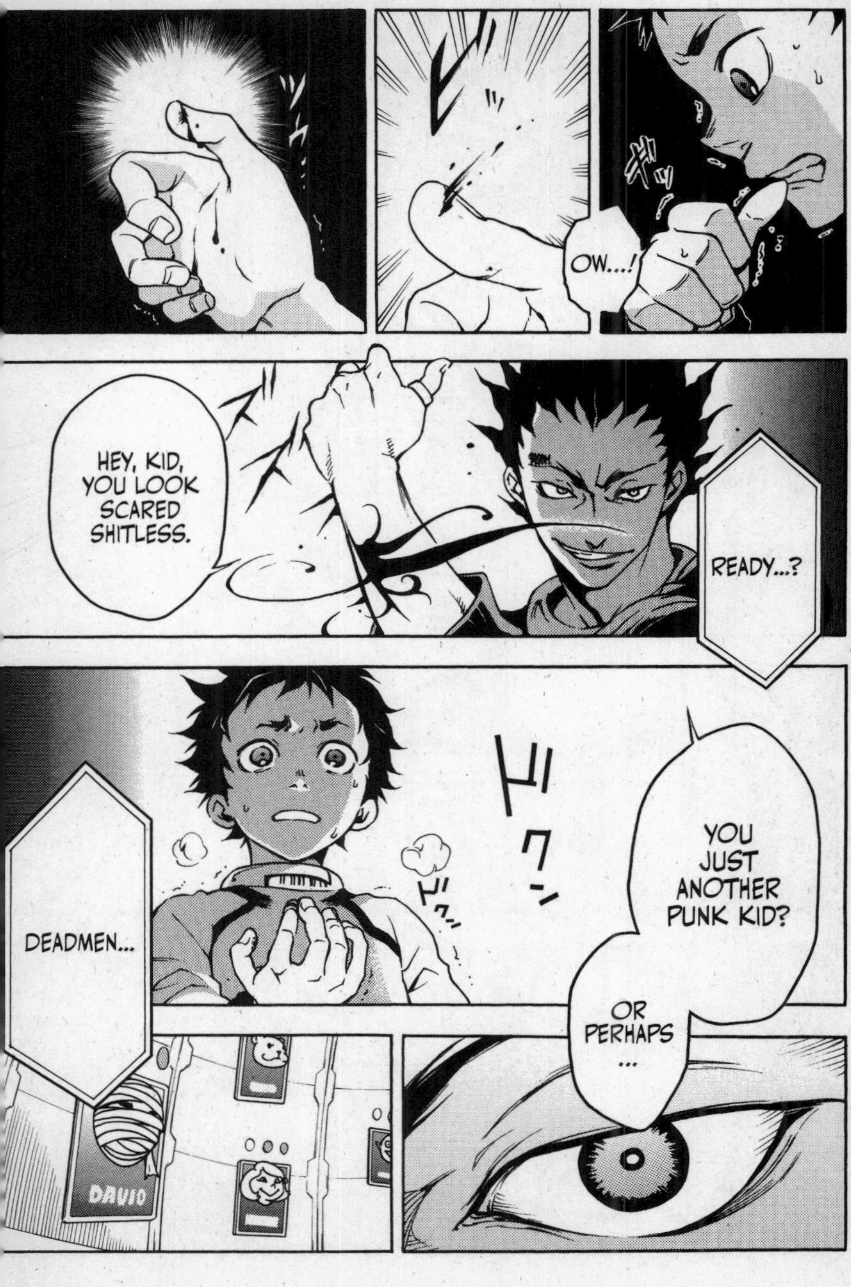
OW...!
READY...?
HEY, KID, YOU LOOK SCARED SHITLESS.
YOU JUST ANOTHER PUNK KID?
OR PERHAPS ...
DEADMEN...

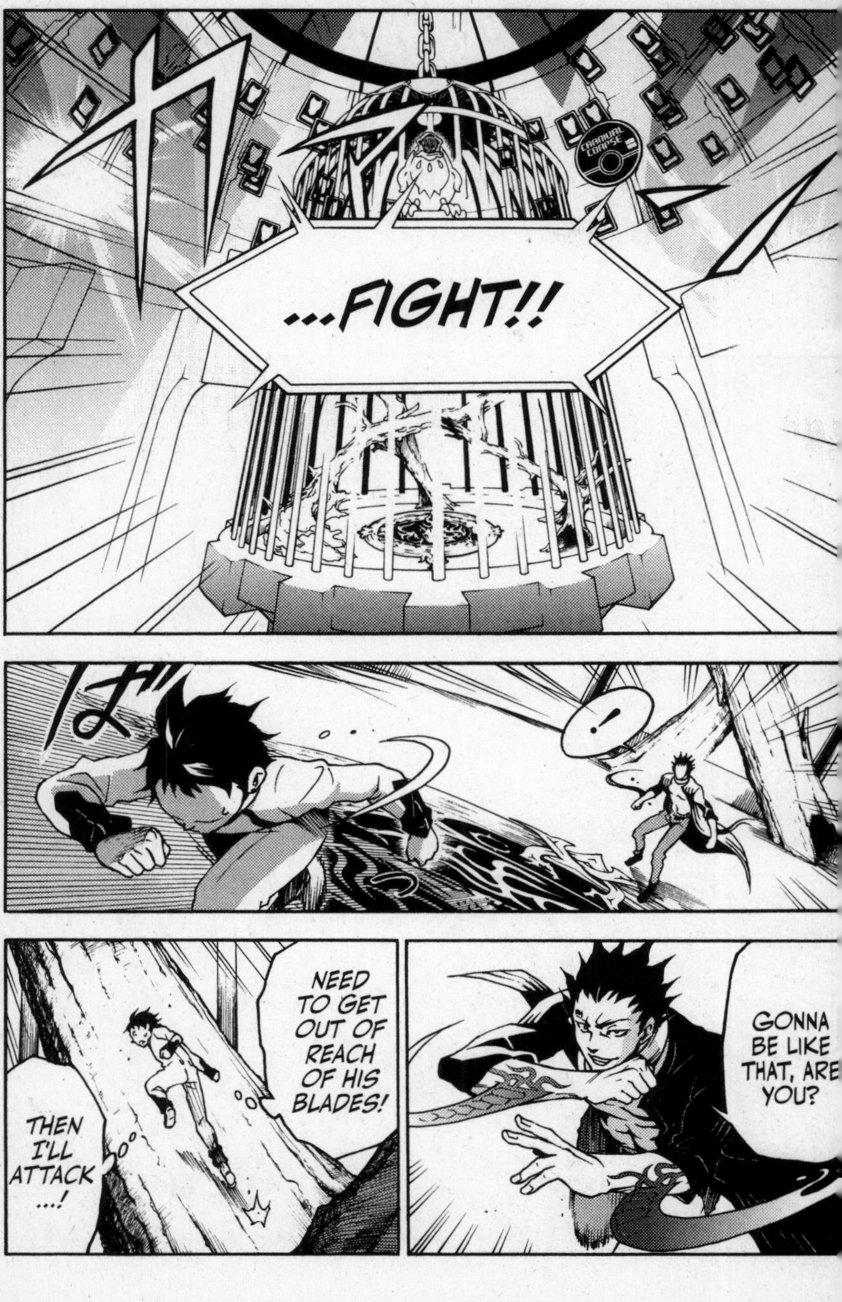
CARNIVAL CORPSE
...FIGHT!!
!
GONNA BE LIKE THAT, ARE YOU?
NEED TO GET OUT OF REACH OF HIS BLADES!
THEN I'LL ATTACK ...!

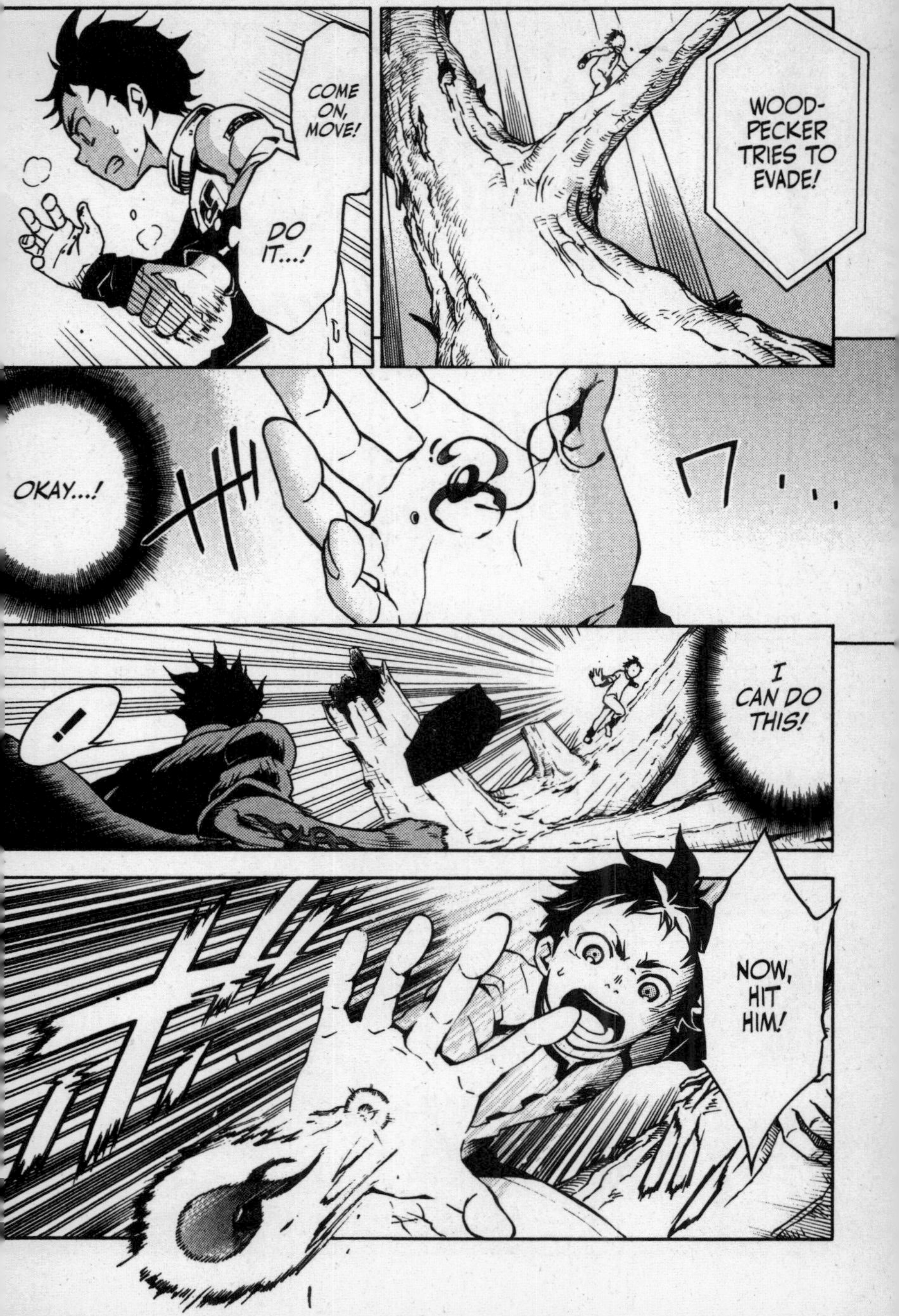
WOOD-PECKER TRIES TO EVADE!
COME ON, MOVE!
DO IT...!
OKAY...!
I CAN DO THIS!
!
NOW, HIT HIM!

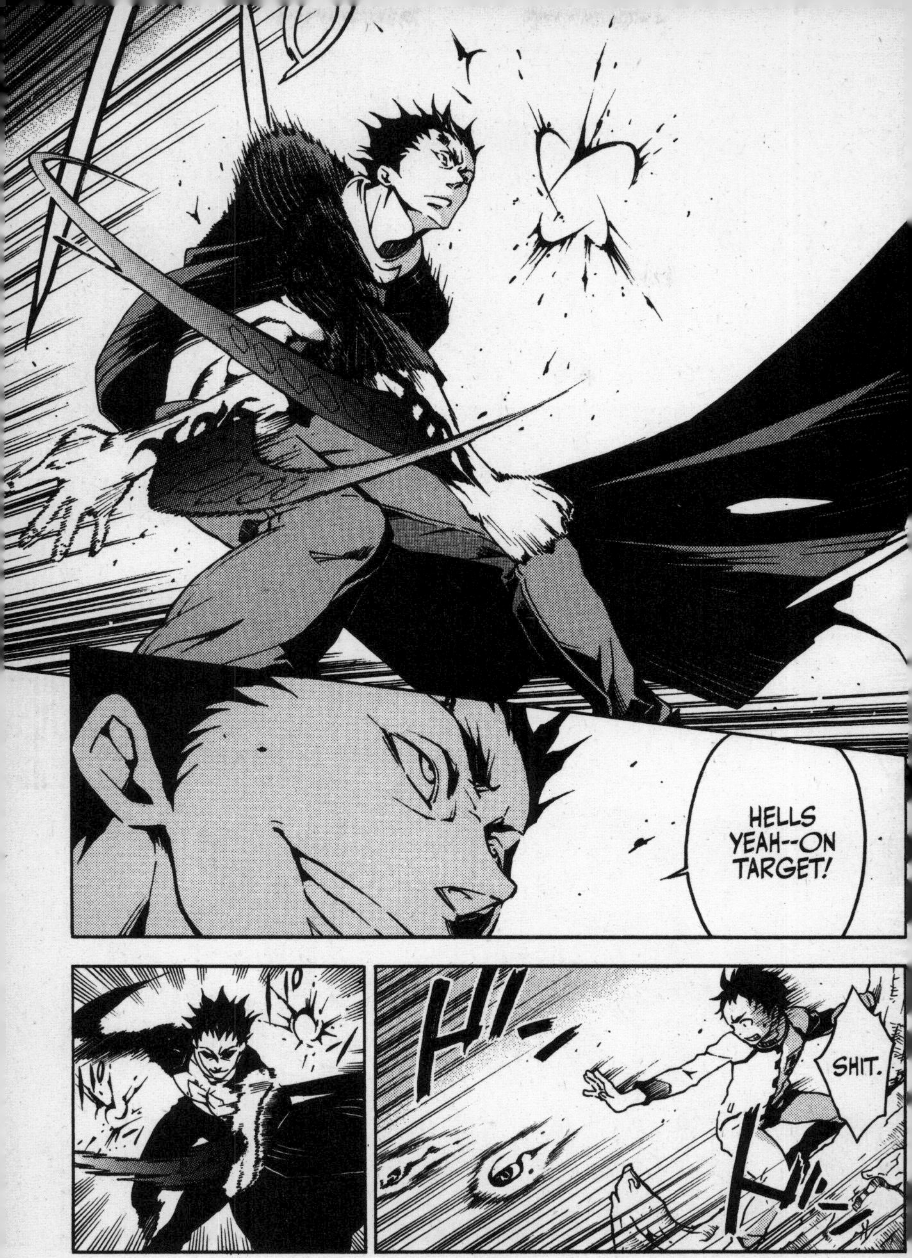
HELLS YEAH--ON TARGET!
SHIT.

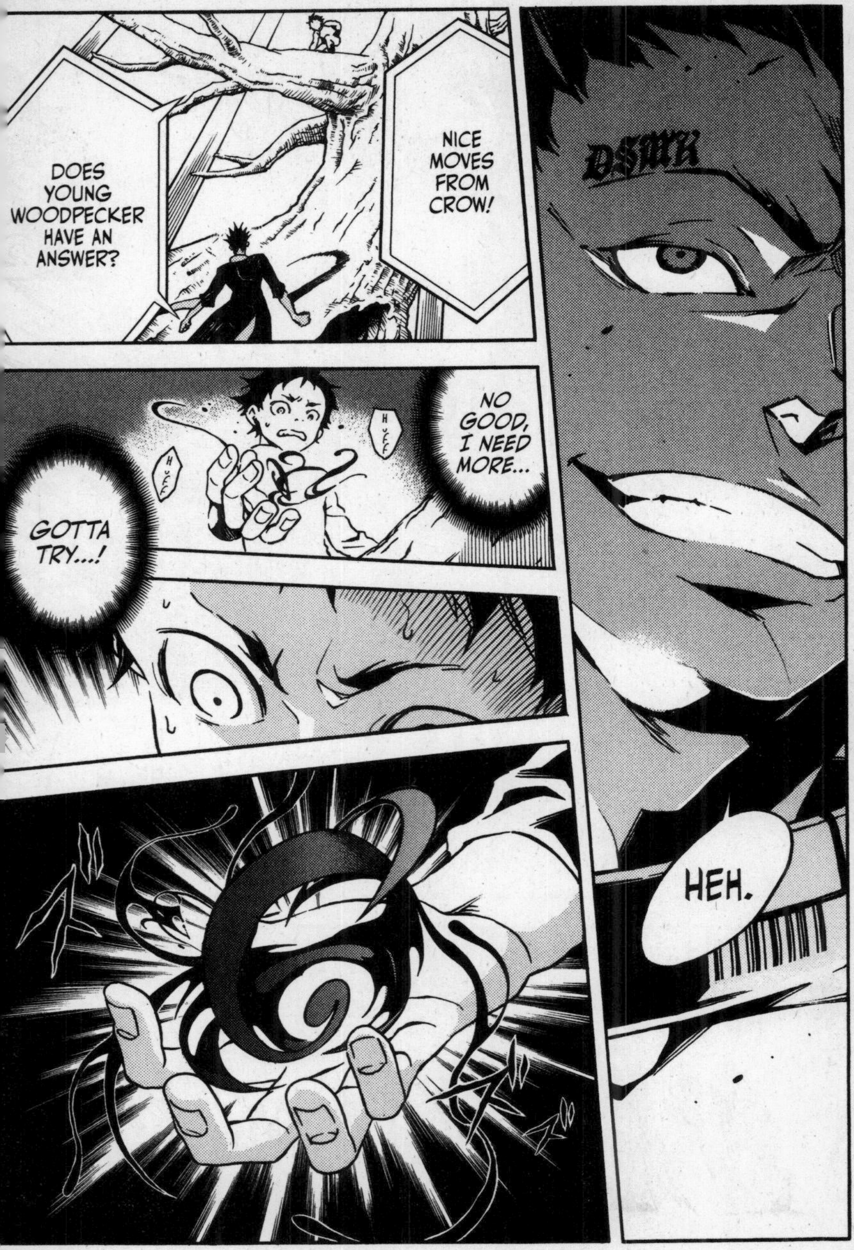
HEH.
NICE MOVES FROM CROW!
DOES YOUNG WOODPECKER HAVE AN ANSWER?
NO GOOD, I NEED MORE...
HUFF
HUFF
GOTTA TRY...!

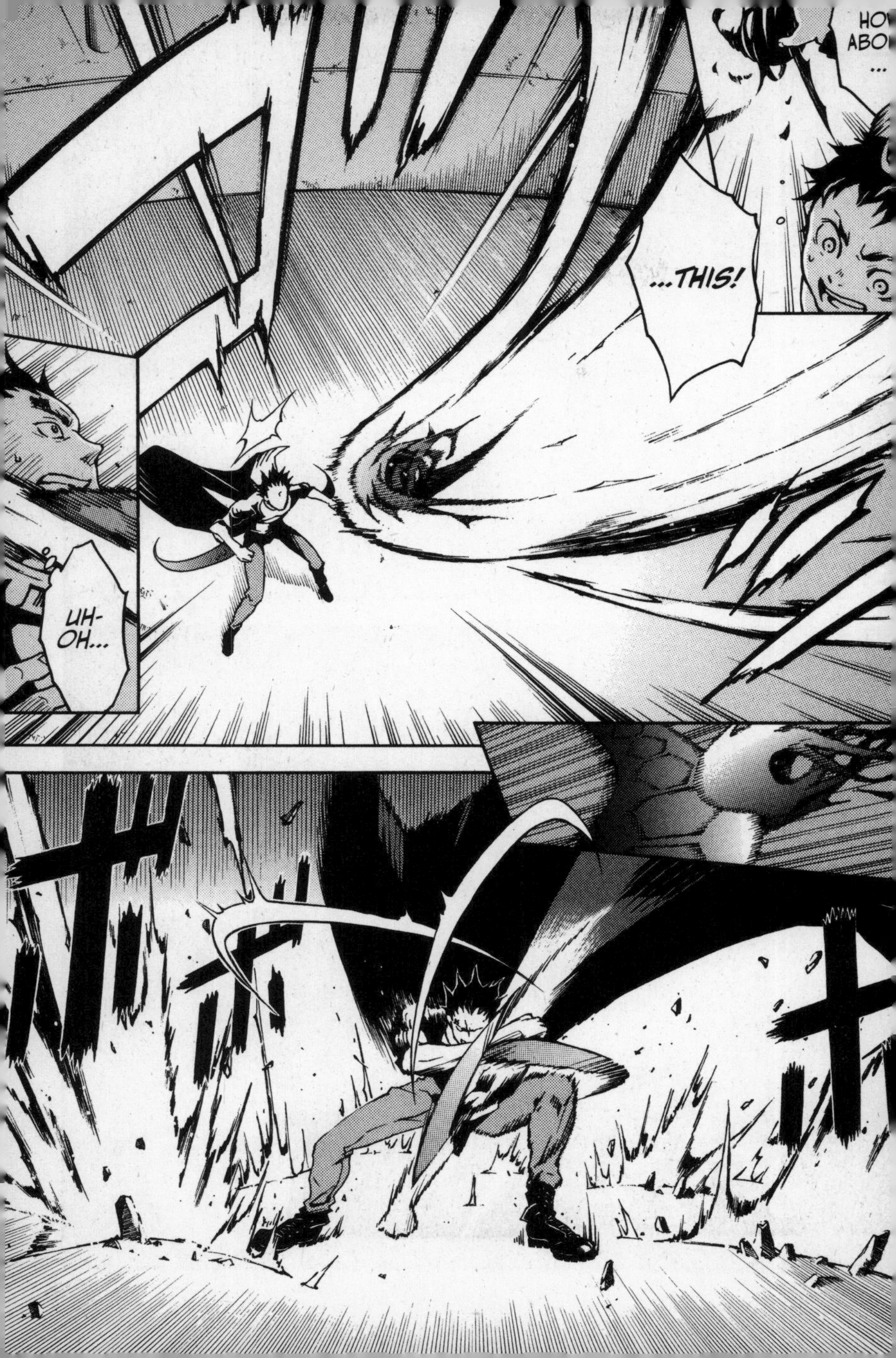
HOW ABOU ...
...THIS!
UH-OH...

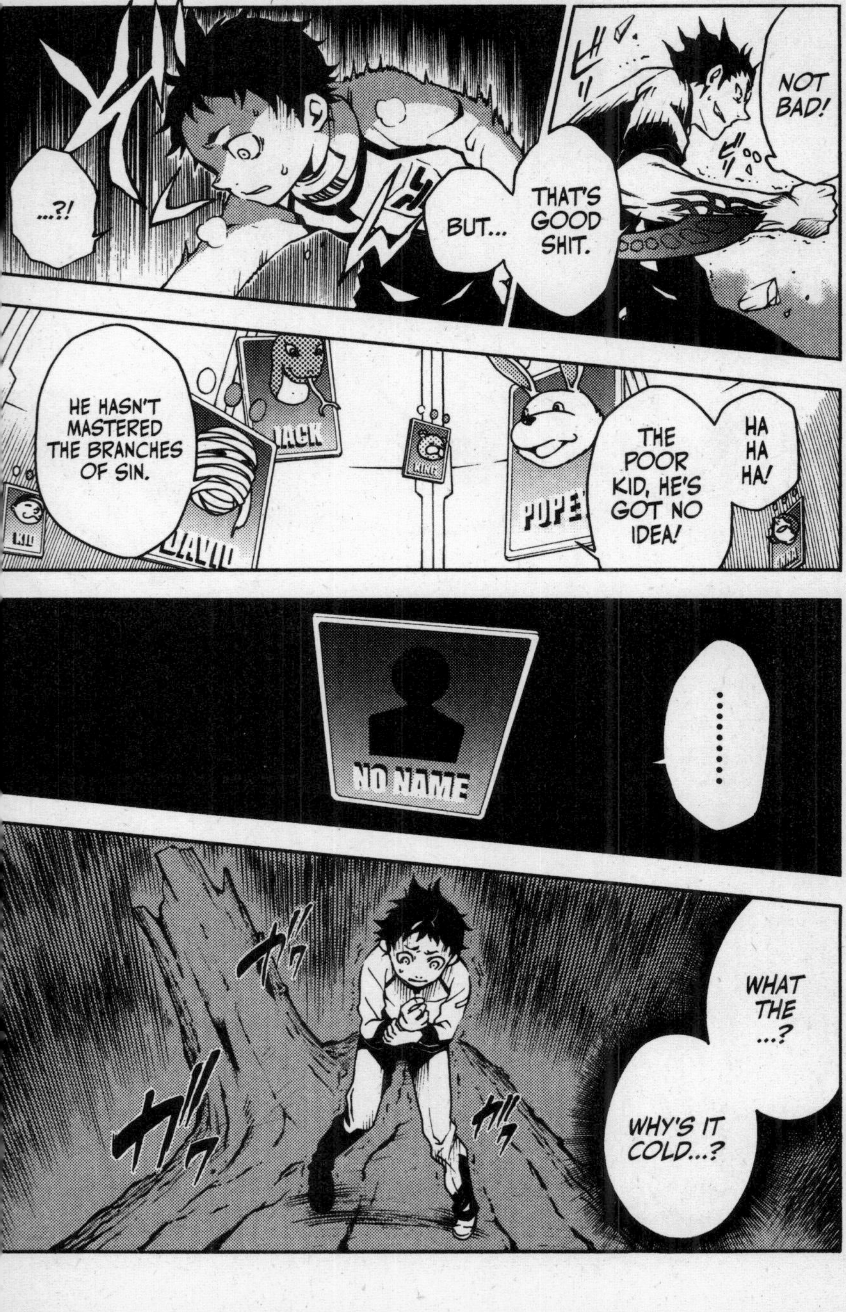
NOT BAD!
THAT'S GOOD SHIT.
BUT...
...?!
HA HA HA!
THE POOR KID, HE'S GOT NO IDEA!
HE HASN'T MASTERED THE BRANCHES OF SIN.
......
NO NAME
WHAT THE ...?
WHY'S IT COLD...?

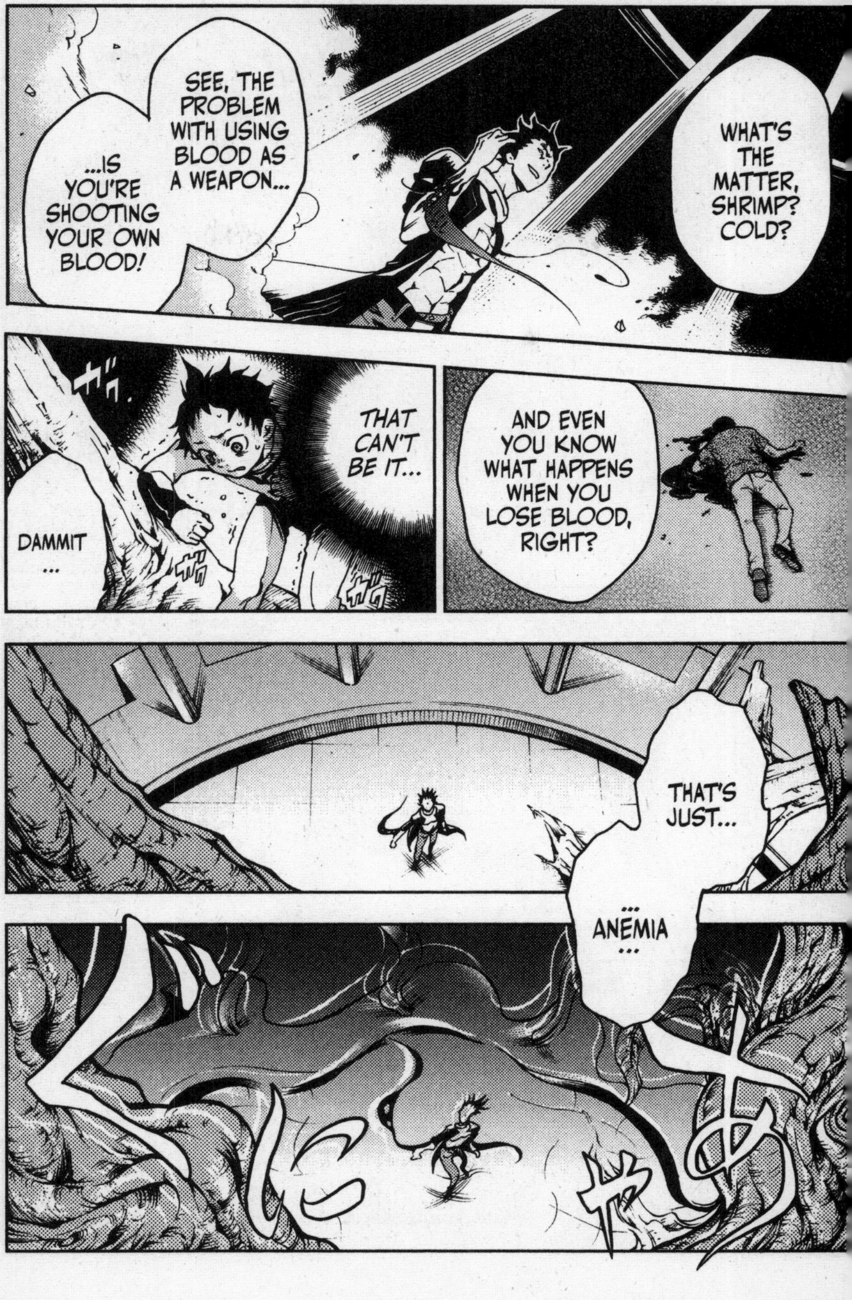
WHAT'S THE MATTER, SHRIMP? COLD?
SEE, THE PROBLEM WITH USING BLOOD AS A WEAPON...
...IS YOU'RE SHOOTING YOUR OWN BLOOD!
AND EVEN YOU KNOW WHAT HAPPENS WHEN YOU LOSE BLOOD, RIGHT?
THAT CAN'T BE IT...
DAMMIT ...
THAT'S JUST...
...ANEMIA...

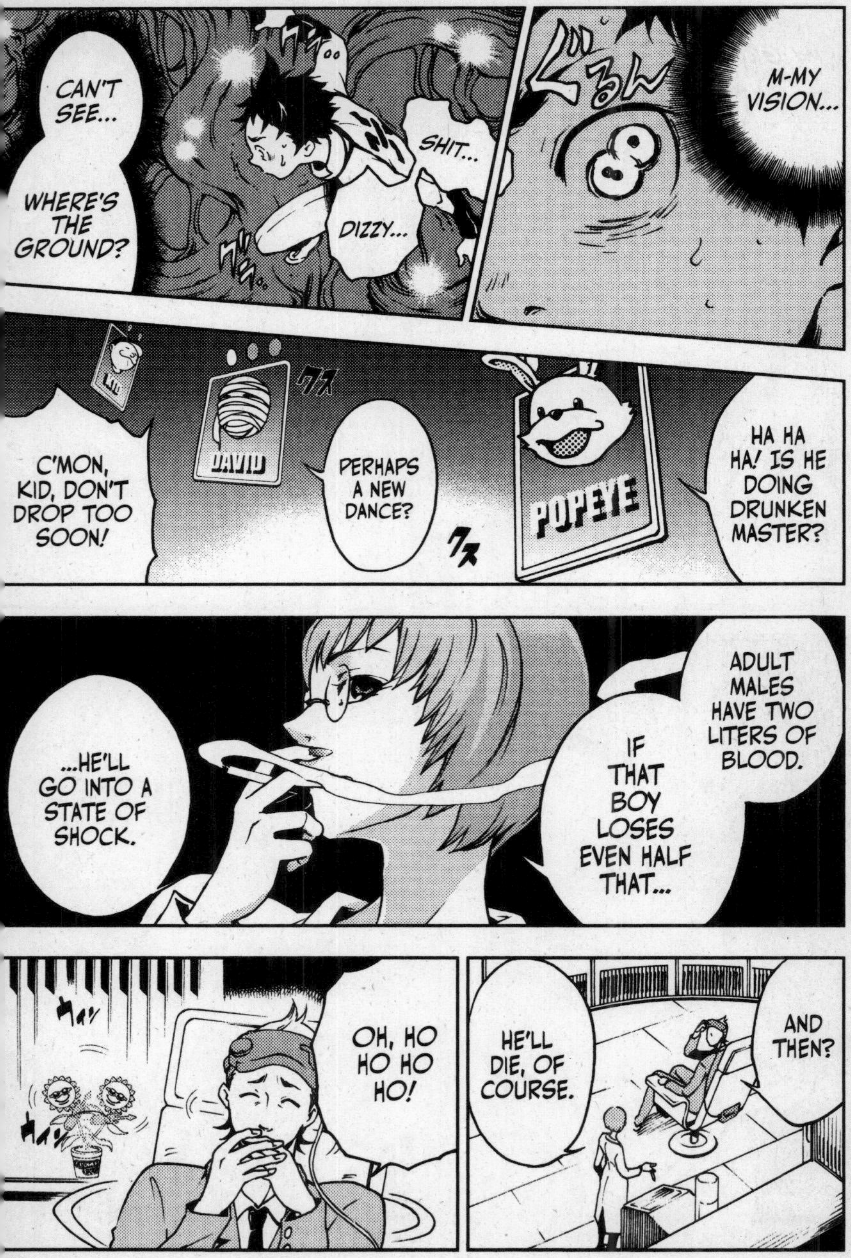
ぐるん
M-MY VISION...
SHIT...
DIZZY...
CAN'T SEE...
WHERE'S THE GROUND?
HA HA HA! IS HE DOING DRUNKEN MASTER?
POPEYE
クス
PERHAPS A NEW DANCE?
クス
DAVID
C'MON, KID, DON'T DROP TOO SOON!
ADULT MALES HAVE TWO LITERS OF BLOOD.
IF THAT BOY LOSES EVEN HALF THAT...
...HE'LL GO INTO A STATE OF SHOCK.
AND THEN?
HE'LL DIE, OF COURSE.
OH, HO HO HO HO!

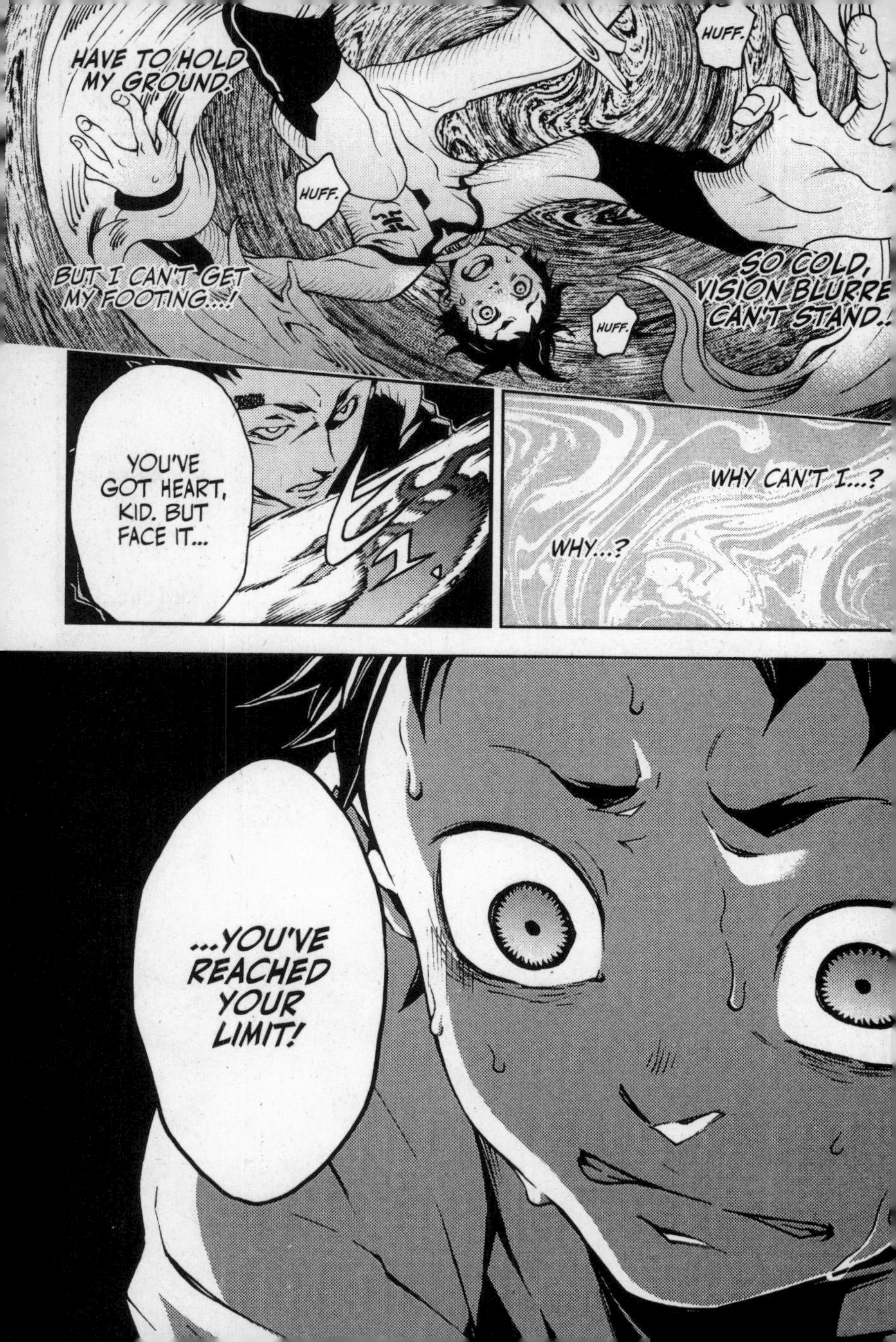
HUFF.
SO COLD, VISION BLURRE CAN'T STAND...
HAVE TO HOLD MY GROUND.
HUFF.
HUFF.
BUT I CAN'T GET MY FOOTING...!
WHY CAN'T I...?
WHY...?
YOU'VE GOT HEART, KID. BUT FACE IT...
...YOU'VE REACHED YOUR LIMIT!

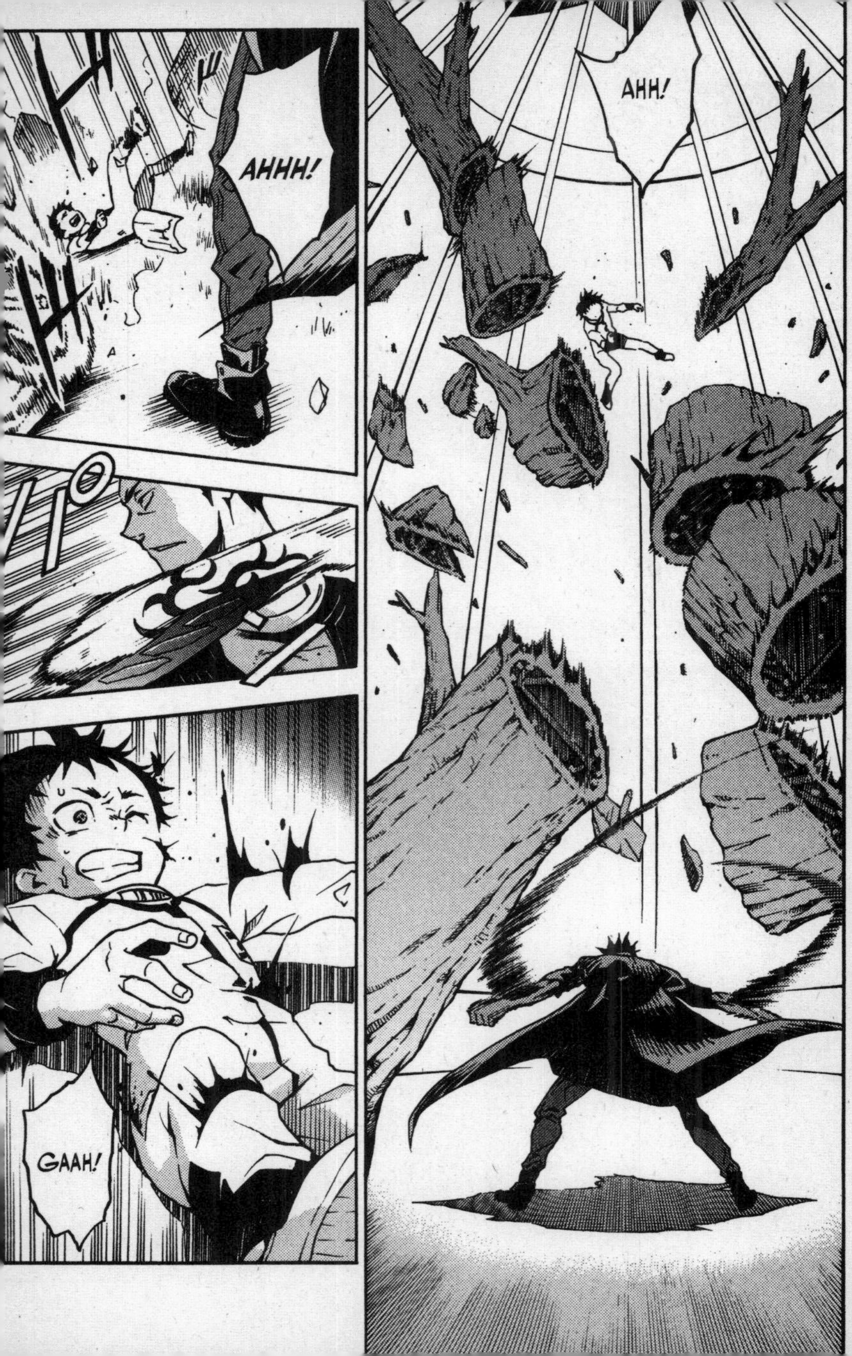
AHH!
AHHH!
GAAH!

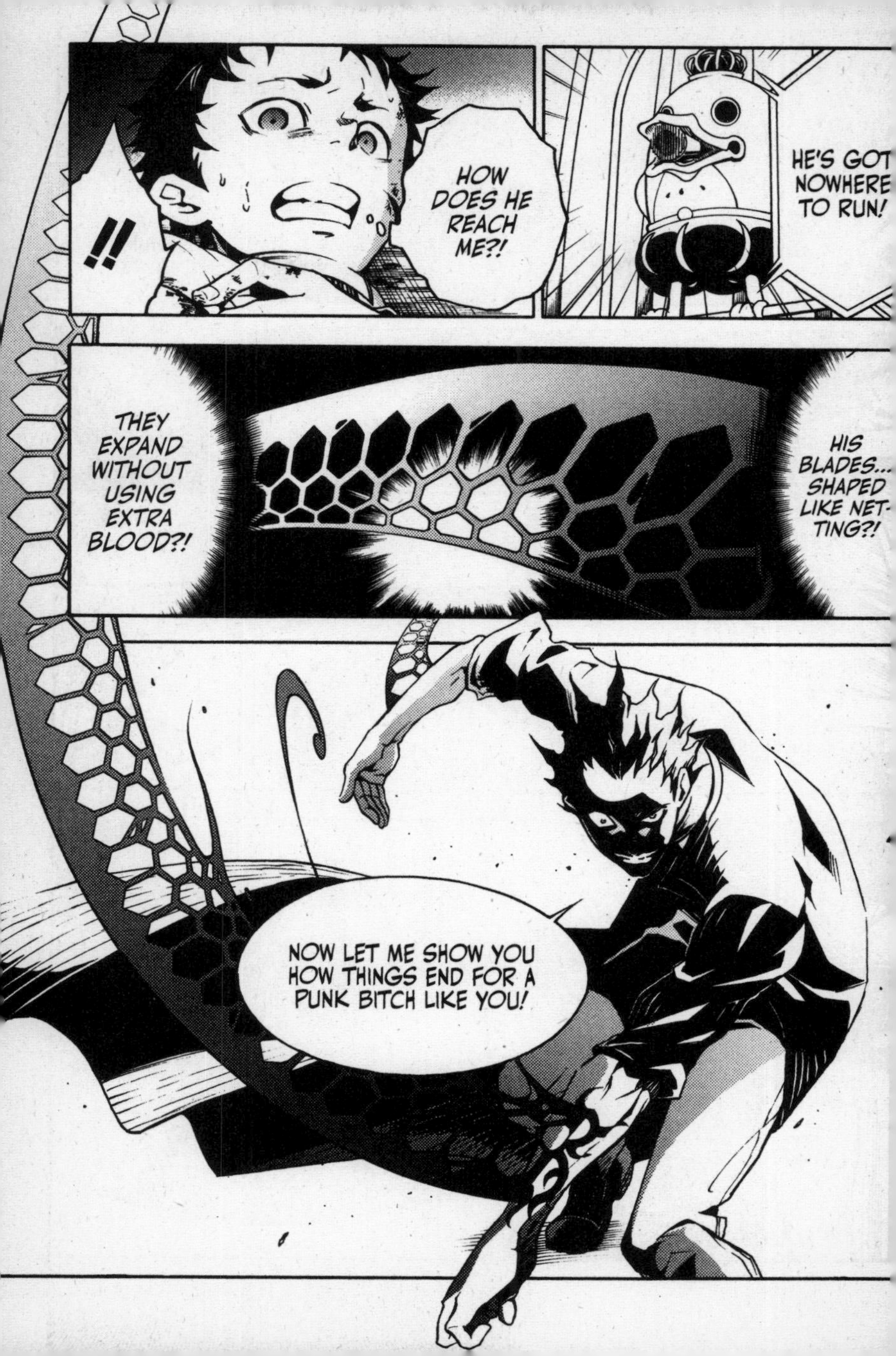
HE'S GOT NOWHERE TO RUN!
HOW DOES HE REACH ME?!
!!
HIS BLADES... SHAPED LIKE NET-TING?!
THEY EXPAND WITHOUT USING EXTRA BLOOD?!
NOW LET ME SHOW YOU HOW THINGS END FOR A PUNK BITCH LIKE YOU!

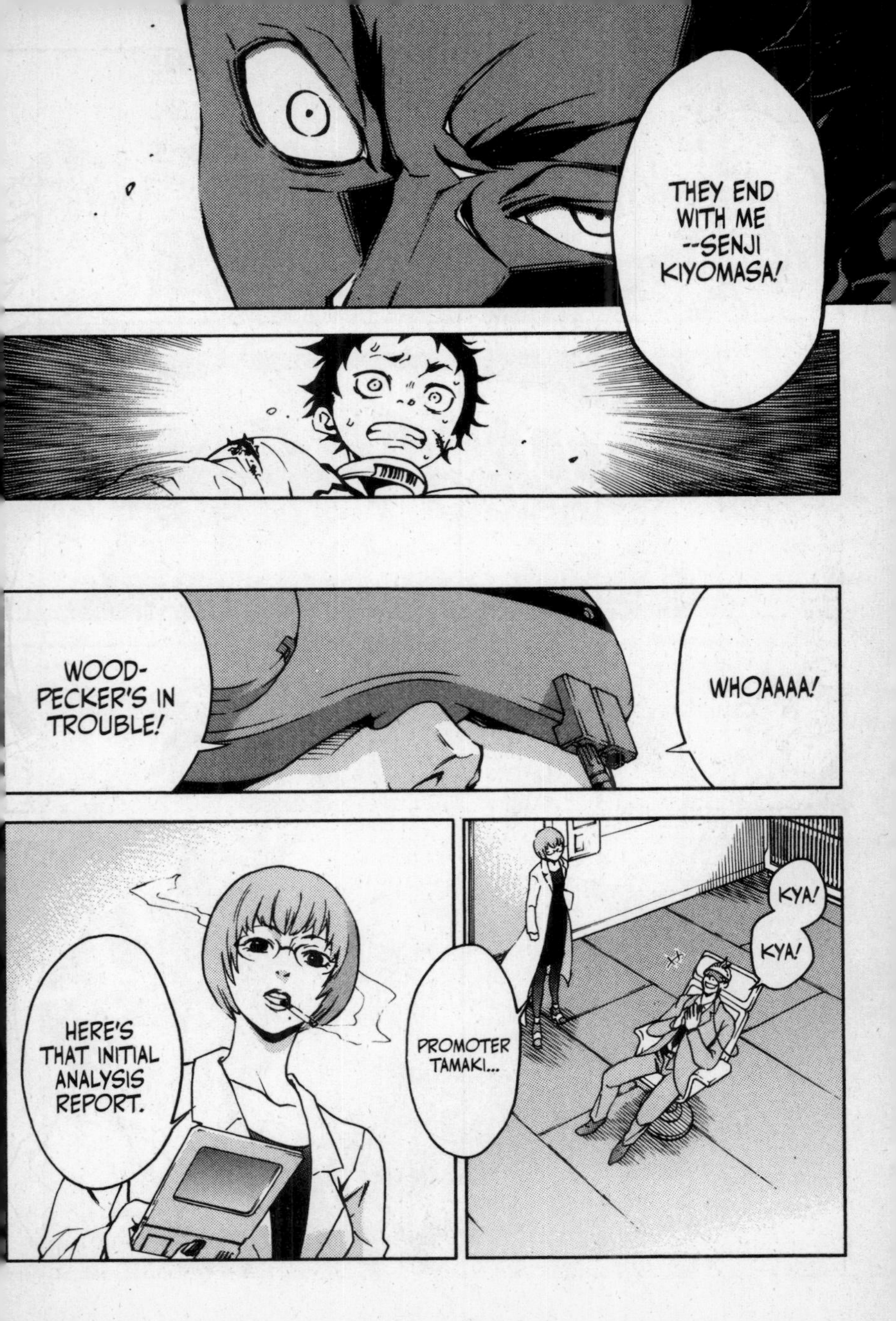
THEY END WITH ME --SENJI KIYOMASA!
WHOAAAA!
WOOD-PECKER'S IN TROUBLE!
KYA!
KYA!
PROMOTER TAMAKI...
HERE'S THAT INITIAL ANALYSIS REPORT.

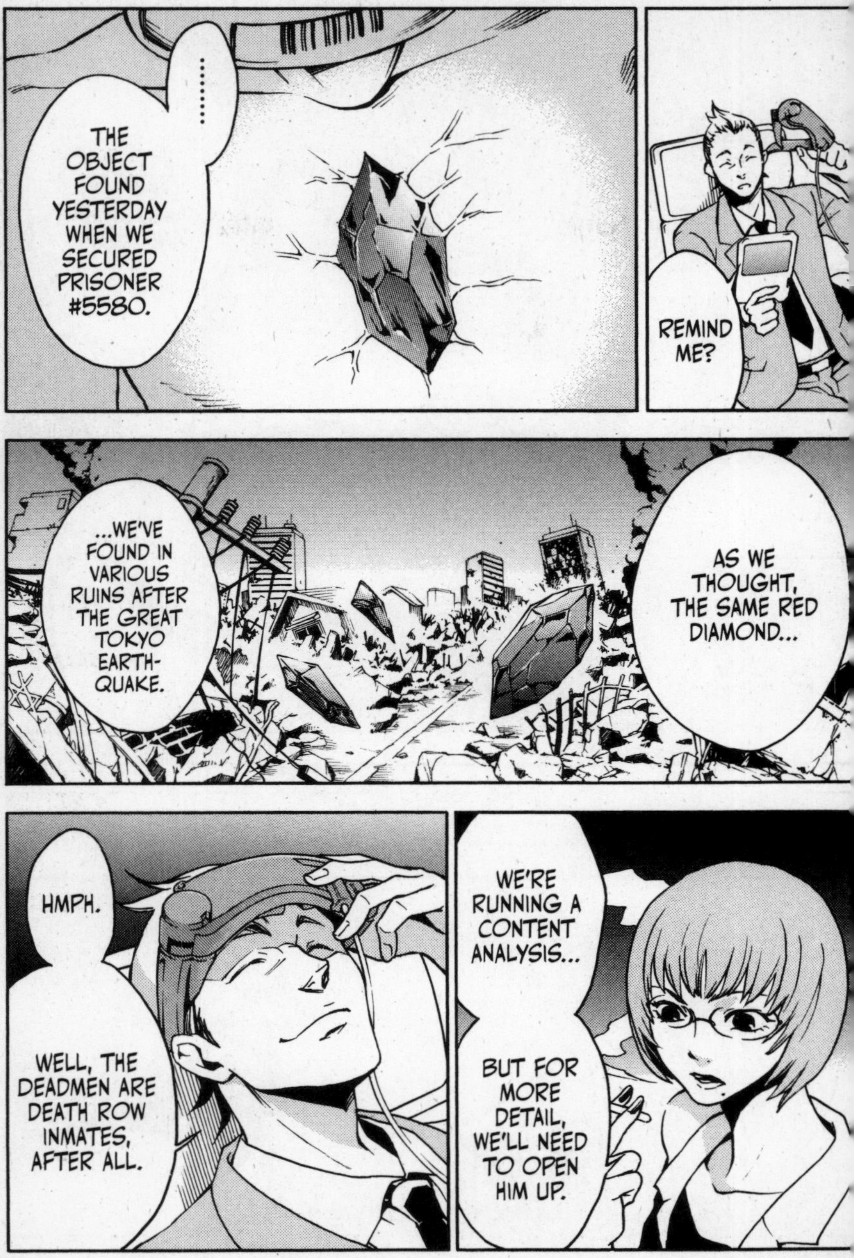
REMIND ME?
......
THE OBJECT FOUND YESTERDAY WHEN WE SECURED PRISONER #5580.
AS WE THOUGHT, THE SAME RED DIAMOND...
...WE'VE FOUND IN VARIOUS RUINS AFTER THE GREAT TOKYO EARTH-QUAKE.
WE'RE RUNNING A CONTENT ANALYSIS...
BUT FOR MORE DETAIL, WE'LL NEED TO OPEN HIM UP.
HMPH.
WELL, THE DEADMEN ARE DEATH ROW INMATES, AFTER ALL.

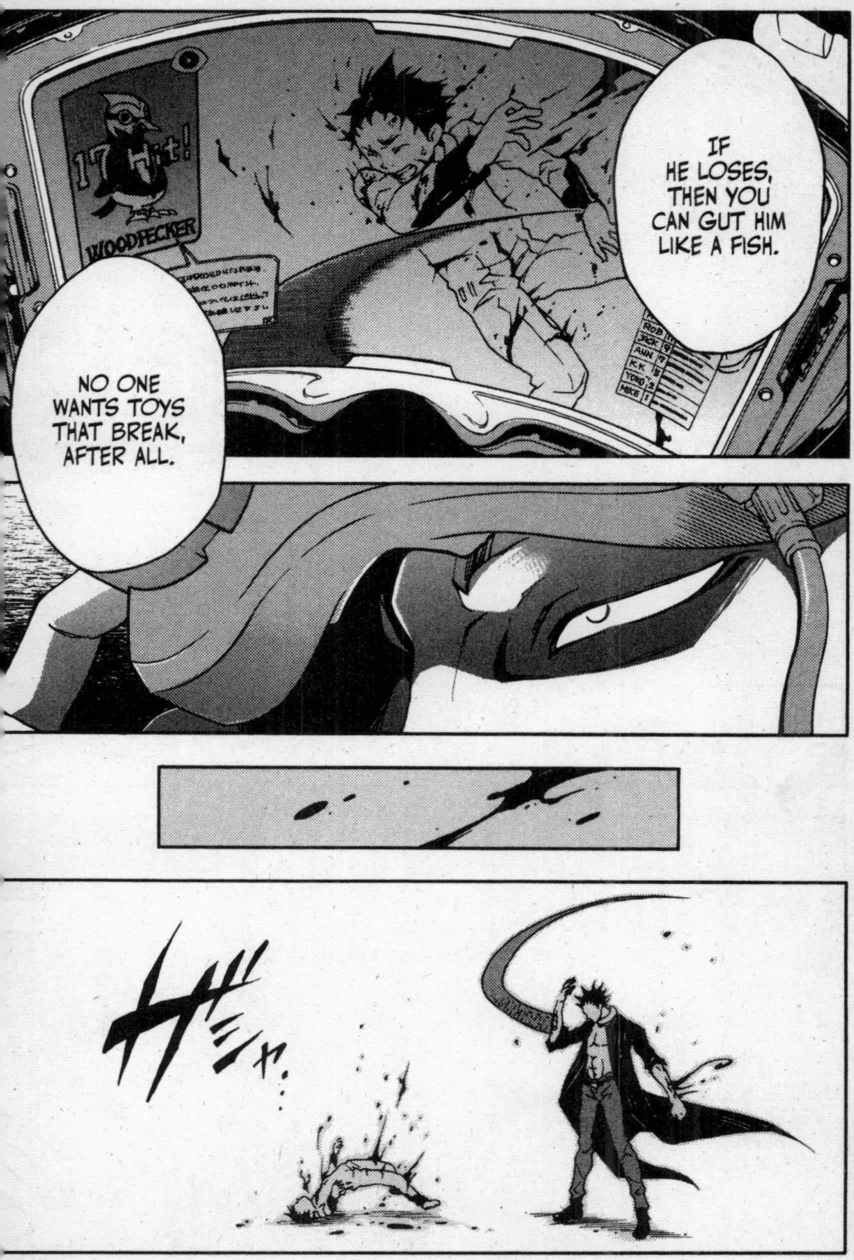
17 Hit!
WOODPECKER
IF HE LOSES, THEN YOU CAN GUT HIM LIKE A FISH.
NO ONE WANTS TOYS THAT BREAK, AFTER ALL.
ザシャ.

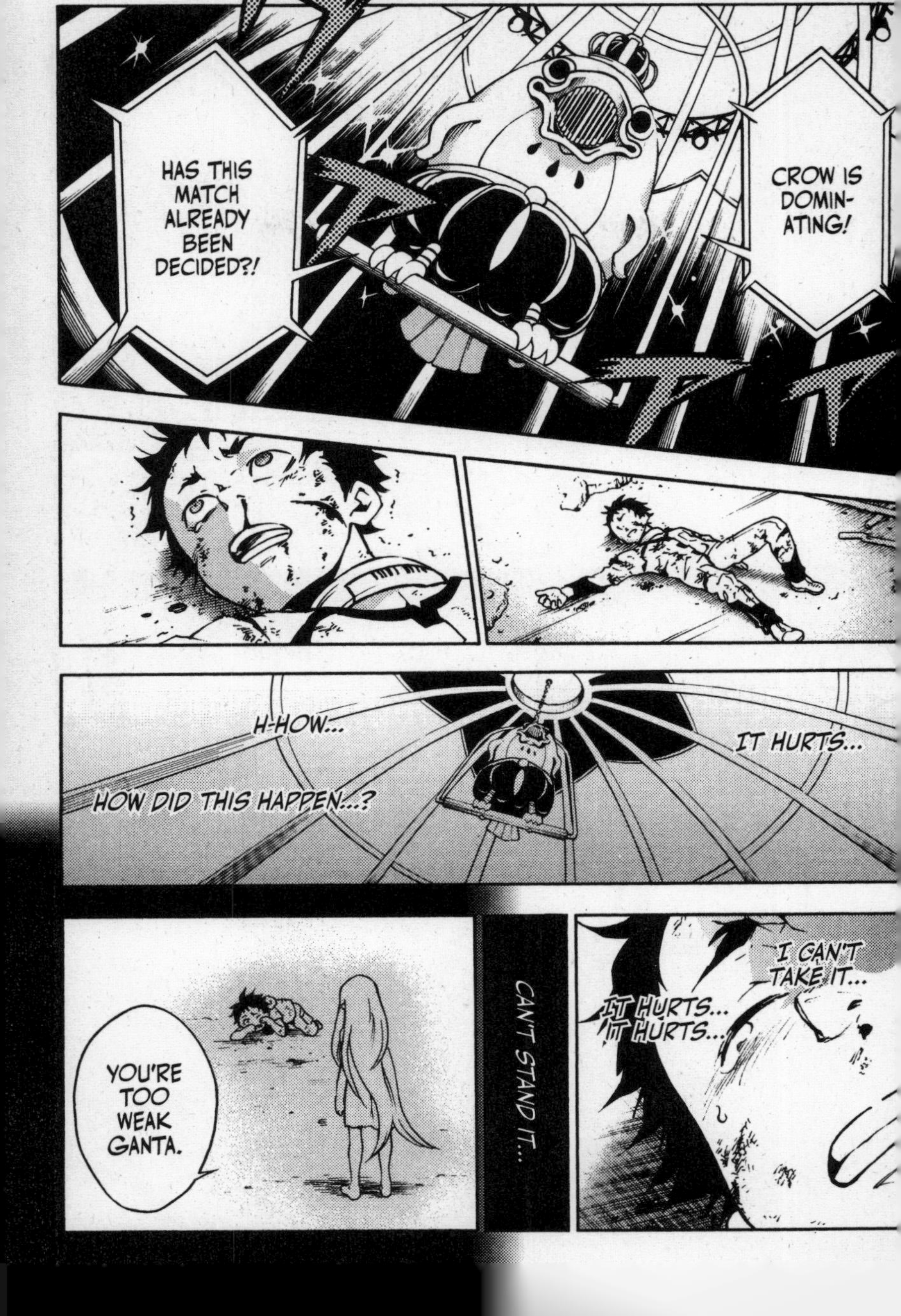
CROW IS DOMIN-ATING!
HAS THIS MATCH ALREADY BEEN DECIDED?!
IT HURTS...
H-HOW...
HOW DID THIS HAPPEN...?
I CAN'T TAKE IT...
IT HURTS... IT HURTS...
CAN'T STAND IT...
YOU'RE TOO WEAK GANTA.

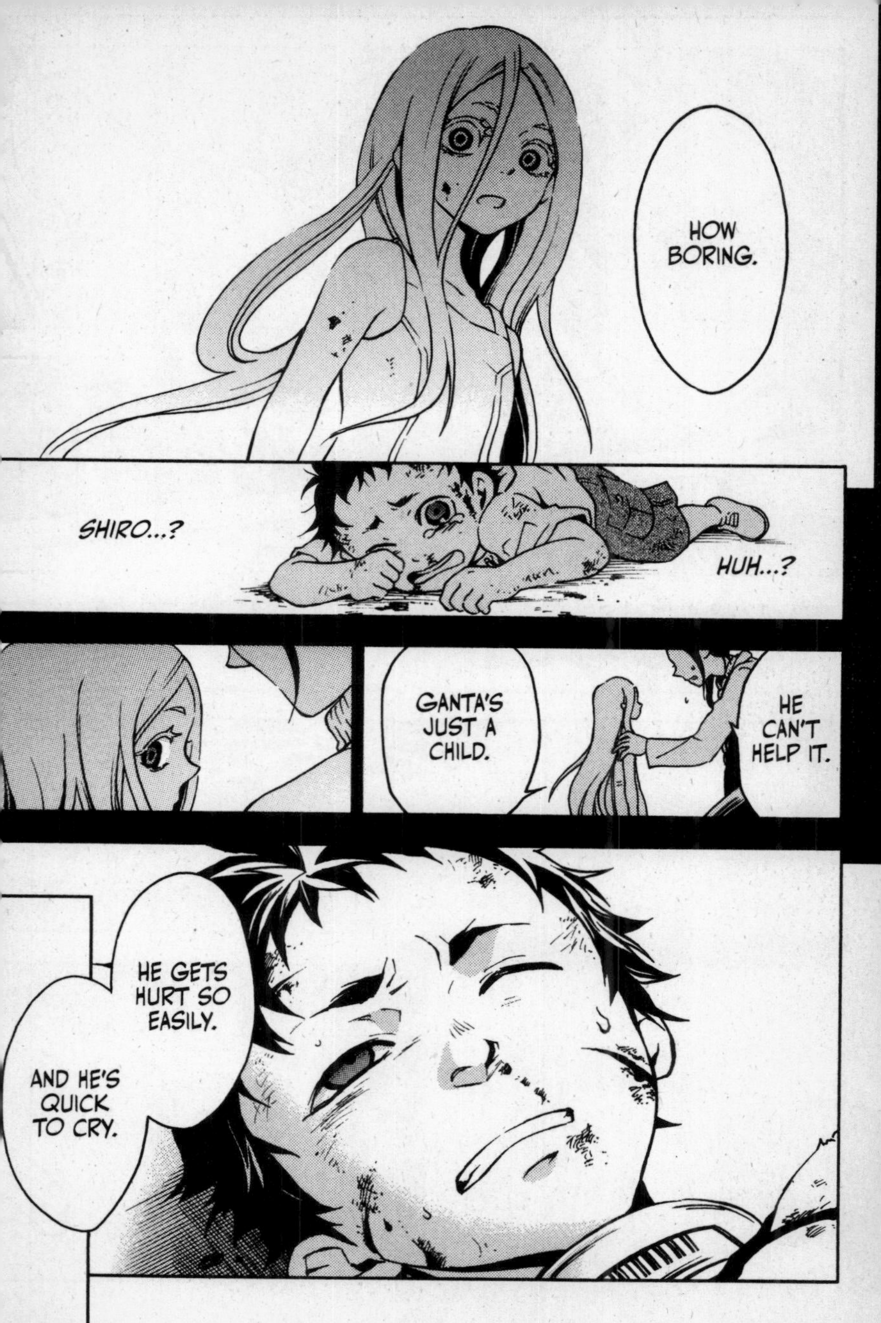
HOW BORING.
HUH...?
SHIRO...?
HE CAN'T HELP IT.
GANTA'S JUST A CHILD.
HE GETS HURT SO EASILY.
AND HE'S QUICK TO CRY.

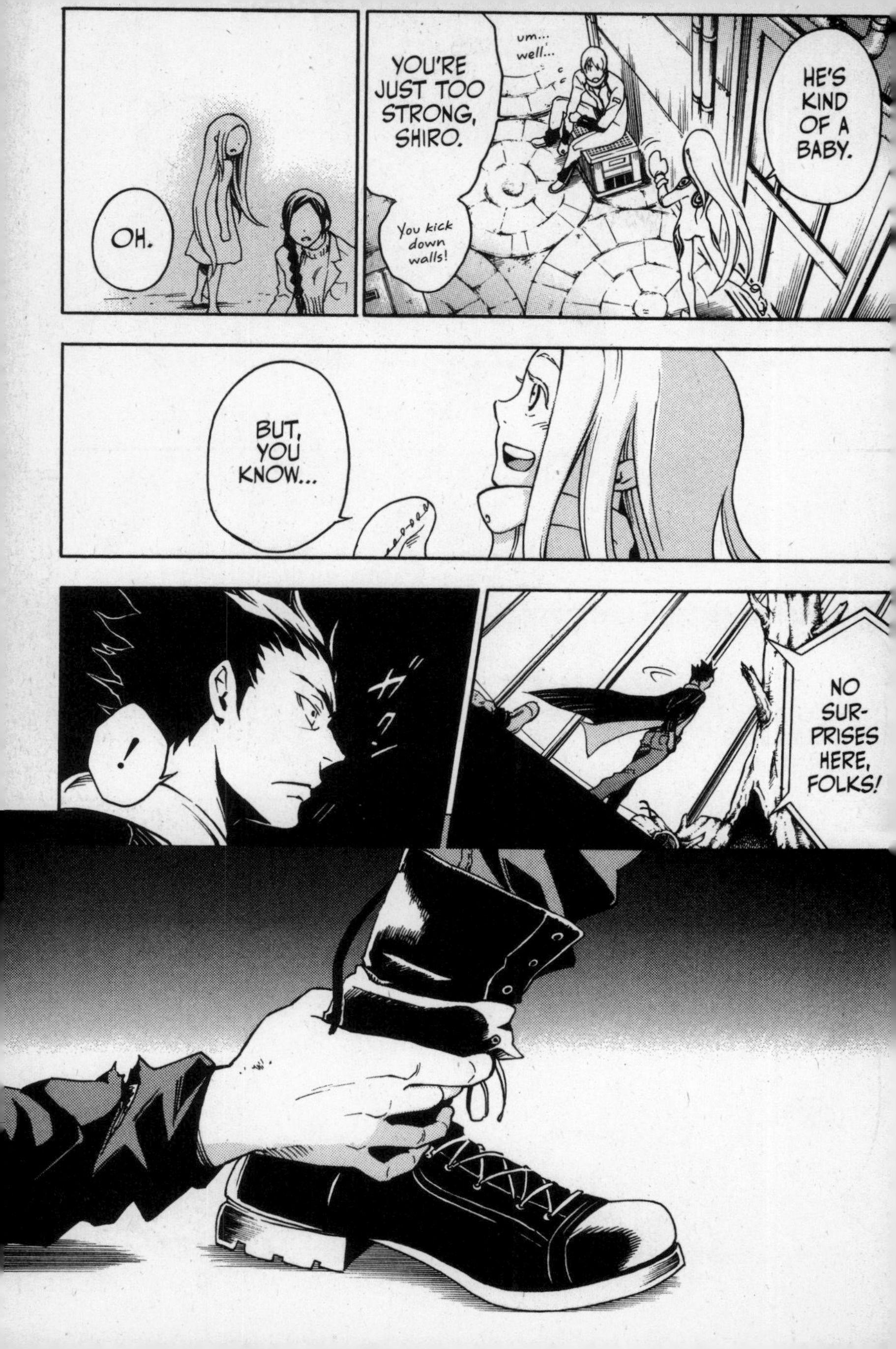
HE'S KIND OF A BABY.
um... well...
YOU'RE JUST TOO STRONG, SHIRO.
You kick down walls!
OH.
BUT, YOU KNOW...
NO SUR-PRISES HERE, FOLKS!
!

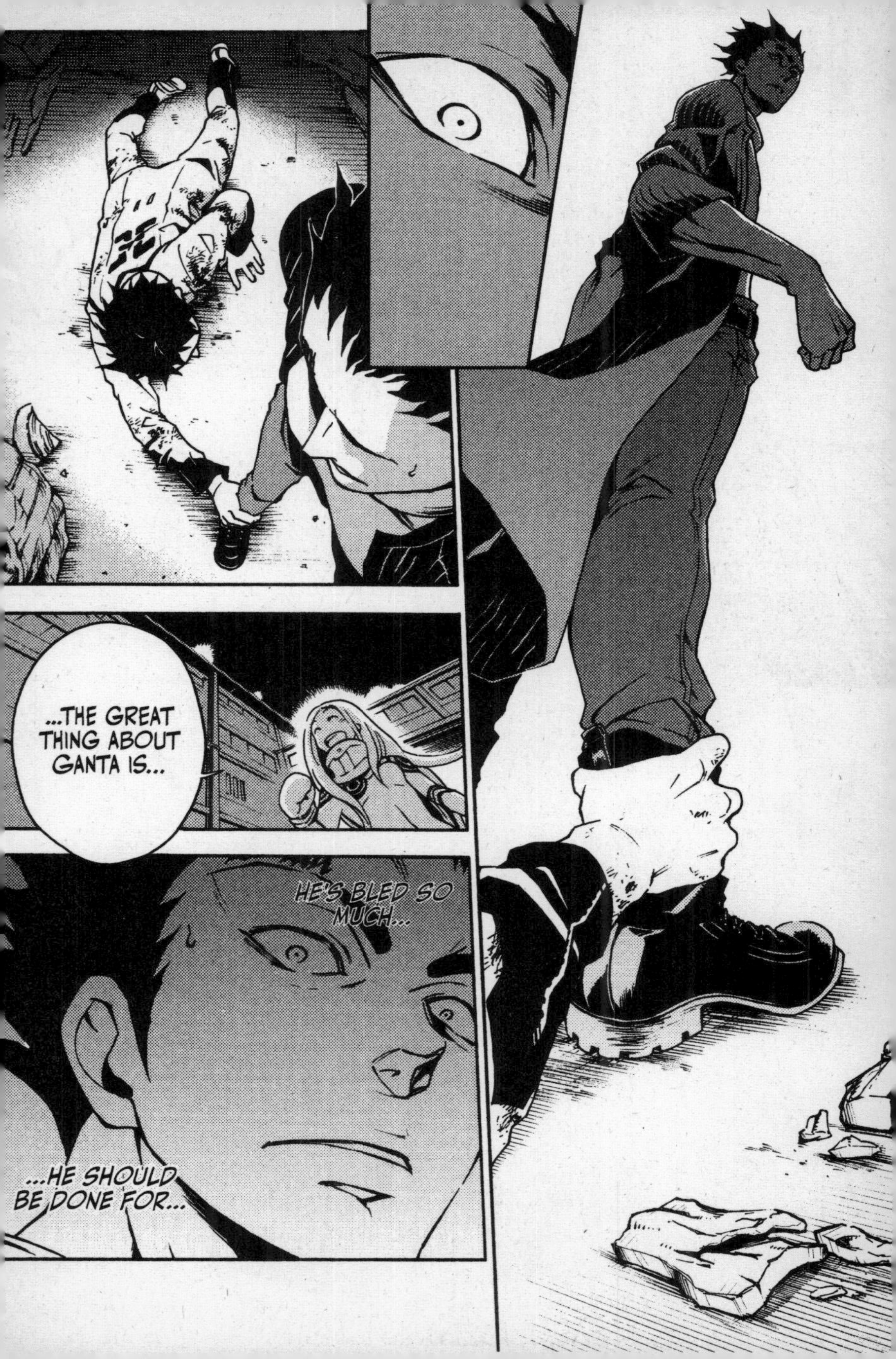
...THE GREAT THING ABOUT GANTA IS...
HE'S BLED SO MUCH...
...HE SHOULD BE DONE FOR...

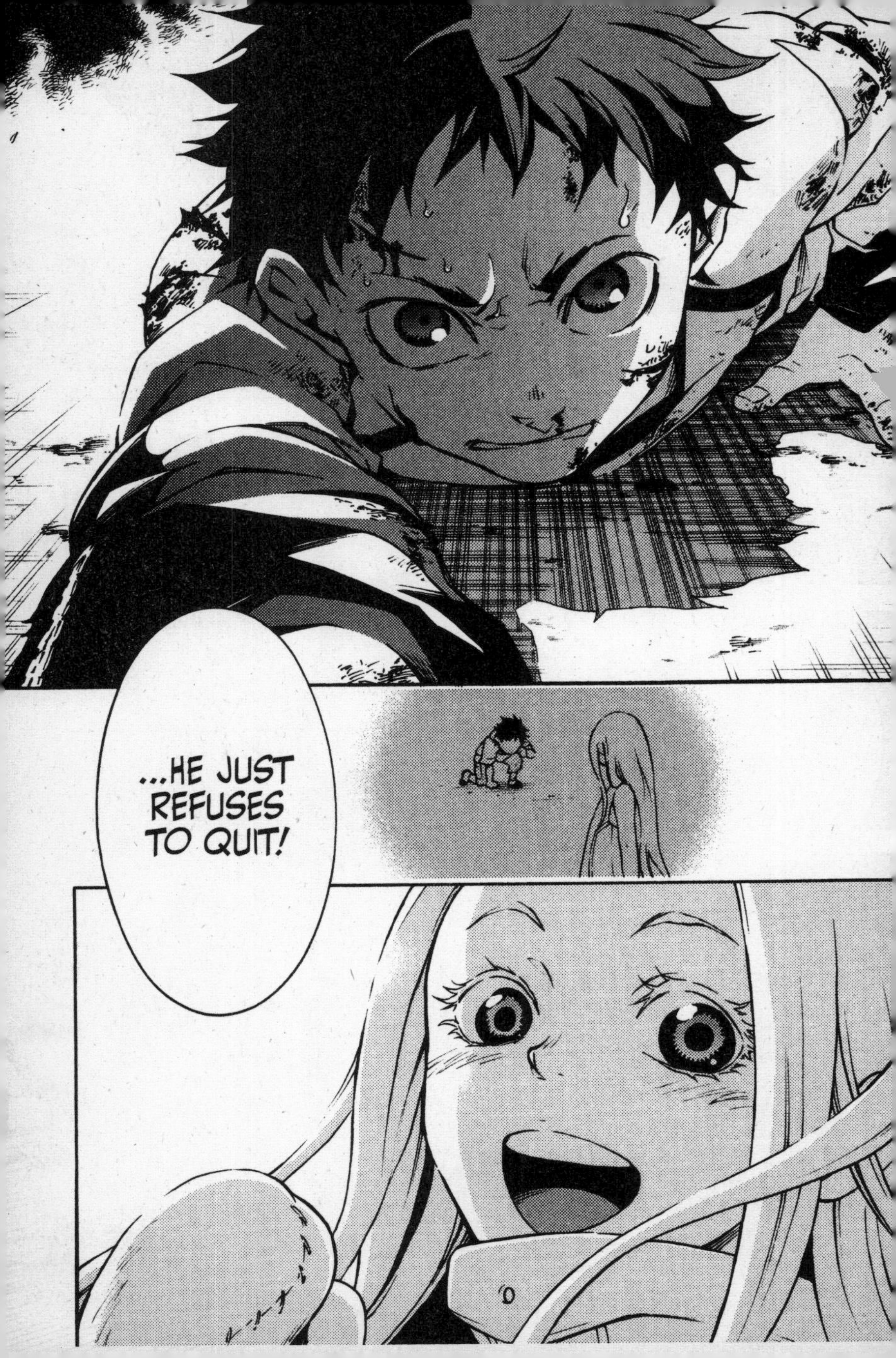
...HE JUST REFUSES TO QUIT!

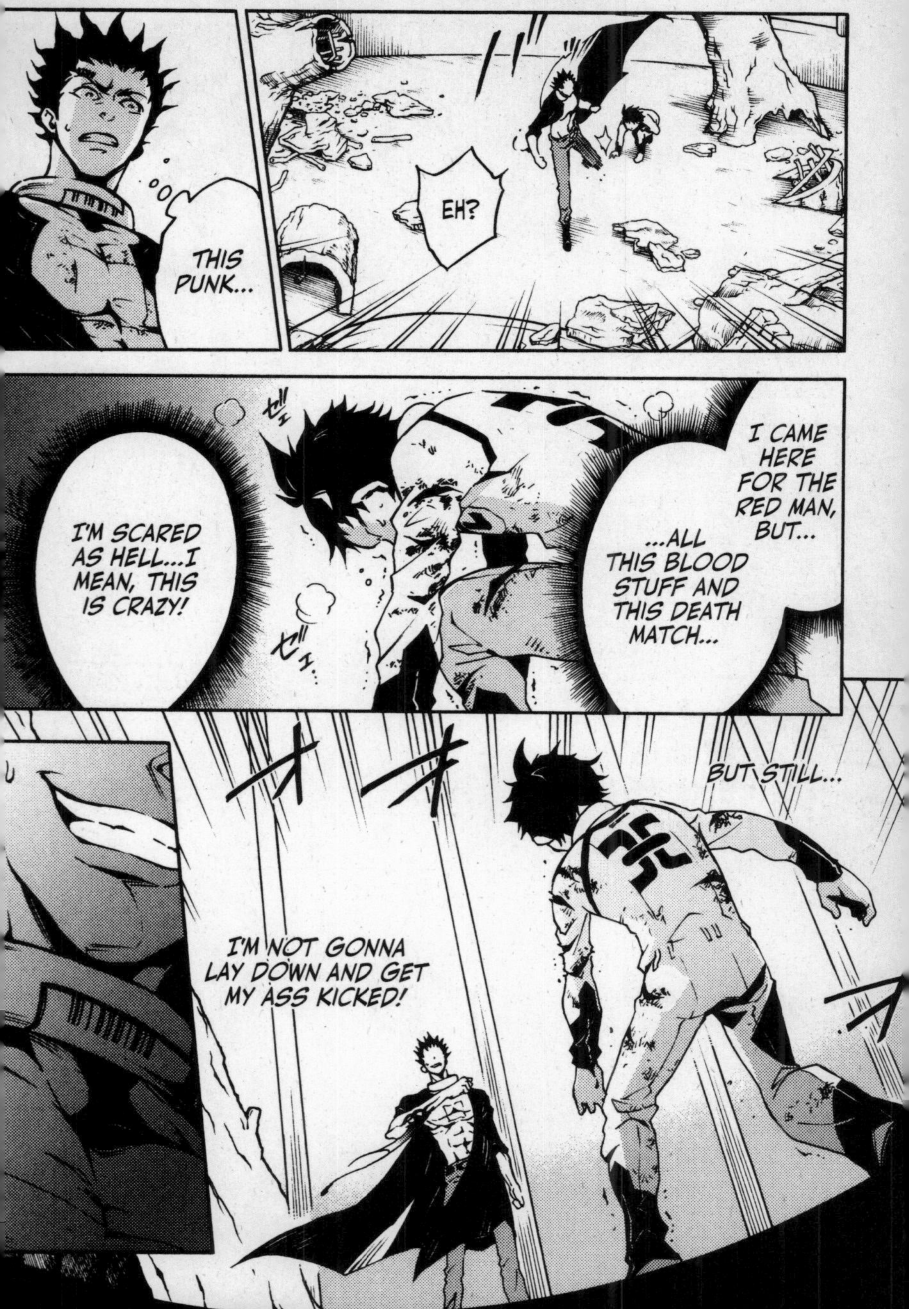
EH?
THIS PUNK...
ゼェ
I CAME HERE FOR THE RED MAN, BUT...
...ALL THIS BLOOD STUFF AND THIS DEATH MATCH...
I'M SCARED AS HELL...I MEAN, THIS IS CRAZY!
ゼェ...
BUT STILL...
I'M NOT GONNA LAY DOWN AND GET MY ASS KICKED!

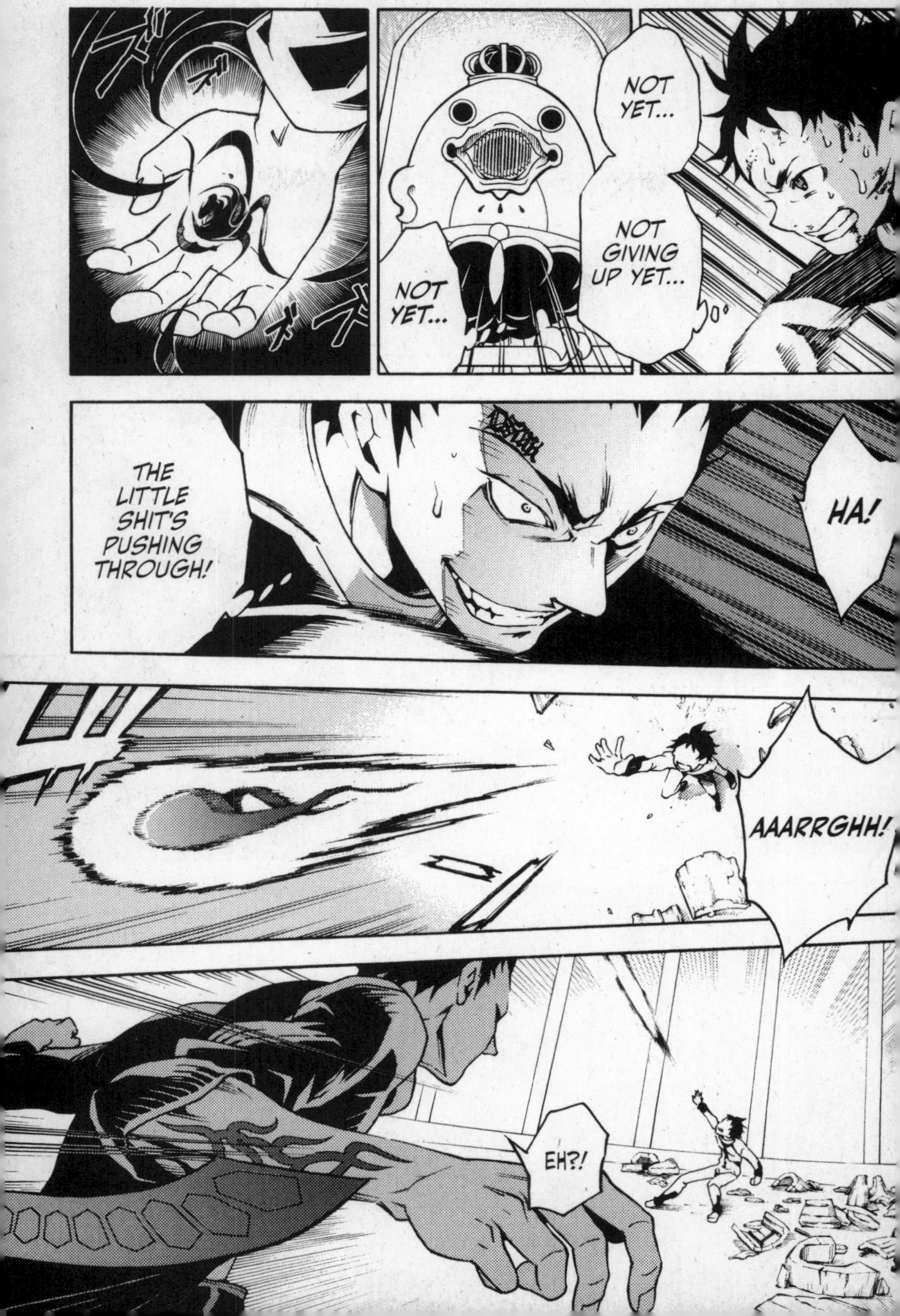
NOT YET...
NOT GIVING UP YET...
NOT YET...
HA!
THE LITTLE SHIT'S PUSHING THROUGH!
AAARRGHH!
EH?!

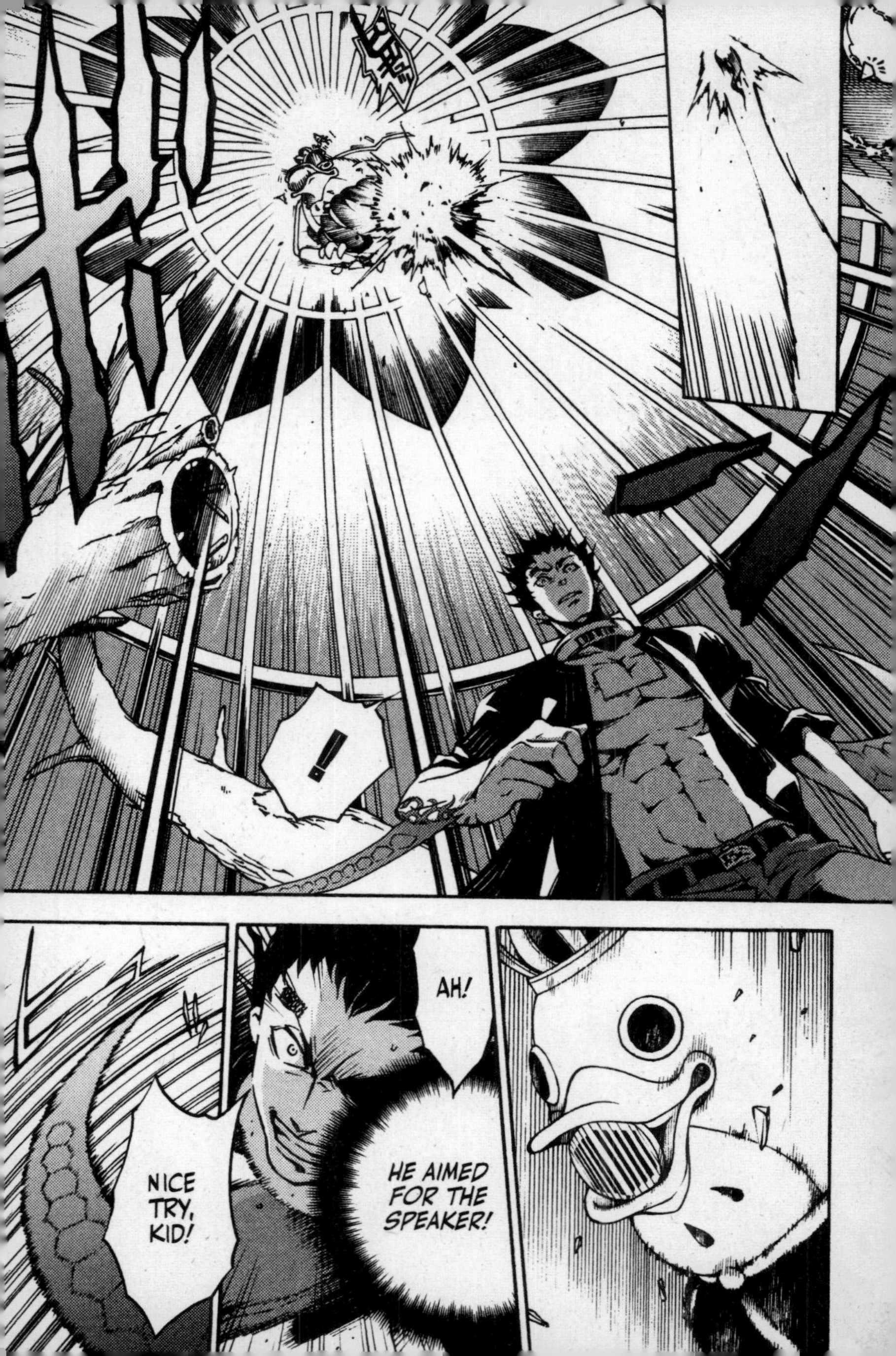
!
AH!
HE AIMED FOR THE SPEAKER!
NICE TRY, KID!

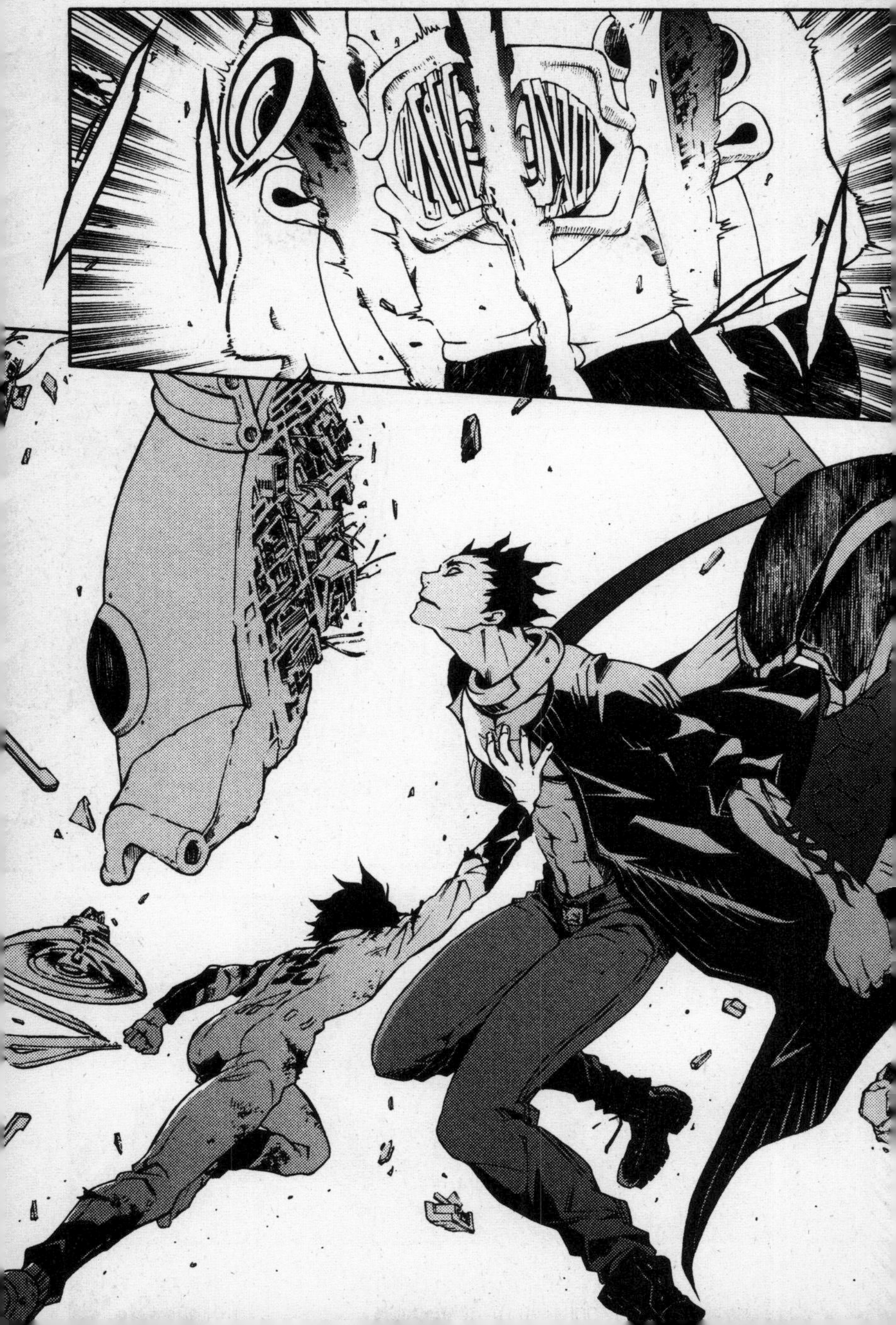

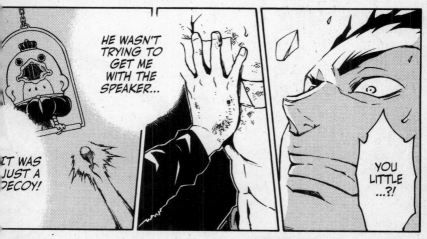

HE WASN'T TRYING TO GET ME WITH THE SPEAKER...

IT WAS JUST A DECOY!

YOU LITTLE ...?!

BUT HE'S GOTTA BE SO LOW ON BLOOD NOW...

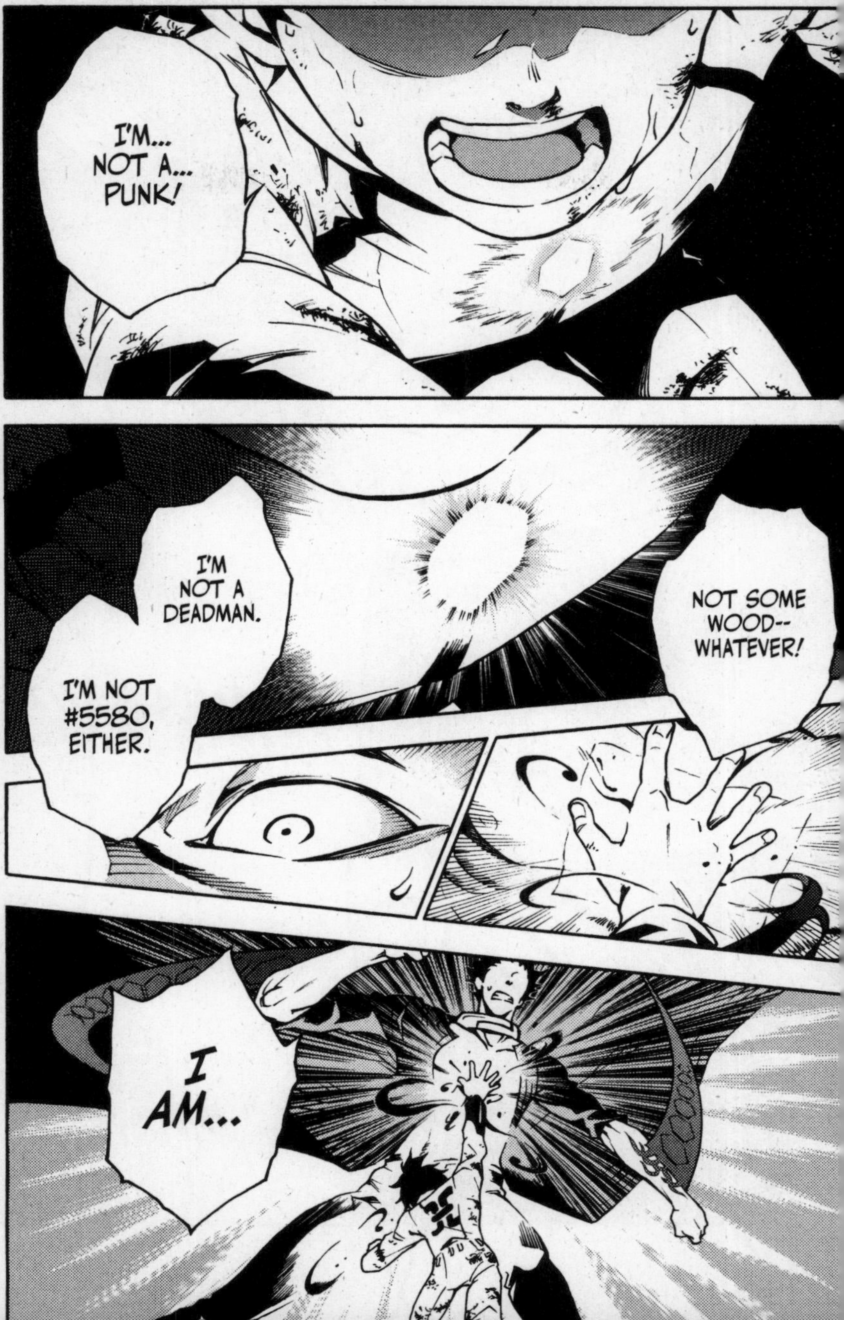
I'M... NOT A... PUNK!
NOT SOME WOOD-- WHATEVER!
I'M NOT A DEADMAN.
I'M NOT #5580, EITHER.
I AM...

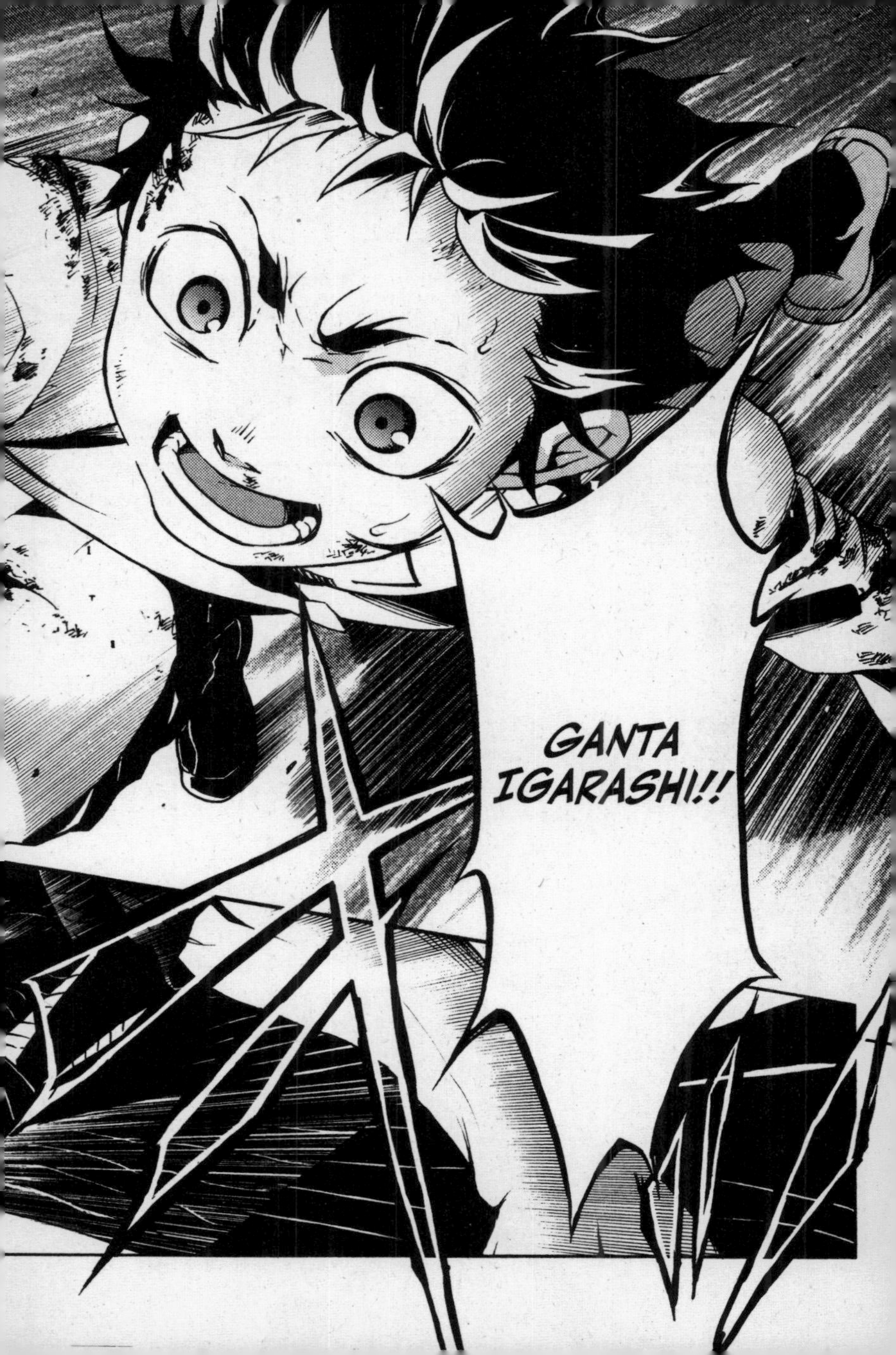
GANTA IGARASHI!!

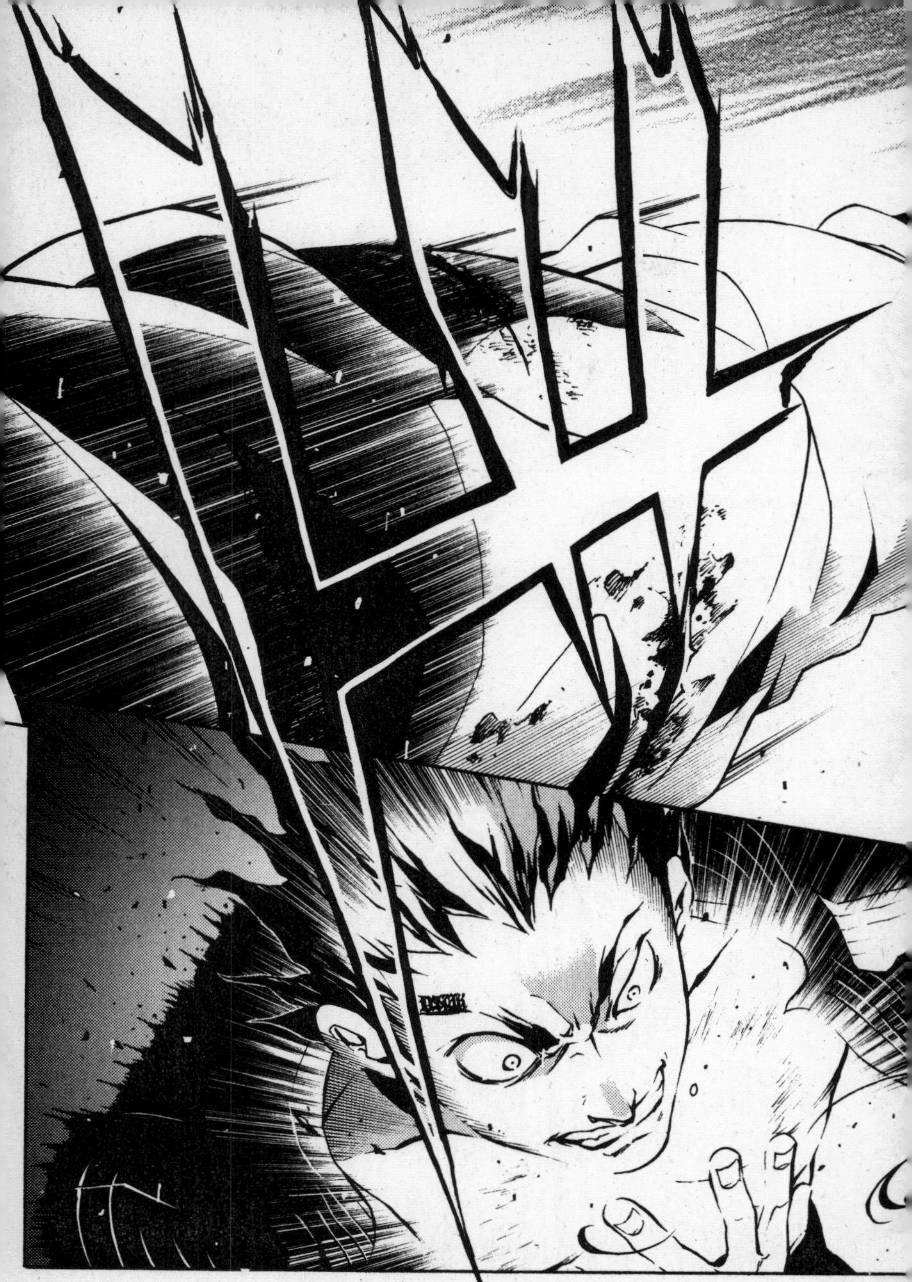

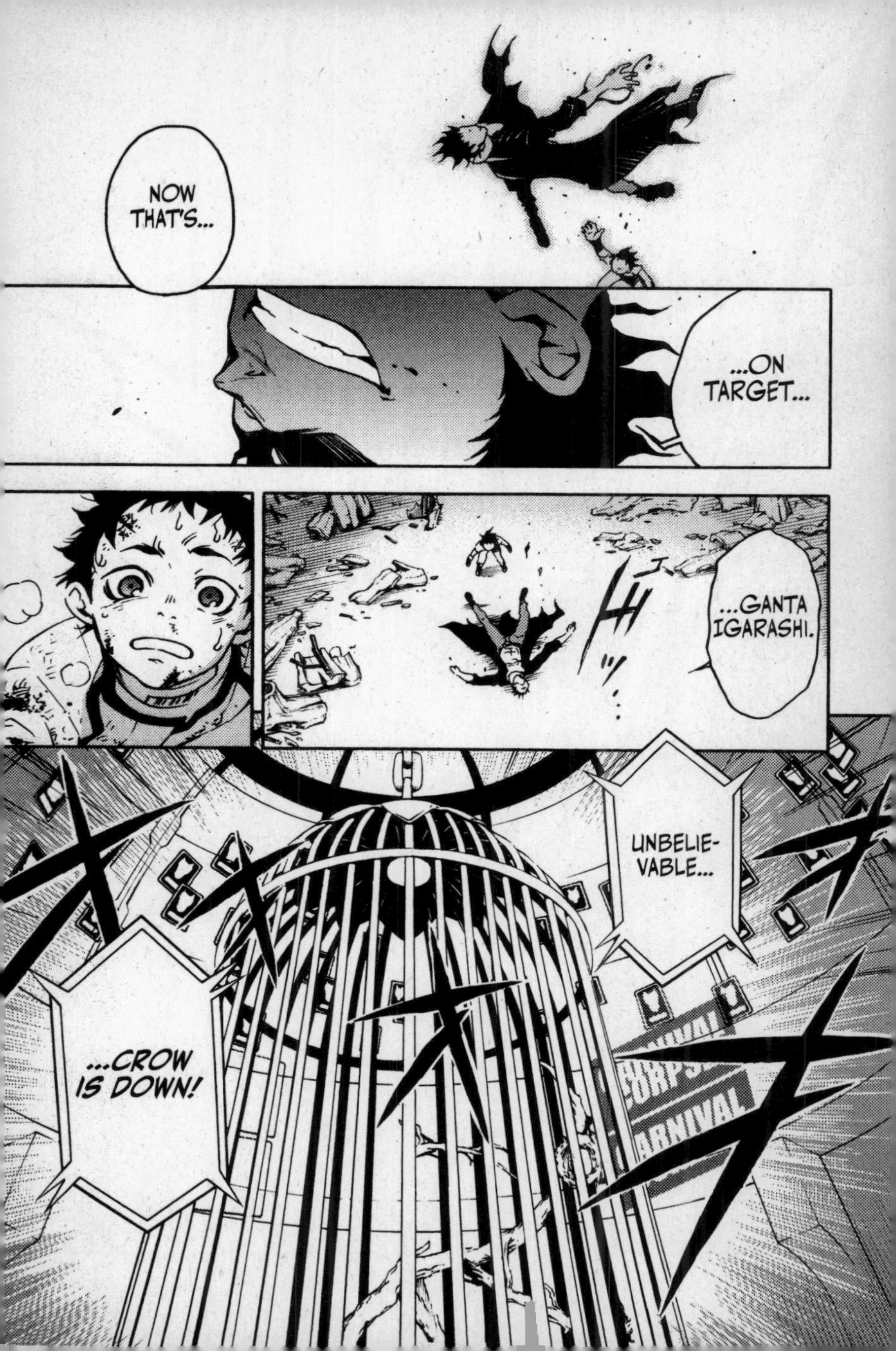
NOW THAT'S...
...ON TARGET...
...GANTA IGARASHI.
UNBELIEVABLE...
...CROW IS DOWN!

DEADMAN WOND
ER LAND

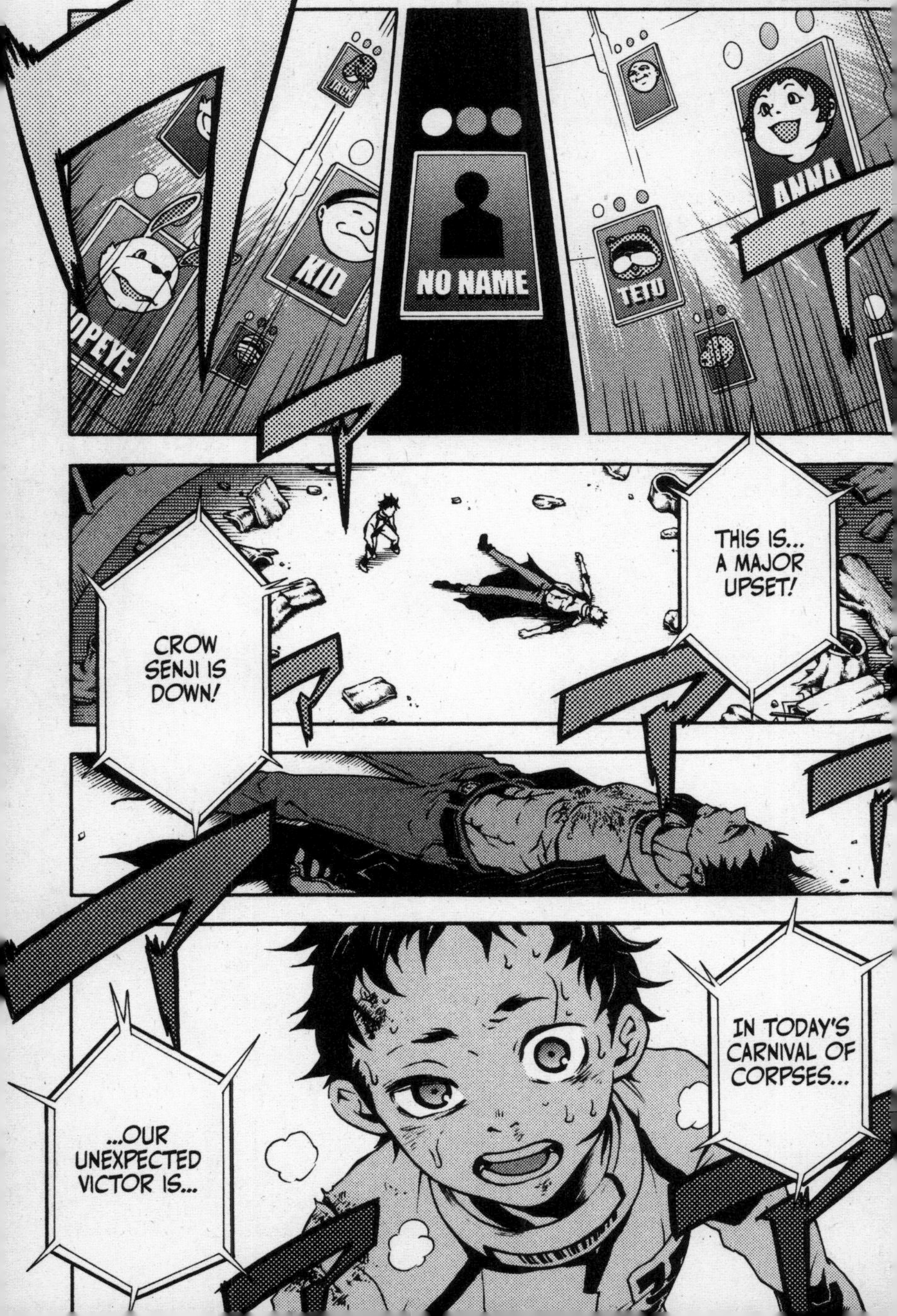
ANNA
TETU
NO NAME
KID
JACK
OPEYE
THIS IS... A MAJOR UPSET!
CROW SENJI IS DOWN!
IN TODAY'S CARNIVAL OF CORPSES...
...OUR UNEXPECTED VICTOR IS...

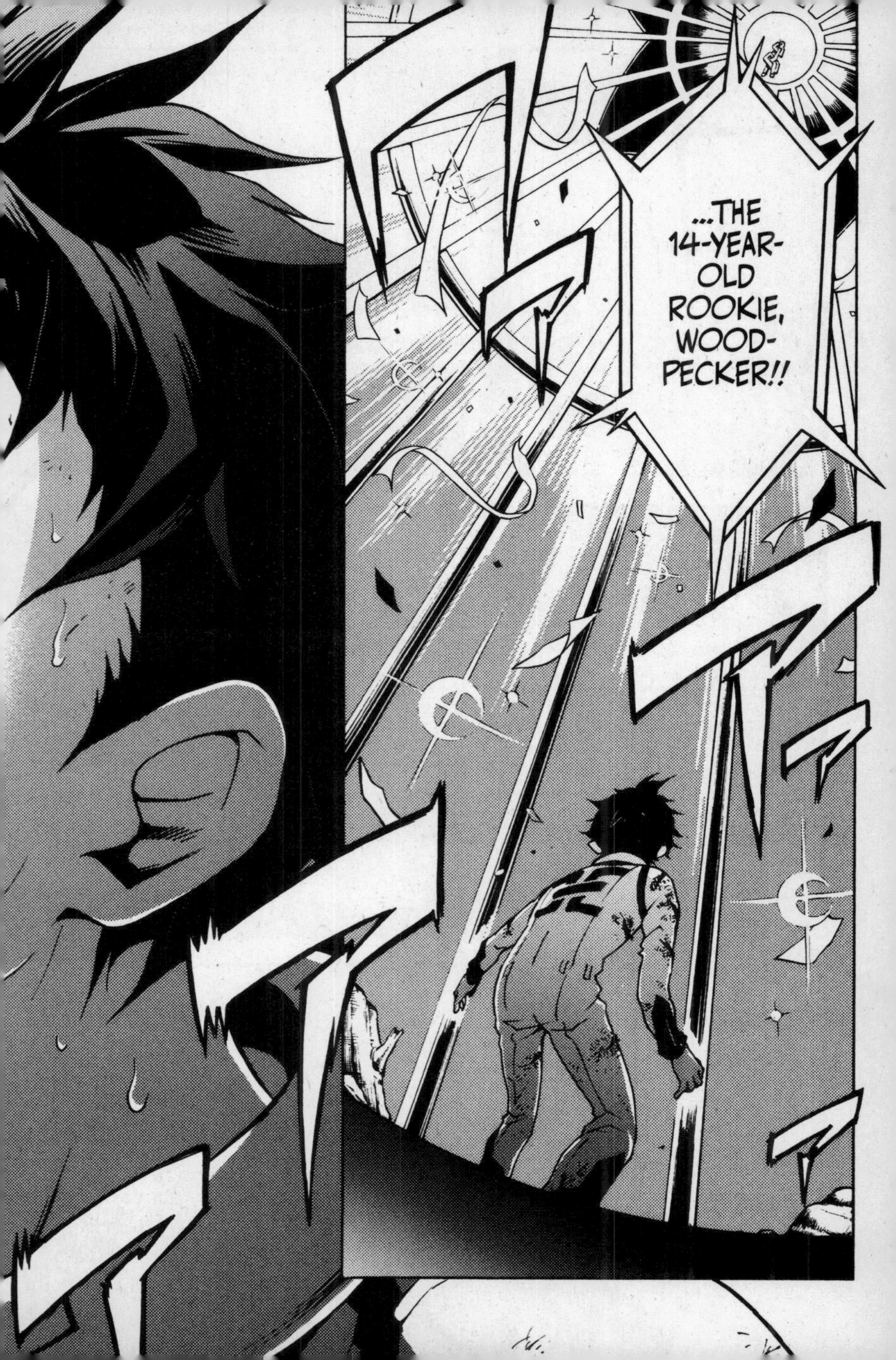
...THE 14-YEAR-OLD ROOKIE, WOOD-PECKER!!

# 08 Bloodthirsty Majesty

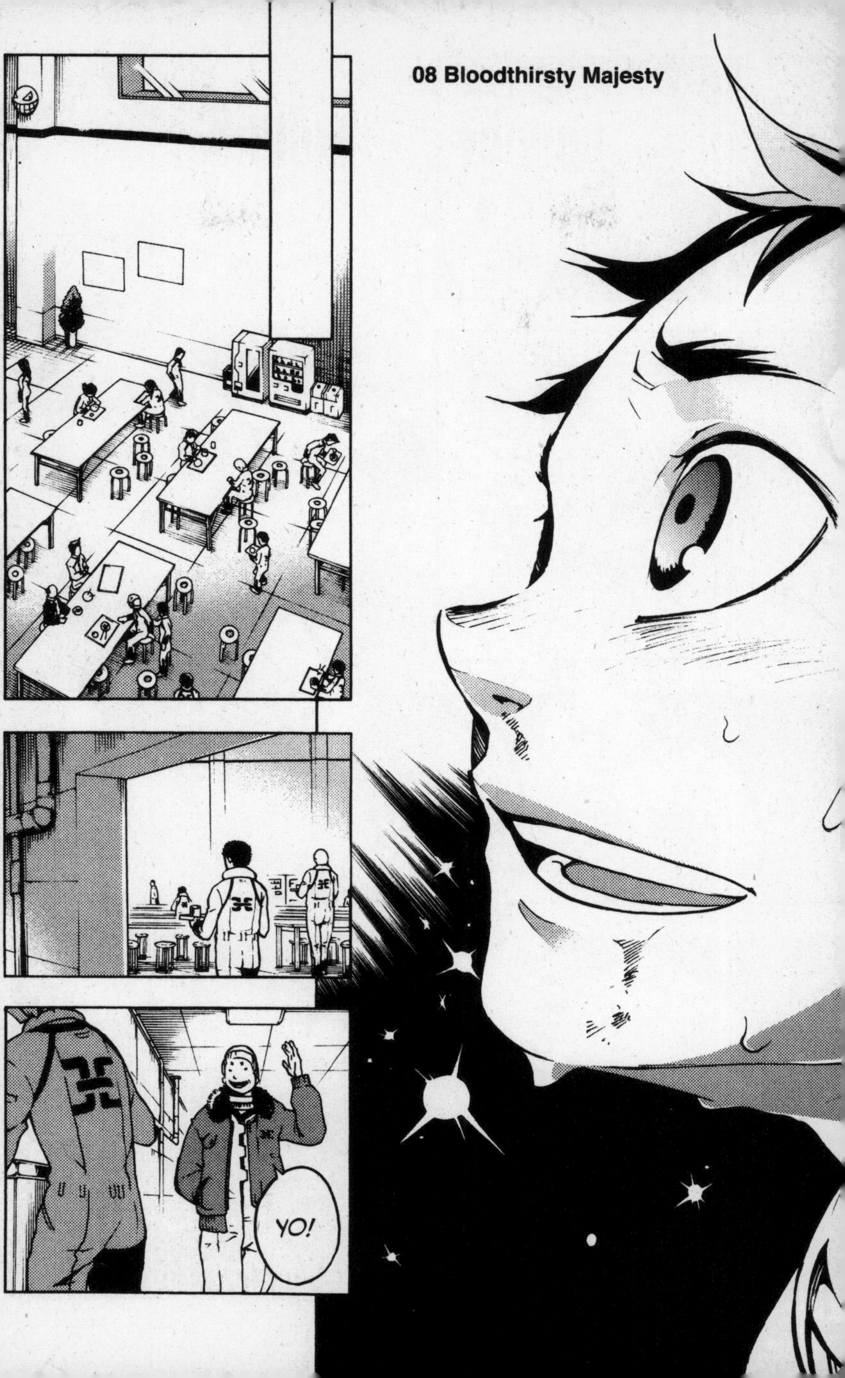
YO!

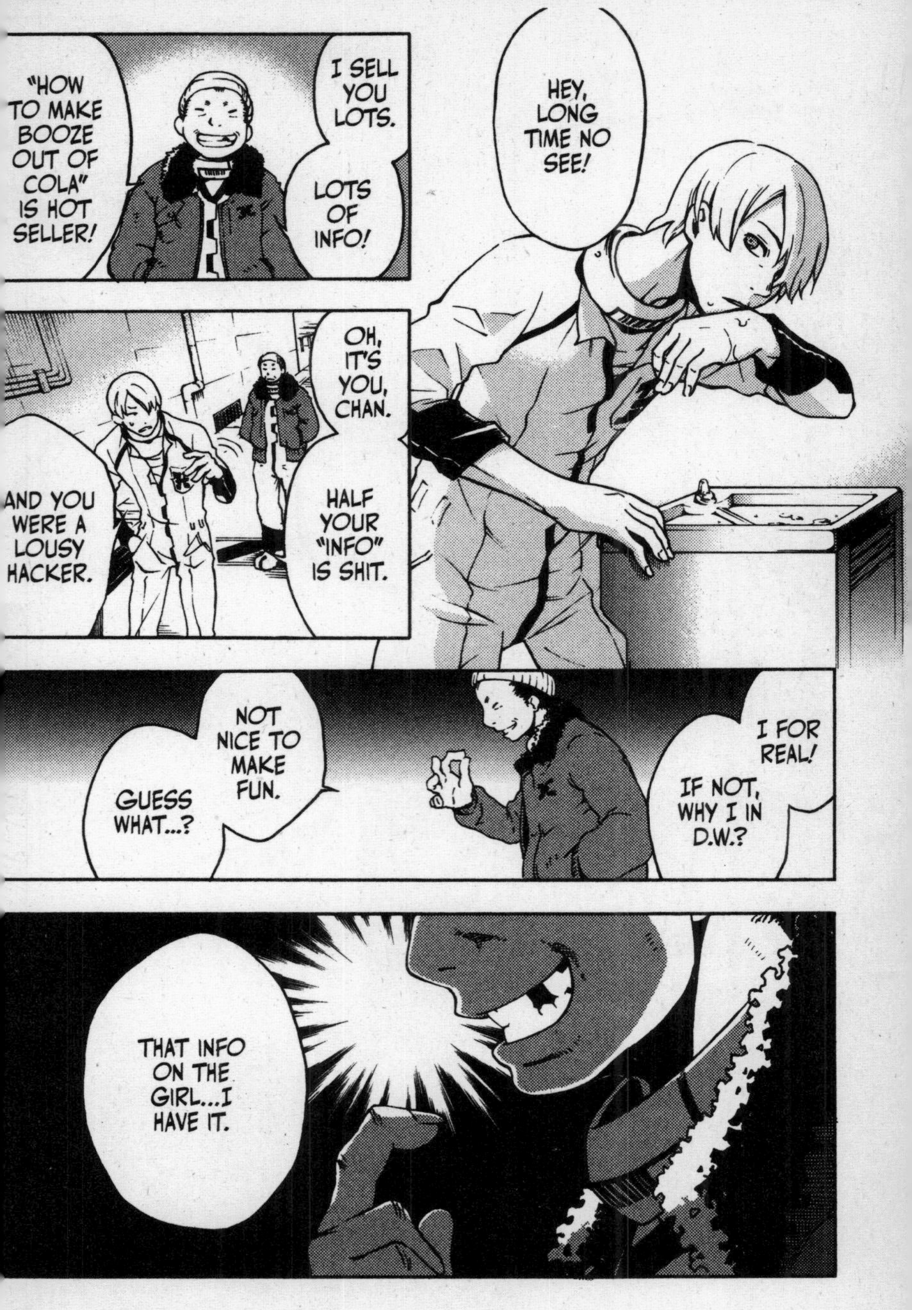
HEY, LONG TIME NO SEE!
I SELL YOU LOTS.
LOTS OF INFO!
"HOW TO MAKE BOOZE OUT OF COLA" IS HOT SELLER!
OH, IT'S YOU, CHAN.
HALF YOUR "INFO" IS SHIT.
AND YOU WERE A LOUSY HACKER.
I FOR REAL!
IF NOT, WHY I IN D.W.?
NOT NICE TO MAKE FUN.
GUESS WHAT...?
THAT INFO ON THE GIRL...I HAVE IT.

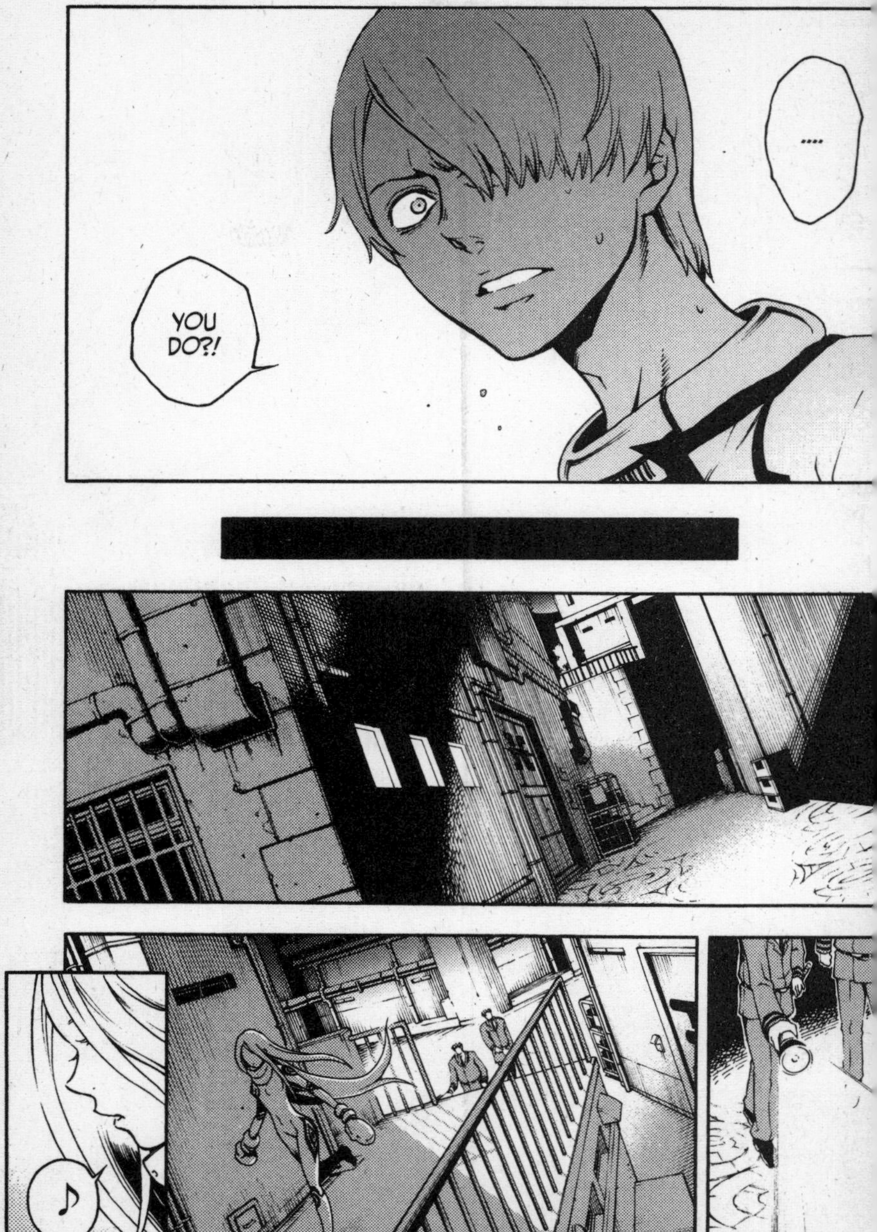
....
YOU DO?!
♪

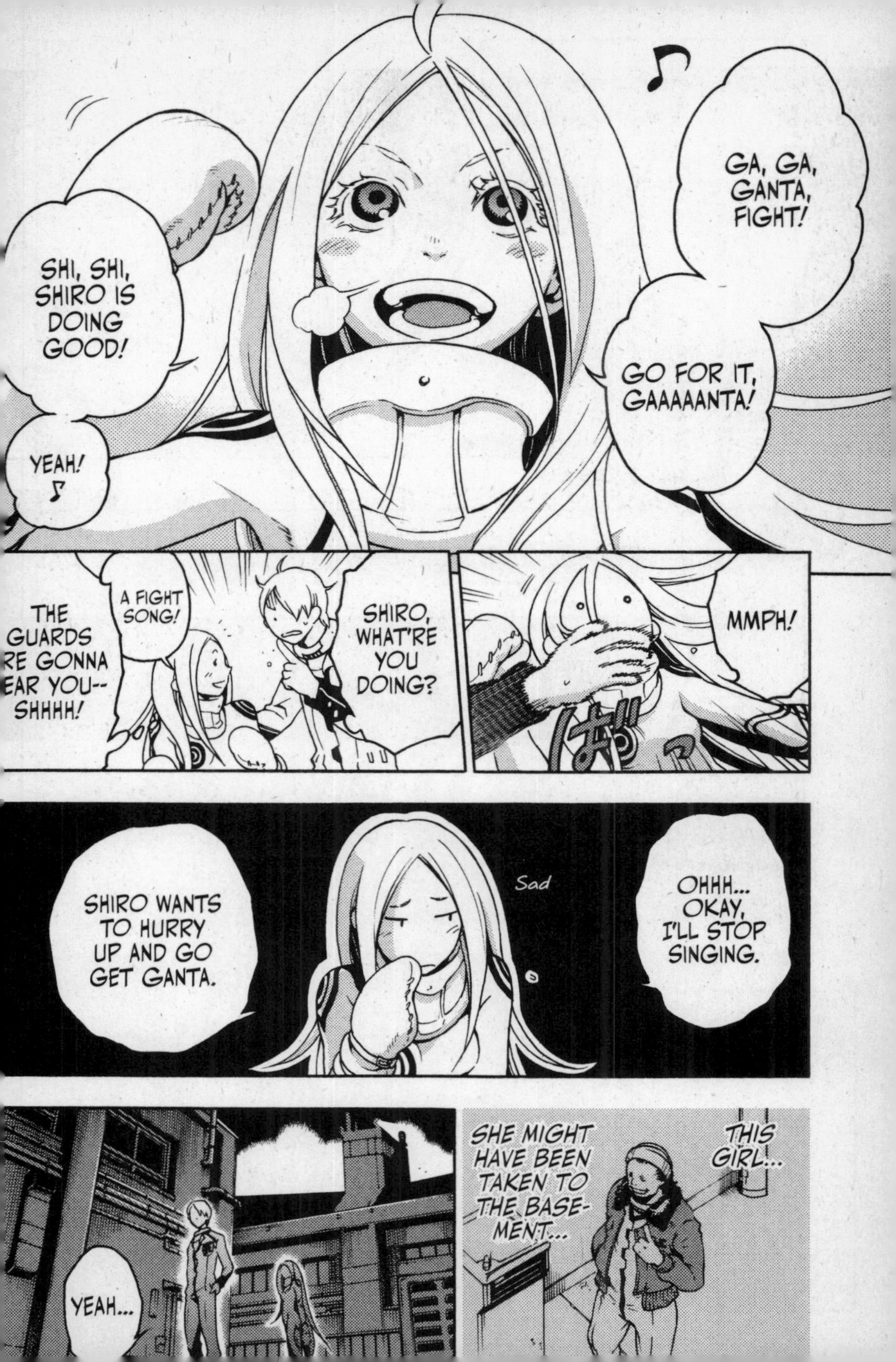
GA, GA, GANTA, FIGHT!
GO FOR IT, GAAAAANTA!
SHI, SHI, SHIRO IS DOING GOOD!
YEAH! ♪
MMPH!
SHIRO, WHAT'RE YOU DOING?
A FIGHT SONG!
THE GUARDS RE GONNA EAR YOU-- SHHHH!
OHHH... OKAY, I'LL STOP SINGING.
Sad
SHIRO WANTS TO HURRY UP AND GO GET GANTA.
THIS GIRL...
SHE MIGHT HAVE BEEN TAKEN TO THE BASE-MENT...
YEAH...

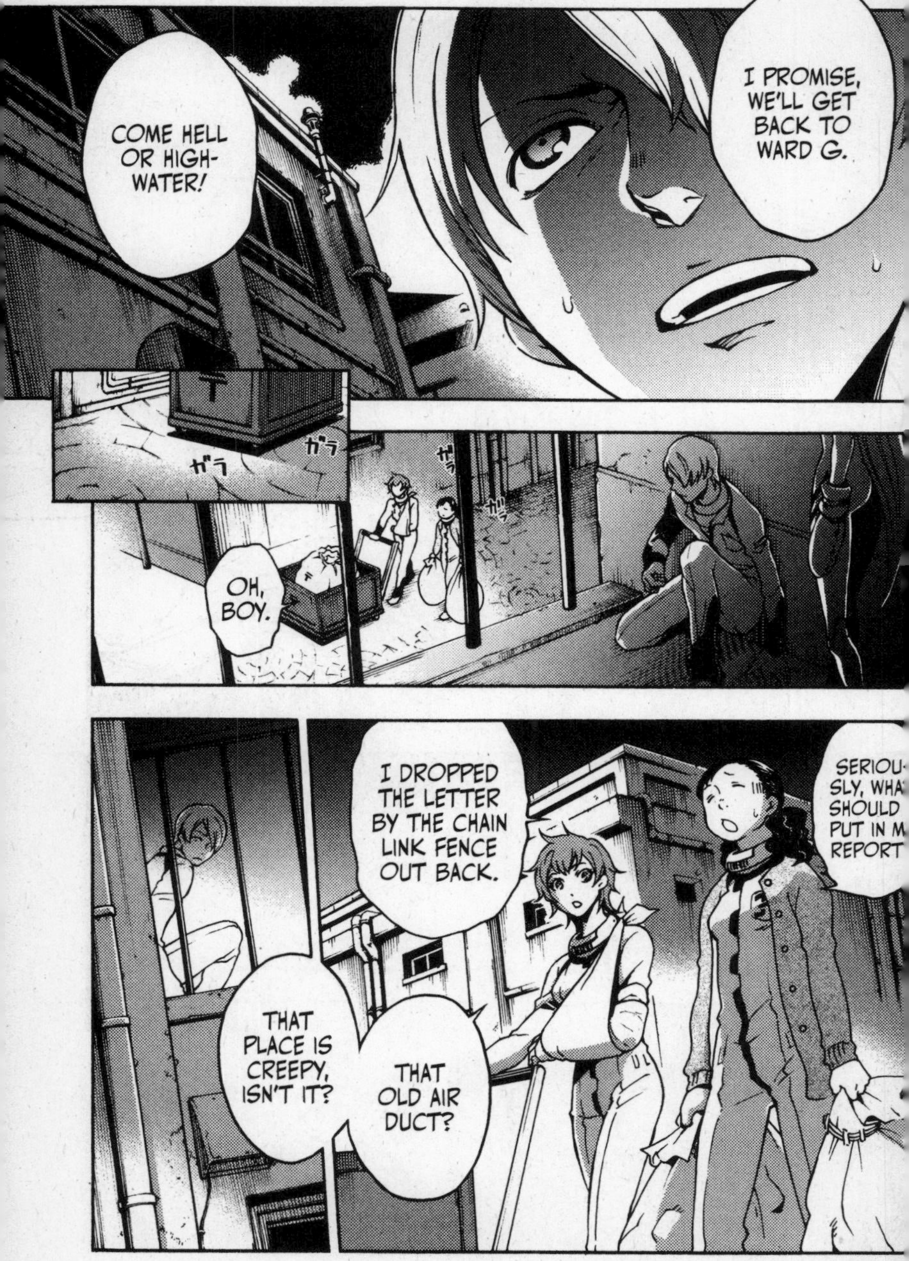
I PROMISE, WE'LL GET BACK TO WARD G.
COME HELL OR HIGH-WATER!
ガラ
ガラ
OH, BOY.
ガラ
ガラ
SERIOU-SLY, WHA SHOULD PUT IN M REPORT
I DROPPED THE LETTER BY THE CHAIN LINK FENCE OUT BACK.
THAT OLD AIR DUCT?
THAT PLACE IS CREEPY, ISN'T IT?

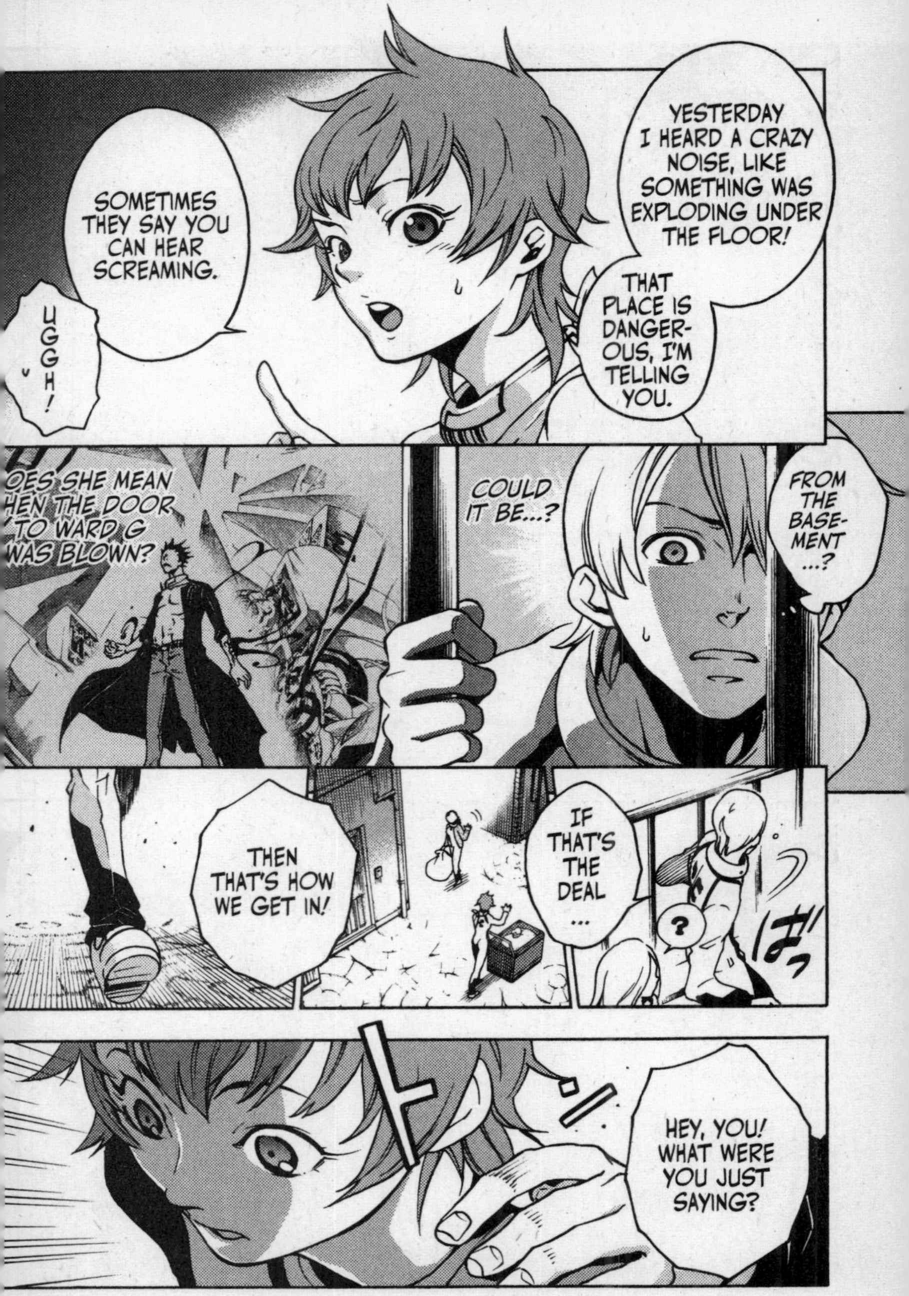
YESTERDAY I HEARD A CRAZY NOISE, LIKE SOMETHING WAS EXPLODING UNDER THE FLOOR!
THAT PLACE IS DANGER-OUS, I'M TELLING YOU.
SOMETIMES THEY SAY YOU CAN HEAR SCREAMING.
UGGH!
FROM THE BASE-MENT ...?
COULD IT BE...?
OES SHE MEAN HEN THE DOOR TO WARD G WAS BLOWN?
IF THAT'S THE DEAL ...
?
ばっ
THEN THAT'S HOW WE GET IN!
ド
HEY, YOU! WHAT WERE YOU JUST SAYING?

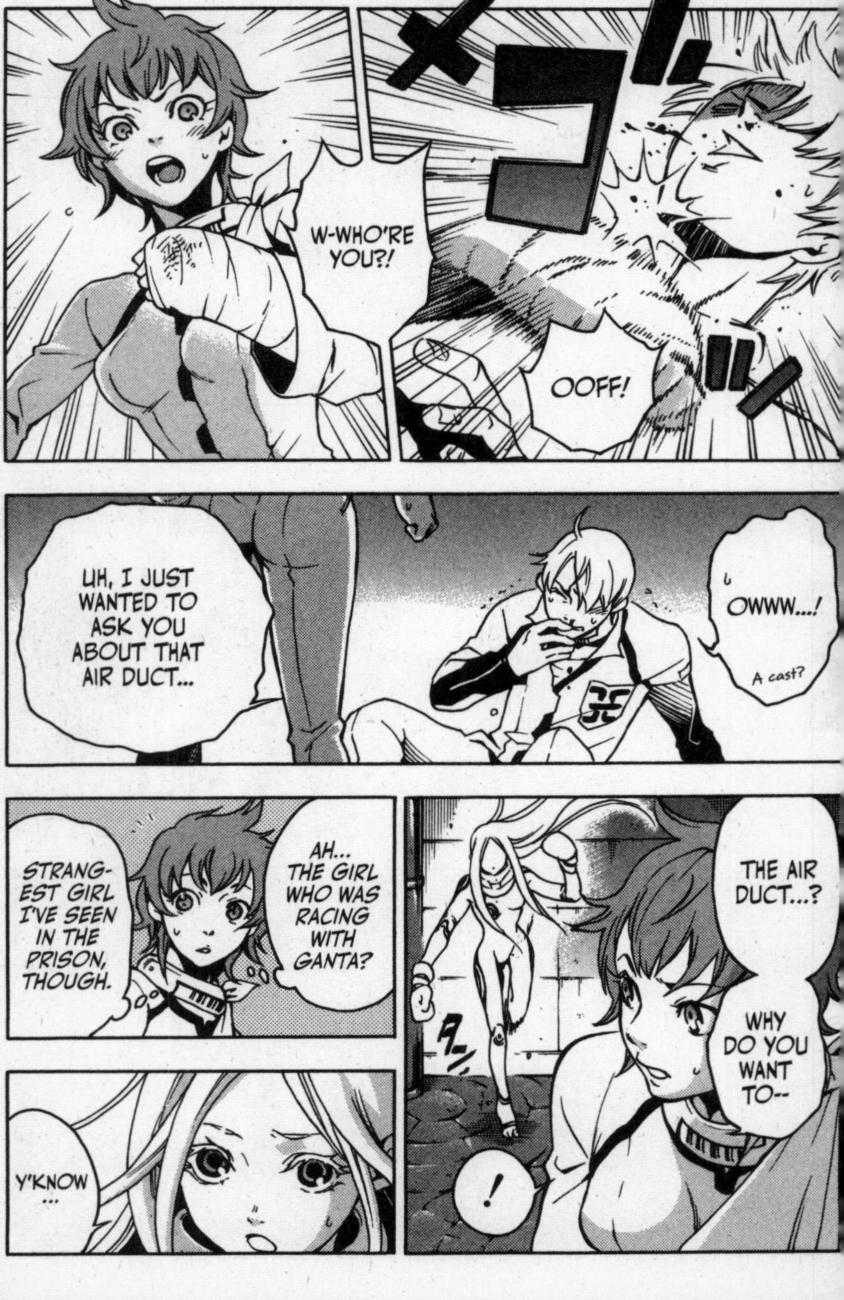
OOFF!
W-WHO'RE YOU?!
OWWW...!
A cast?
UH, I JUST WANTED TO ASK YOU ABOUT THAT AIR DUCT...
THE AIR DUCT...?
WHY DO YOU WANT TO--
!
AH... THE GIRL WHO WAS RACING WITH GANTA?
STRANGEST GIRL I'VE SEEN IN THE PRISON, THOUGH.
Y'KNOW...

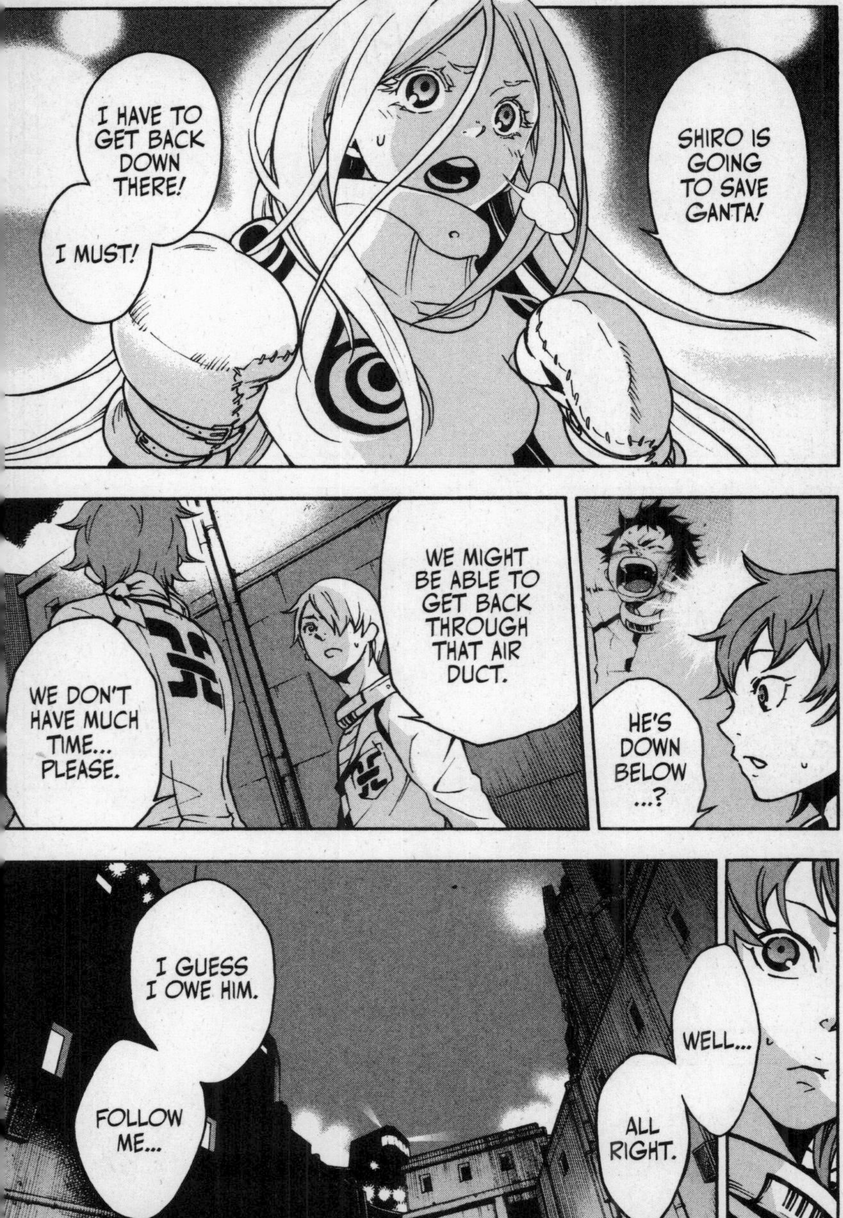
SHIRO IS GOING TO SAVE GANTA!
I HAVE TO GET BACK DOWN THERE!
I MUST!
HE'S DOWN BELOW ...?
WE MIGHT BE ABLE TO GET BACK THROUGH THAT AIR DUCT.
WE DON'T HAVE MUCH TIME... PLEASE.
WELL...
ALL RIGHT.
I GUESS I OWE HIM.
FOLLOW ME...

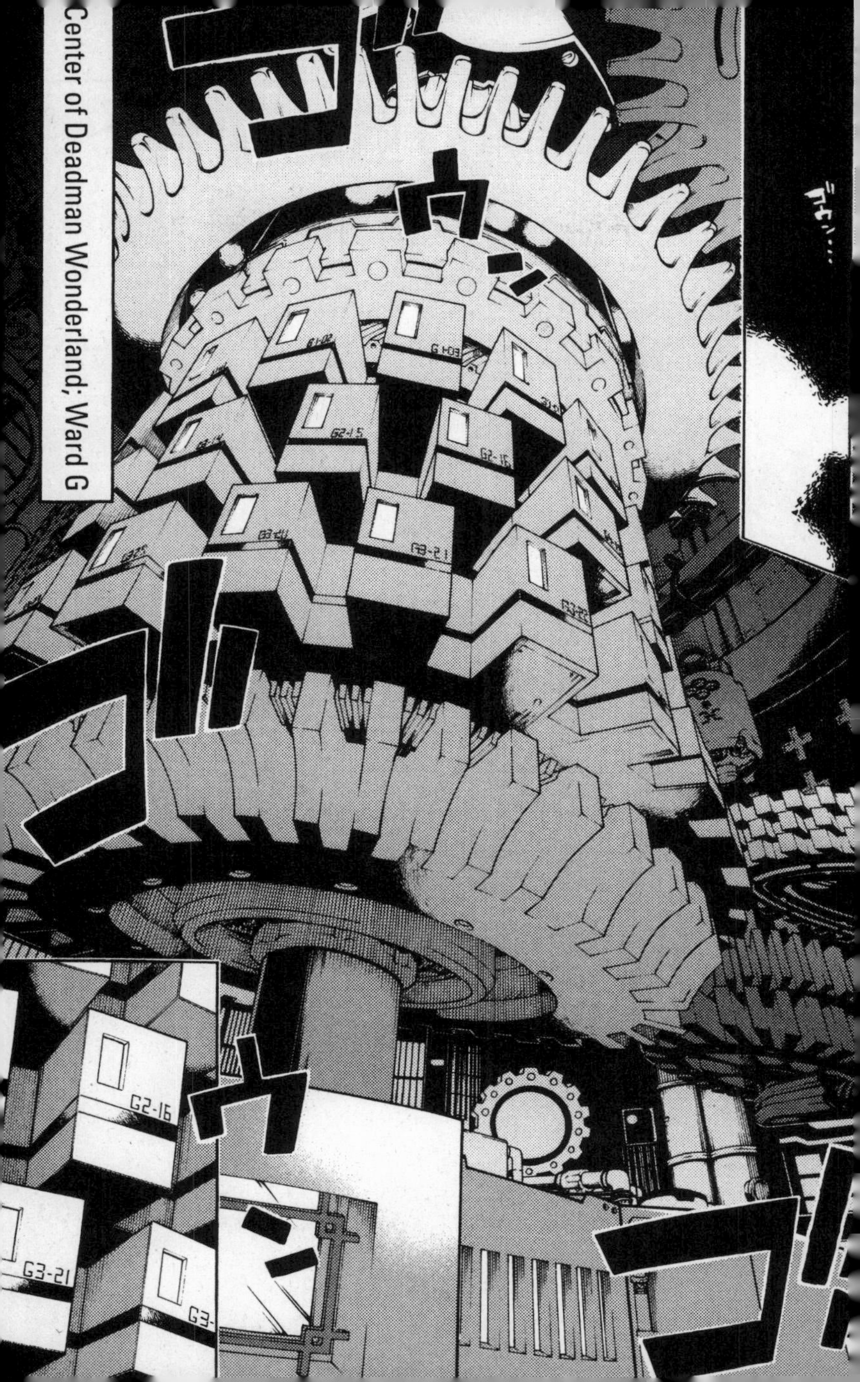
Center of Deadman Wonderland; Ward G
G2-16
G3-21

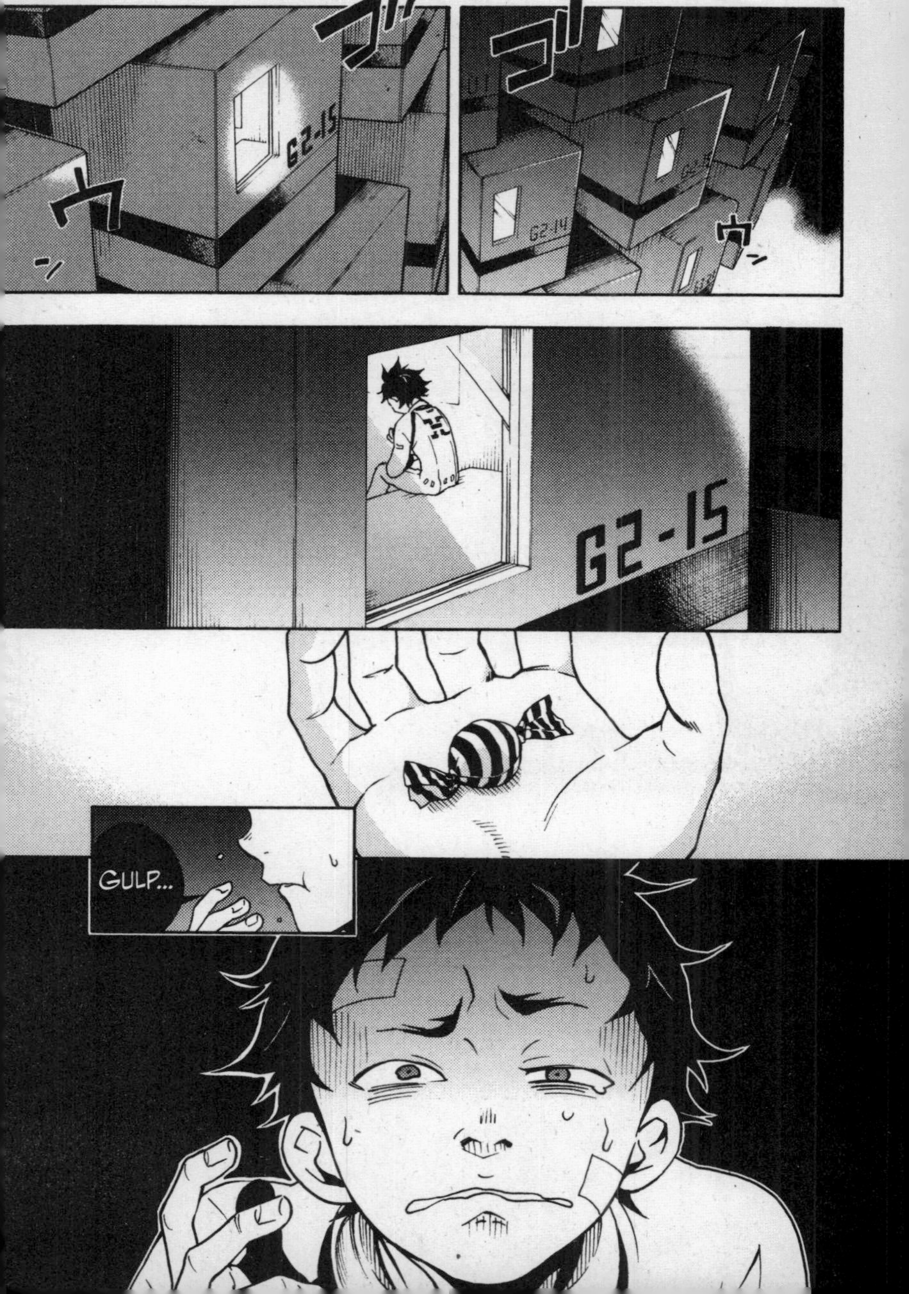
ゴ
G2-14
ウン
ゴ
G2-15
ウン
G2-15
GULP...

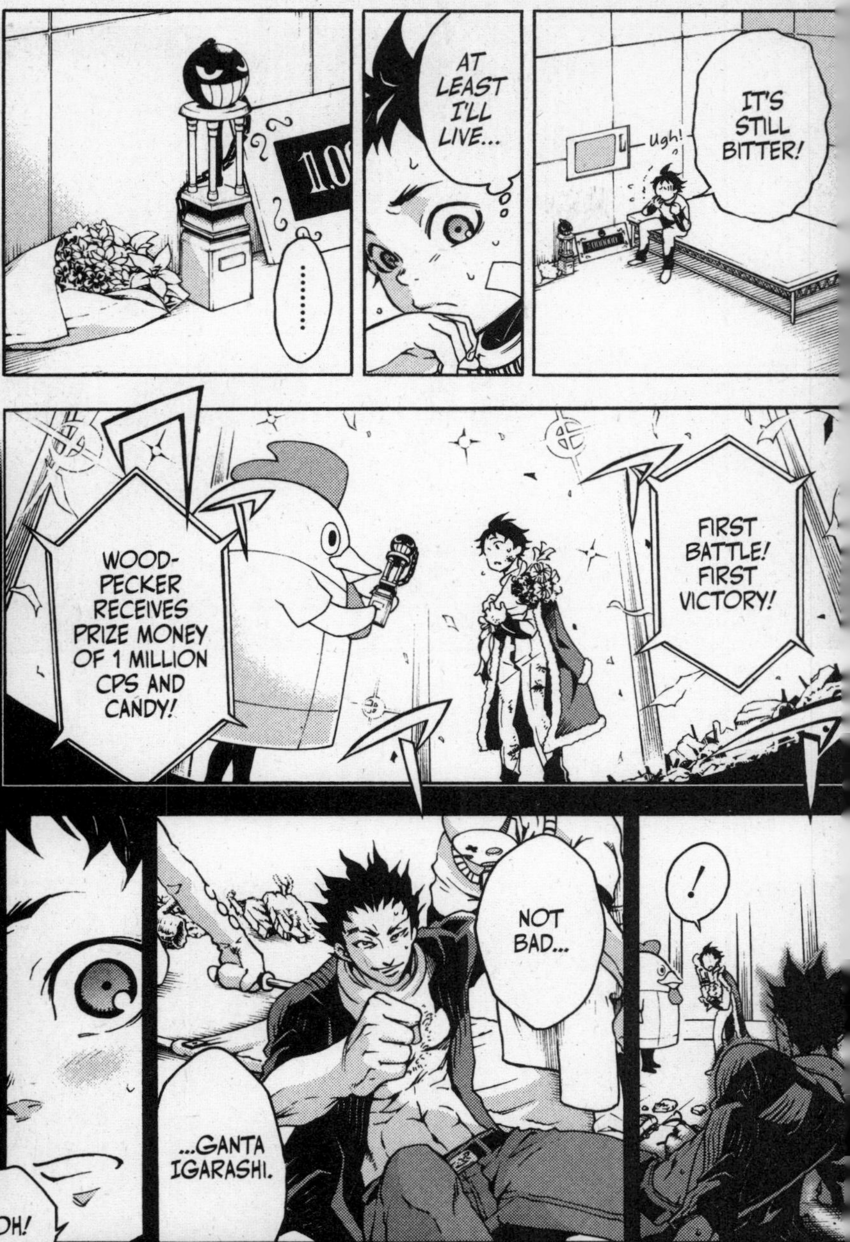
IT'S STILL BITTER!
Ugh!
AT LEAST I'LL LIVE...
......
FIRST BATTLE! FIRST VICTORY!
WOOD-PECKER RECEIVES PRIZE MONEY OF 1 MILLION CPS AND CANDY!
!
NOT BAD...
...GANTA IGARASHI.
OH!

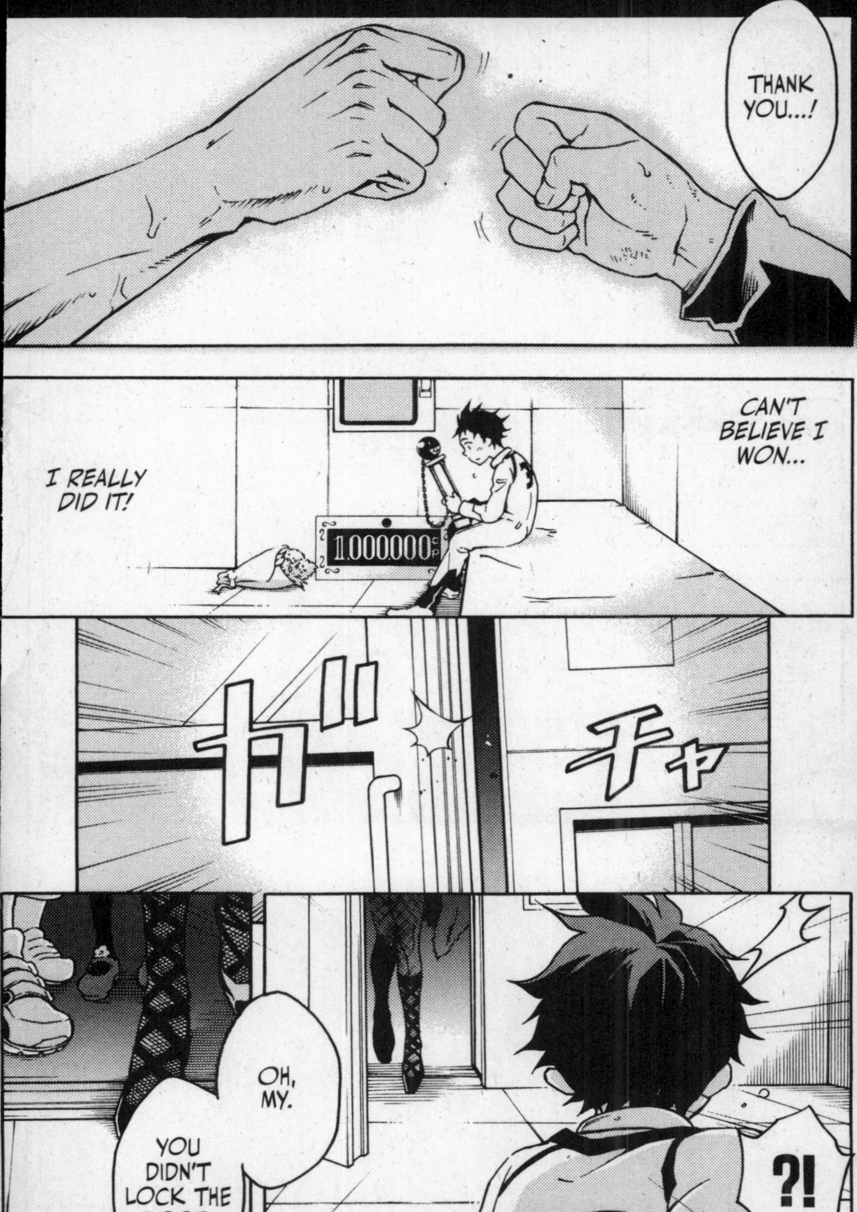
THANK YOU...!
CAN'T BELIEVE I WON...
I REALLY DID IT!
1,000,000
ガ
チャ
?!
OH, MY.
YOU DIDN'T LOCK THE DOOR. SILLY.

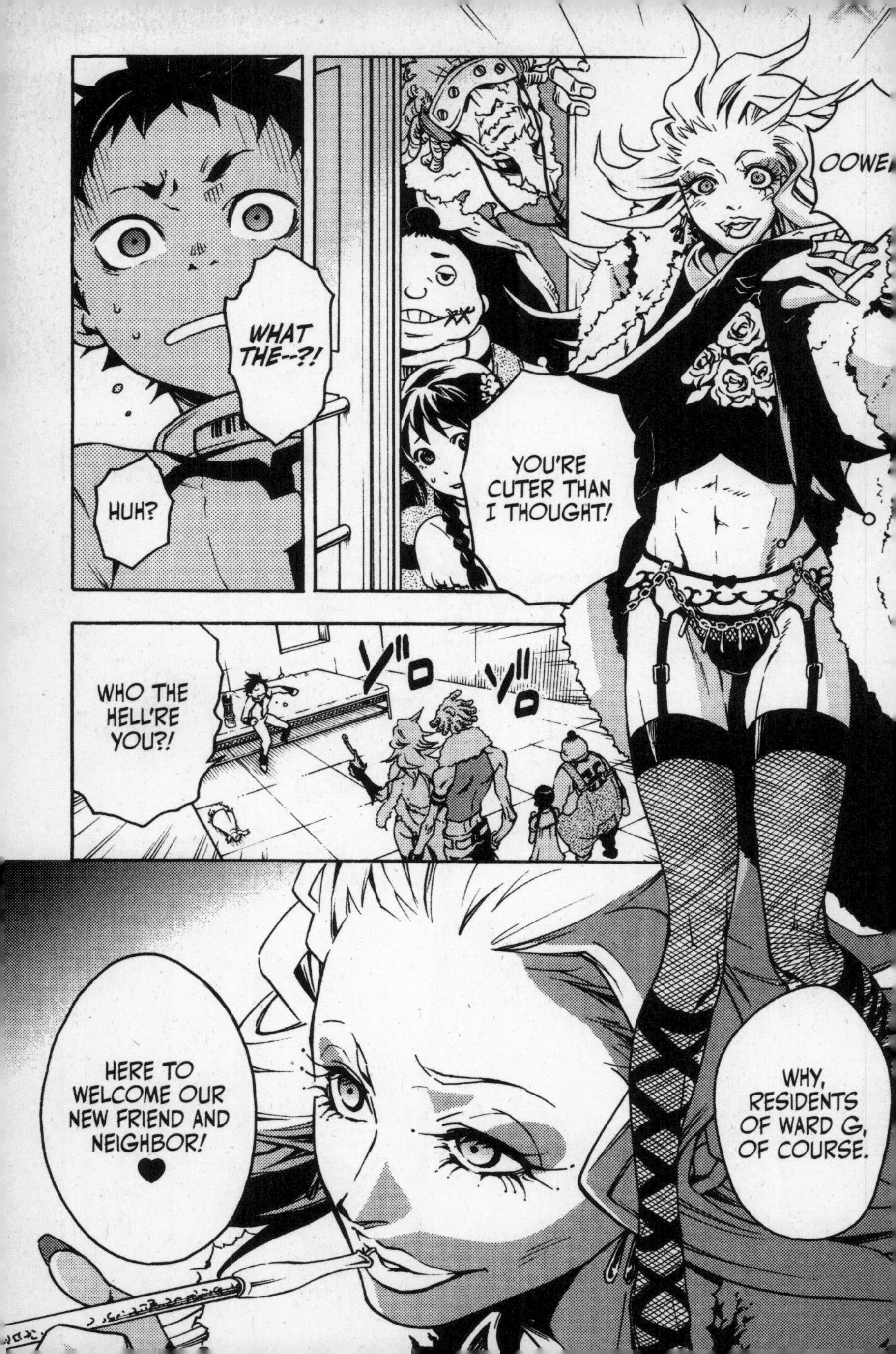

OOWE
YOU'RE CUTER THAN I THOUGHT!
WHAT THE--?!
HUH?
ゾロ ゾロ
WHO THE HELL'RE YOU?!
WHY, RESIDENTS OF WARD G, OF COURSE.
HERE TO WELCOME OUR NEW FRIEND AND NEIGHBOR! ♥

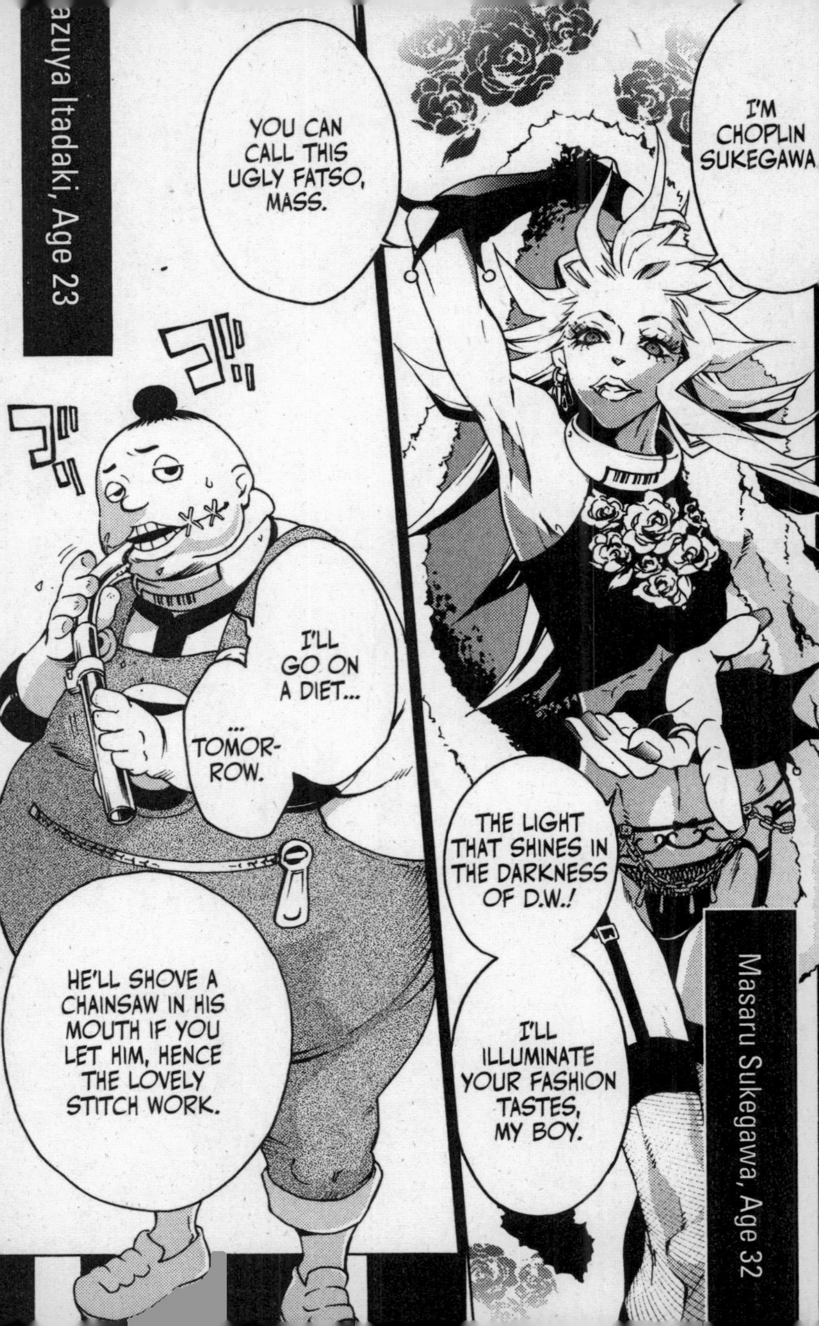
I'M CHOPLIN SUKEGAWA
THE LIGHT THAT SHINES IN THE DARKNESS OF D.W.!
I'LL ILLUMINATE YOUR FASHION TASTES, MY BOY.
Masaru Sukegawa, Age 32
YOU CAN CALL THIS UGLY FATSO, MASS.
I'LL GO ON A DIET...
...TOMORROW.
HE'LL SHOVE A CHAINSAW IN HIS MOUTH IF YOU LET HIM, HENCE THE LOVELY STITCH WORK.
azuya Itadaki, Age 23

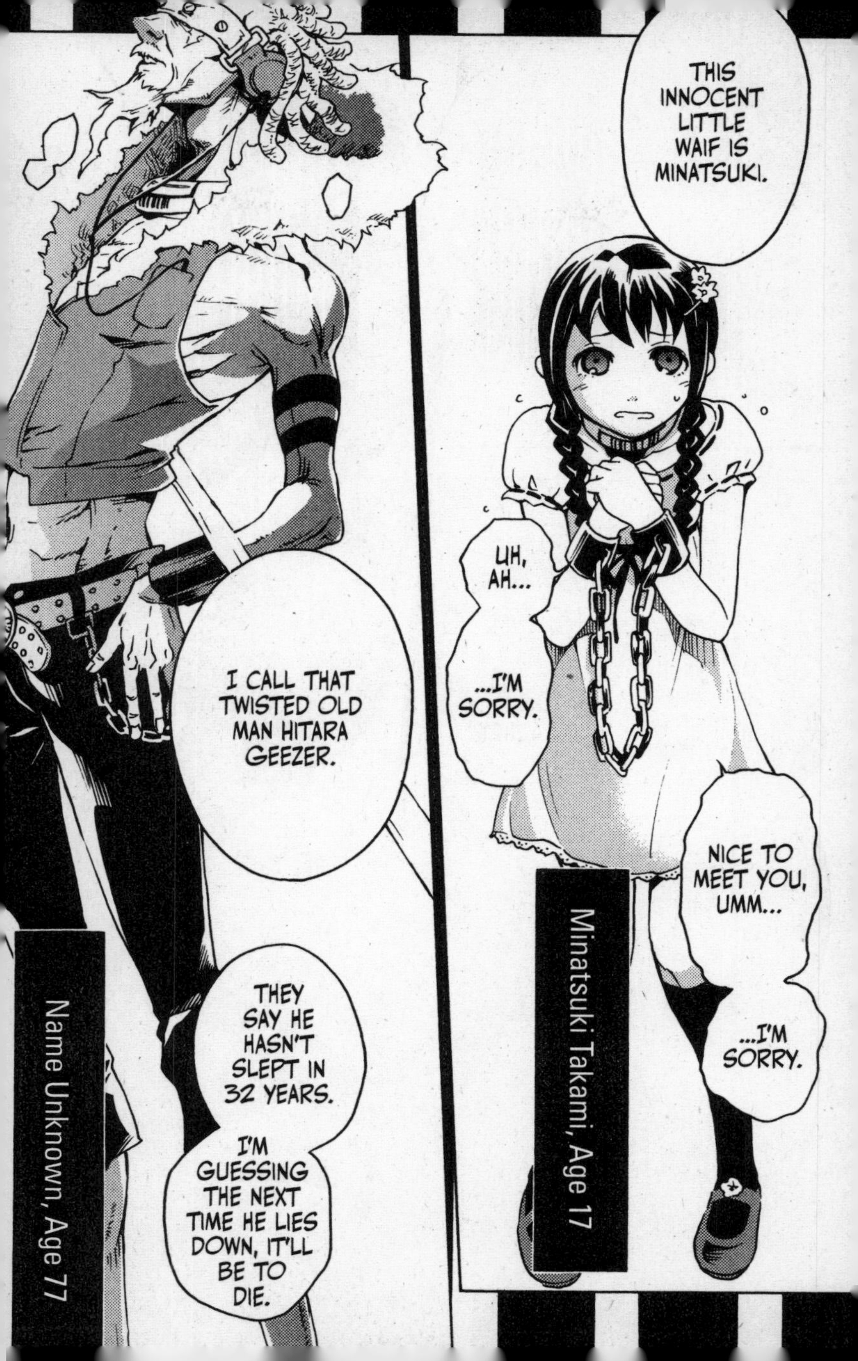
THIS INNOCENT LITTLE WAIF IS MINATSUKI.
UH, AH...
...I'M SORRY.
NICE TO MEET YOU, UMM...
...I'M SORRY.
Minatsuki Takami, Age 17
I CALL THAT TWISTED OLD MAN HITARA GEEZER.
THEY SAY HE HASN'T SLEPT IN 32 YEARS.
I'M GUESSING THE NEXT TIME HE LIES DOWN, IT'LL BE TO DIE.
Name Unknown, Age 17

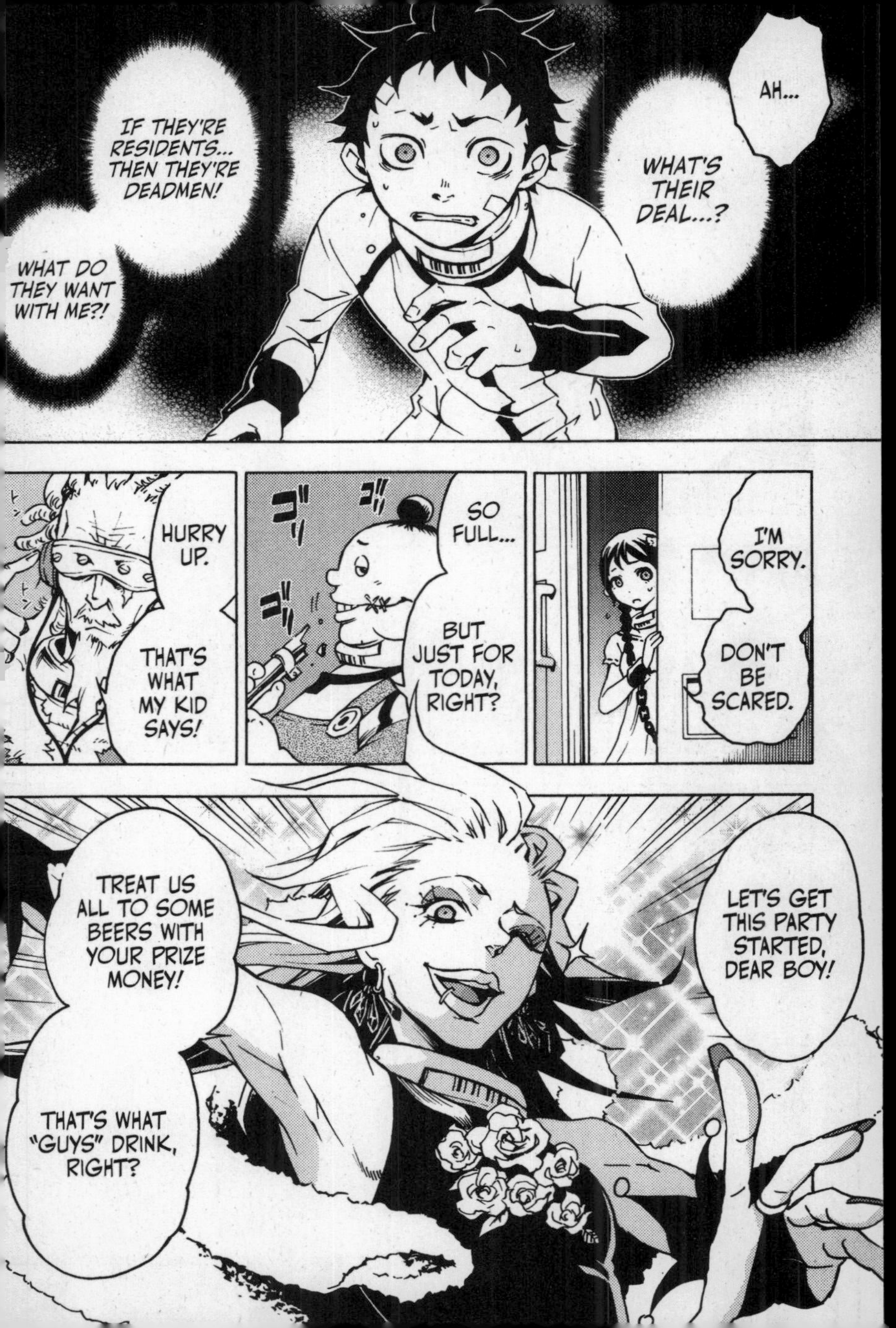
AH...
WHAT'S THEIR DEAL...?
IF THEY'RE RESIDENTS... THEN THEY'RE DEADMEN!
WHAT DO THEY WANT WITH ME?!
I'M SORRY.
DON'T BE SCARED.
SO FULL...
BUT JUST FOR TODAY, RIGHT?
HURRY UP.
THAT'S WHAT MY KID SAYS!
LET'S GET THIS PARTY STARTED, DEAR BOY!
TREAT US ALL TO SOME BEERS WITH YOUR PRIZE MONEY!
THAT'S WHAT "GUYS" DRINK, RIGHT?

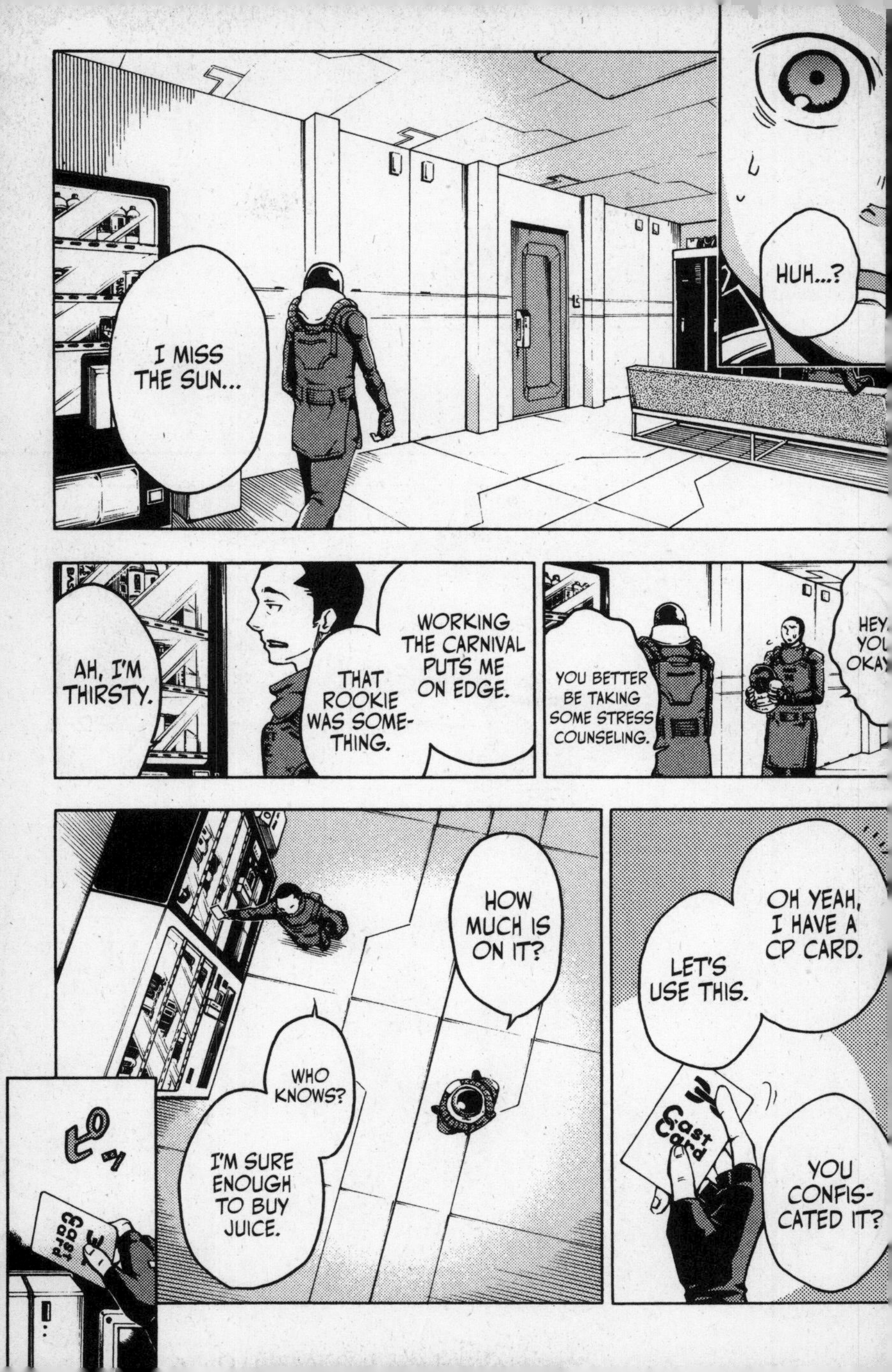
HUH...?
I MISS THE SUN...
HEY. OKAY
YOU BETTER BE TAKING SOME STRESS COUNSELING.
WORKING THE CARNIVAL PUTS ME ON EDGE.
THAT ROOKIE WAS SOME-THING.
AH, I'M THIRSTY.
OH YEAH, I HAVE A CP CARD.
LET'S USE THIS.
Cast Card
YOU CONFIS-CATED IT?
HOW MUCH IS ON IT?
WHO KNOWS?
I'M SURE ENOUGH TO BUY JUICE.
ピッ
Cast Card

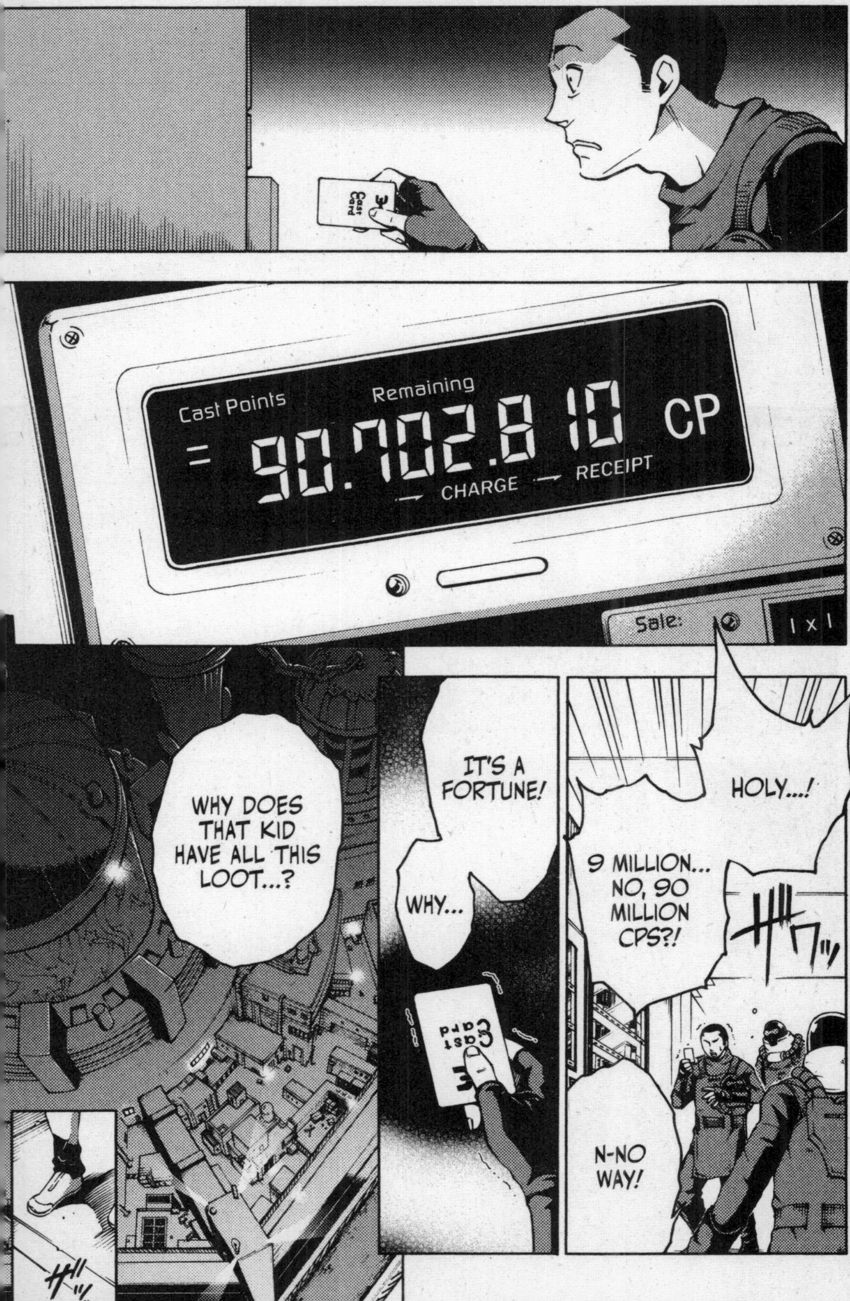
Cast Card
Cast Points
Remaining
= 90.702.810 CP
CHARGE
RECEIPT
Sale:
1x1
HOLY...!
9 MILLION... NO, 90 MILLION CPS?!
ザワッ
N-NO WAY!
IT'S A FORTUNE!
WHY...
Cast Card
WHY DOES THAT KID HAVE ALL THIS LOOT...?
ザッ

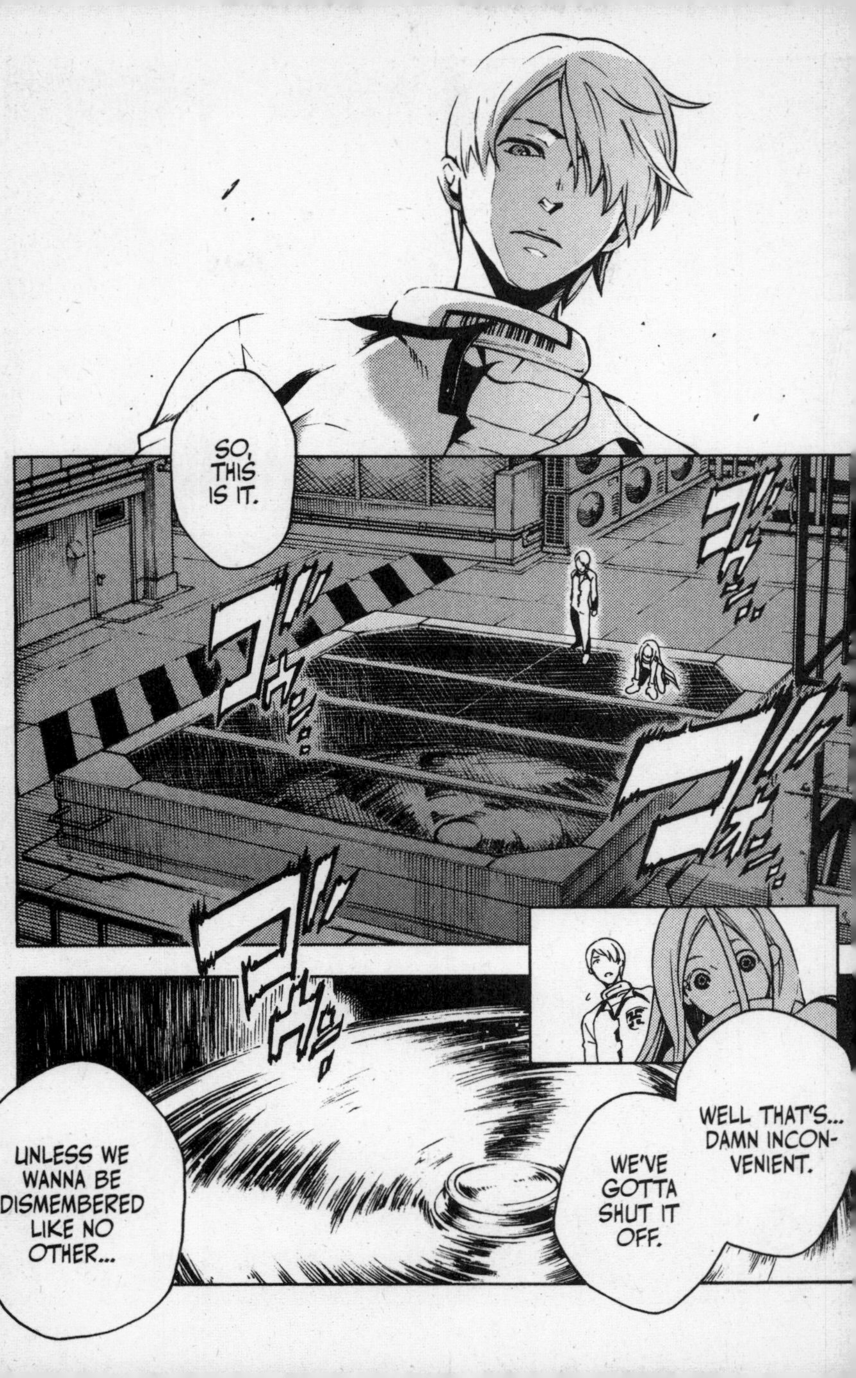
SO, THIS IS IT.
WELL THAT'S... DAMN INCON-VENIENT.
WE'VE GOTTA SHUT IT OFF.
UNLESS WE WANNA BE DISMEMBERED LIKE NO OTHER...

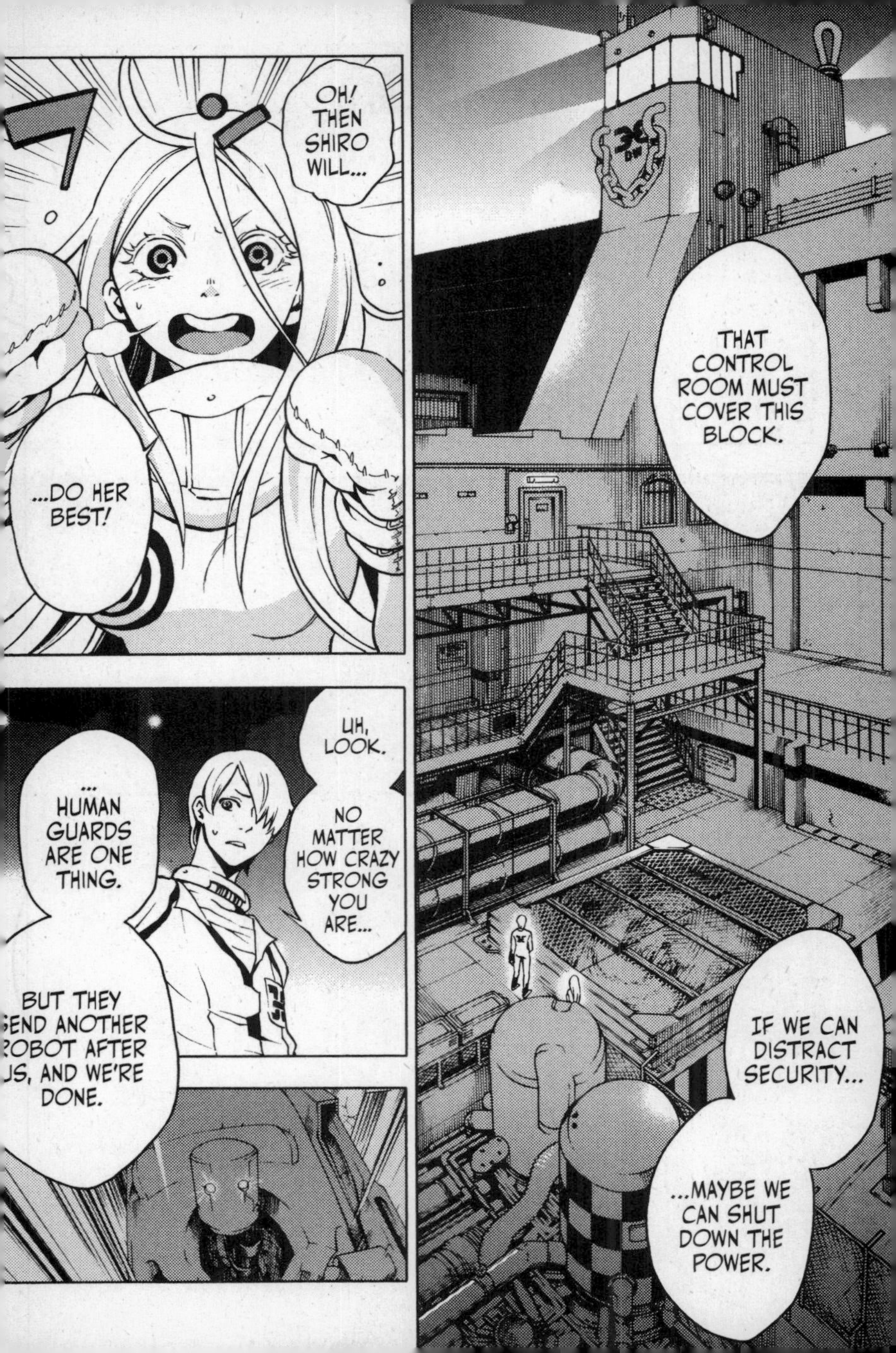
THAT CONTROL ROOM MUST COVER THIS BLOCK.
IF WE CAN DISTRACT SECURITY...
...MAYBE WE CAN SHUT DOWN THE POWER.
OH! THEN SHIRO WILL...
...DO HER BEST!
UH, LOOK.
NO MATTER HOW CRAZY STRONG YOU ARE...
... HUMAN GUARDS ARE ONE THING.
BUT THEY SEND ANOTHER ROBOT AFTER US, AND WE'RE DONE.

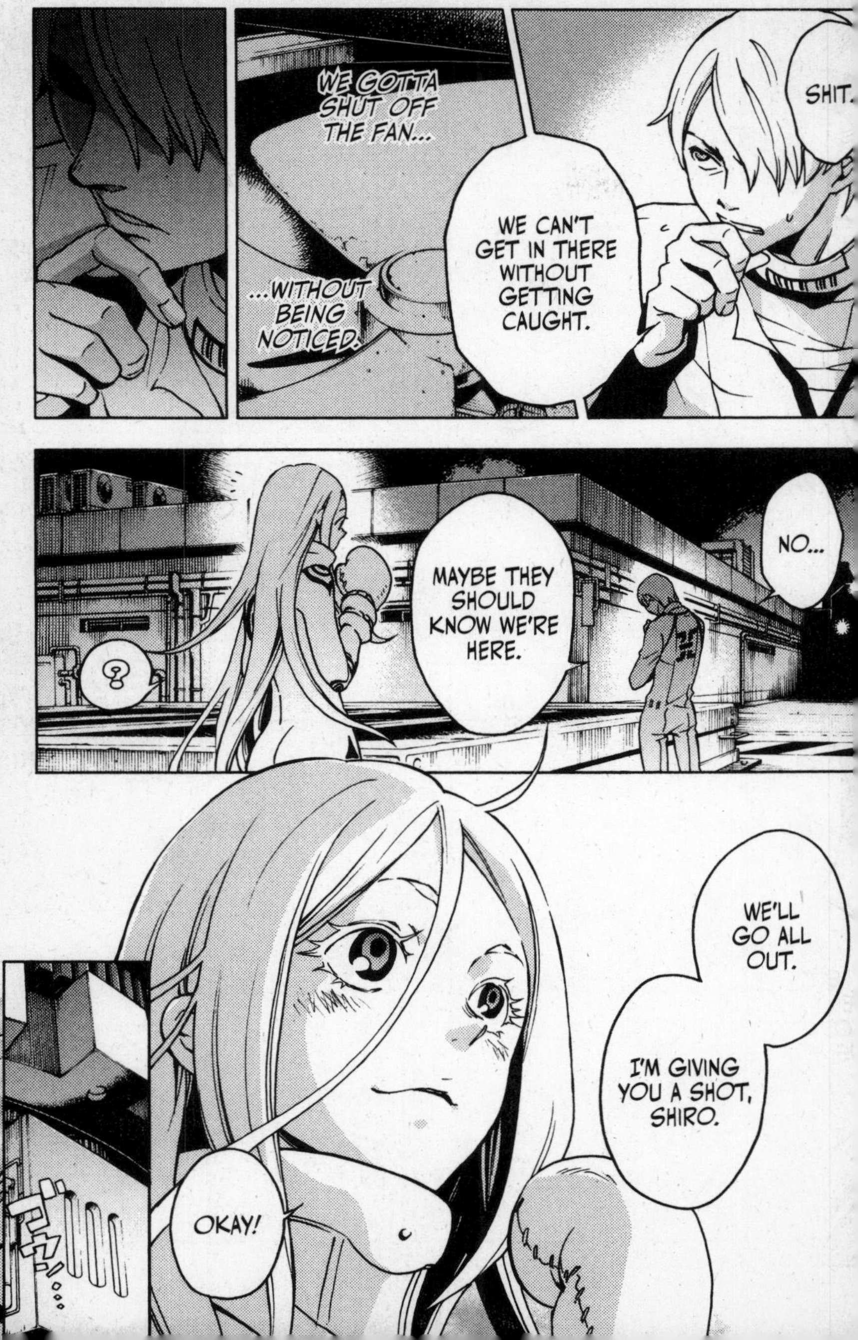
SHIT.
WE CAN'T GET IN THERE WITHOUT GETTING CAUGHT.
WE GOTTA SHUT OFF THE FAN...
...WITHOUT BEING NOTICED.
NO...
MAYBE THEY SHOULD KNOW WE'RE HERE.
?
WE'LL GO ALL OUT.
I'M GIVING YOU A SHOT, SHIRO.
OKAY!

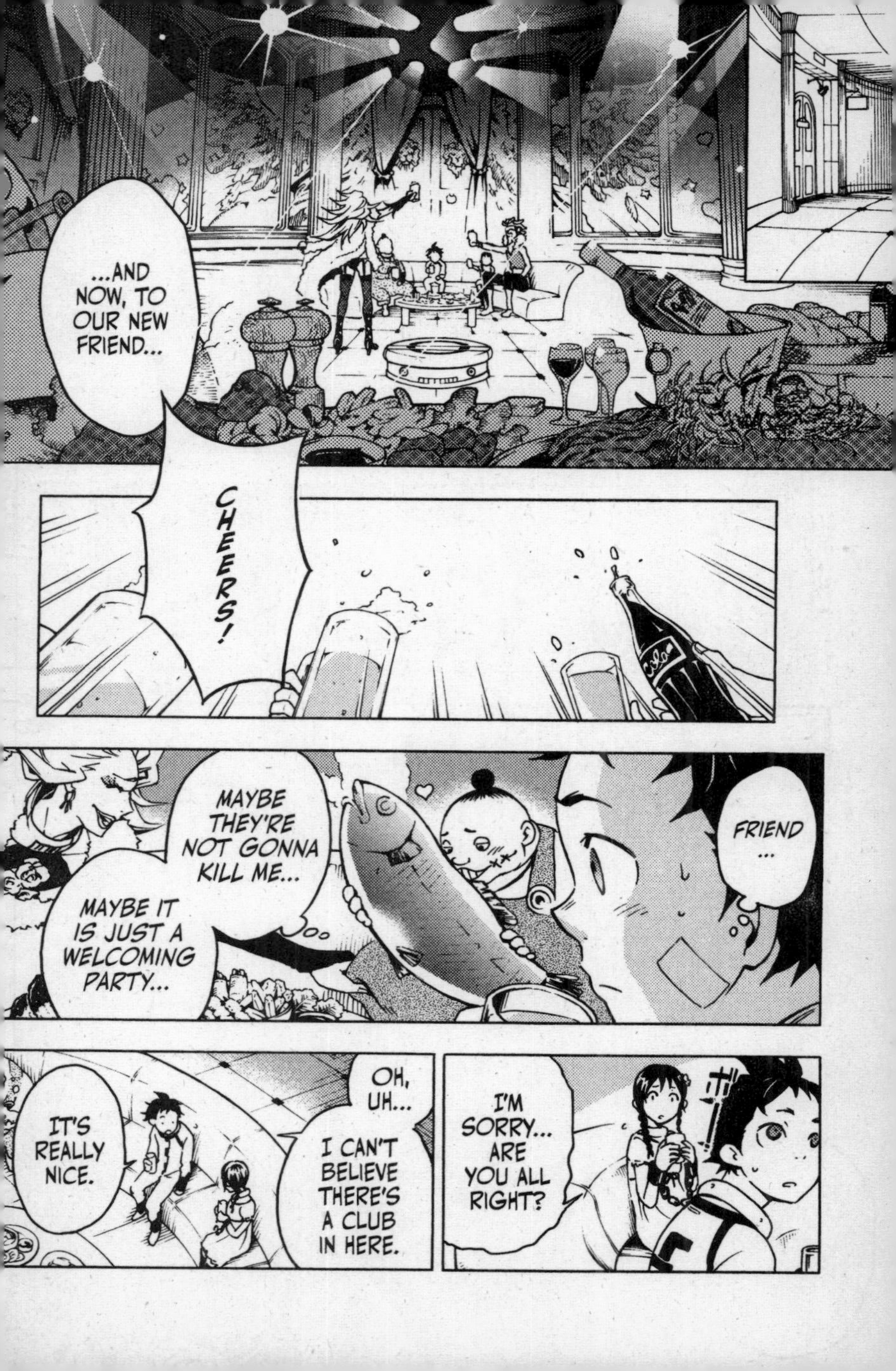
...AND NOW, TO OUR NEW FRIEND...
CHEERS!
FRIEND ...
MAYBE THEY'RE NOT GONNA KILL ME...
MAYBE IT IS JUST A WELCOMING PARTY...
I'M SORRY... ARE YOU ALL RIGHT?
OH, UH...
I CAN'T BELIEVE THERE'S A CLUB IN HERE.
IT'S REALLY NICE.

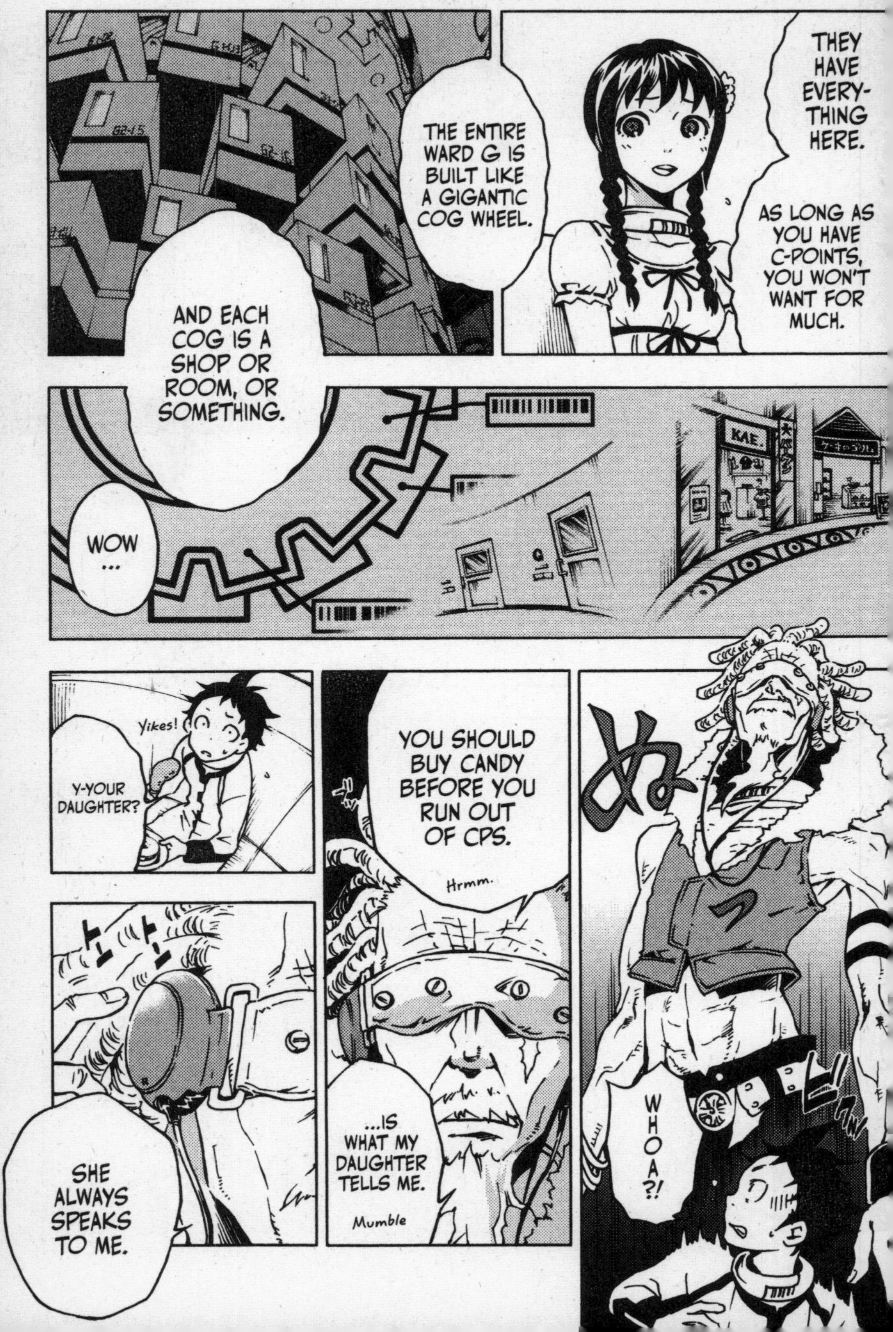
THEY HAVE EVERY-THING HERE.
AS LONG AS YOU HAVE C-POINTS, YOU WON'T WANT FOR MUCH.
THE ENTIRE WARD G IS BUILT LIKE A GIGANTIC COG WHEEL.
AND EACH COG IS A SHOP OR ROOM, OR SOMETHING.
KAE.
WOW ...
ぬ
WHOA?!
YOU SHOULD BUY CANDY BEFORE YOU RUN OUT OF CPS.
Hrmm.
...IS WHAT MY DAUGHTER TELLS ME.
Mumble
Yikes!
Y-YOUR DAUGHTER?
SHE ALWAYS SPEAKS TO ME.

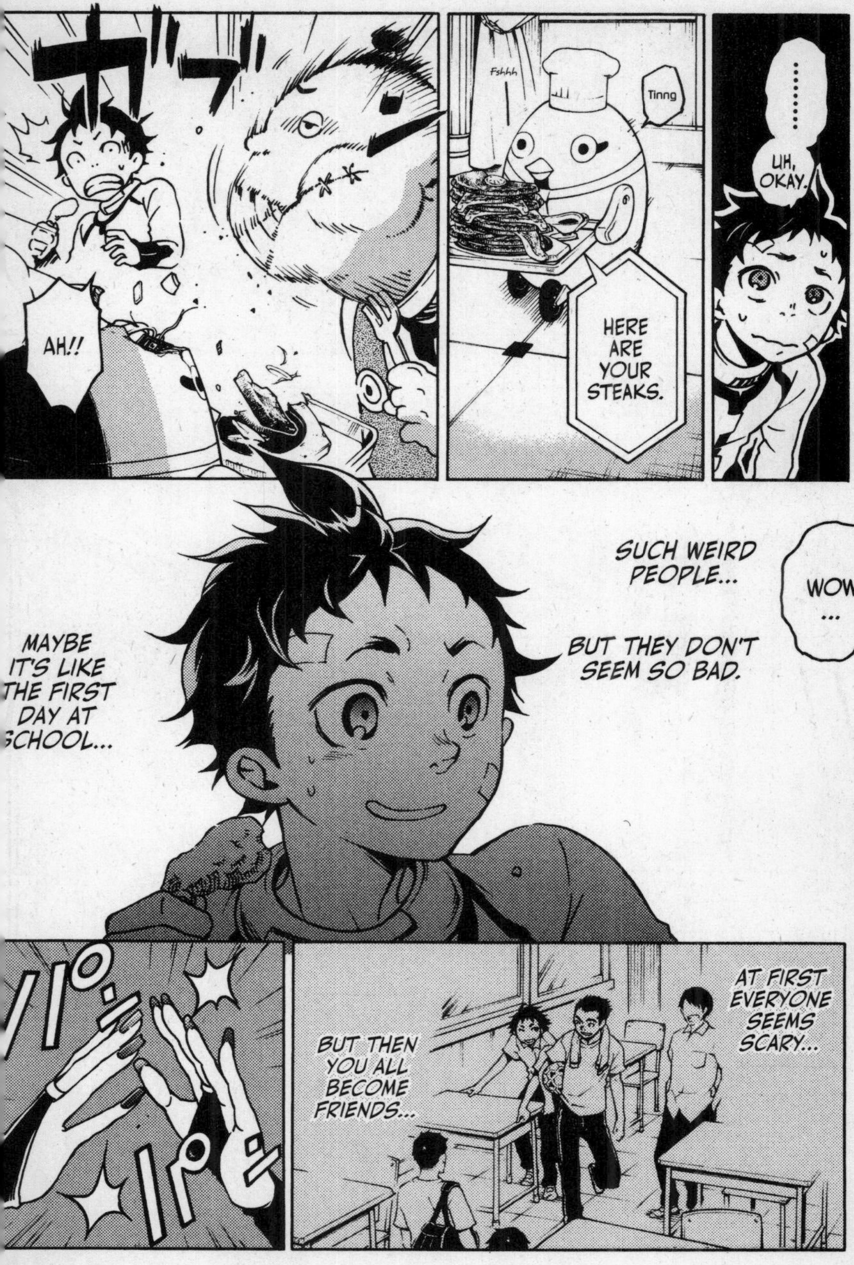
......!
UH, OKAY.
Fshhh
Tinng
HERE ARE YOUR STEAKS.
AH!!
WOW ...
SUCH WEIRD PEOPLE...
BUT THEY DON'T SEEM SO BAD.
MAYBE IT'S LIKE THE FIRST DAY AT SCHOOL...
AT FIRST EVERYONE SEEMS SCARY...
BUT THEN YOU ALL BECOME FRIENDS...

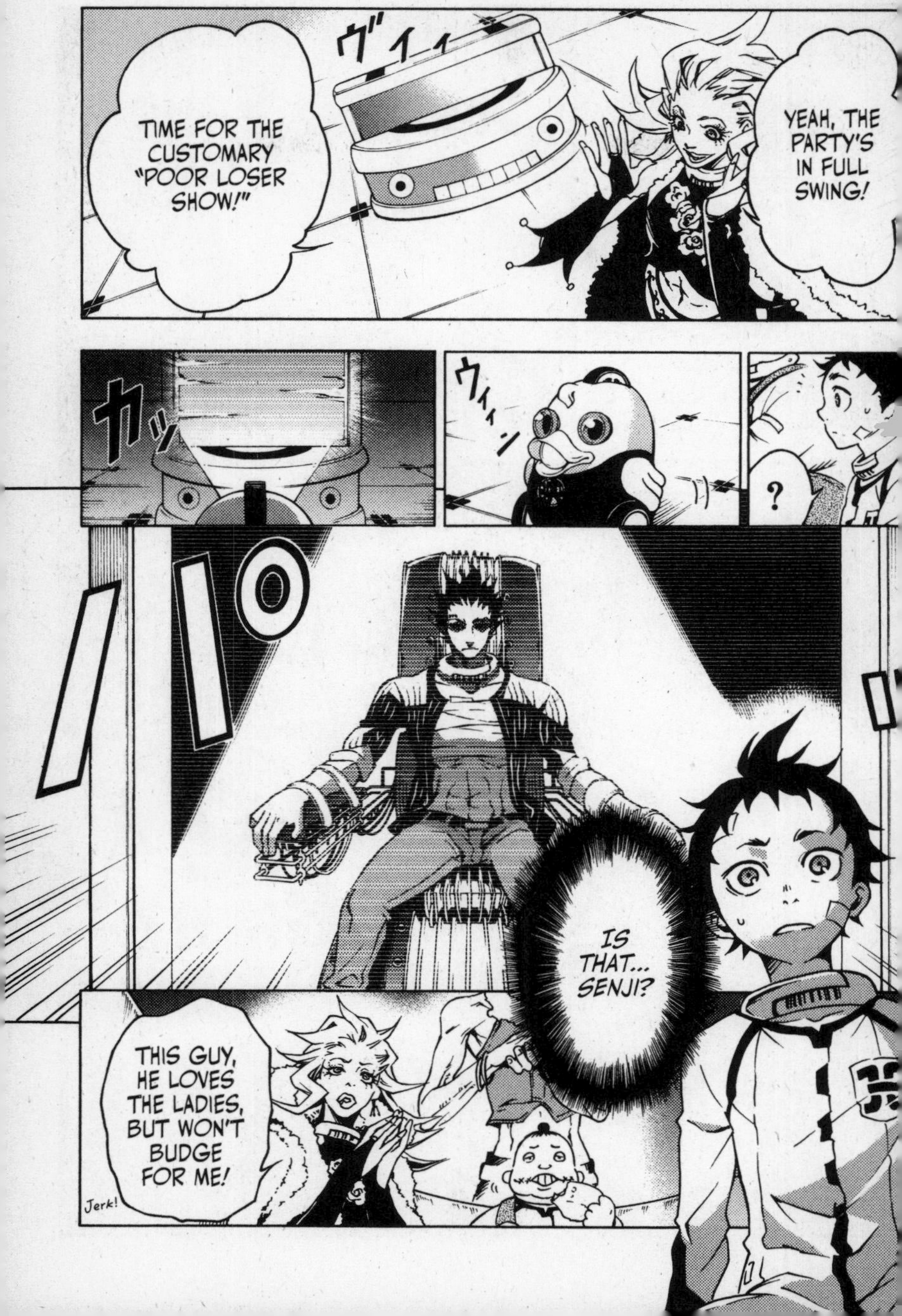
YEAH, THE PARTY'S IN FULL SWING!
ヴィィ
TIME FOR THE CUSTOMARY "POOR LOSER SHOW!"
?
ウィィン
カッ
IS THAT... SENJI?
パッ
THIS GUY, HE LOVES THE LADIES, BUT WON'T BUDGE FOR ME!
Jerk!

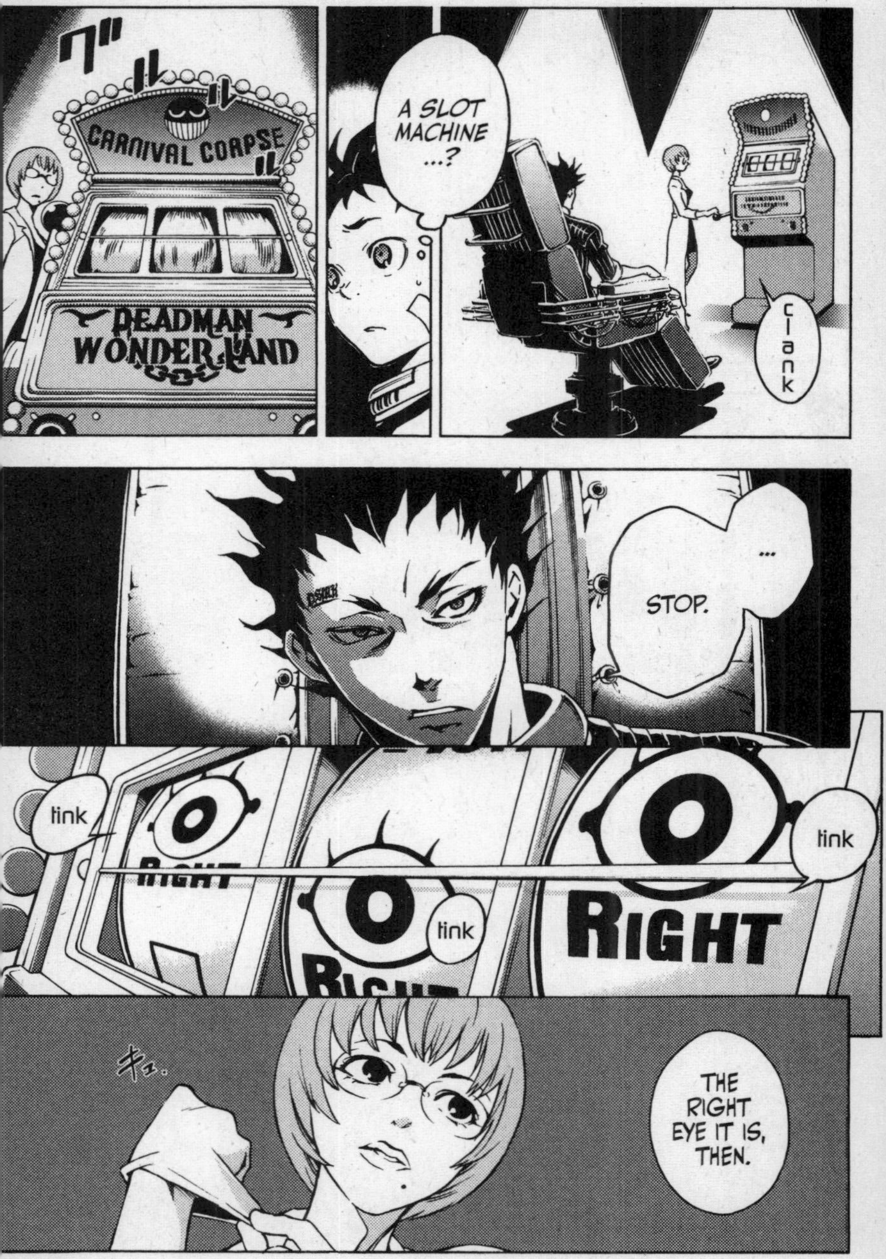
clank
A SLOT MACHINE ...?
CARNIVAL CORPSE
DEADMAN WONDER LAND
... STOP.
tink
tink
tink
RIGHT
キュ。
THE RIGHT EYE IT IS, THEN.

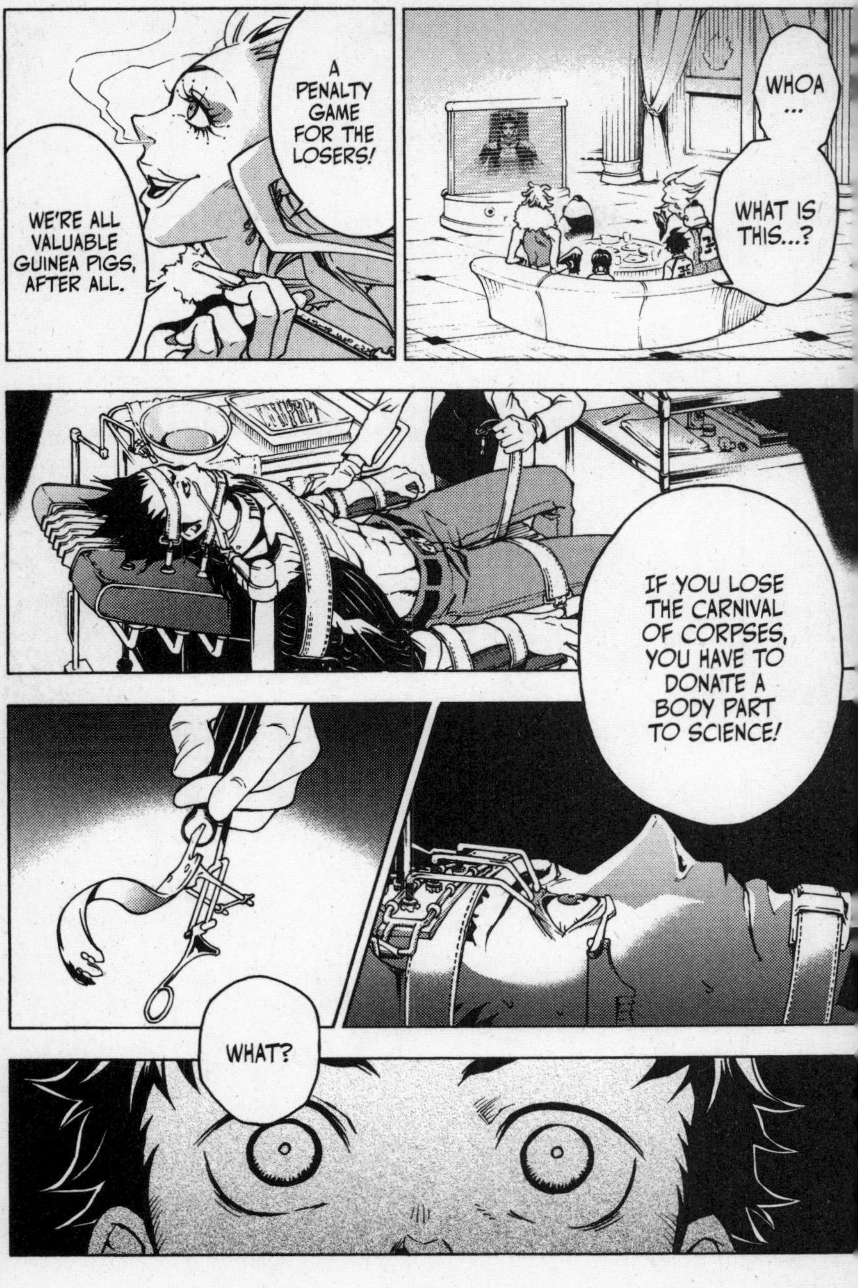
WHOA ...
WHAT IS THIS...?
A PENALTY GAME FOR THE LOSERS!
WE'RE ALL VALUABLE GUINEA PIGS, AFTER ALL.
IF YOU LOSE THE CARNIVAL OF CORPSES, YOU HAVE TO DONATE A BODY PART TO SCIENCE!
WHAT?

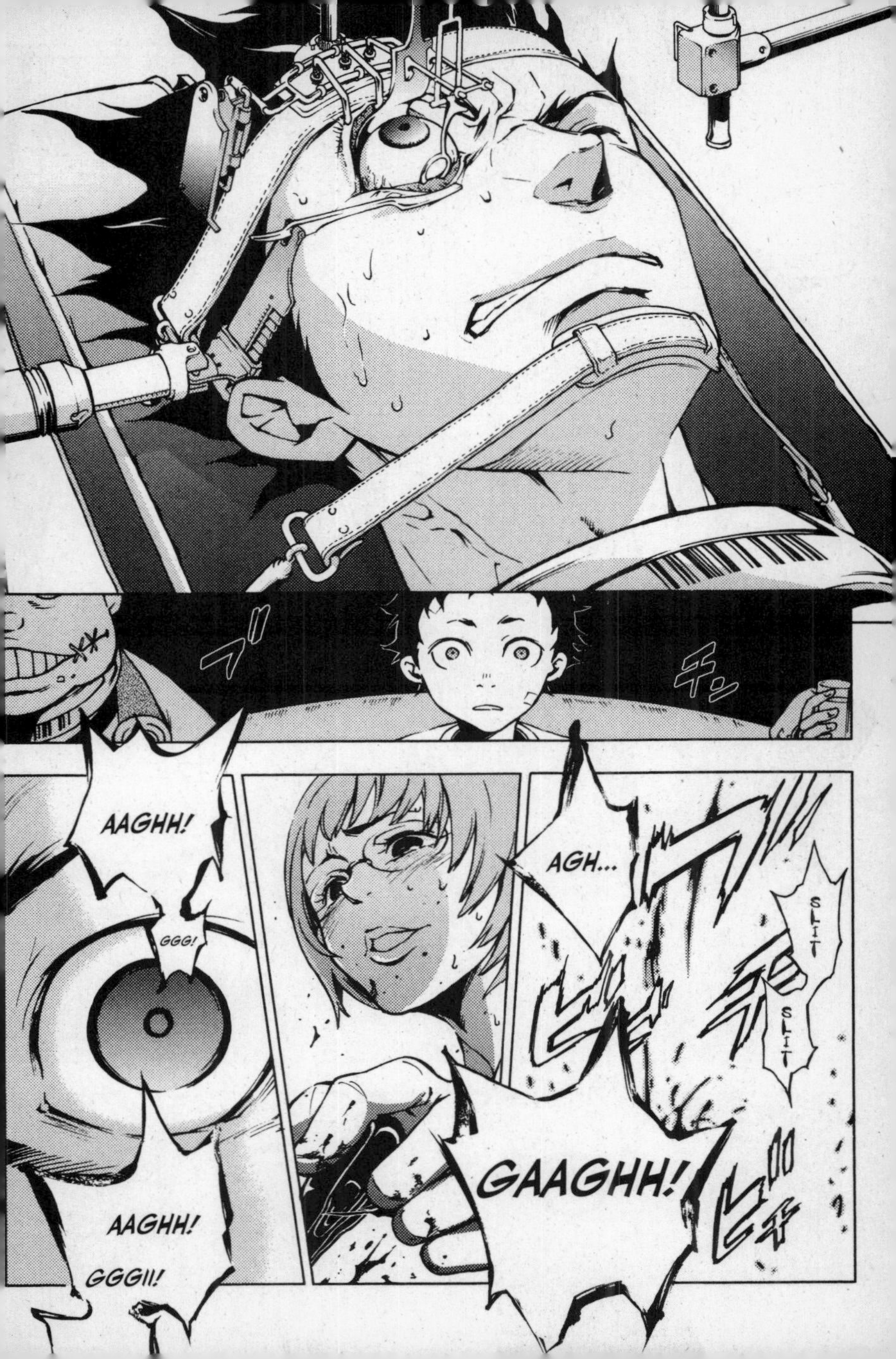
チン
ブ
AGH...
SLIT
SLIT
GAAGHH!
AAGHH!
GGG!
AAGHH!
GGGII!

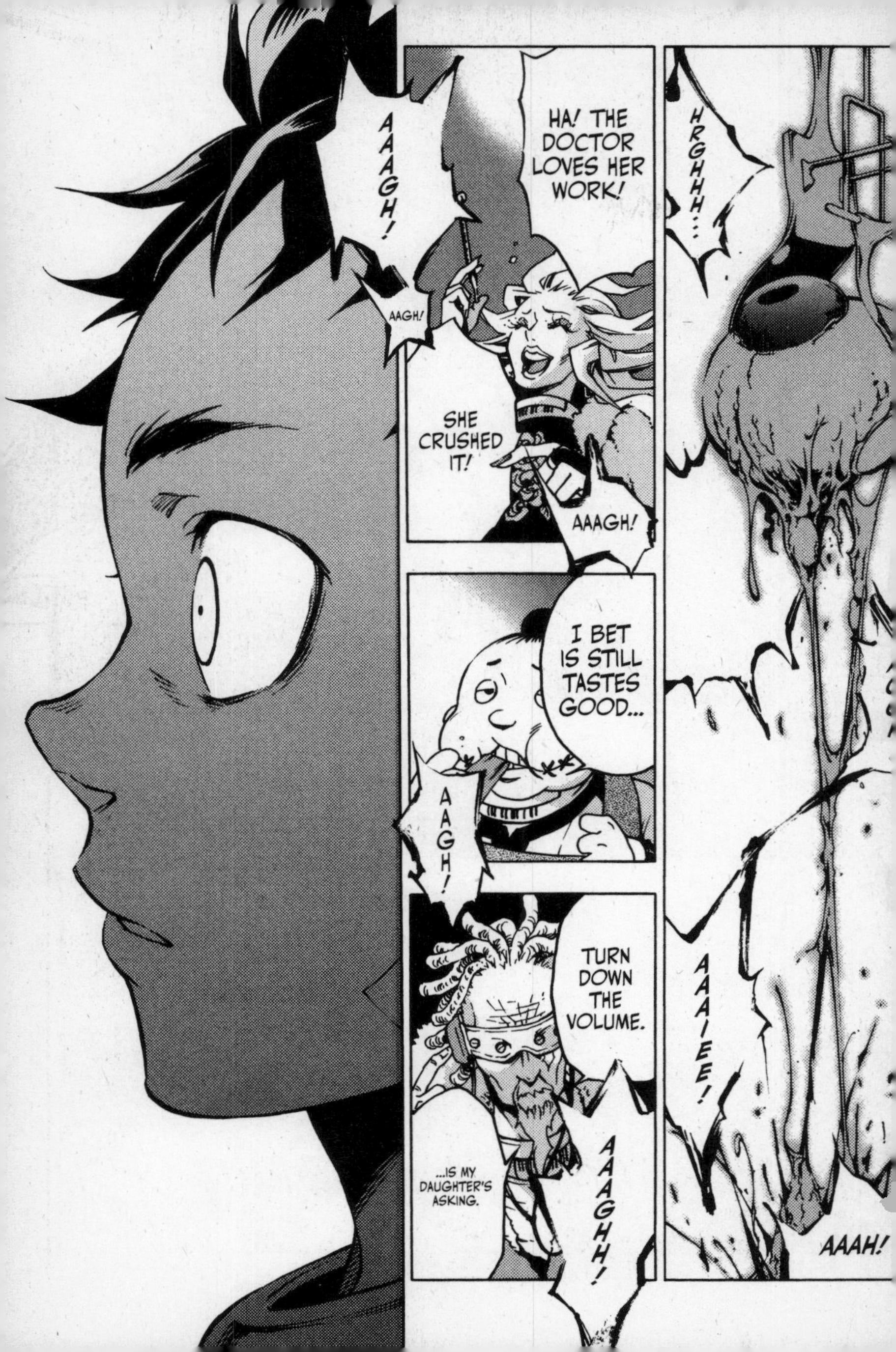
HRGHHH...
AAAIEE!
AAAH!
HA! THE DOCTOR LOVES HER WORK!
AAAAGH!
AAGH!
SHE CRUSHED IT!
AAAGH!
I BET IS STILL TASTES GOOD...
AAGH!
TURN DOWN THE VOLUME.
AAAAGHH!
...IS MY DAUGHTER'S ASKING.

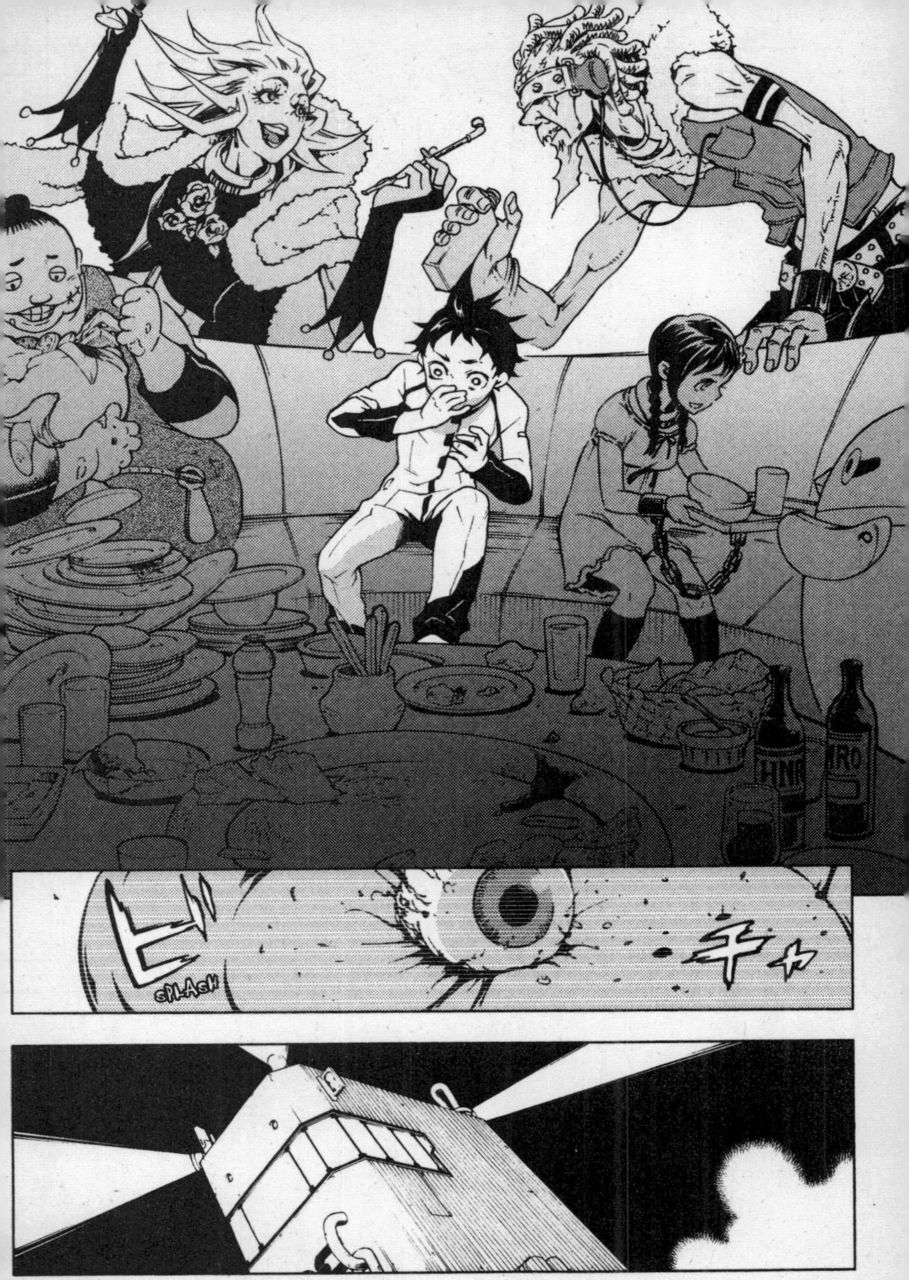
チャ
ビ
SPLASH

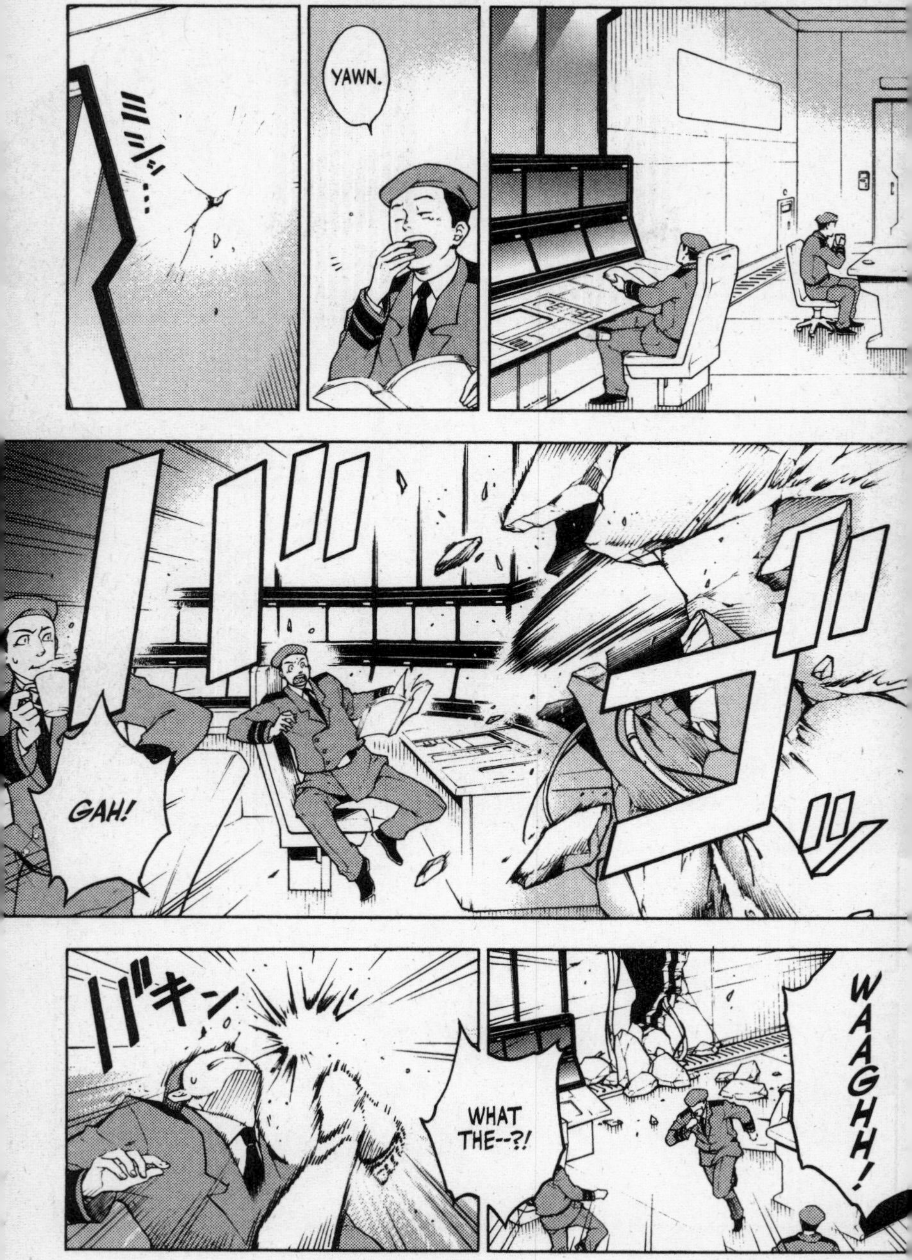
YAWN.
ミシッ…
GAH!
WAAGHH!
WHAT THE--?!
バキン

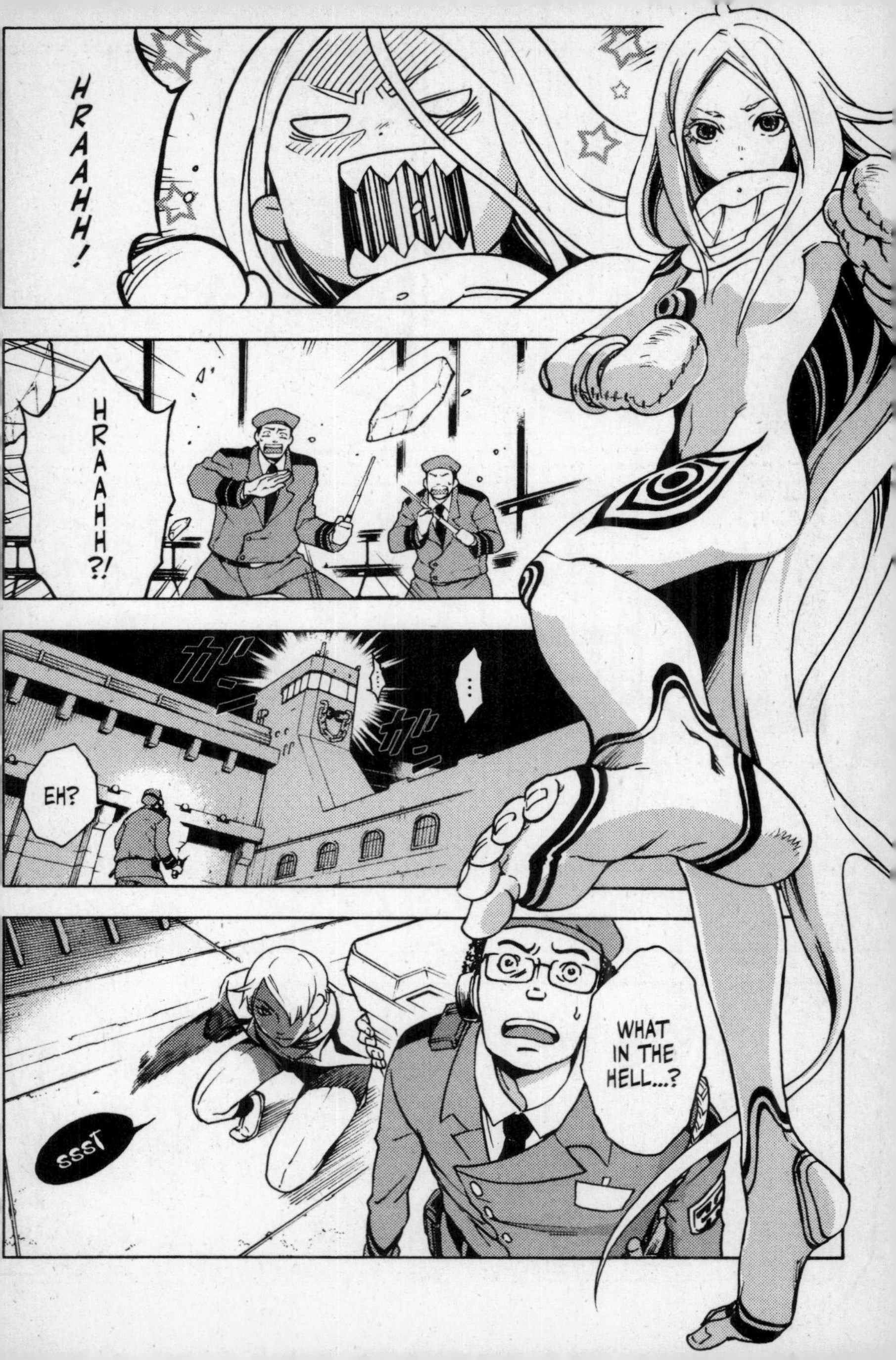
HRAAAHH!
HRAAAHH?!
...
...
ガーン
ガーン
EH?
WHAT IN THE HELL...?
SSST

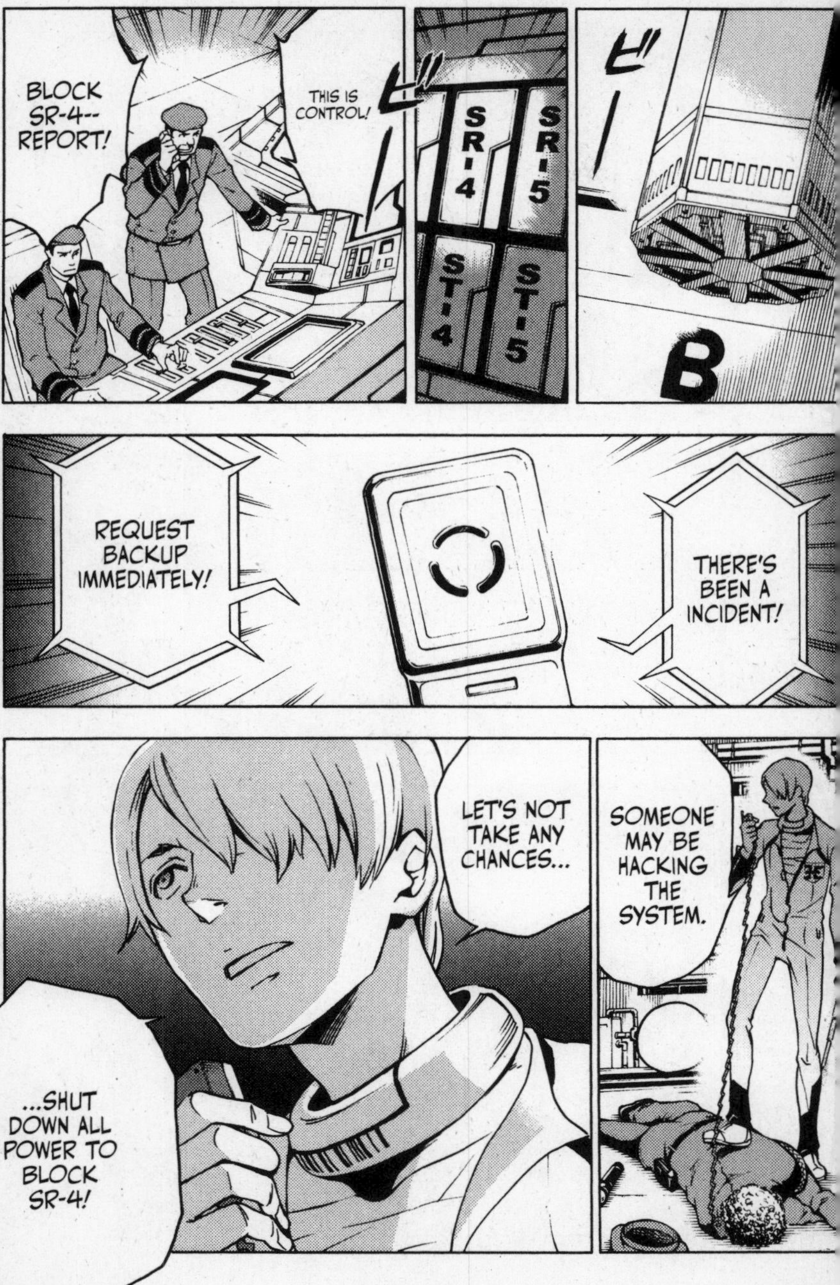
ビー
B
SR-4
SR-5
ST-4
ST-5
ビー
THIS IS CONTROL!
BLOCK SR-4-- REPORT!
THERE'S BEEN A INCIDENT!
REQUEST BACKUP IMMEDIATELY!
SOMEONE MAY BE HACKING THE SYSTEM.
LET'S NOT TAKE ANY CHANCES...
...SHUT DOWN ALL POWER TO BLOCK SR-4!

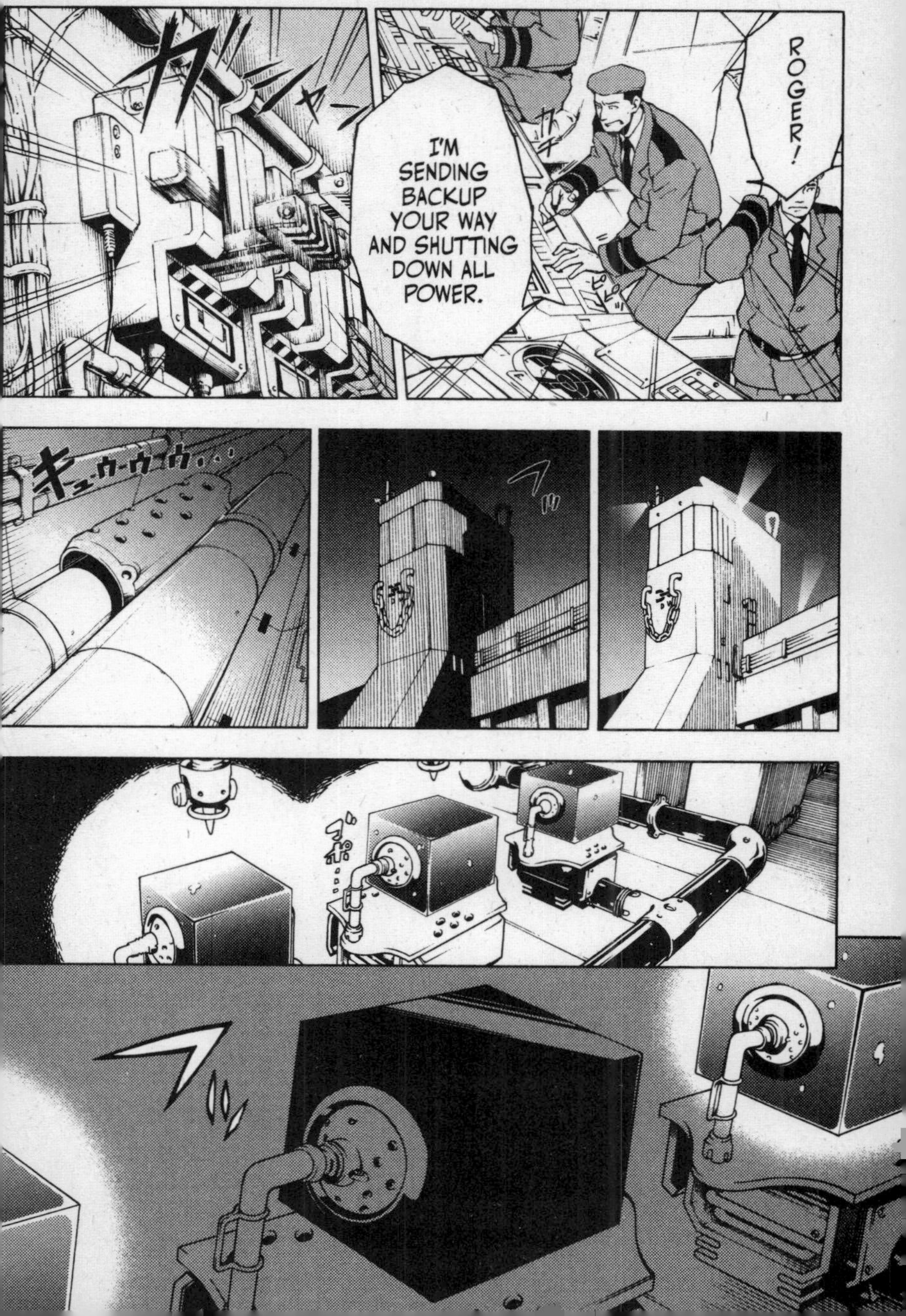
I'M SENDING BACKUP YOUR WAY AND SHUTTING DOWN ALL POWER.
ROGER!

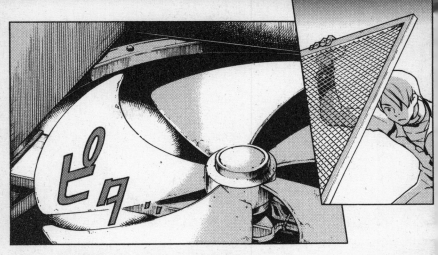

NOW I CAN GET TO WARD G...!

OKAY ...!

ALL THAT'S LEFT...

THIS IS HQ CONTROL ROOM...

HAVE YOU SPOTTED THE INTRUDER?

YES...

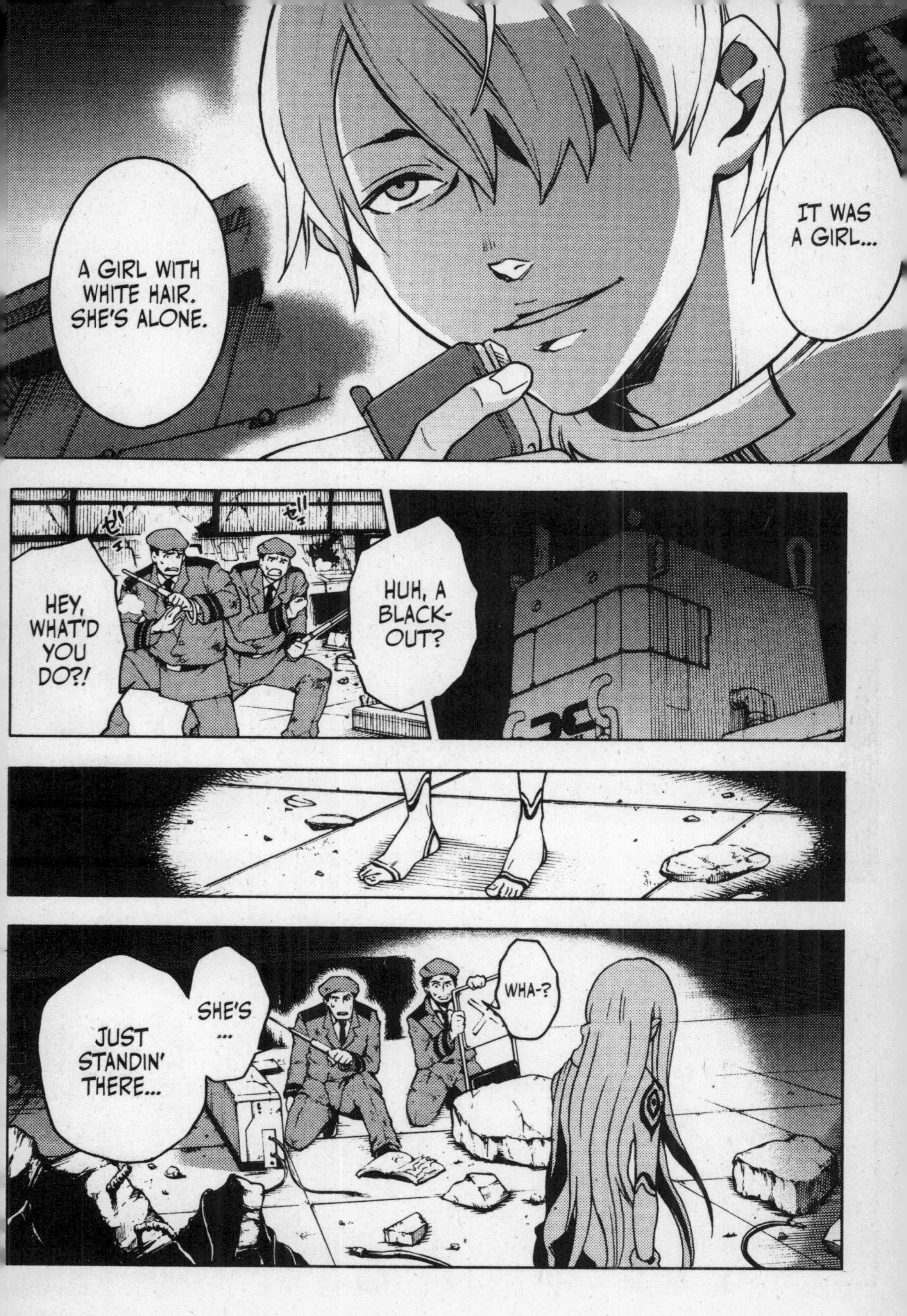
IT WAS A GIRL...
A GIRL WITH WHITE HAIR. SHE'S ALONE.
HUH, A BLACK-OUT?
HEY, WHAT'D YOU DO?!
WHA-?
SHE'S ... JUST STANDIN' THERE...

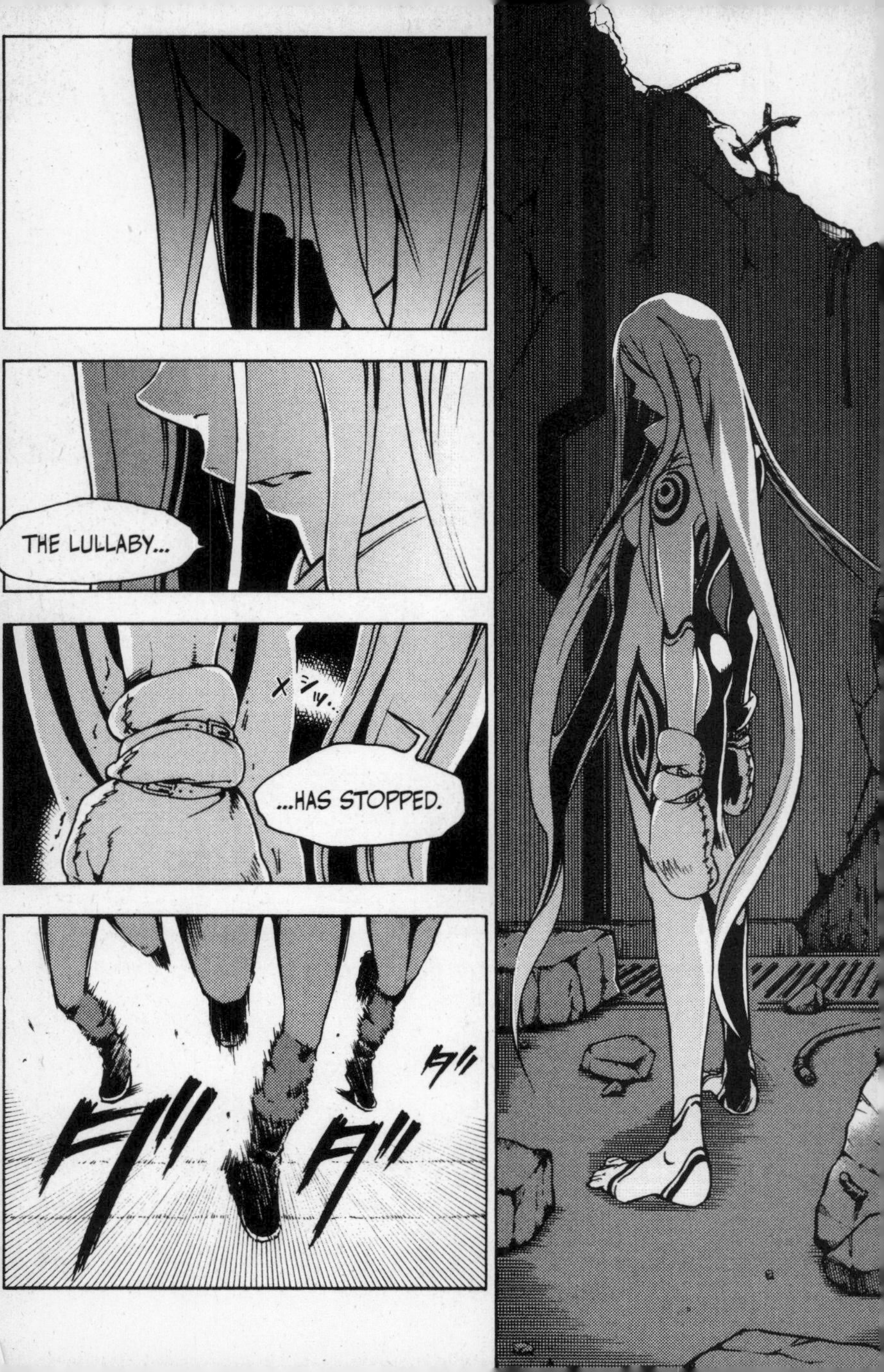
THE LULLABY...
...HAS STOPPED.

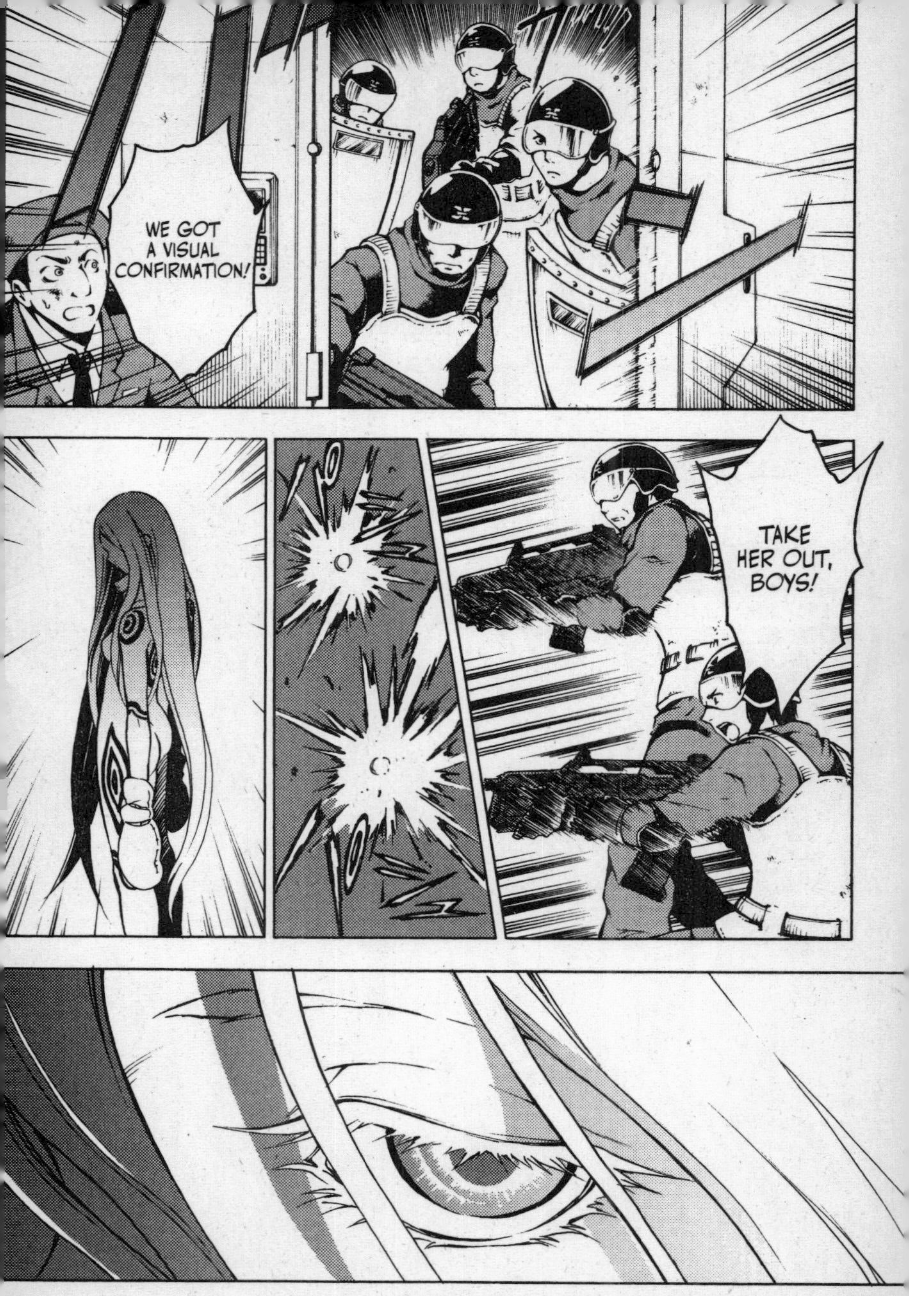
WE GOT A VISUAL CONFIRMATION!
TAKE HER OUT, BOYS!

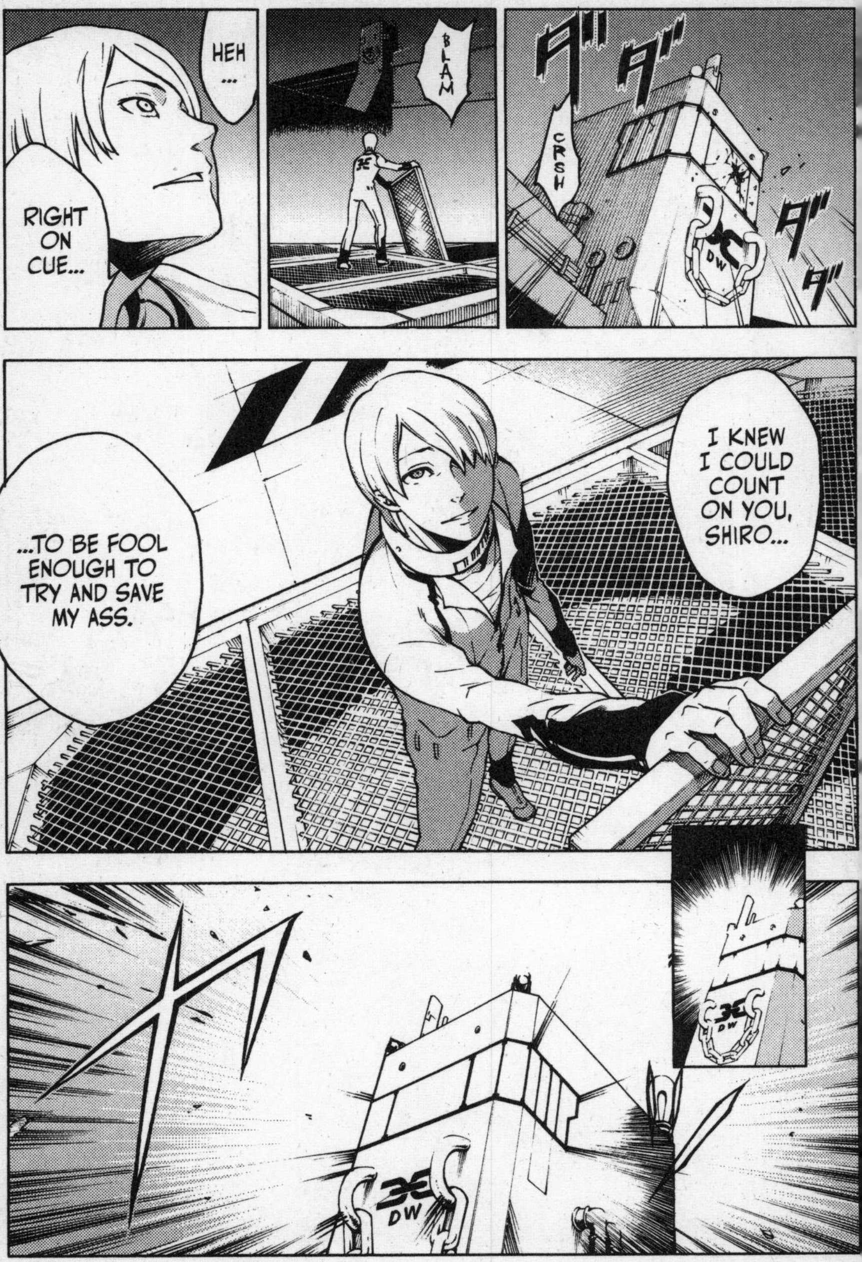
ダ
ダ
CRSH
ダ
ダ
BLAM
HEH ...
RIGHT ON CUE...
I KNEW I COULD COUNT ON YOU, SHIRO...
...TO BE FOOL ENOUGH TO TRY AND SAVE MY ASS.

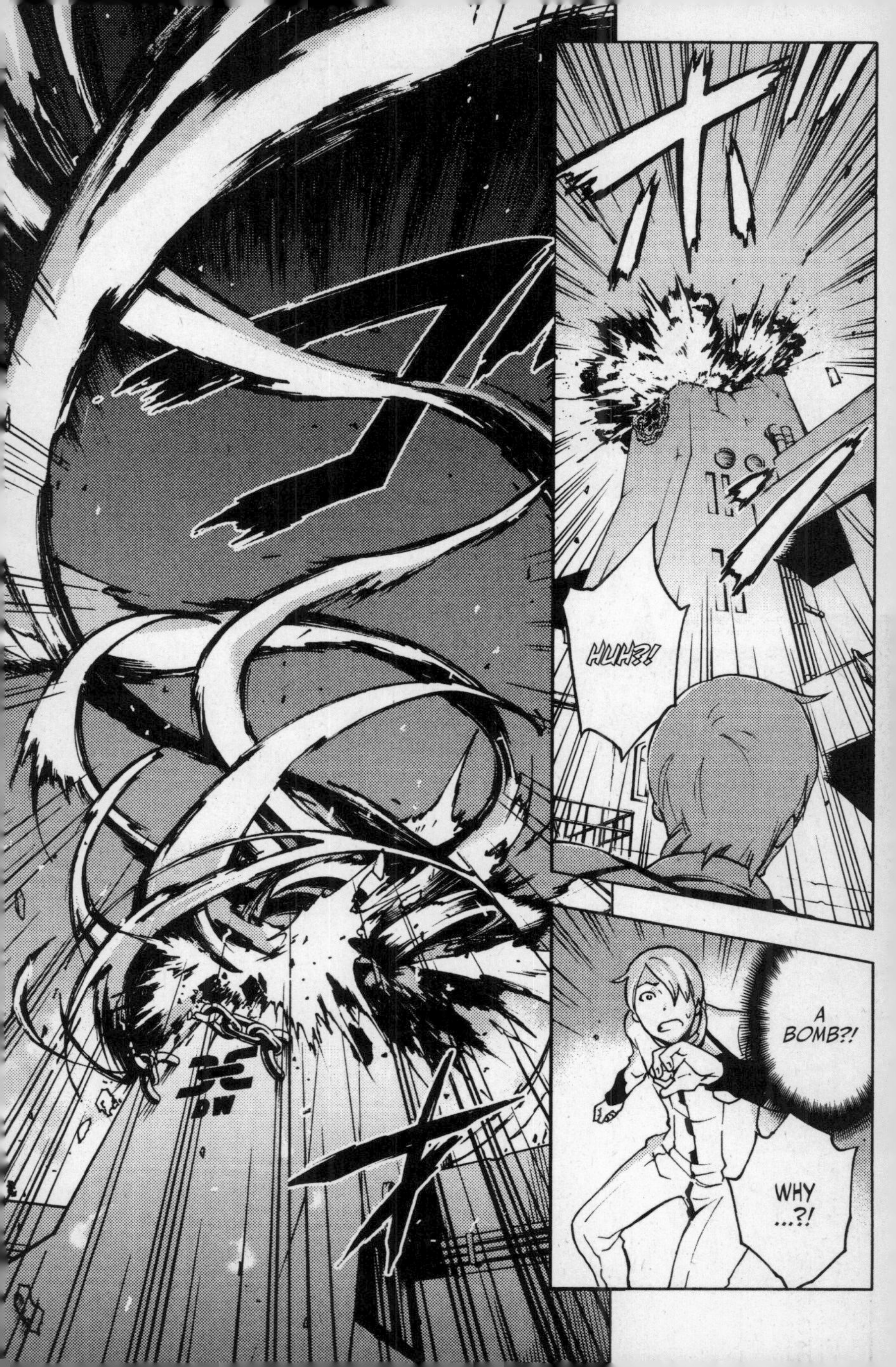
HUH?!
A BOMB?!
WHY ...?!

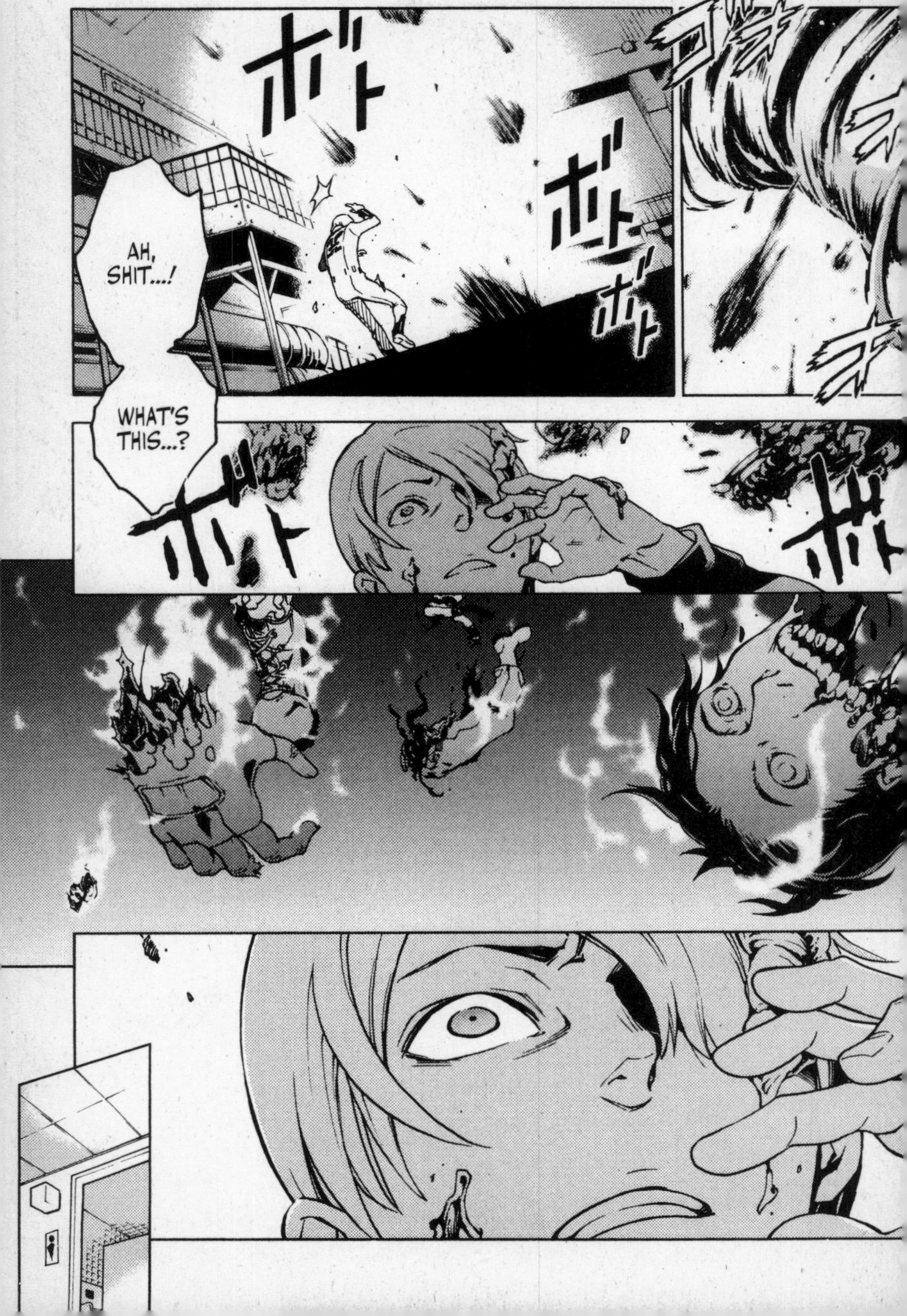
ボト
ボト
ボト
AH, SHIT...!
WHAT'S THIS...?
ボト
ボト

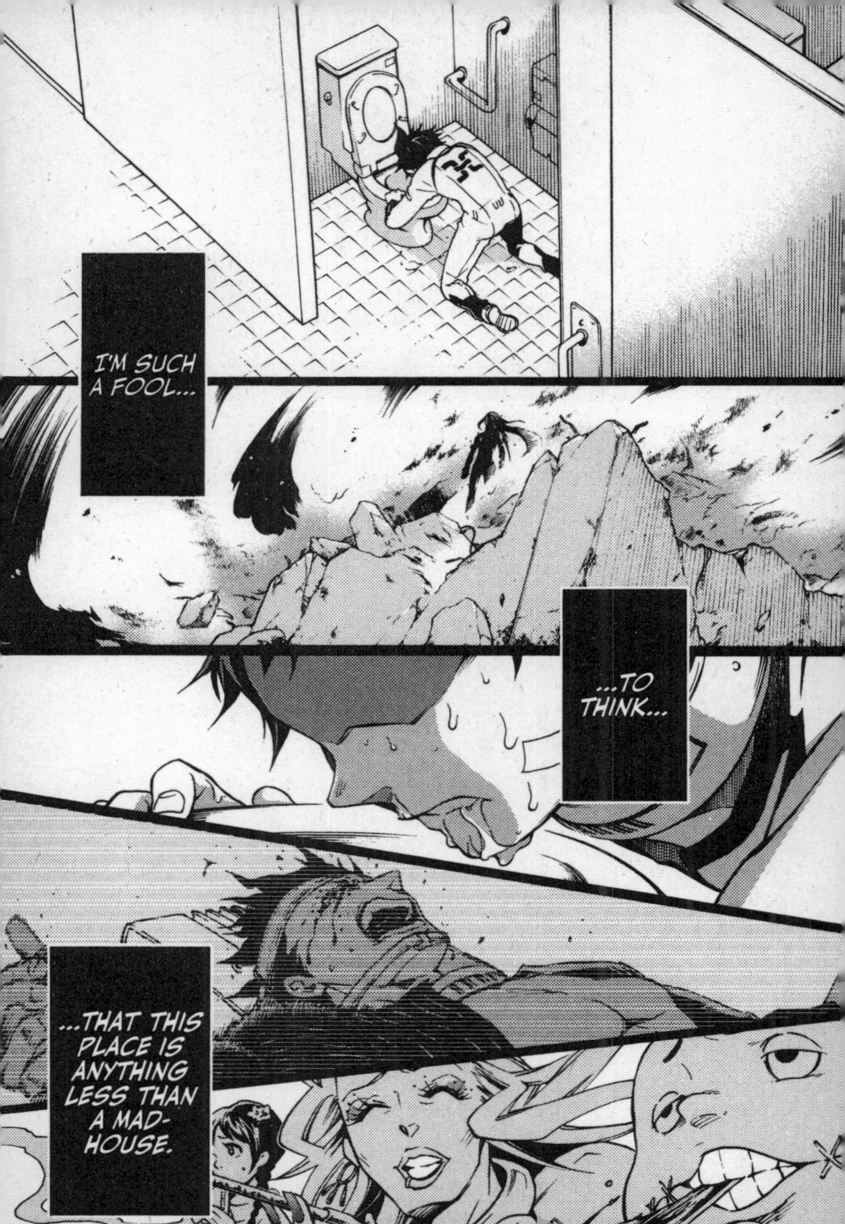
I'M SUCH A FOOL...
...TO THINK...
...THAT THIS PLACE IS ANYTHING LESS THAN A MAD-HOUSE.

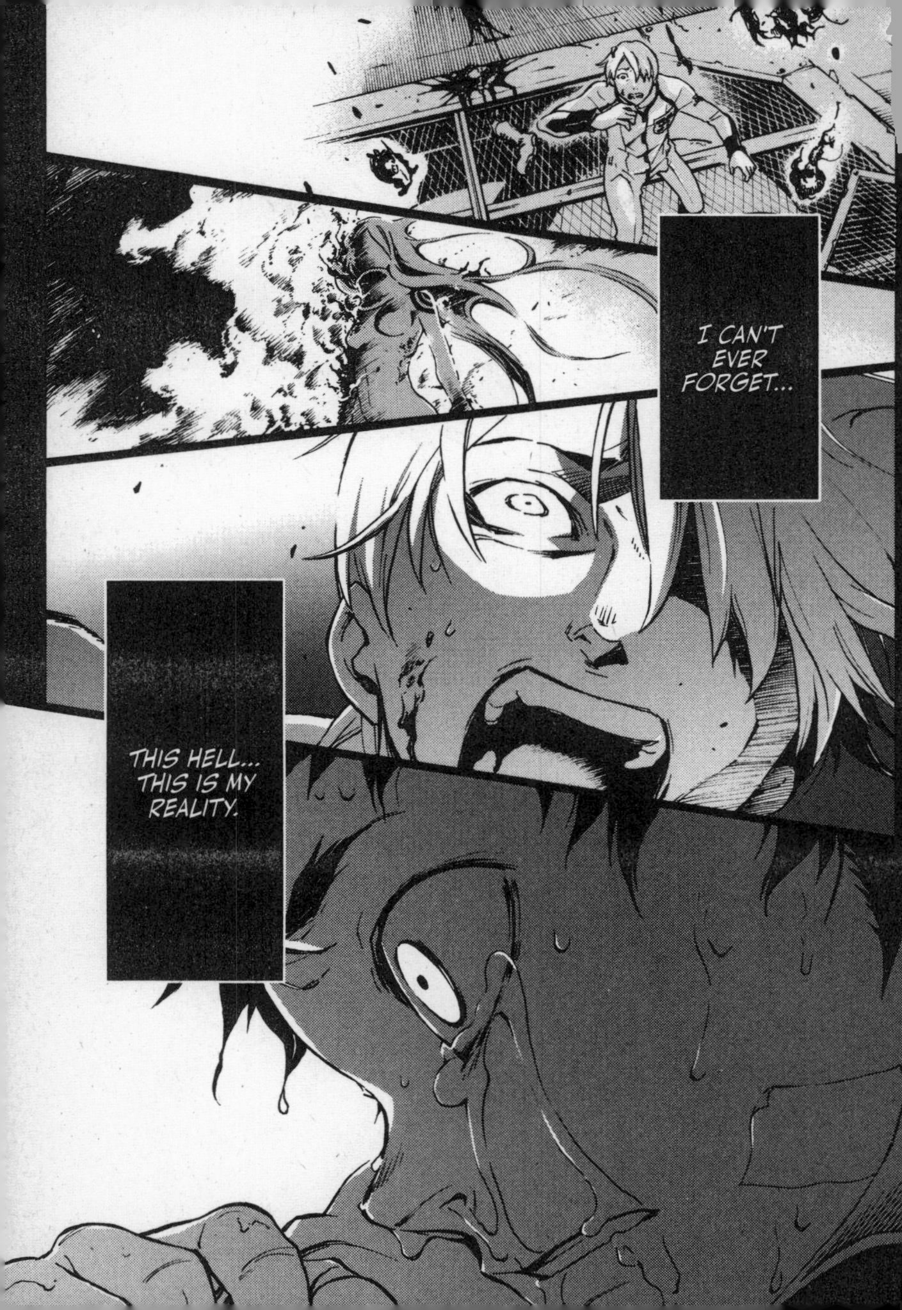
I CAN'T EVER FORGET...
THIS HELL... THIS IS MY REALITY.

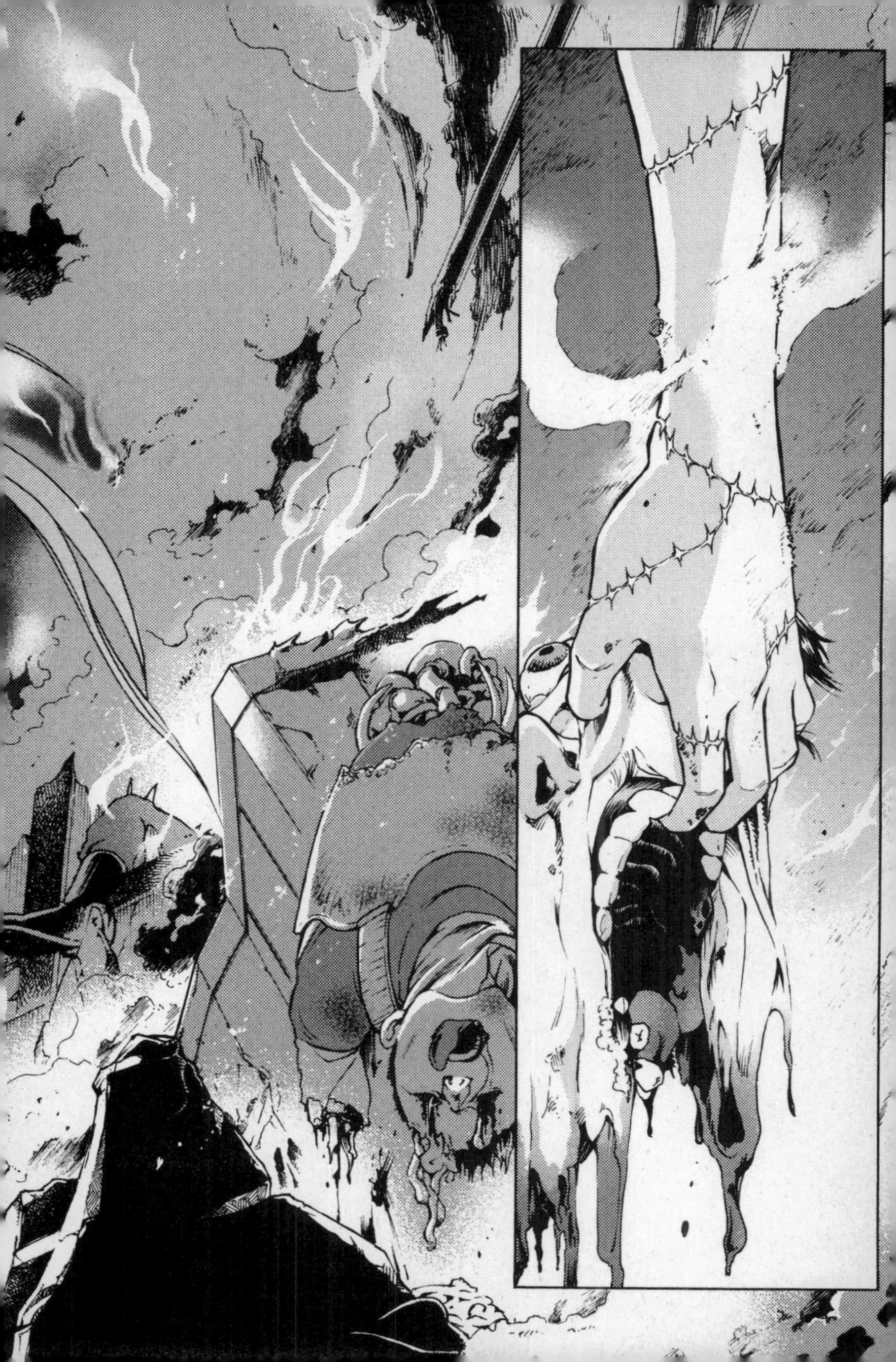

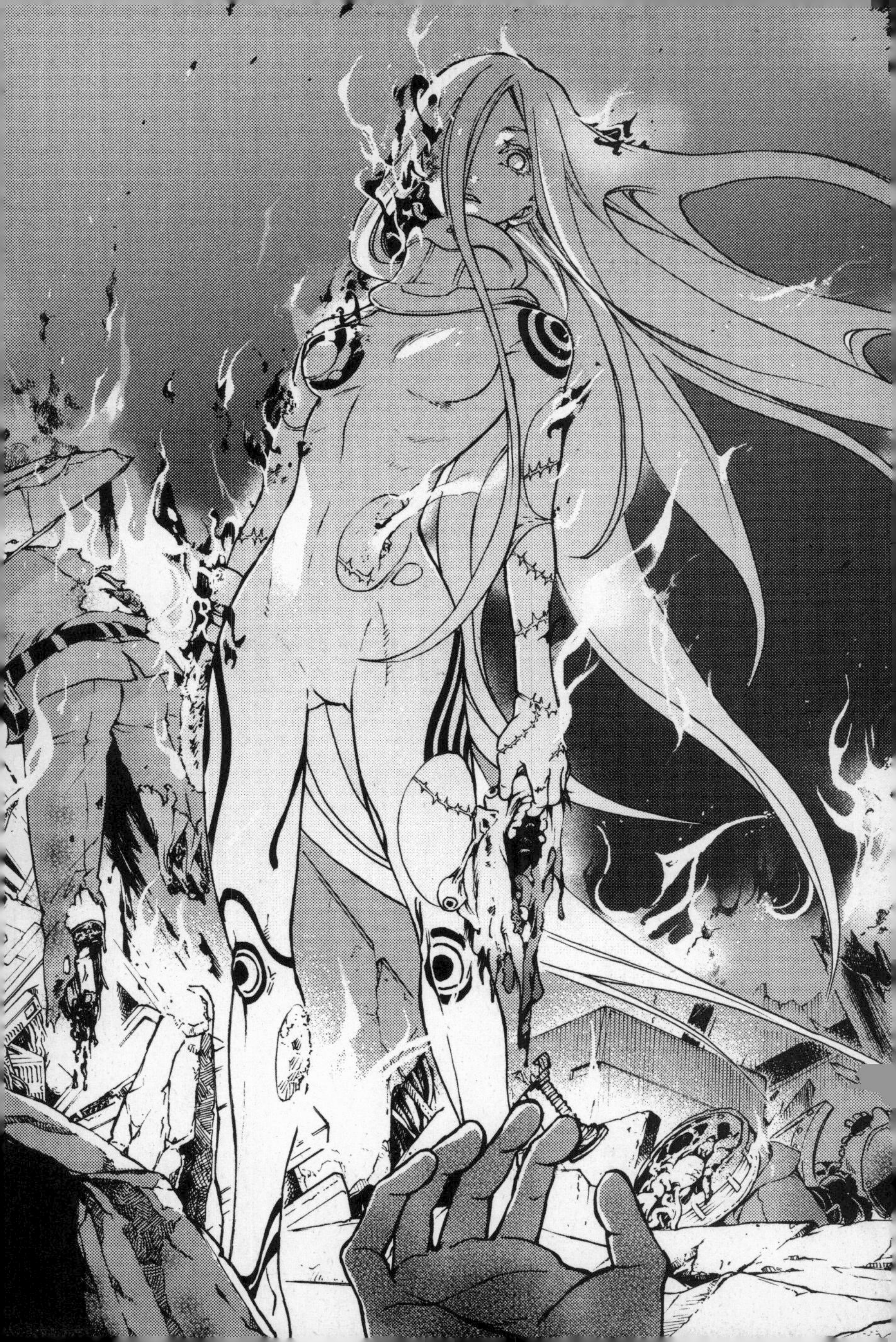

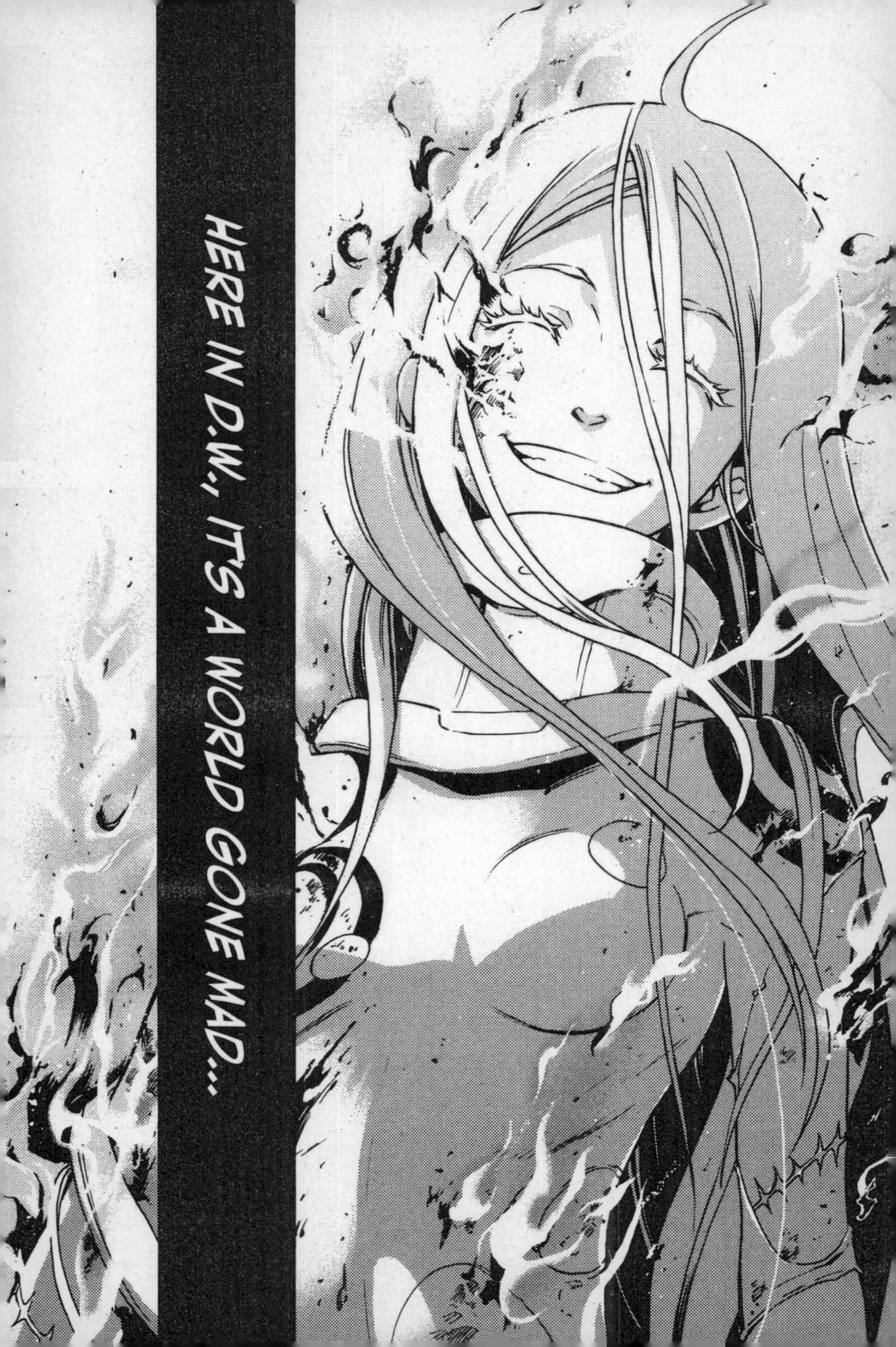
HERE IN D.W., IT'S A WORLD GONE MAD...

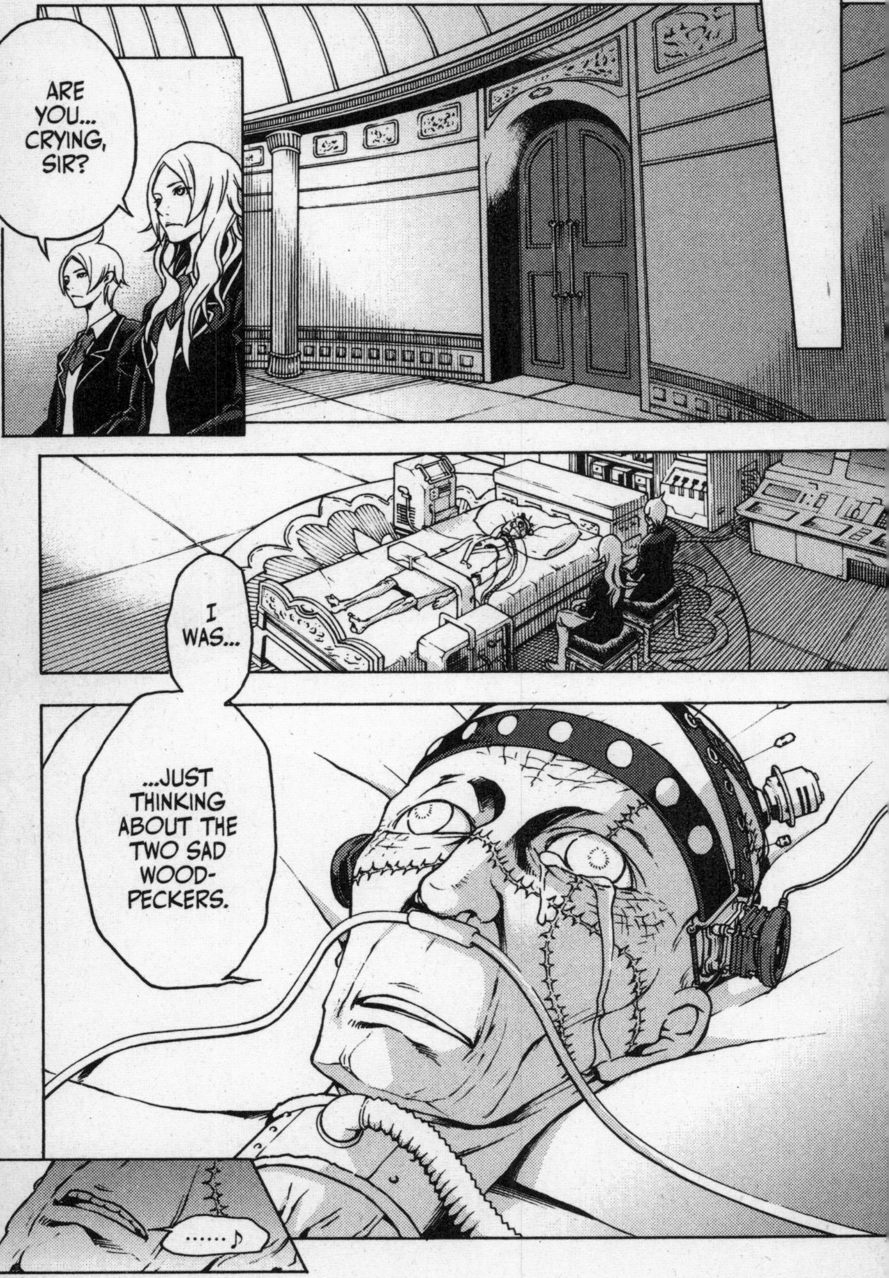
ARE YOU... CRYING, SIR?
I WAS...
...JUST THINKING ABOUT THE TWO SAD WOOD-PECKERS.
......♪

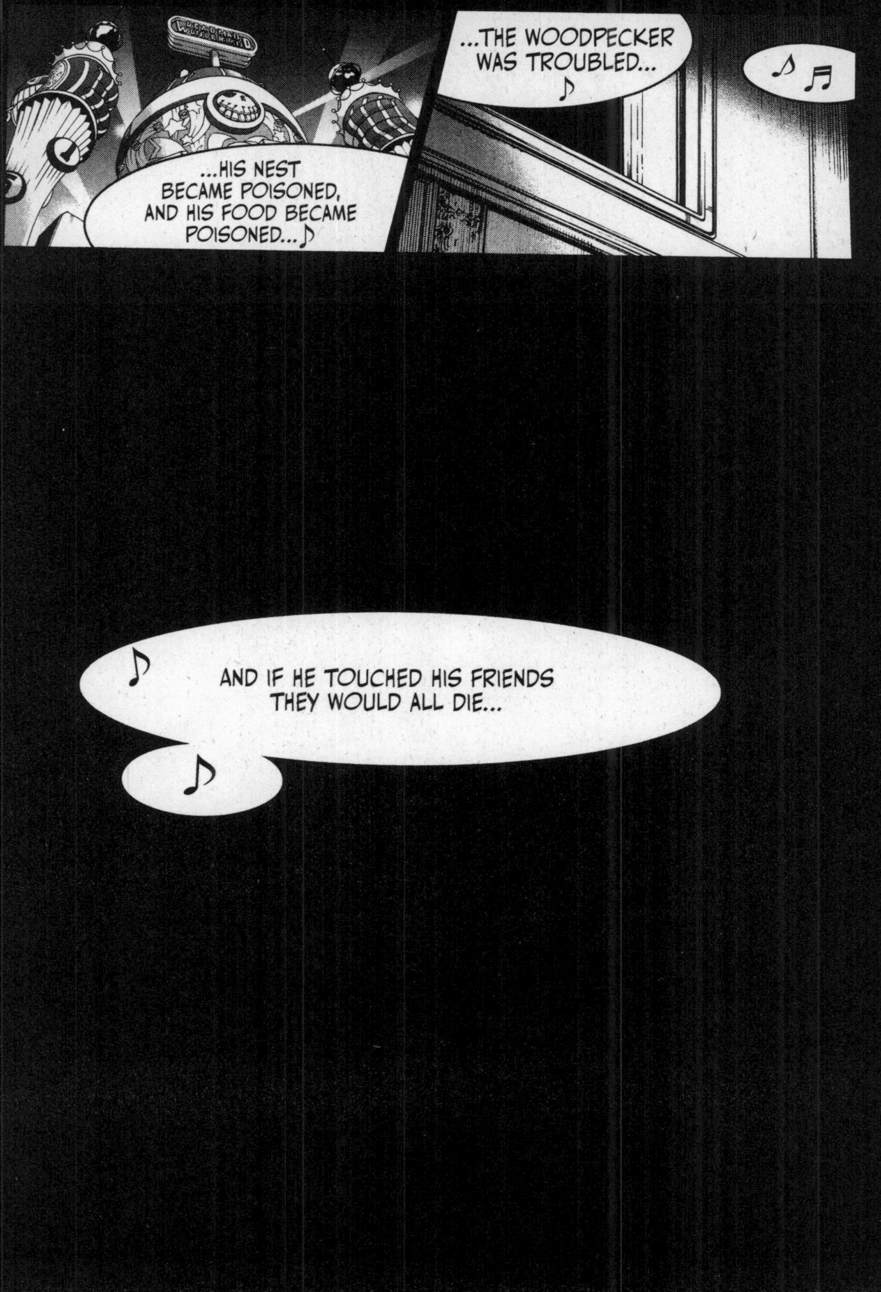
...THE WOODPECKER WAS TROUBLED... ♪
♪ ♬
...HIS NEST BECAME POISONED, AND HIS FOOD BECAME POISONED...♪
♪ AND IF HE TOUCHED HIS FRIENDS THEY WOULD ALL DIE...
♪

# DEADMAN
# WONDERLAND
# 2

# CONTINUED
# TO VOLUME
# 03

# DEADMAN WONDERLAND

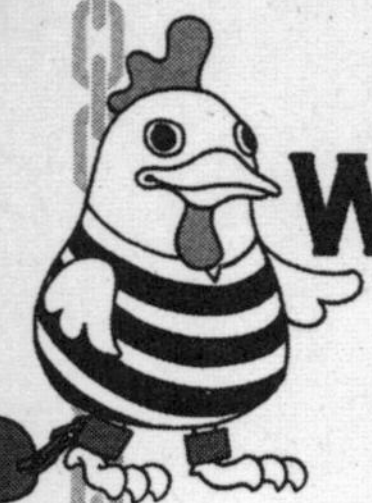

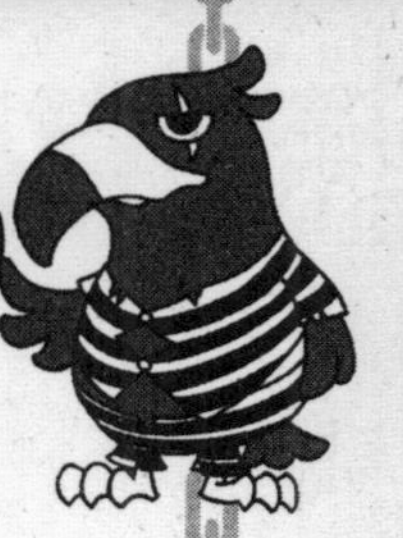

## Secrets of Deadman Wonderland!

### This is Necro Macro!

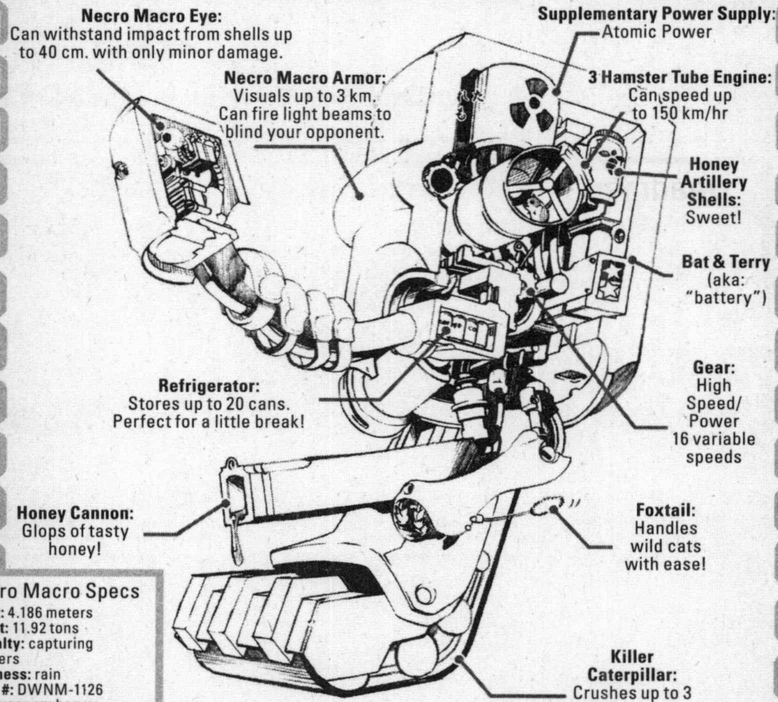

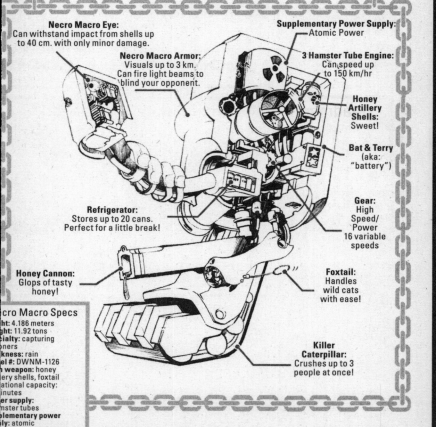

Necro Macro Eye:
Can withstand impact from shells up to 40 cm. with only minor damage.
Necro Macro Armor:
Visuals up to 3 km. Can fire light beams to blind your opponent.
Supplementary Power Supply:
Atomic Power
3 Hamster Tube Engine:
Can speed up to 150 km/hr
Honey Artillery Shells:
Sweet!
Bat & Terry
(aka: "battery")
Gear:
High Speed/ Power
16 variable speeds
Refrigerator:
Stores up to 20 cans. Perfect for a little break!
Honey Cannon:
Glops of tasty honey!
Foxtail:
Handles wild cats with ease!
Killer Caterpillar:
Crushes up to 3 people at once!


ecro Macro Specs
**ht:** 4.186 meters
**ght:** 11.92 tons
**cialty:** capturing
oners
**kness:** rain
**el #:** DWNM-1126
**n weapon:** honey
lery shells, foxtail
ational capacity:
inutes
**er supply:**
mster tubes
**plementary power**
**ly:** atomic

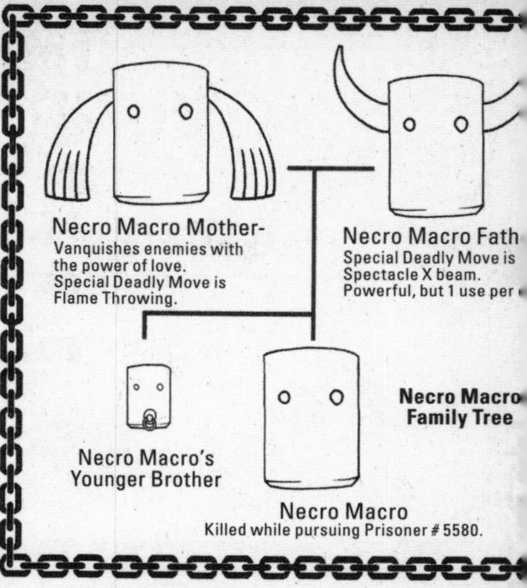

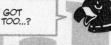

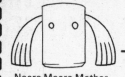

Necro Macro Mother-
Vanquishes enemies with the power of love.
Special Deadly Move is Flame Throwing.
Necro Macro Fath
Special Deadly Move is Spectacle X beam.
Powerful, but 1 use per
Necro Macro Family Tree
Necro Macro's Younger Brother
Necro Macro
Killed while pursuing Prisoner #5580.

HEY...HOW CAN A MACHINE HAVE A FAMILY... THERE'S A LIMIT EVEN TO RIDICULOUSNESS, YOU KNOW!

SINCE SENJI KILLED HIS SON, APPARENTLY HIS FATHER IS ANGRY.
AND BY THE WAY, HIS FATHER STANDS 40 METERS TALL.

SO THEY'VE GOT EMOTIONS, TOO...?

THEY'RE PRETTY ADVANCED!

# Deadman Wonderland Product Information

- **Deadman Russian Bean Jam Bun**
  The gentle sweetness of pureed sweet red bean jam paste. One of the 12 buns is a bun-shaped eraser. Anyone who takes a bite is sure to be surprised! The perfect gift.
- **Deadman Bat**
  Wooden bat crafted with the latest technology, with a cork-stuffed center. You'll increase your long ball hitting by leaps and bounds. Use the attached steel ball for unexpected brawls!
- **Deadman Flavored Miso Paste**
  Healthy, made with low sodium. Comes in white & red.

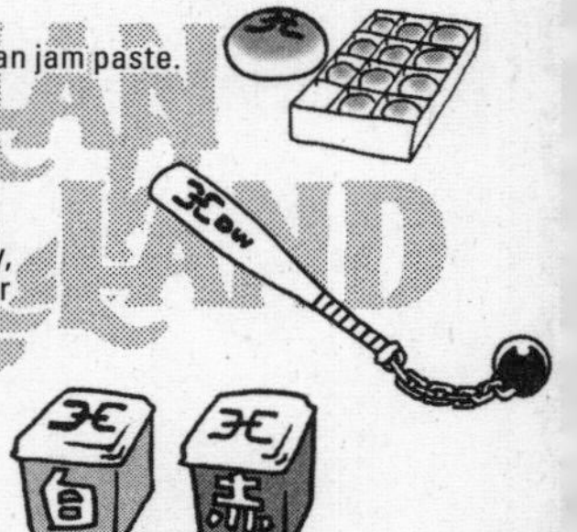

MOST OF THESE PRODUCTS AT D.W. ARE CRAFTED BY INMATES WITH LOVING CARE. PLEASE BUY SOME!

BUY THEM, EVEN IF YOU HAVE TO GO INTO DEBT! THAT MONEY GOES TOWARDS FEEDING US!

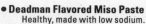

**Thanks for shopping at Deadman Wonderland!**

# IIIII!

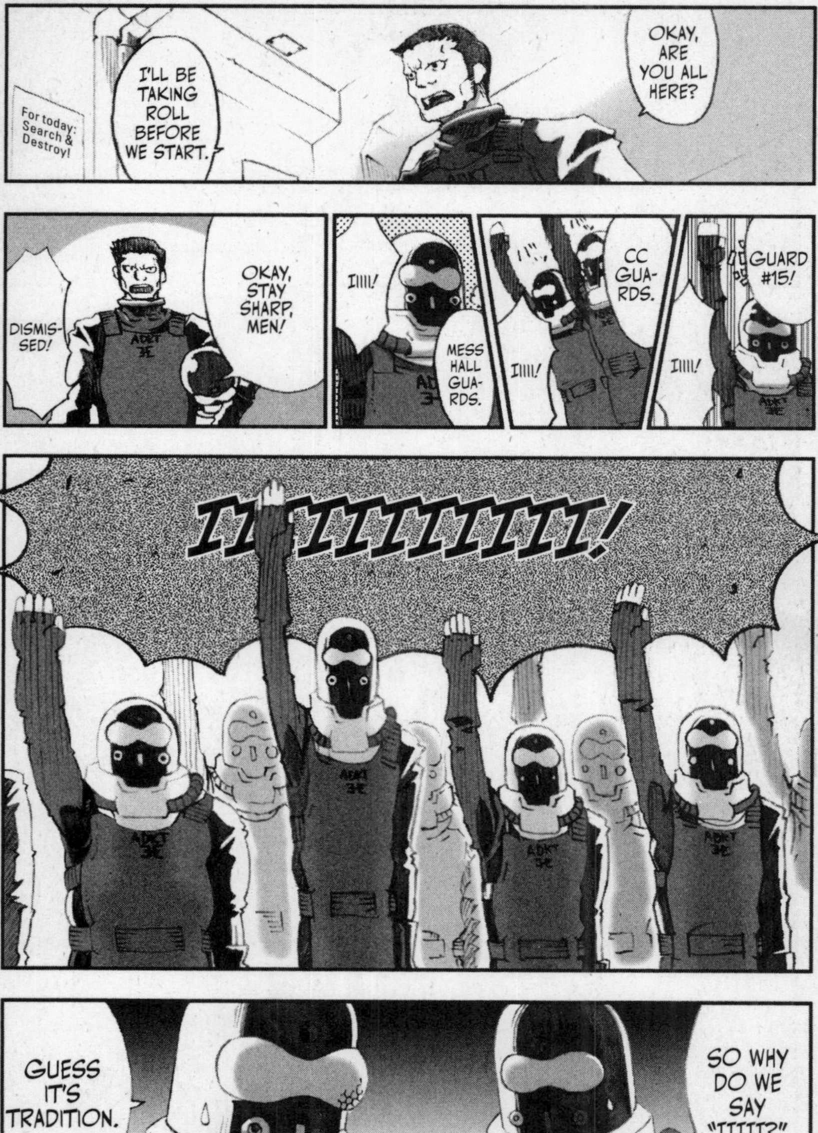
OKAY, ARE YOU ALL HERE?
I'LL BE TAKING ROLL BEFORE WE START.
For today: Search & Destroy!
GUARD #15!
IIIII!
CC GUARDS.
IIIII!
MESS HALL GUARDS.
IIIII!
OKAY, STAY SHARP, MEN!
DISMISSED!
IIIIIIIIIII!
SO WHY DO WE SAY "IIIII?"
GUESS IT'S TRADITION.

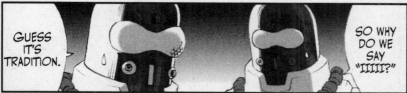

## On Target

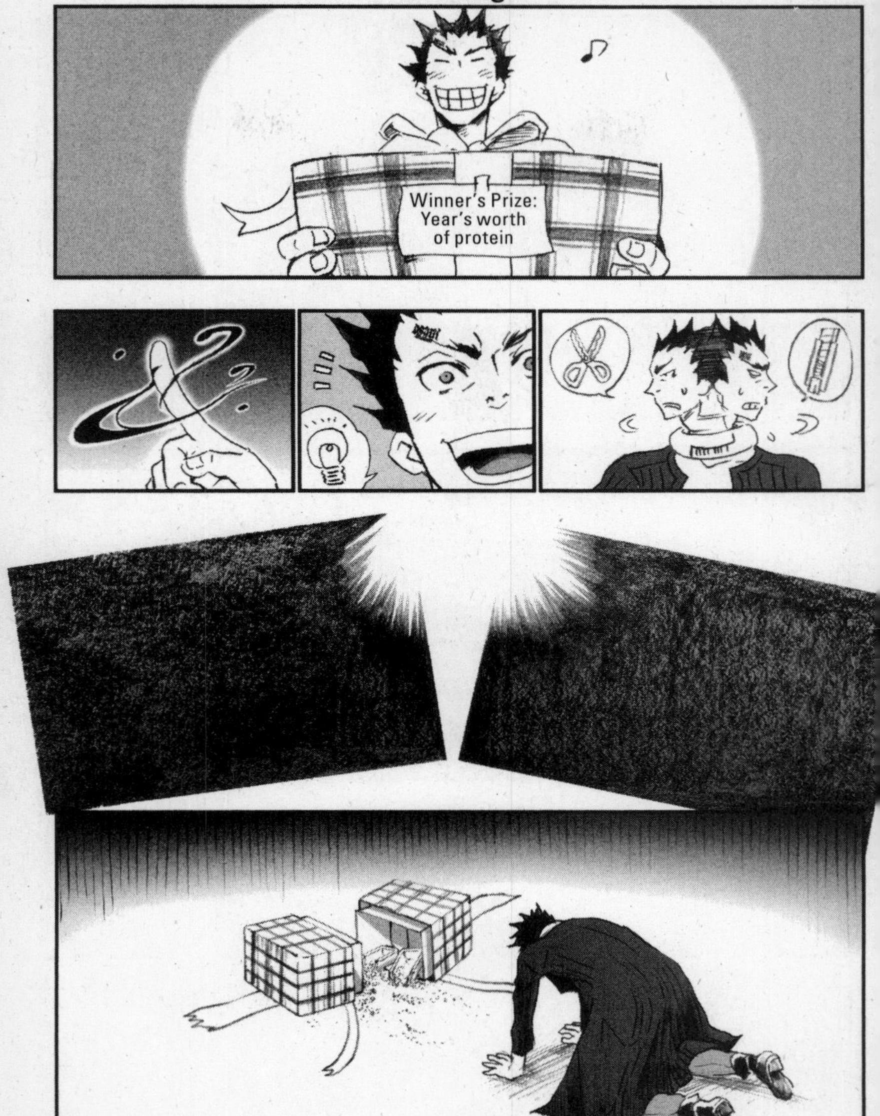
Winner's Prize: Year's worth of protein

## A Present

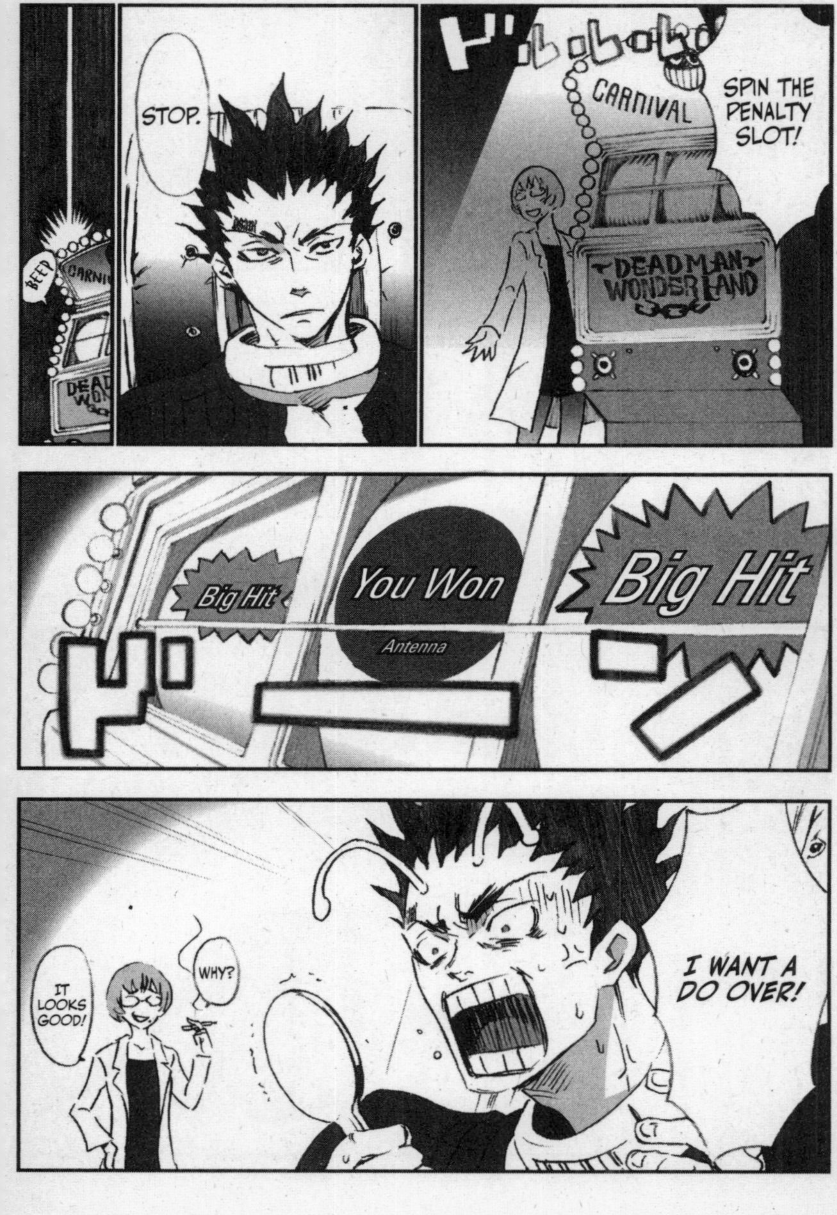

CARNIVAL
SPIN THE PENALTY SLOT!
DEADMAN WONDERLAND
STOP.
BEEP
Big Hit
You Won
Antenna
Big Hit
I WANT A DO OVER!
WHY?
IT LOOKS GOOD!

# New Product

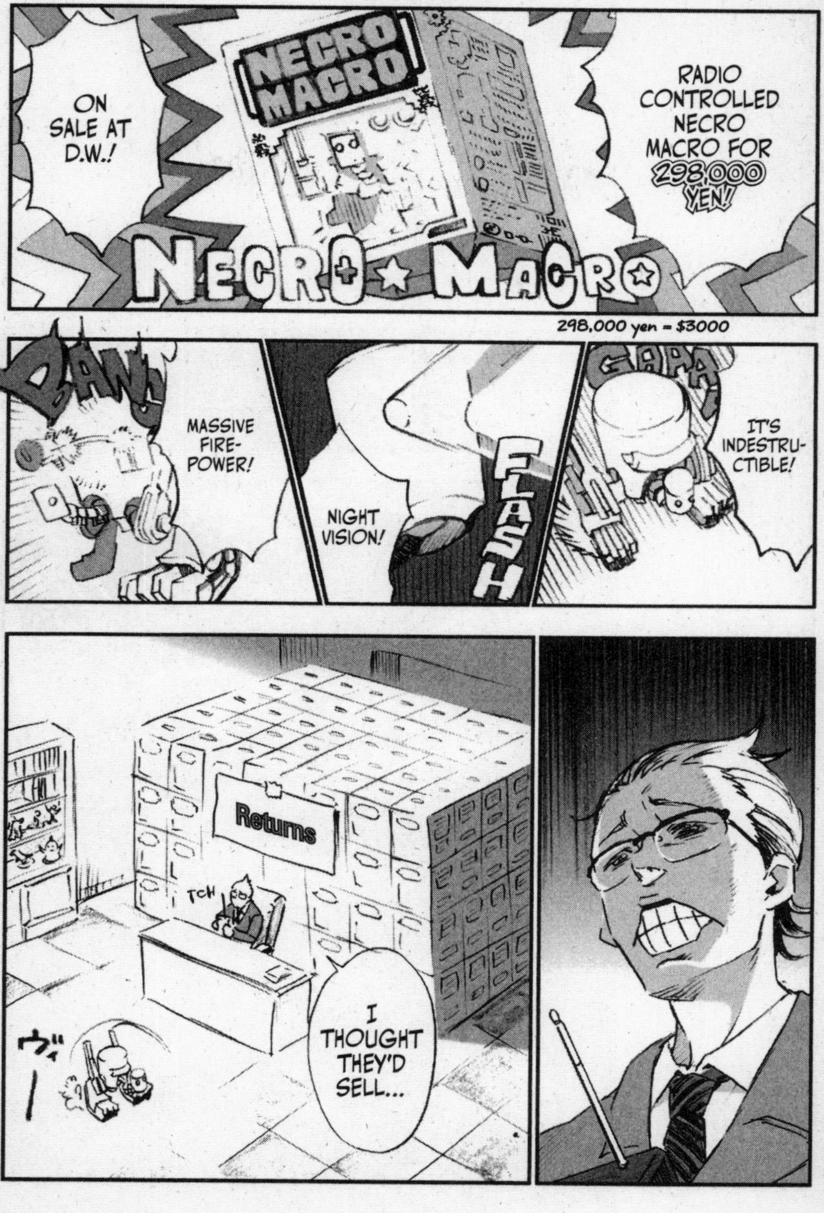

RADIO CONTROLLED NECRO MACRO FOR 298,000 YEN!
ON SALE AT D.W.!
NECRO MACRO
NECRO★MACRO
298,000 yen = $3000
GAPA
IT'S INDESTRUCTIBLE!
FLASH
NIGHT VISION!
BAN
MASSIVE FIRE-POWER!
I THOUGHT THEY'D SELL...
Returns
TCH
ヴィ

IN THE NEXT VOLUME OF...

# DEADMAN
## WONDERLAND

AS GANTA SETTLES INTO WARD G, HE BEFRIENDS MINATSUKI, A FELLOW BRANCH OF SIN. BUT WHAT WILL SWEET MINATSUKI DO WHEN THE TWO ARE FORCED TO FIGHT EACH OTHER IN THE NEXT CARNIVAL OF CORPSES? AND WHEN GANTA GETS MIXED UP WITH A GROUP OF WARD G GUERILLAS, THE IDENTITY OF THE ORIGINAL SIN IS REVEALED!

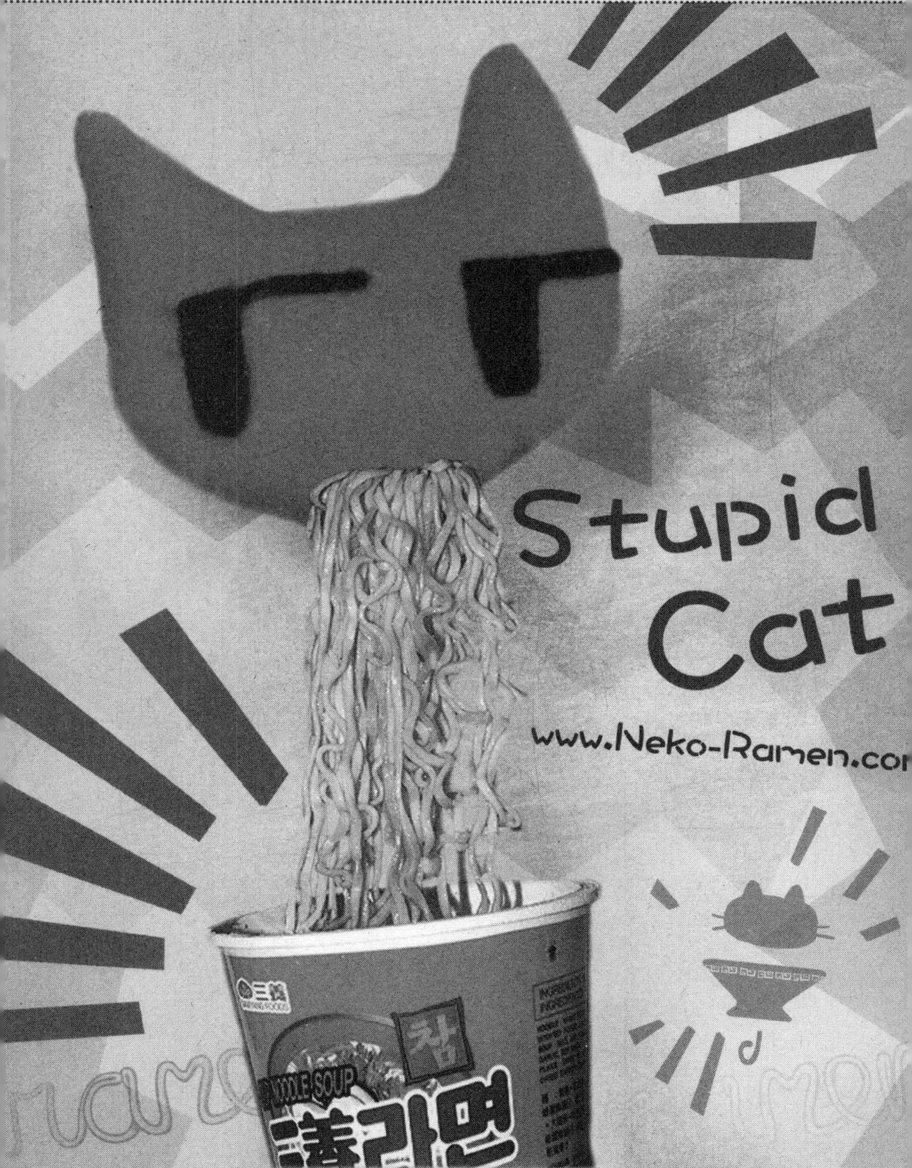
Stupid
Cat
www.Neko-Ramen.co
NOODLE SOUP

# THE SMALLEST HERO!?
# RATMAN
ラットマン

Shuto Katsuragi is a superhero otaku. Only problem is, he's a shrimp always getting teased for his height…especially when he tries to emulate his favorite superhero! To make matters worse, Shuto suddenly gets abducted by his classmate and tricked into participating in some rather sketchy and super-villainous experiments! Why is it always one step forward and a hundred steps back for this little guy?

ACTION

OT OLDER TEEN AGE 16+

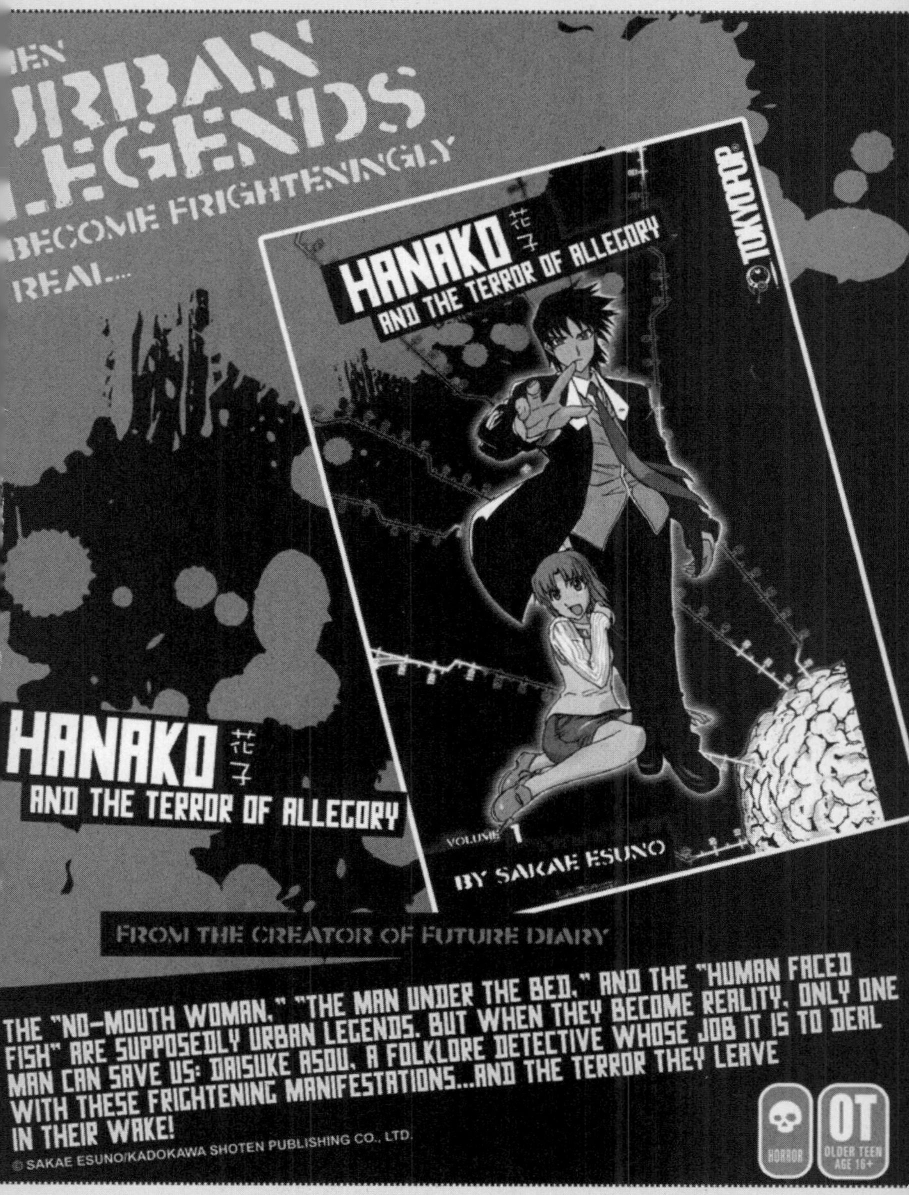
URBAN LEGENDS BECOME FRIGHTENINGLY REAL....
HANAKO 花子 AND THE TERROR OF ALLEGORY
TOKYOPOP
VOLUME 1
BY SAKAE ESUNO
FROM THE CREATOR OF FUTURE DIARY
THE "NO-MOUTH WOMAN," "THE MAN UNDER THE BED," AND THE "HUMAN FACED FISH" ARE SUPPOSEDLY URBAN LEGENDS. BUT WHEN THEY BECOME REALITY, ONLY ONE MAN CAN SAVE US: DAISUKE ASOU, A FOLKLORE DETECTIVE WHOSE JOB IT IS TO DEAL WITH THESE FRIGHTENING MANIFESTATIONS...AND THE TERROR THEY LEAVE IN THEIR WAKE!
© SAKAE ESUNO/KADOKAWA SHOTEN PUBLISHING CO., LTD.
HORROR
OT
OLDER TEEN AGE 16+

# STOP!

## This is the back of the book.
## You wouldn't want to spoil a great ending!

This book is printed "manga-style," in the authentic Japanese right-to-left format. Since none of the artwork has been flipped or altered, readers get to experience the story just as the creator intended. You've been asking for it, so TOKYOPOP® delivered: authentic, hot-off-the-press, and far more fun!

# DIRECTIONS

If this is your first time reading manga-style, here's a quick guide to help you understand how it works.

It's easy... just start in the top right panel and follow the numbers. Have fun, and look for more 100% authentic manga from TOKYOPOP®!